THE **GUINNESS** BOOK OF

MUSIC

FACTS AND FEATS

CATALOGUE
de la Musique
de Monsieur
Le Comte
D'Ogny.

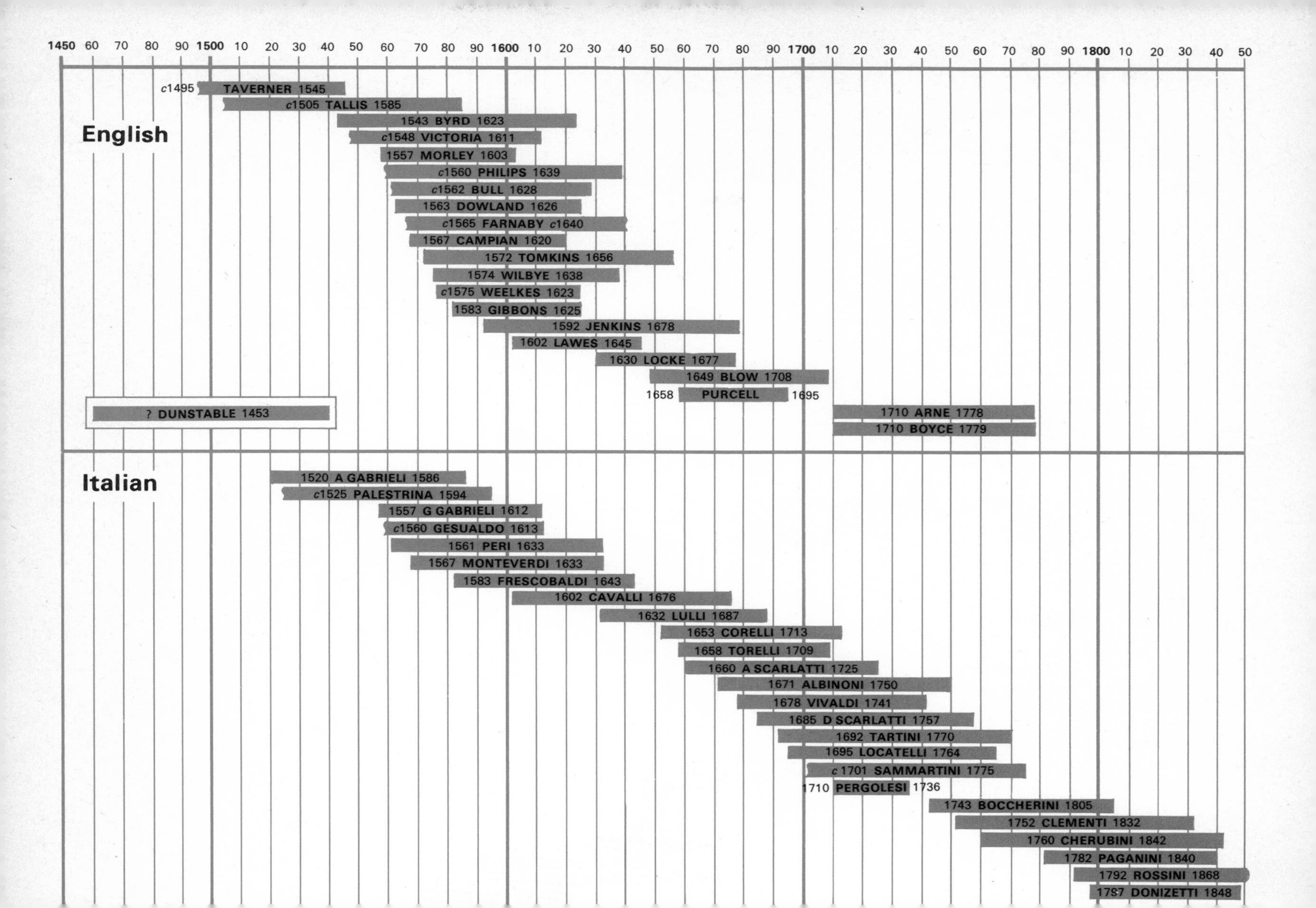
1450 60 70 80 90 1500 10 20 30 40 50 60 70 80 90 1600 10 20 30 40 50 60 70 80 90 1700 10 20 30 40 50 60 70 80 90 1800 10 20 30 40 50
English
c1495 TAVERNER 1545
c1505 TALLIS 1585
1543 BYRD 1623
c1548 VICTORIA 1611
1557 MORLEY 1603
c1560 PHILIPS 1639
c1562 BULL 1628
1563 DOWLAND 1626
c1565 FARNABY c1640
1567 CAMPIAN 1620
1572 TOMKINS 1656
1574 WILBYE 1638
c1575 WEELKES 1623
1583 GIBBONS 1625
1592 JENKINS 1678
1602 LAWES 1645
1630 LOCKE 1677
1649 BLOW 1708
1658 PURCELL 1695
? DUNSTABLE 1453
1710 ARNE 1778
1710 BOYCE 1779
Italian
1520 A GABRIELI 1586
c1525 PALESTRINA 1594
1557 G GABRIELI 1612
c1560 GESUALDO 1613
1561 PERI 1633
1567 MONTEVERDI 1633
1583 FRESCOBALDI 1643
1602 CAVALLI 1676
1632 LULLI 1687
1653 CORELLI 1713
1658 TORELLI 1709
1660 A SCARLATTI 1725
1671 ALBINONI 1750
1678 VIVALDI 1741
1685 D SCARLATTI 1757
1692 TARTINI 1770
1695 LOCATELLI 1764
c1701 SAMMARTINI 1775
1710 PERGOLESI 1736
1743 BOCCHERINI 1805
1752 CLEMENTI 1832
1760 CHERUBINI 1842
1782 PAGANINI 1840
1792 ROSSINI 1868
1797 DONIZETTI 1848

THE GUINNESS BOOK OF MUSIC FACTS AND FEATS

Robert and Celia Dearling
with Brian Rust

Guinness Superlatives Limited
2 Cecil Court, London Road, Enfield, Middlesex

Published in Great Britain by
Guinness Superlatives Ltd,
2 Cecil Court, London Road, Enfield,
Middlesex

ISBN 0 900424 63 X

Set in 'Monophoto' Plantin Series 110
Printed and bound in Great Britain by
Jarrold and Sons Ltd, Norwich

Frontispiece: Title-page of the thematic catalogue of music in the collection of Le Comte d'Ogny, Paris. See page 218 (British Museum)

OTHER GUINNESS SUPERLATIVES TITLES

Facts and Feats Series:

Air Facts and Feats, *2nd ed*
John W R Taylor, Michael J H Taylor and David Mondey

Rail Facts and Feats, *2nd ed*
John Marshall

Tank Facts and Feats, *2nd ed*
Kenneth Macksey

Yachting Facts and Feats
Peter Johnson

Plant Facts and Feats
William G Duncalf

Structures – Bridges, Towers, Tunnels, Dams . . .
John H Stephens

Car Facts and Feats, *2nd ed*
Anthony Harding

Business World
Henry Button and Andrew Lampert

Animal Facts and Feats, *2nd ed*
Gerald L Wood

Guide Series:

Guide to Freshwater Angling
Brian Harris and Paul Boyer

Guide to Mountain Animals
R P Bille

Guide to Underwater Life
C Petron and J B Lozet

Guide to Formula 1 Motor Racing
José Rosinski

Guide to Motorcycling, *2nd ed*
Christian Lacombe

Guide to Bicycling
J Durry

Guide to French Country Cooking
Christian Roland Délu

Other titles:

English Furniture 1550–1760
Geoffrey Wills

English Furniture 1760–1900
Geoffrey Wills

The Guinness Guide to Feminine Achievements
Joan and Kenneth Macksey

The Guinness Book of Names
Leslie Dunkling

Battle Dress
Frederick Wilkinson

Universal Soldier
Martin Windrow and Frederick Wilkinson

History of Land Warfare
Kenneth Macksey

History of Sea Warfare
Lt-Cmdr Gervis Frere-Cook and Kenneth Macksey

History of Air Warfare
David Brown, Christopher Shores and Kenneth Macksey

The Guinness Book of Answers
edited by Norris D McWhirter

The Guinness Book of Records, *23rd ed*
edited by Norris D McWhirter

The Guinness Book of 1952
edited by Kenneth Macksey

CONTENTS

PREFACE

The aim of this book is to bring to the music-lover and to the collector of superlatives an assortment of facts and feats about music. The subject is a wide one, as are the authors' objectives, and although the general reader has been borne in mind throughout, 'difficult' subjects have not been avoided. On the contrary, such is the fascination of some of the esoterica of music that it has been considered useful to expend a disproportionate number of words on explaining some of them in order to make them intelligible to all. On the other hand, a specialist finding a particular subject overloaded, in his opinion, with elementary bases will perhaps forgive the authors for the sake of the music-lover with a less sophisticated view.

In attempting to amass an interesting and accurate assembly of facts the authors have consulted a great number of reference books, but a large amount of the material is the result of original research among periodicals, documents and many other sources. Nevertheless, the task could not have been completed without the help of a number of individuals and organisations who have unhesitatingly supplied assistance of the most valuable kind. Sincere thanks are due in particular to Oliver Neighbour of the Music Library in the British Museum for much patient co-operation over the years in laying bare some of the secrets of that Institution; to Robert Layton of the BBC, Michael Downey of Sevenoaks, and Antony Hodgson of Ascot, all of whom made available information not otherwise easily obtained; and to the composers Alan Hovhaness of Seattle and Patrick Moore of Selsey, Sussex, for answers to specific queries.

The imminent, if not altogether welcome, conversion to metrication in the UK has forced upon the authors the decision to render all measurements, weights, etc, into metric values, parenthetically converting these into the more familiar values. The task of conversion has been undertaken by Dr Stephen Jackson of Bedford, to whom are due our grateful and relieved thanks.

It fell to Brian Rust to provide the greater part of Section VIII and valuable material for Section IX. His name will be well known to readers, particularly those fascinated by the lighter musical scene of pre-Second World War, and he made available his astonishing fund of knowledge, much of it obtained direct from the artists themselves.

Acknowledgement is also made to Miss Mary Kennard for permission to print two of her many poems at the heads of Sections III and VI, and to Mrs Mary Morgan for invaluable help in the preparation of the typescript.

Our special thanks go to Norris McWhirter and the editorial staff of Guinness Superlatives Ltd who, by their endless patience, courtesy, tact and constructive advice, have brought this book to a form which we believe the reader will find helpful and interesting. If the book hits its target it will be due entirely to their correction of the aim.

The mass of information collected for inclusion, often scribbled on scraps of paper or small cards, presented a problem of decision for all concerned. Some items would fit equally well into more than one category and it was then a matter of making an arbitrary decision as to where the final resting-place should be. For instance, should a fact concerning a modern opera be of more use to the reader in Section V or in Section VIII? Most of these problems were solved satisfactorily, but even so some facts refused to fit anywhere. The attention of an editorial meeting was caught by the patchy career of Robert Nicholas Charles Bochsa, the French harpist and composer who spent his non-musical hours forging signatures for fraud. He was forced to flee France and, arriving in London, he continued his dissolute ways by committing bigamy. Faced with a law suit, he ran away to Australia with the wife of one of the most prominent English composers of the time, Sir Henry Bishop. 'What shall we put *him* under?' Immediately, if unhelpfully, someone supplied the obvious answer: 'Guard!'

With a subject as wide as music, unavoidably certain areas have had to be neglected, but we believe that these are only a minor facet of the over-all picture. A conscientious book centred mainly upon extremes and priorities can be entertaining and at times surprisingly useful. It is also, however, provocative. If any reader, kind or less than kind, wishes to take us to task for some solecism, we shall accept their rival authority as a constructive lead to renewed researches. A philosophical attitude has been adopted by the authors over these matters because it is simply impossible to issue a revised edition first.

Robert and Celia Dearling,
Harlington, Beds, July 1976

Section I

SETTING THE SCENE

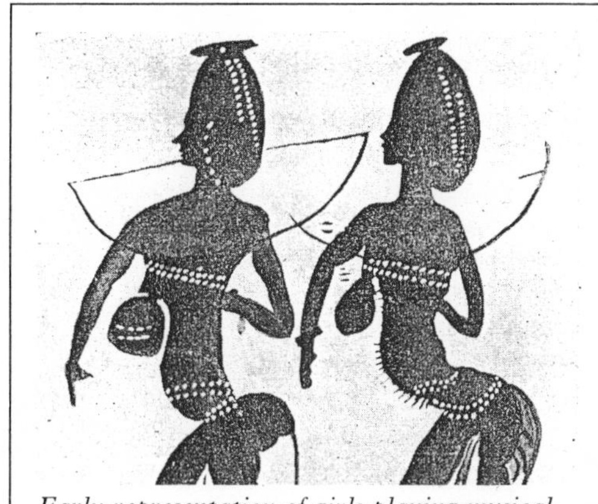

Early representation of girls playing musical bows. Cave-drawing from South Africa (copyright Government of the Union of South Africa)

Intelligent man has existed on this planet for nearly 2000000 years. At the very core of man's nature is an urge to produce music, either of the rhythmic, percussive variety, or of the sort to awaken echoes in his surroundings by raising his voice in joyful cries. As far as we can guess, primitive man was as fascinated by these sounds as is man of the 20th century, and we may, therefore, take a bold step and assert, with only instinct and common sense to back us up, that music, too, has existed on this planet for nearly 2000000 years. Plenty of time for the art form to have reached a degree of complexity and perfection, perhaps; yet we must point out parenthetically that the greater part of music performed today is organised according to rules and principles laid down in an extremely short period by a handful of composers between 250 and 300 years ago. Before that, different rules applied, and if we look back far enough we come to the days before there were any rules, to the days when music was merely a spontaneous expression of uncivilised man. As this Section unfolds it will be seen that the word 'merely' in the previous sentence is out of place; uncivilised man's musical expressions were among the most important of his activities–there was nothing inconsequential or simple in them.

The first musician who ever lived was a member of a nomadic tribe who unexpectedly lifted his voice in a canyon between high, smooth rocky walls. Through the combination of the vibrations he produced and the echo thrown back at him, he discovered the mysterious pleasure of sound which had abruptly taken a first step along the path towards organised music. Vaguely perceiving the possibilities he had unleashed, he spent a few minutes experimenting with shouts and calls of various pitches until other members of the tribe, fearful of the invisible spirits he had aroused in the cliffs, called him away. The game was abandoned until another day–or another generation.

In time, groups of these primitive cave-dwellers would be found experimenting vocally among the cliffs and among themselves, and we may be sure that the experiments became more complex necessitating some kind of code of discipline, since spontaneous music quickly becomes boring, and unruly extemporisation by several voices soon turns into a competition to see who can shout the loudest. Clearly rules had to be made, and we may visualise one of these savages taking it upon himself to attempt to control and regulate his companions' enthusiasm, indicating with threatening gestures his displeasure at some sounds and his boredom with others. An image is emerging of the **first chorus master** encouraging his performers with a bovine femur in his hand.

Gradually it was realised that high notes travelled farther and were more penetrating than low ones, and they were thus suitable for long-distance communication. Deep notes, on the other hand, were lost in open spaces, but in confined areas such as caves they set up a powerful resonance which excited the performers at the same time as frightening the listeners. For these superstitious peoples, who trembled as the echoes of the caves reverberated round them, certain sounds came to possess certain magical significances, and those with the loudest and most powerful voices gradually found that they had a power over the rest with which they could control and influence. **The first enchanting** had come into being. Through a series of lucky coincidences it was found that certain incantations augured well for a successful hunt or ensured a plentiful supply of drinking water from the skies.

We shall have occasion to return to the influence which these chanters wielded among their tribes.

About the same time, plus or minus a few thousand years, **the first instrumentalist** lived. Swinging his club at a potential meal, he missed and accidentally struck a rock. The resulting sound terrified him, for the rock rang like a gong. Emerging from his hiding-place later with a curiosity stronger than his fear, he tentatively hit the rock again, revelling in the deep, resonant sound which, as he struck harder and harder, rolled round the area, attracting other tribe members who had travelled some distance to discover what strange phenomenon was disturbing for the first time a world of natural animal and elemental noises. The carrying properties of the sound having thus been proved, the rock was thereafter used as a signal to tribe members who were out of shouting range. It signalled to them of danger or of success in the hunt; the first utility music had arrived, simultaneously with the first musical instrument.

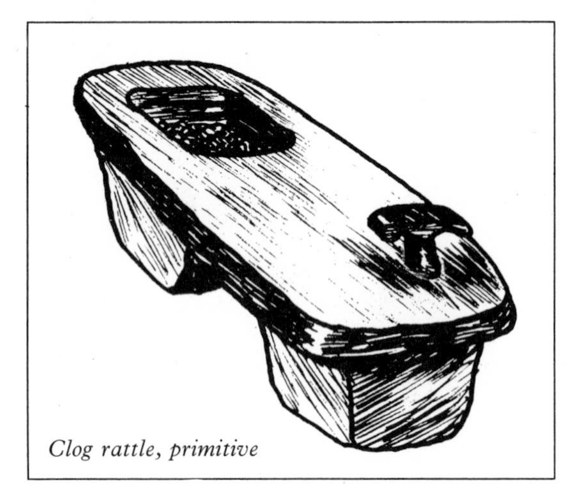
Clog rattle, primitive

If such spectacular results were obtainable from a piece of rock and a club, perhaps other materials would also yield results. Experiments were made in tapping and hitting a variety of substances, and it was merely a question of time before a number of different types of non-membrane drum were evolved. It was discovered that thigh-slapping and hand-clapping produced a sharp rhythmic sound, and that an animal skin, when pegged tightly over a shallow pit, would resonate the air inside the pit and produce an eerie, penetrating noise when hit with a stick. A covering of bark made a stronger membrane which would withstand the impact of dancers' heels; it was found also that the charm bracelets worn on wrist and ankle by these dancers made a pleasing jingling sound in time to the rhythm of the dance. Therefore, open rattles were soon cultivated and, alongside them, enclosed rattles in which seeds or pebbles were put into a gourd to be shaken at the end of a short handle.

The first wind instruments were also invented in a haphazard manner. An old straw or hollow reed was found to produce a note when blown in a particular way, and modifications to the length of the tube produced alterations in the note. A major discovery was made by a native with a sharp stone and the time to experiment; by cutting holes in the length of the tube and then 'stopping-up' the holes successively with the fingertips, a whole range of notes could be produced. The increase in variety of the first flutes over the first drums inevitably led to further experiments, and a wedding of instrumental and vocal techniques brought about the voice-flute (a simple flute through which the player hums or sings) which is still in use even today in some areas of Europe and Asia.

A thin sliver of wood or grass in the airway was found to change the sound of the instrument into something more piercing (children still stretch a blade of grass between thumbs for the same purpose), and the foundation was laid for the invention of single- and double-reed instruments.

A curious kind of 'wind-percussion' instrument developed from the stamping-pit principle. The sticks which were used to strike the skin or bark were sometimes hollow, and it was found that the column of air within the stick resonated with the vibration of the concussion. With a shaped top, these 'stamping-sticks' were promoted from their role of producing the sound in the pit-drum to having the status of independent musical instruments.

An animal horn, truncated and hollowed out, was found to possess a strange new character which, when blown from the narrow end, thrilled the blood of the hunter. Consequently, animal horns came to typify the sound of the hunt for food on the hoof, and **the first hunting-horns** had arrived, ripe for development through incredible sophistications over the ages until their modern perfection, which has removed from them all traces of their savage origins. A whole family of instruments grew from these early experiments with animal horns, a family ranging in size from the massive Wagner tuba to the tiny Baroque trumpet, and in shape from the slender simplicity of the herald trumpet and post-horn to the intestinal complexities of some specimens in the history of the development of the modern orchestral horn. The finger-holes bored in the early cow-horn represent the first step in the attemps to wrest more than the basic notes from the instrument, and modern machinery appended

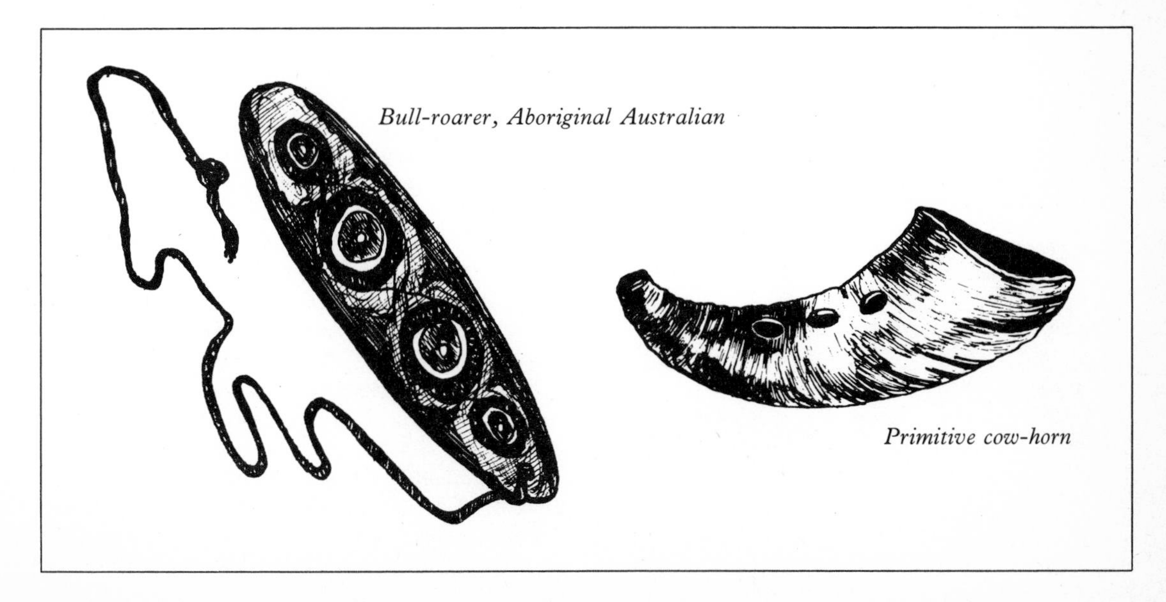

Bull-roarer, Aboriginal Australian

Primitive cow-horn

to the cow-horn's descendants range from the subtle perfection of the horn's rotary valves to the spectacular sliding action of the trombone.

Animals provided the material also for two other early instruments; the scraper, made from a notched bone which might be pressed against a resonator of some kind, and the conch-shell trumpet.

Non-intrumental music, too, was developing. Experimenters were discovering that the human voice is capable of a wide range of pitch, volume, and quality, and that the blending of some tones pleased more readily than others. Gradually, through aeons of trial and error, experience produced results which led ultimately to the great traditions of unison choral singing, and to polyphony. Doubtless many of these early experiments included both vocalists and instrumentalists. The imagination reels at the sound which must have been produced by a handful of players on crudely fashioned instruments, blowing and banging with abandon, accompanying (or, more accurately perhaps, vying with) vocalists giving forth in the coarse, throaty, tortured voices, often modified by hand-to-windpipe or fist-to-chest rhythmic embellishments, which they had cultivated for carrying power and penetration, rather than artistic, purposes. The phases of self-control, discipline, experiment, and sophistication undergone between such occasions and a modern performance of, for example, Handel's *Messiah,* are too numerous to imagine.

It is probable that stringed instruments were the last of the main groups to appear on that prehistoric scene. A hunting-bow, when not being used for its meat-winning purpose, might have indicated to some idle cave-man that the taut string, when plucked, would resound, and that by altering its tension or length a different note would result. Two bows, if treated with powdered rock or animal fat to encourage abrasive action, and then rubbed together crosswise, may have set off a developing stream of ideas which led to the violin family, a group which has evolved alongside the plucked lute family (but often merging with it, see Part I of Section II) until the development of the wide differences between the stringed instruments which we encounter today. It should be pointed out in the interest of accuracy that the first representation of a bowed instrument shows a player holding a bow some 3 m (10 ft) long, much longer than the Danish Bronze Age hunter's bow and the military long-bow of the Middle Ages, and unwieldy in the extreme for both musical and aggressive purposes. This enormous bow may have been constructed for a specific purpose which is now obscure, but it hardly affects the image of the archer experimenting with two crossed bows.

Conch shell trumpet, Tibet (Horniman Museum, London)

It will be seen that, in the everyday accoutrements of a cave-man's life, all the ingredients existed for the development of the instruments and the vocal techniques of today. Even the ultra-sophisticated grand piano has developed from a simple frame of strings which were struck with a little hammer (see Dulcimer and Psaltery, Part I of Section II), while the Stradivarius violin is basically a wooden box and strings developed to a point of loving perfection by skills and techniques which have evolved over centuries of gradual advancement and improvement.

The reader may be forgiven for feeling cheated by the above. He is presumably reading this book in search of facts, several of which have been enumerated, but not a single one has been, or can be, substantiated in detail or even placed in its correct chronology. However, it is hoped that the foregoing will illustrate the extreme antiquity of the origins of music, and that these origins were certainly, and in every case, the results of chance or coincidence.

From the quicksands of conjecture we move to the slightly less hazy area of educated guesses.

The concept of form was a late factor in the history of music. The performances given by the artists discussed above would have had little or no over-all design from the constructional viewpoint, apart perhaps from rudimentary devices such as a recurring motif, but there is likely to have been one exception. Of all the forms and styles of music with which the 20th-century listener is familiar, one, and one only, was known to music's earliest performers: **descriptive music.**

One of the most natural things for a performer to attempt, once he has become familiar with his instrument's characteristics, is to try to imitate the sounds he hears round him. Thus the player of a primitive reed-pipe might try to reproduce on his instrument the vocalisations made by birds and singers; the horn-player might imitate the bellowing of a bull; and our primitive violinist, with bow and box and strings, might try to reproduce all the natural sounds of a thunderstorm. Folk-musicians of this century still tell stories on their instruments, as A L Lloyd has illustrated so clearly in his broadcast talks. Single performers will recount long and involved folk-tales entirely in music, reproducing dances, dramatic happenings, the calls of animals, and even the emotions of the narrator; it is difficult to imagine that our proto-musicians did not indulge their feelings also. What more natural than for the player of a reed-pipe to convey his moods of depression or elation through music? The 'Age of Sensibility' was merely reawakened by the mid-18th-century Germans!

These musical tales might have been aided by a vocalist to tell the story. Perhaps he would act a part in order to clarify and enhance the narrative, the logical step then being for another 'character' to join in. Thus commenced the long line of development which led, through an infinite variety of plays, masques, passion dramas, entertainments, dramatic madrigals, cantatas, etc, to the most sophisticated and artificial of all musical activities: **opera.**

Early singers would certainly have praised their deities in song, at the same time asking a few meteorological or hunting favours in return, and even if the music bounded with enthusiasm, it was still technically a **hymn.**

In prehistoric times, therefore, the foundations were laid for tone poem, opera, and hymn, forms which were still to take countless thousands of years to become the stylised works we know today but which nevertheless cannot be called by other names.

These are essentially benign forms. They were joined by something less innocuous; a use for music which has already been hinted at: **magic.**

We know that a deep male voice, used with imagination in the right surroundings, could strike dread into primitive souls. There can be no doubt that this knowledge was exploited by some singers to gain power within the community, and this strange connection between music and what has become known as 'the black arts' has persisted in greater or lesser intensity to the present day. In the days of the primitives, life, music, superstition, and religion were, as it were, one entity. Once a certain stage has been reached in civilisation, a stage at which man realised that there existed greater things than his imagination could grasp, the unknown powers of the spirits began to be equated with the mysterious power of music. A force which possessed the power to stir and move the soul and yet was intangible and invisible must have been sent by the spirits, and, therefore, the spirits must be rewarded or placated. Early civilisations frequently buried their dead with provisions for the journey to, and residence in, the next world, and among these provisions often were to be found musical instruments, whether or not the deceased had had musical connections. Mythologies of all countries and all periods are awash with references to music and musicians. Musical instruments figure in early rock-carvings and

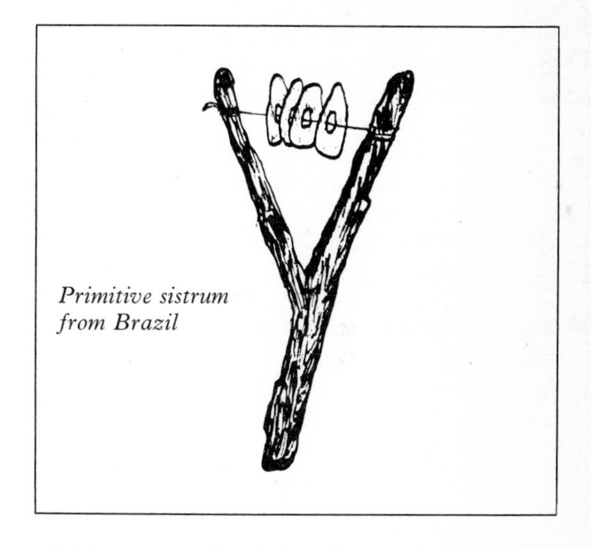
Primitive sistrum from Brazil

cave-paintings. Everywhere music existed to assist in work, sleep, combat and relaxation, but most potently of all in magic.

In some primitive communities the individuals who sang or played upon instruments were so feared that they took on a position only slightly less exalted than gods. Theirs was the power to control the elements. It was they who officiated at spring fertility rites, at circumcisions, at harvest gatherings, at solstices and equinoxes, and at all the other important functions and festivals of those superstition-ridden years. They were held in equal, if not greater, awe than priests and medicine-men. So great was their influence, and so jealously did they guard their power, that countless cruel activities grew up round the mystique of music. For instance, only men were allowed to operate the bull-roarer (see Part I of Section II), women had to be rounded up and put out of sight before that piece of wood might be lifted aloft to sound its strange message. If by chance a feminine eye fell on a bull-roarer, the possessor of that prying eye would summarily be put to death. And if a man had been responsible for the forbidden feminine viewing, he too would be executed. A similar mystique surrounded certain kinds of trumpet. Very often the death would be hideously slow and excruciating in an effort to appease the offended invisible spirit residing within the instrument. Similar taboos and penalties exist even today in certain backward countries, females being forbidden to touch, or even to see, certain 'sacred' instruments. Little wonder that the mythologies of the world became saturated with stories of musicians with their magic powers, of men and gods dwelling in instruments or adopting each others' identities.

The 'power' of music, then, to regulate the lives of men and women is as old as music itself. We may wonder at the gullibility of the ancients in allowing sounds to so influence and control their emotions, working, eating, sleeping, and battle activities, yet are things so different today? The first few notes of a familiar entertainer's signature tune are enough to trigger the modern brain to signal the appropriate action of the body–to listen or to switch off; advertisers realise the potent subliminal power of music in TV and radio commercials. In factories and hospitals, and even in farming, music is used to obtain better results, relaxed patients, or more milk! The last ten years or so have witnessed the realisation that carefully chosen music is of use in the relief and perhaps the cure of some nervous disorders, but before we enter ultra-technical areas let us remember the simple and basic use made of music in impelling large groups of individuals to rise, to eat, to do battle, or to sleep.

The army bugle is still fulfilling these functions.

Section II

MUSICAL INSTRUMENTS

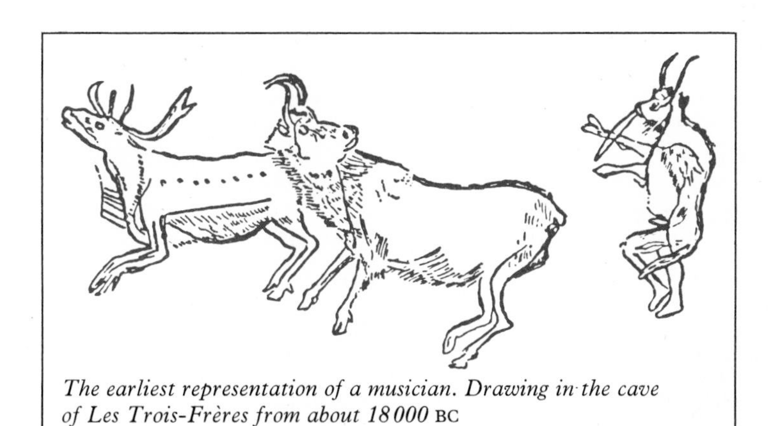

The earliest representation of a musician. Drawing in the cave of Les Trois-Frères from about 18 000 BC

1. PRIMITIVE, ANCIENT AND OBSOLETE

Possibly the earliest known indication that man played musical instruments in prehistoric times comes from an engraving in the Cave of Les Trois-Frères (named after the three sons of Count Bégouen, one of whom discovered the cave on 20 July 1914) in the Pyrenees of the extreme south-west of France. The engraving is of a figure wearing a stag's head, horns, coat, and tail, and dancing. In, or near, his mouth is what appears to be a flute (or perhaps a bow), and it is possible that he is dancing to his own music. Before him prance two oxen, one with its head turned towards him as if listening. This cave-drawing dates from some 20000 years ago.

No other representation which might be construed as human musical activity is known between this date and the 7th century BC. A drummer, in a mural in Anatolia discovered in 1961, plays for a group of twelve dancers dressed in leopard skins.

Thereafter, musical representations are common in the cultures of Egypt, Greece, and Rome, as the following instrumental details show. It has been considered most useful to group together under one heading primitive, ancient, and obsolete instruments since they do not easily separate from each other. Some primitive and ancient instruments, for instance, are still in use in virtually unaltered form while many obsolete instruments are of no great antiquity.

The generally adopted divisions of wood-wind, brass, strings, and percussion which are adhered to in Part II of this Section despite the occasional inadequacy of the system, collapses completely when primitive and ancient instruments are considered, the categories being stretched to their utmost until their edges merge imperceptibly. For this reason the alternative grouping originated by Curt Sachs in his *The History of Musical Instruments* is used. Brief explanations of the contents and boundaries of each group are followed by discussions of the most prominent instruments therein. The actual number of different instruments known from the earliest times is truly vast and it is, of course, not possible to give details of each and every one, nor the alternative names by which many of them are known.

It will be seen that many primitive and ancient instruments developed into designs which are still in use, and the reader is therefore advised to use Parts I and II of this Section in conjunction so that a true historical picture may emerge.

The basic principle by which instruments work is very simple: they set up vibrations in the air with which they are in contact. These vibrations may be brought about in four[1] different ways and instruments, therefore, divide into the following categories, which were worked out by Curt Sachs:

1. Idiophones.
2. Aerophones.
3. Membranophones.
4. Chordophones.

1. IDIOPHONES

This group comprises instruments made of materials which produce a sound when scraped, rubbed, or hit, without further modification having been made to that material, and without the intervention of other materials. Modern instruments in this group include the xylophone, cymbals, gongs, and castanets; less common are the following examples:

Bull-roarer

One of the simplest of all instruments, the bull-roarer consists of a flat piece of wood to be whirled round the player's head on the end of a piece of string. Its passage through the air produces a frightening sound, often of elemental proportions, and primitive peoples considered that this 'sound from nothing' represented the voices of dead ancestors. It was also believed to have magical, medical, and meteorological powers. Although of world-wide distribution, its best-known association today is with the Aboriginal tribes of Australia, and it has been used in the Suite from the ballet *Corroboree* (1946) by the Australian composer John Antill.

[1] Or five, see page 30.

Sansa

Thus named after the Congolese tribe among whom the instrument was first discovered, it is also known by the following names: Kaffir piano; likembe; marimba (but not to be confused with the instrument described on page 40); mbira; thumb piano; toum; zeze.

Its metal plates were fastened at one end to the sounding-board, the free ends being sprung down and released by the fingers and thumbs. It is this principle of vibrating metal which led to the construction of the first musical-boxes (see Section IX).

Sistrum

An extremely early and simple coloristic instrument, widely distributed throughout the world at the dawn of history. Two of its many varieties are depicted here. (Below and p. 15). The instrument could be used as a rattle or struck with a stick.

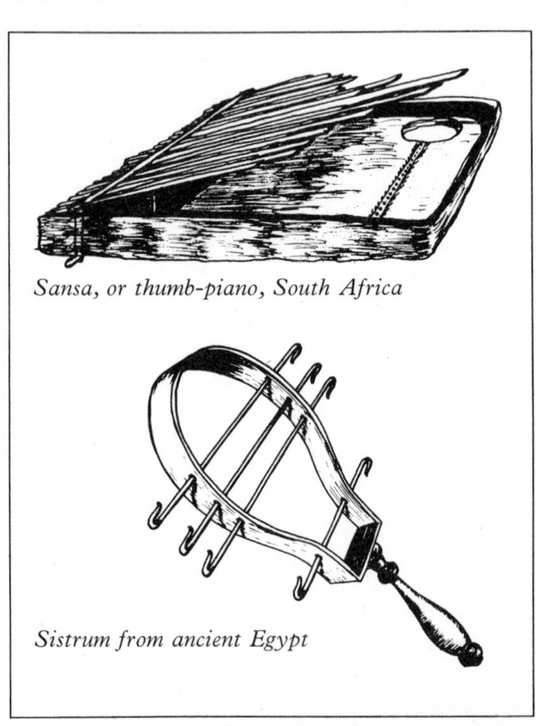

Sansa, or thumb-piano, South Africa

Sistrum from ancient Egypt

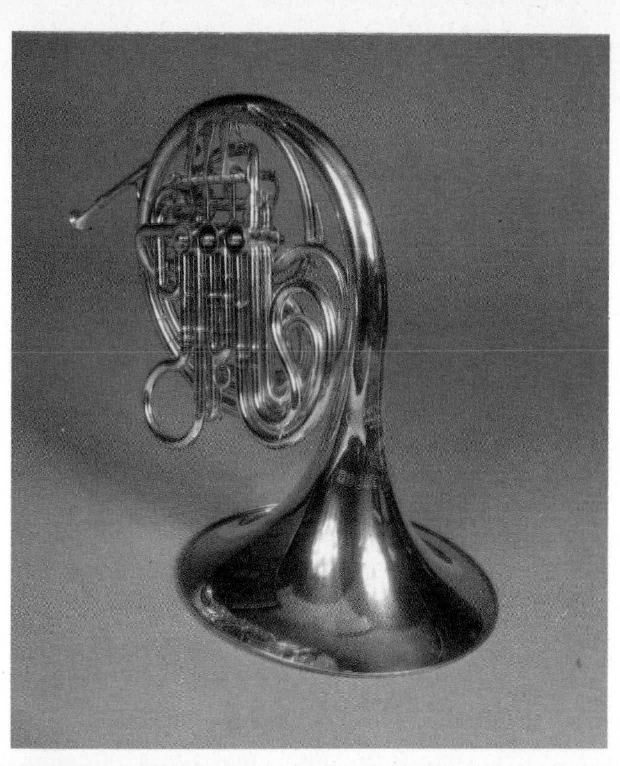

A modern French Horn (courtesy Boosey and Hawkes Group)

Interior of San Petronio Cathedral, Bologna, setting for some of the earliest symphonies

Trinidad steel drum

Trinidad steel drum

The West Indian steel drum consists of an oil-drum the head of which has been divided into a number of sections, each of which produces a different note when hit with a rubber beater. Although essentially a percussion instrument, the steel drum is well suited to the production of melodies, and 'steel bands' possess a remarkably sophisticated repertoire in which melody, harmony, and rhythm all play a vital part. The writer has heard a thoroughly acceptable performance of Mozart's *Eine Kleine Nachtmusik* played by a West Indian steel band.

Yamstick

An Australian Aboriginal instrument of the most basic kind: a simple stick used to beat out the rhythm on trees, shields, the ground, or anyone or anything which happens to be near by, to heighten the excitement at the wild ceremonial totemic dances known as 'corroborees'.

2. AEROPHONES

Instruments which contain a column of air within a cylinder or cone. A sound is produced when this air is vibrated by the player's lips or a single or double reed, or (most primitive of all) by air passing across the top of a tube, as in the flute and the recorder. Modern instruments in this group include the flute, oboe, trumpet, horn, and saxophone families. These were preceded, or are supplemented, by more primitive instruments.

Alphorn or Alpenhorn

A long wooden horn used for signalling in the Alps, its first references date from the 15th century although it is undoubtedly of prehistoric origin. Best known for its use in Alpine districts, it is nevertheless widespread in Europe.

The alphorn has attracted the attention of classical composers on rare occasions: Rossini imitated its call in his *William Tell* Overture (1829), but Leopold Mozart actually wrote a concerto for alphorn and string orchestra. At one of the famous Hoffnung Music Festival Concerts at London's Royal Festival Hall (13 November 1956) Dennis Brain played part of the concerto, using an ordinary garden hosepipe fitted with a horn mouthpiece. The modern Swiss composer Jean Daetwyler has also written a concerto for alphorn and orchestra.

Aulos

The aulos is the ultimate origin of all double-reed wind instruments. The strident tones of the aulos were produced by a double reed which was actually inserted into the mouth-cavity. The pressure required to vibrate this reed was so great that players had to wear bandages to prevent their cheeks from bursting. Due to its flexibility–its range was two and a half octaves–the aulos was a widespread and highly popular instrument in antiquity, and it survives in double-pipe, and even triple-pipe, form in Mediterranean areas today.

Basset-horn

The origin of the basset-horn is attributed to the instrument-making firm of A and M Mayerhofer of Passau, in Bavaria, about 1770, and was designed to extend the lower range of the clarinet. The name possibly derives from a German diminutive of 'bass', and the name–'Horn'–of the actual inventor. The first composer to use the instrument extensively was Mozart who, from about 1781, wrote a series of chamber, choral, and orchestral works exploiting its subtly different qualities. The first concerto for the instrument is now thought to be Mozart's A major work, K 622, written for the 'basset clarinet' which extends four semitones below the standard clarinet, thus equating with the lower part of the basset-horn range. Isolated works for the instrument exist by Beethoven and Mendelssohn, and a basset-horn concerto in F by Alessandro Rolla in manuscript at Einsiedeln bears the date 24 April 1829, although the work itself carries internal evidence of considerably earlier composition.

Bass horn

A Frenchman named André Frichot developed the bass horn from the serpent at the beginning of the 19th century (it was also known as the 'English horn'–not to be confused with the cor anglais–since Frichot lived in London) but it survived barely 40 years, and then only in military bands, before being superseded by the ophicleide and the tuba.

Cornet; Cornett

The name is a diminutive of Italian *corno*: literally 'a small horn', but the word has stood for two entirely different instruments in musical history which have alternated in prominence. In English the method of differentiation is simple: 'cornett', with double 't', was a medieval wooden or ivory instrument with finger-holes which operated like a brass instrument and was used mainly for the upper melody in open-air bands and in church music, usually in association with trombones (earlier, sackbuts). The instrument might be straight (muto) or gracefully curved (ronto). It was incorporated in the orchestra from the inception of such organisations, but its last appearance seems to have been in the Viennese production of Gluck's *Orfeo* in 1762, although it continued in use in churches until the next century.

'Cornet', with one 't', is a species of piston-valved bugle which was developed (in France?) in the mid 1820s. It appeared in Parisian opera in 1830 and in Berlioz's *Symphonie Fantastique* the same year; it also found a place as the upper melody instrument in brass/wind bands in England, and during the present century this has been its main role, its orchestral use fading out apart from exceptional instances. A performance of Berlioz's symphony with the authentic cornet parts is today, despite the modern taste for faithfulness in performance and instrumentation, still a rarity.

With this interest in authentic performances of old music, however, has come a revival in popularity of old instruments, among them the cornett, which is no longer a rarity.

While English terminology allows no confusion between cornet and cornett, when other languages, particularly German, are considered, room for error is introduced. The following list of names may be of assistance:

	Cornett (wood or ivory; medieval)	Cornet (brass; 19th century)
Ger:	*Zinke; Zink; Kornett*	*Piston; Pistonkornett; Kornett; Ventilkornett*
Fr:	*cornet à bouquin* = 'goat cornett'	*cornet à pistons pistons*
It:	*cornetto*	*cornetta; pistone sopranino; cornettino pistone*

The earliest cornetts were of animal horn: the German word *Zink* means the smallest branch of a stag's antlers. Finger-holes were first bored in the instrument in the 11th century, and with the use of wood and ivory allowing greater possibilities in construction, a family developed ranging from the tiny cornettino to the S-shaped bass member, the serpent.

Crumhorn

The Old English word 'crump', meaning crooked, led to the name 'crumhorn' for a wooden instrument, with finger-holes, which curved upwards at the end like a hockey-stick.

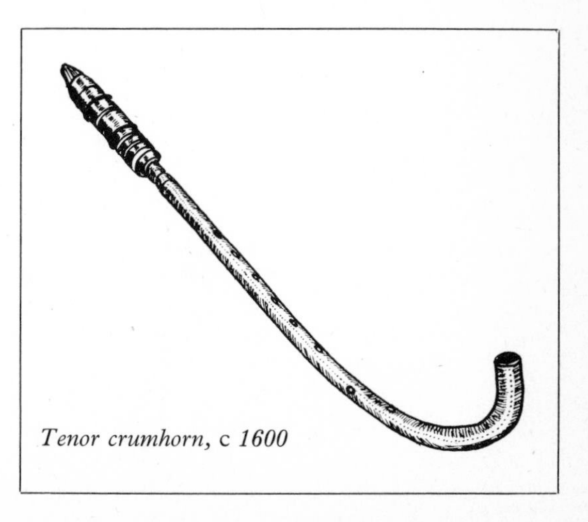

Tenor crumhorn, c 1600

Its names, in various countries, were subject to a certain overlapppng:

Eng/Ger: crumhorn/krummhorn
Fr/Eng: cromorne
Fr: *tournebout*
Ger: *Schreierpfeife*
It: *schryari*
Fr: *cornemusa* (not to be confused with *cornemuse* and *cornamusa,* both of which mean 'bagpipe', qv)

The crumhorn was a double-reed instrument which was popular from the Middle Ages but which died out during the 17th century.

Didjeridoo and Ilpirra

An Australian Aboriginal instrument consisting of a hollowed-out tree branch into which the player hums or whistles. Its origin is probably prehistoric.

Bass recorder

Lur

Constructed of bronze in the shape of mammoth tusks, these early trumpets were widespread in northern Europe in the Bronze Age. They are relatives of the Roman *lituus* and the Irish *karnyx,* and examples have been found with remarkably sophisticated mouthpieces. The main use for such instruments was in religious festivals, where they were employed in pairs.

Panpipes or syrinx

Said to have been played by the god Pan to the water-nymph Syrinx, the simple panpipes are of extreme antiquity. Each pipe produces only one note (in this respect the panpipes are in fact the simplest form of organ): a collection of pipes is bound together in order of size, the lower ends being blocked. The instrument has played very little part in concert music through the ages, being regarded mainly as a pastoral instrument, although Telemann included a tiny *Flauto Pastorale* for syrinx and continuo in his *Der Getreuen Music-Meister* (1728). Romanian folk-orchestras still make extremely effective use of the panpipes.

Recorder

It: *flauto à becco; flauto d'eco*
Fr: *flûte-à-bec; flûte douce*
Ger: *Blockflöte; Schnabelflöte*='beak-flute'

The earliest recorders were made from the bones of animals and have been discovered in Upper Palaeolithic ('Late Dawn Stone') sites of the Aurignacian period (*c* 25000–22000 BC). The instrument seems to have entered Europe from the East via the Slav countries, and its popularity outshone that of the shawms during the Middle Ages. The name 'recorder' comes from the Old Anglo-French *recordour,* which meant an imitation of the song of a bird.

In 1510 King Henry VIII kept a large collection of instruments at Westminster, including 76 recorders and a similar number of side-blown flutes, and a quarter of a century later, by which time there were four distinct sizes of the instrument, the first recorder manual was written by Sylvestro Ganassi dal Fontego, 'Musician to the illustrious authorities of Venice'. By the beginning of the 17th century there were as many as nine sizes of the basically unaltered design, but thereafter a decline set in. Only three sizes were in general use at the start of the 18th century (descant, alto, bass) but the instrument was well established in serious music circles, both Bach and Handel writing extensively for it. During the 18th century the superior power of the flute, together with some prominent propaganda on the latter instrument's behalf by King Frederick the Great, contributed to the eclipse of the recorder until the revival in about 1912 by Arnold Dolmetsch, who also encouraged interest in old music for the instrument. Among modern composers to have written for the recorder are Hindemith (Sonata for recorder and piano, 1932) and Luciano Berio (*Gesti*, for recorder alone).

During the 19th century the English flageolet, derived from the higher members of the recorder family, held a certain popularity among amateurs, leading to the construction of double and even triple flageolets, after the double recorders and double shawms of earlier times.

Early trumpets (see also Lur)

The trumpet had wide distribution throughout the East and Africa in the days before the Romans. Its earliest examples were straight, without modification of any kind to the simple tube, and, therefore, severely limited in melodic possibilities. The dividing-line between horns and trumpets is, to say the least, hazy until modern times, the two types developing along much the same lines and being used for similar purposes: mainly signalling on the hunting and battlefields. However, the true trumpet first appeared in Sicily in the 11th century; called *busine,* it evolved from the Roman *buccina*. The trumpet also held ceremonial responsibilities until its decline during the 18th century, before which, in the Late Baroque era, it enjoyed a spectacular development. At the time, trumpeters were regarded as among the most important personages at royal courts, occupying, with their drumming colleagues, a position physically above the rest of the orchestra.

The loss of high trumpet (clarino) technique led to interest being shown in extending the number of notes available in the lower register;

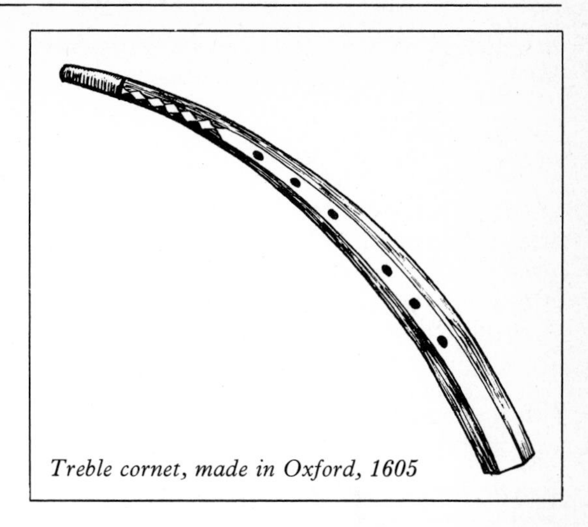

Treble cornet, made in Oxford, 1605

the invention of keyed trumpets, and subsequently of valve trumpets during the early 19th century leading to the perfect instrument we know today.

3. MEMBRANOPHONES

These are instruments in which a membrane is stretched across a hollow body (the resonator) and then made to vibrate by rubbing or hitting. Modern membranophone instruments include the drums and tambourine; only a selection of the huge number of more primitive instruments may be mentioned.

Bongos

Small, high-pitched, basin-shaped drums, joined together in pairs and held between the knees. They are struck by the fingers and thumbs which set up a sharp resonance from the vellum heads. Although of great antiquity, they have never become established in the modern orchestra; they have spread, instead, from their Cuban surroundings, via Latin American dance bands, into many areas of popular music.

Slit-drum

Often of enormous length, the slit-drum consists of a hollowed-out tree-trunk in the upper face of which is a slit of varying width and shape. When hit with heavy beaters, these drums can be heard over great distances and are used for signalling in the African jungles in which they originated. Virtually every village, no matter how small, possesses a slit-drum, as much as a status symbol as a musical necessity.

Frame drum

A membrane is stretched over a simple round or square frame and is struck by a beater or by the fingers, depending upon the size of the instrument. Early examples date from Asian prehistory, but they are still in use in the East, and a sophisticated form has entered the orchestra as the tambourine.

Friction drum

This describes the method of playing rather than the instruments themselves, which may be of widely varying types. In some friction drums the fingers or hands are rubbed over the membrane (as is the case in the modern orchestral tambourine for sustained notes), but in the majority of instances the skin is pierced by a stick or a chord, which is rubbed or revolved to produce a vibration at the membrane. Once again the principle is extremely old but still survives in primitive cultures.

Hourglass drums

These are double-headed drums with narrow waists, almost like two flattened tumbler-shaped basins joined at their pointed ends. Chords run outside the instrument between the two heads, and pressure on these chords produces increased tension at the skins. The notes obtainable, therefore, are infinitely variable, and a proficient drummer will cause the drums to 'speak' in an eloquent and excitable manner. These hourglass drums, which might be struck by fingers and thumbs or by a wooden beater, originated in India at least 2000 years ago and have spread into Africa and as far east as Japan. The capacity to 'speak' in an almost human way has led to the hourglass drum being employed in Africa as one of the 'talking' or 'message' drums.

Mirliton

Mirlitons of great variety are found throughout the last few thousand years. Today the best-known example, and an ideal illustration of the principle, is the simple comb-and-paper. The voice is projected against a membrane, which resonates in sympathy, producing a rasping sound. The toy kazoo is another example, as are the Chinese flute in which one hole is covered by a membrane, and the African mirliton, in which one end of a horn is covered by a type of tough spider-web.

Tabor

This old word for 'drum' (compare Fr: *tambour*) might refer to almost any type of ancient drum. More specifically, it is used for the tiny drum that formed half of the equipment of the pipe-and-tabor artist, who marched along with a pipe in one hand and a beater in the other with which he played upon a drum suspended from a strap round his neck. Recently, tabor has come to mean a species of narrow, long drum with a single snare. This latter was the instrument called for by Bizet in his Suite from the opera *L'Arlesienne*, and by Copland in *El Salon Mexico* and *Appalachian Spring*.

4. CHORDOPHONES

The two basic parts of these instruments are a chord and a resonator, the two joined together. The chord might be scraped by a bow or plucked with a finger, and when the chord vibrates the resonator amplifies the sound. Modern instruments in this group include the

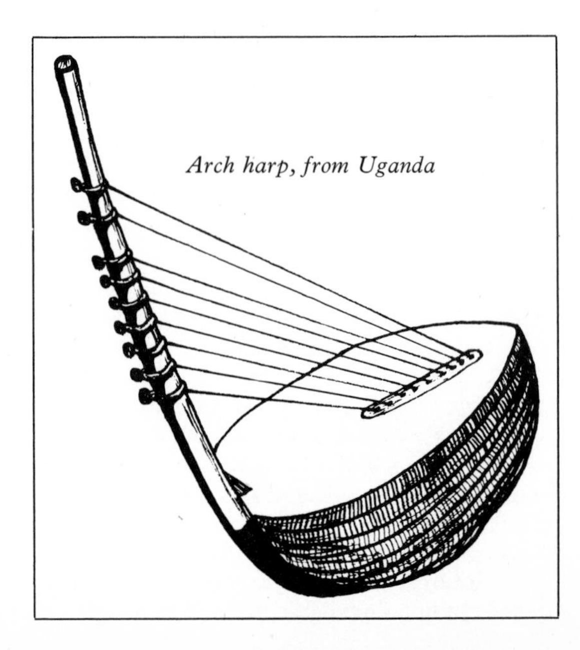

Arch harp, from Uganda

violin, guitar, harp, and piano families, in the last of which, of course, the strings are hit by hammers; less well-known examples of chordophones cover an extremely wide field.

Balalaika and Domra

An early stringed instrument allied to the lute and the guitar which was widespread as a folk-instrument in Europe from about the 17th century. The balalaika, together with its larger relative the domra, were modernised towards the end of the 19th century, and the improved form is now considered to be the national instrument of Russia. It is made in six sizes: piccolo, primo, secunda, viola, bass, and contrabrass; the domra family is similarly constituted.

Clavichord

The principle behind the operation of the clavichord dates from the Late Middle Ages; the oldest dated example was built by Domenico da Pesaro in 1543 and is preserved in Leipzig University. Like the virginals, the strings run parallel to the keyboard, but the method of sound reproduction is totally different from the harpsichord group: metal blades, called 'tangents', strike the strings from below, and the note produced is dependent upon the length of string left to vibrate. With this principle of not more than one note obtainable per string, some chords become impossible to produce, but this is no disadvantage since the instrument was basically melodic and was the most essentially intimate of all keyboard instruments, its sound being barely loud enough to be heard through a closed door.

Crwth

This is the Welsh name for an instrument also known as the 'crowth' or 'crowd' (Eng), *cruit* or *crot* (Celt) which was last used in Wales at the beginning of the last century. It originated in the 1st century BC and was developed from the lyre. Later versions (*c* 1300) were equipped with a finger-board and played with a bow. This modification made the instrument into an ancestor of the violin family. Alternative names from the Middle Ages stress this connection: *fiedel*='fiddle', *vielle*='viol'.

Dulcimer

Fr: *tympanon*
It: *Salterio tedesca*='German psaltery'
Ger: *Hackbrett*
(See also Psaltery, below)

One of the instruments which contributed to the invention of the pianoforte, the dulcimer consists of a rectangular box across which strings are stretched; the strings are hit with little mallets. The dulcimer was introduced into Europe from Persia during the 15th century and has survived well into the modern age, even though it has only rarely found a place in serious music.

The 'zither', a fretted, plucked relative of the dulcimer, was used occasionally in the serious music of the 19th century, notably by Johann Strauss II, but it is as a café instrument that it achieved fame for its prominent part in the film music for Carol Reed's *The Third Man* (1946), the 'Harry Lime Theme' played by Anton Karas becoming immensely popular. The American 'Appalachian dulcimer' is in fact a true zither.

Pantaleon Hebenstreit constructed a large and complicated dulcimer early in the 18th century and this had a hundred years or so of currency as the 'pantaleon'. The composer Christian Siegmund Binder was said to have been an excellent pantaleonist.

A local variety of dulcimer is the east European 'cymbalom'. Zoltan Kodály incorporated the instrument in his Suite from the opera *Háry János* (1926), and the Byelorussian composer Valter Kaminsky has composed a concerto for cymbalom and folk-orchestra. The instrument is also used, often with incredible virtuosity, in Romanian folk-bands.

Fiedel; fidel; fidula

Introduced into Europe from the East in about the 9th century, and played vertically in front of the player supported on his knee, the fiedel developed into the chin-held design during the Renaissance. It gave rise to the whole family of viols and violins, and the type cross-fertilised with the lute-type to such an extent that there may be found, scattered about the history of music, a confusing array of allied instruments, including bowed lutes and

Italian harpsichord, late 17th century (Horniman Museum, London)

plucked viols. In short, it is true to say that this family of instruments has undergone continuous modification right up to the peak of perfection in Italy early in the 18th century.

Gusli

This is not to be confused with the Yugoslavian bowed lute, *gusla*. The gusli is a Russian folk-instrument related to the psaltery and the zither and is called for by Rimsky-Korsakov in his opera *Sadko* (1898). The instrument had its virtuoso in the person of Vasilii Fiodorovich Trutovski, who played a variety of gusli, probably fitted with a keyboard.

Harpsichord

Fr: *clavecin*
It: *clavicembalo; cembalo; gravicembalo*
Ger: *Clavicymbel*

The earliest origins of the harpsichord can be traced to the 14th century. In the Victoria and Albert Museum, London, there is preserved a harpsichord built by Hieronymus of Bologna: it is dated 1521 and is the oldest harpsichord to which a date can be ascribed with certainty.

King David is seen playing an instrument in some early representations: it is plucked, has a sounding-board behind the strings, and resembles the psaltery which was brought to

Europe by the Saracens and Moors in the Early Middle Ages. The psaltery, giving birth on its way to the dulcimer which led ultimately to the development of the pianoforte, eventually evolved into the harpsichord family, which reached its greatest popularity during the first half of the 18th century. Literally thousands of harpsichord sonatas appeared in print (see, for example, Domenico Scarlatti in Section IV). Perhaps because of the limited carrying power of the instrument when in the company of even a small string orchestra, the harpsichord was slow to achieve solo status in a concerto. It is thought that the Brandenburg Concerto No 5, BWV 1050 (before 1723) of J S Bach was the first to include a solo harpsichord part, and even then it is merely an episode, although one of great length, in the first movement; for the rest of the work it 'concertises' with the other soloists, a violin and a flute. Bach's own harpsichord is still to be seen in the Museum of the Music Highschool in Charlottenburg. His seven solo harpsichord concertos all appear to be arrangements of concertos for other instruments.

From the earliest symphonies the harpsichord was, or could have been on an ad lib basis, included in the bass line as part of the continuo, but the first symphonic part specifically designed for the instrument (although, ironically, evidence suggests that it may have been played after all on a fortepiano since that instrument was popular at the time in England) is a series of arpeggios introduced for performance by the composer towards the end of Haydn's Symphony No 98 in B flat, first performed in March 1792 in the Hanover Square Rooms in London.

From the fourth quarter of the 18th century the harpsichord began to give way to the more flexible, wider-ranging, powerful pianoforte until it became completely eclipsed in the 19th century, but during the past few decades composers have come to recognise its value again as a soloist, and concertos have been written for it by Manuel de Falla (1926), Frank Martin (1952), and others.

Lute

The earliest forms of lute were already widespread at the beginning of recorded history. Illustrations exist of lute-players from Mesopotamia of 3000 BC, and tomb-paintings prove that lute-like instruments were well known to the Egyptians of the 18th Dynasty (1567–1320 BC). Similar evidence shows that the lute was played in ancient Greece and Rome: Nero, it is said, fiddled while Rome burned. In fact, he played the lute.

From its possible origins in the Near and Middle East, the lute spread in most directions, as the name chart which follows demonstrates, changing its form and name but still remaining basically the same in over-all principle and design. It was introduced into Europe by the Moors and Saracens who brought also its Arabic name *al'ud* or *el'ud*, from which the word 'lute' is derived. The meaning of *al'ud* is 'flexible stick'; the translation adopted in some reference books, 'the wood', appears to be incorrect.

It is pointless to discuss the matter of the instrument's first orchestral appearance since the lute has always been one of the stand-bys of art, as well as folk, bands since the beginning of organised music. It was still being employed in the orchestra at the beginning of the 18th century (J S Bach wrote for it in his *St John's Passion*, BWV 245, of 1723) and possibly its last orchestral appearance was in Handel's opera *Deidamia* in 1741.

Vivaldi wrote a concerto for the lute (P 209), the lightly scored orchestra of two violins and bass balancing the delicate tone of the soloist. He also wrote a concerto in D minor (P 266, of 1740) for lute and viola d'amor, accompanied by muted strings and muted harpsichord, and there exists also a large concerto (P 16, also of 1740) which includes in its scoring parts for two *theorbos*, or large lutes.

Although it is not possible to give here a list of the names by which many of the obsolete instruments were known, an exception is made in the case of the lute (and of the bagpipe, below). From its beginnings the lute had a wide influence on instrumental design, its successful construction being taken by following makers as a pattern for a vast variety of instruments which are widely spread throughout the ancient and modern world. Whether the lute is the true ultimate ancestor of the violin is an arguable point; what is plain is that the clear divisions which developed later between lute, lyre, guitar, and viol families become increasingly fuzzy the further one looks back into history, and it is a rash person who will attempt to describe definite lines of evolution.

The list which follows is not complete (and it would be neither useful nor possible to make it so), but it will serve to illustrate the wide range of the lute, geographically and constructionally. Asterisked names indicate bowed varieties.

_al'ud_	Arabia
angelica	England
angélique	France
archicistre	France
archlute	England
arcicetera	Italy
arciluta	Italy
balalaika	Russia
bandola	Italy
banlira	Ukraine
barbat	Persia
biwa	Persia
bugaku biwa	Japan
cai dan nguyet	Annam
cartar[1]	Persia
chicuzen	Japan
chitarra battente	Italy
chitarrone	Rome
cithare	England
cither	England
Cithrinchen	Germany
citole	England
cittern	Europe
cobza	Romania
colascione	Italy
dital-harp	England
domra	Central Russia
dutar[1]	Persia
_el'ud_	Arabia
*_erh hu_	China
Erzcister	Germany
esrar	India
*_fandur_	Caucasus
gadulka	Bulgaria
gambus	North Africa/Asia
gekkin	Japan
genkwan	Japan
guitar	Europe
*guitar-fiddle	Europe
gunbri	Sudan
gunibri	Morocco/Arabia
gusle	Yugoslavia
harp guitar	England
harp lute	England
*_hu'ch'in_	China
*_hu hu_	China
jamisen	Japan
kabosa	North Africa/Asia
*_kaccapi vina_	India
kamanga a'guz	Egypt
*_kamanje_	Persia
*_kinnari vina_	India
kobus	Arabia
*_kobuz_	Greece/Central Asia
*_koca vina_	India
_ku_	Japan
*_la ch'ing_	China
laghoute	Greece
laud	Spain
Laute	Germany
*_lira_	Greece
liuto	Italy
lute guitar	England
luth	France
lutina	Italy
machete	Portugal
mandola	Italy
mandolin(e)	Italy
mandora	Italy
mandore	Italy
mandorin	Italy
Mandürchen	Germany
mandurina	Italy
*_masenqo_	Ethiopia
mayuri[2]	India
mizhar	Arabia
ourumi	Nigeria
outi	Greece
paduan	Italy
panctar[1]	Persia
pandora	Europe
pandurina	Europe
pandurion	Greece
panturi	Georgia
_p'ip'a_	China
prasarini vina	India
qabus	Arabia
qitara	North Africa
qupuz	East Europe
*_rabob_	India
rabob assa'ir	Egypt
*_rebab_	Europe/North Africa
*rebec	Europe
rebob	Tajikistan/Afghanistan

san hsien	China
sanktika	India
★*sanktika vina*	India
★*sarangi*	India
★*sarinda*	India
sarod	India
satsuma	Japan
saz	Turkey
shamisen	Japan
shuang ch'in	China
sitar[1]	Persia/India
su hu	China
★*ta hu ch'in*	China
tambura	India
tanbur or *tanpur*	Afghanistan/Iran/Turkey/ West Pakistan
★*tan ch'in*	China
tar	Armenia
tayus[3]	India
theorbo	Europe
theorbo-lute	Europe
★*ti ch'in*	China
trichordon	Greece
★troubadour-fiddle (=guitar-fiddle)	Europe
vihuela de mano	Spain
vihuela de peñola	Spain
★*vina*	India
wol kum	Korea
★*ya cheng*	China
yueh ch'in	China
𓄤[4]	Egypt

It is left to etymologists and historians to develop the significance of some of the word resemblances, but geographical lines are suggested by *al'ud, el'ud, laud, luth, laute, lute;* and by *quitara, chitarra, cittern, guitar, cither, tar, sitar*. Further, the similarity of the last group to 'zither' is noted.

[1] These Persian words originally described the number of strings possessed by each instrument:
dutar = two strings *sitar* = three strings
cartar = four strings *panctar* = five strings
The Indian *sitar*, however, has from four to seven strings.
[2] Sanscrit for 'peacock.
[3] Hindustani for 'peacock'.
[4] This Egyptian hieroglyph, or, more correctly, pictograph, represents the non-vowelled sound 'n-f-r'. From this one may assume that the instrument was known to the ancient Egyptians by a name somewhere between *nafir, nofer, nefur,* etc.

Lyra; Lyre

A prehistoric instrument which has had enormous influence on the construction and development of stringed instruments through the ages, the lyra was originally made from the horns of an antelope, across the top of which was attached a yoke from which a maximum of seven strings ran to the body of a tortoise-shell with a membrane stretched across the top. The lyra was probably the root of instruments such as the harp, and indeed of many instruments from all over the world which incorporated strings fixed directly on to an amplifying membrane. In Roman times orchestras consisting of many hundreds of lyra-players were assembled.

Psaltery

(see also Dulcimer)

Early Biblical references to the psaltery seem to be confused with a species of harp, an instrument with which its development was approximately contemporary. In its early forms the psaltery consisted of a shallow rectangular box across which usually about a dozen strings were stretched. These were plucked with a plectrum or the fingertips, the instrument being stood or held vertically. As it developed, the instrument acquired more strings and a triangular shape and came to be laid flat. Some species came to be played with hammers; this led to the eventual invention of the pianoforte, on the way branching off into local varieties of psaltery such as the east European cymbalom. The plucked psaltery, on the other hand, led, with the invention of mechanical plucking agents operated from a keyboard, to the harpsichord family.

Spinet

Fr: *eschiquier*
It: *spinetto*
Ger: *Schachtbrett*

The spinet, originally called 'clavicymbalum', dates from the start of the 15th century but did not become widespread until the 17th; thereafter it co-existed with the harpsichord and clavichord until all three instruments gave way to the fortepiano towards the end of the 18th century. Opinions vary as to the origin of the name. It may be from the Lat: *spina* = 'spines' = 'quills', with which the strings were plucked, or from an Italian instrument-maker Spinetti. It was an even more domestic instrument than the harpsichord and its comparatively simple construction encouraged amateur makers to design and build their own, often widely differing, models. The 'clavicytherium', also known as 'couched harp', was a type of upright spinet.

Virginals

The name does not derive from the fact that the instrument was played by Queen Elizabeth I since it was known as that before her birth. It comes instead from the Lat: *virga* = 'rod' = 'jack', the rod which carries the quill past the string. Popular in England from the time of the first printed music for the instrument (*Parthenia,* 1611), its use paralleled that of the harpsichord and spinet and like the latter it possessed only one string to each note. Although exceptions existed, the easiest way to remember the basic difference in playing position relative to the instruments is to imagine the strings as viewed from the player running across from right to left in the viRginaLs, but away, or from south to north, in the SpiNet.

5. AQUAPHONE

This category does not appear in Curt Sachs's study; it has been found necessary to institute it to accommodate just one instrument, the 'glass harmonica', which, by its very oddness, refuses to fit into any of the other four categories. Considerable modification has taken place to the materials used in its construction so it cannot be classed as an idiophone; there are no strings or air columns to vibrate, thus ruling out chordophone and aerophone classes; and there are no membranes.

Glass harmonica

Also known as the 'euphon' and 'clavicylindre', the glass harmonica was a product of the imagination and sensitivity of the middle of the 18th century. Basically the principle stems from the idea of producing notes from glasses or tumblers which are tuned by being filled to different levels with water. 'Musical glasses' were performed by the Irishman Richard Pockrich in London in 1743 (but in 1759 he was burned to death in a fire which also engulfed his glass-and-water instrument); in 1746 Gluck played 'a concerto on 26 drinking glasses tuned with spring water' at the Haymarket Theatre in London, although it is not recorded whether the work was adapted or specifically written for the new instrument, nor by whom.

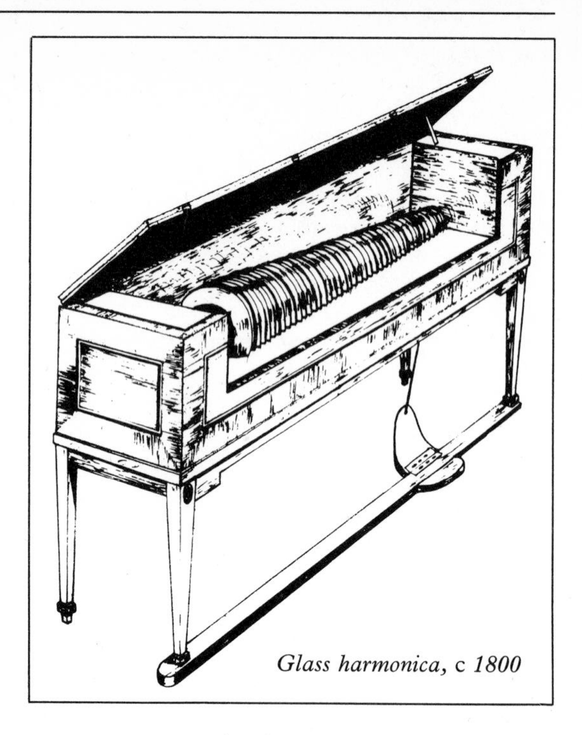

Glass harmonica, c *1800*

Benjamin Franklin, often given the credit for inventing the glass harmonica, merely adapted existing principles when he completed his instrument in 1763. The glasses, fitted one in another, were half submerged in water and were rotated by a treddle, the edges being activated by wetted fingertips.

Much value was put on the ethereal sound thus produced. It was said to have magical soothing qualities, and the German composer Franz Xaver Joseph Peter Schnyder von Wartensee wrote a descriptive piece entitled *Der durch Musik überwundene Wüterich* ('The Angry Man Calmed by Music') in about 1830, in which the volatile temper of the pianoforte is gradually calmed by the soothing ministrations of the glass harmonica. Saint-Saëns included the 'harmonica' in the 'Aquarium' movement of his *Carnival of the Animals,* Op 22 (1886): probably the glass harmonica was the instrument he required.

2. ORCHESTRAL INSTRUMENTS TODAY

No attempt is made here to describe the construction or working of the instruments of the modern orchestra, apart from a table of the extreme upper and lower notes obtainable from each, since technical and constructional details may be obtained from numerous reference books. What *is* attempted for each instrument is a brief note concerning its origin and, in order to pinpoint its 'acceptance' into so-called 'serious' music, the dates of its first use in the orchestra (concert or opera), its first true concerto, and its first use in the symphony. Usually, these appearances were preceded by the instrument's use in chamber or solo works, but as this field of intimate music-making is the proving ground for most instruments, the earliest uses often being undocumented and lost in antiquity, these particular origins have not been followed up, especially as the resulting details would be of little interest and no help in the understanding of the history of the instrument.

The grouping employed here is that of the modern orchestra: woodwind, brass, strings, percussion. Also included are the concert keyboard instruments (piano and organ) which lead a separate activity as well as being featured from time to time in the orchestra.

WOODWIND

Piccolo

It: *flauto piccolo; ottavino*
Fr: *petite flûte*
Ger: *Kleine Flöte*

1. Prehistoric; via flute and sopranino recorder. The name is an abbreviation of It: *flauto piccolo* = 'little flute'.
2. Handel's *Water Music* (1717).
3. Vivaldi's three concertos, P 78, P 79, P 83 (all before 1741).
4. Beethoven's Symphony No 5 in C minor, Op 67 (1805), last movement.
5. Arcady Dubensky, the Russian violinist and composer, wrote a capriccio for solo piccolo in 1948.

Key

1. Origin (with name derivation if known).
2. First use in the orchestra.
3. First true concerto.
4. First use in the symphony.
5. Additional facts.

Flute

It: *flauto*
Fr: *flûte*
Ger: *Flöte*

1. Prehistoric; via recorder. Lat: *flatus* = 'breath' or 'blowing'. Alternative names, referring to the angle at which the instrument is played, are 'cross flute' and 'transverse flute':

It: *flauto traverso*
Fr: *flûte traversière*
Ger: *Traversflöte; Querflöte*

2. Lully was the first specifically to call for the flute in 1672 in his operatic scores. All earlier, and many later, requests for 'flute' meant the then more usual recorder.
3. Vivaldi's *VI Concerti à Flauto Traverso* Op 10, printed by Le Cene, Amsterdam, in *c* 1729/30.
4. Alessandro Scarlatti's twelve symphonies (after 1715). These include one or two flutes in a semi-soloistic capacity and, therefore, antedate Vivaldi's Op 10 (see above) by a decade or so. By 1750 the flute was being used coloristically, rather than as a solo instrument, in the symphonies of the Mannheim School (Fils, Jan Stamič, etc).
5. Henry Brant may be said to have composed the first 'exclusive' flute concerto: his *Angels and Devils* (1931) is for solo flute with an orchestra consisting of three piccolos, five flutes, and two alto flutes.

Oboe

It: *oboe*
Fr: *hautbois*
Ger: *Hoboe* or *Oboe*

1. Middle Ages; via the schalmey family. The name comes from Fr: *hautbois* = 'loud wood'.
2. Lully's ballet *L'amour malade* (1657)

Names and frequencies of notes

The system used is the standard one based on the piano keyboard for easy reference, taking the note C at 261.6 cps as 'middle C'. In this system, the octave middle C to the B above serves as a reference upon which the upper and lower octaves depend. The C above middle C is noted as C′ (ie the first C above middle C), the next as C′′, and so on. Octaves below middle C are noted as C, to B, and C,, to B,, and so on.

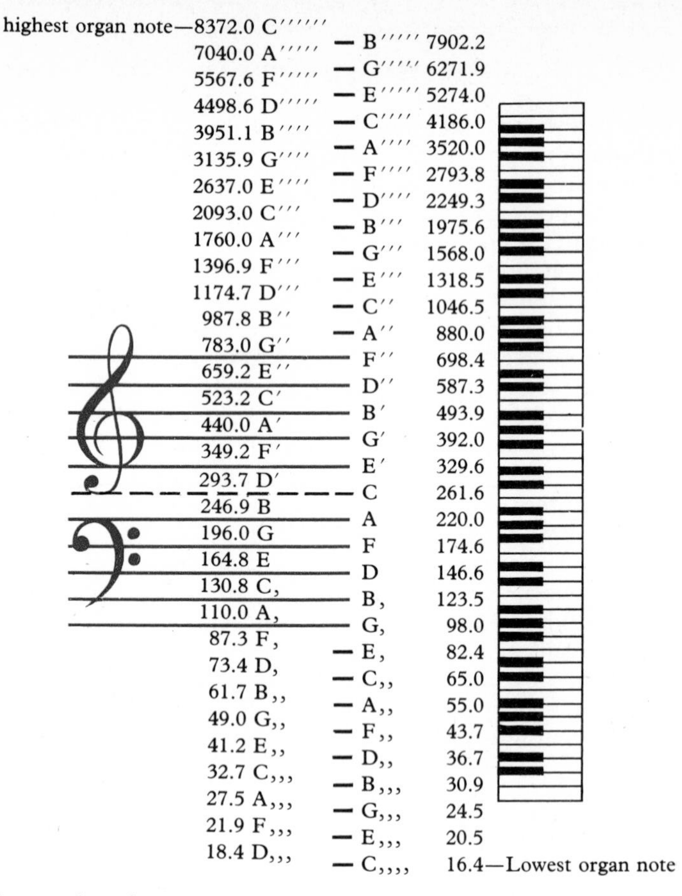

Highest and lowest notes of familiar modern instruments.

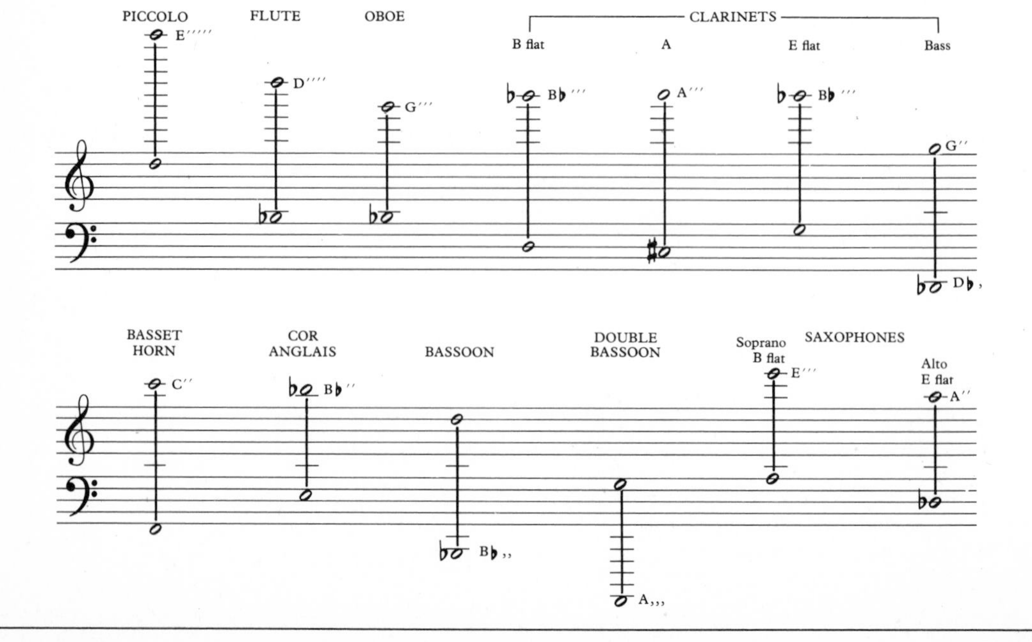

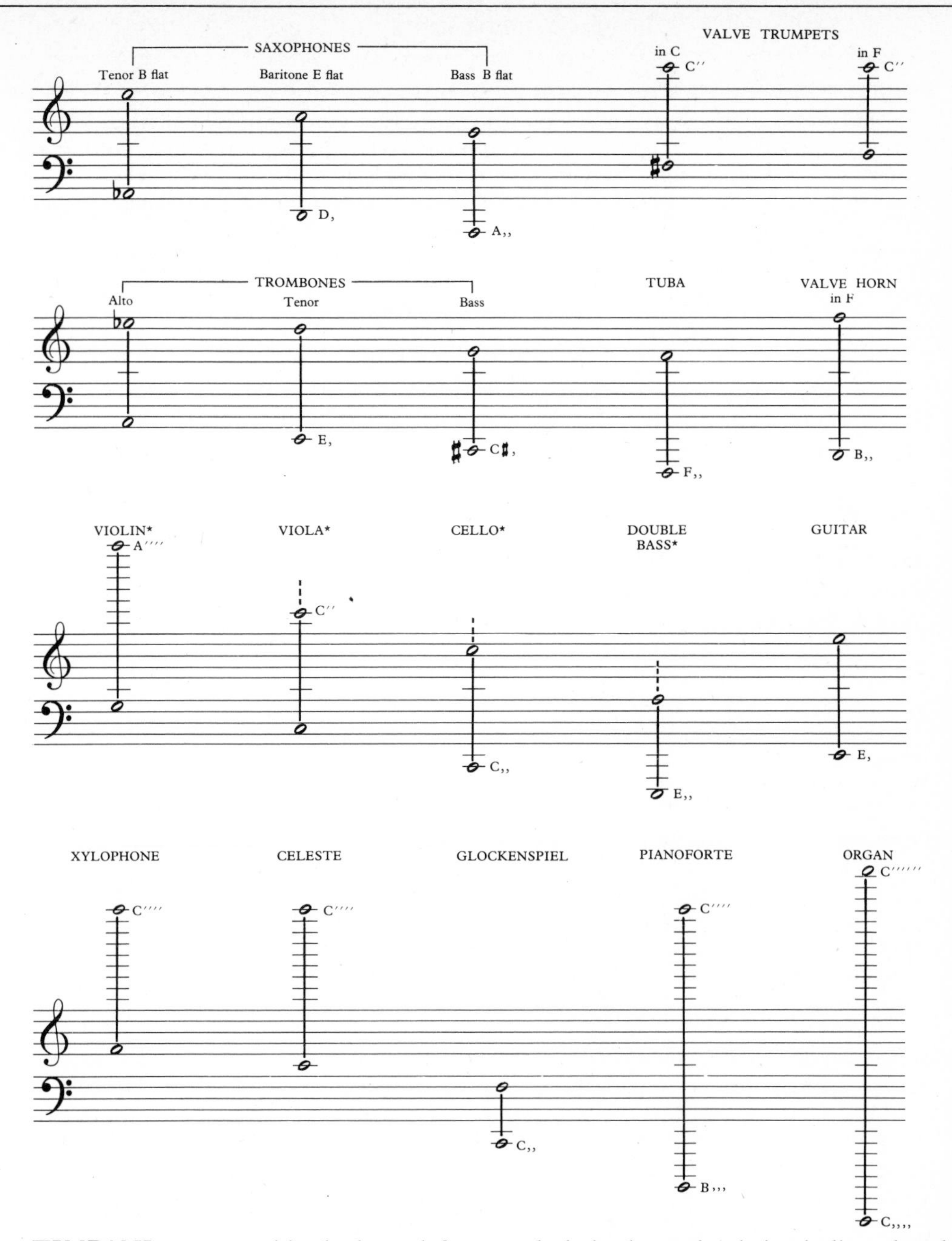

TIMPANI are notated in the bass clef at actual pitch, the tuning being indicated at the start of the piece; changes of tuning during a work are indicated by a direction in the score: for example, *change C to C#*, or *muta C in C#*.

The normal extremes of range are

*The purity and quality of extreme upper notes on bowed stringed instruments depends upon the skill of the players, and may be several tones higher than those shown for viola, cello and double bass. The usual upper extreme of the violin is given as B''' (1975.6), but an extension up to F'''' (2793.8) is not unusual today. Richard Strauss demands G'''' (3135.9) in *Also Sprach Zarathustra*, and Tchaikovsky's Violin Concerto requires the soloist to reach A'''' (3520.0).

3. Marcheselli (1708), but the instrument was used in solo and duet in the symphonies of Torelli before the end of the 17th century.
4. Torelli: several symphonies, for example G 31.

Clarinet

It: *clarinetto*
Fr: *clarinette*
Ger: *Klarinette*

1. Invented by J C Denner (1655–1707) during the last decade of the 17th century; via the recorder and schalmey families. The name means literally 'little clarino', since early examples had a tone similar to that of a trumpet.
2. Faber's *Mass for Assumption Day* (1726). Handel's *Riccardo Primo* of 1726/27 contains two clarinet parts written for August Freudenfeld and Franz Rosenberg.
3. Vivaldi's P 73 and P 74 (before 1741). In 1742 in Dublin, a Mr Charles played a (solo?) clarinet concerto which is unidentified and may be an arrangement from a work for a different instrument.
4. In 1753 the Concerts Spirituel in Paris included symphonies by Jan Stamič with clarinets replacing the oboe parts; three such works were published by Bayard in Paris in 1755–60.
5. The principal differences between clarinet and oboe, both of which occupied much the same range in the early years of the former's development, are that the oboe is of the double-reed family of conical bore while the clarinet family possess a single reed and are cylindrical in bore. The first clarinet virtuoso was Joseph A Beer (1744–1811), whose two clarinet concertos were written in about 1780, at about the time he became a member of the Berlin Hofkapelle. He was an associate of Karel Stamič, who also composed a number of clarinet concertos. The development of the clarinet family had reached such perfection by the beginning of the 20th century that a performance of Mozart's Symphony No 40 in G minor, K 550 could be given at the Brussels Conservatory in which all parts, in their correct registers, were taken by varieties of clarinet.

Key

1. Origin (with name derivation if known).
2. First use in the orchestra.
3. First true concerto.
4. First use in the symphony.
5. Additional facts.

English horn

It: *corno inglese*
Fr: *cor anglais*
Ger: *Englisches Horn*

1. Purcell wrote for a 'tenor oboe', but the first reference to a cor anglais is in Vienna in the 1760s. The origin of the name is obscure but it may refer to the use by Purcell.
2. As 1, above.
3. J M Haydn: lost. The earliest extant concertante work is Donizetti's Concertino in G (*c* 1820).
4. Haydn's Symphony No 22 in E flat, 'Philosopher' (1764).

Bassoon

It: *fagotto*
Fr: *basson*
Ger: *Fagott*

1. Italy, about 1540, introduced as the lowest of the double-reed group and known as the *dulzian*. The name 'bassoon' comes from It: *bassone* = 'big bass'.
2. Early 17th century.
3. Vivaldi wrote some 38 bassoon concertos, none of which is easy to date. All were composed before 1741, of course (Vivaldi's death date), but it is not possible to state whether any antedate Boismortier's Op 26 (1730) which includes a bassoon concerto.
4. End of the 17th century. Although not usually specified at this time, the bassoon was employed as a part of the continuo in symphonies, as in other orchestral music, from early days.
5. Johann Ernst Galliard wrote a so-called 'sonata' for 24 bassoons and four double bassoons. It was performed at Lincoln's Inn Fields Theatre, London, in 1745. Concertos for the instrument are still being written, as the recent example by Peter Hodgson illustrates.

Double bassoon

It: *contrafagotto*
Fr: *contre basson*
Ger: *Kontrafagott*

1. Its development and use followed closely after those of the bassoon. It appeared in Berlin in 1620.
2. Handel introduced it to England from the Continent for special effects in opera and oratorio.
3. No double bassoon concerto has come to the notice of the writer.
4. Beethoven's Symphony No 5 in C minor, Op 67 (1805).
5. Haydn used the instrument to good effect in his oratorio *The Creation* (1797/98).

Saxophone

It: *sassofono*
Fr: *saxophone*
Ger: *Saxophon*

1. Invented by Adolphe Sax (hence the name) in about 1840, and patented in Paris six years later.
2. J G Kastner's oratorio *The Last King of Judah* (1844).
3. Debussy's *Rhapsody* (1903); Holbrooke's concerto (1928).
4. Vaughan Williams' Symphony No 4 in F minor (1935).

BRASS

Trumpet

It: *tromba*
Fr: *trompette*
Ger: *Trompete*

1. Prehistoric; used as a signalling and warlike instrument from the beginnings of human awareness when wooden or animal horns were blown to attract attention. Our name for the instrument has considerable antiquity; it may be of onomatopoeic origin.
2. Trumpets were a part of the very earliest orchestras and, until the 18th century, they virtually dictated the development of orchestral groups and the music played on religious and ceremonial occasions.
3. Cazzati, in 1665. Although his works were called 'sonatas', they are in fact concertos for solo trumpet and orchestra.
4. Torelli, before 1700. Many of the works written for the San Petronio Cathedral in Bologna by Torelli and his associates were entitled 'sinfonia', 'sonata', or 'concerto' virtually indiscriminately. Therein, the trumpets were used soloistically. Non-solo parts appeared in symphonies at Mannheim and elsewhere in the 1740s.
5. The keyed trumpet dates from 1796, and Haydn's famous Trumpet Concerto of that year was written for it; the valve trumpet appeared in 1835 and was first used in Halévy's opera *La Juive* in the same year. The first sonatas for trumpet and continuo were published by Fantini, together with his trumpet instruction book, in 1638. The earliest work for clarino trumpet was a 'method' by Cesare Bendinelli, published in 1614 with his *Tutta l'arte delle Trombetta*.

Saxophone (Popperfoto)

Horn

It: *corno*
Fr: *cor*
Ger: *Horn*

1. Prehistoric. The development of the horn is so inextricably bound up with that of the trumpet that names, uses, and shapes have been frequently confused and were often indistinguishable. The word 'horn' may be onomatopoeic in origin, but the instrument's origin as the prepared horn from the head of an animal must not be overlooked.
2. Cavalli's opera *Le Nozze di Teti e di Peleo* (1639).
3. Vivaldi: there are two concertos for two horns, P 320 and P 321, but as their dates are not known they may have been antedated by J S Bach's Brandenburg Concerto No 1 in F, BWV 1046 (between 1717 and 1723), which also employed a pair of horns. The first concertos for a solo horn were probably the five of Op 4, published in London in 1742, by Hasse, and played in Dublin that year (but see 5, below).
4. Torelli, before 1700: G 37. The two horns in this work are used for orchestral colour, without solo parts.
5. Mattheson reports that there was a blind travelling horn-player in Hamburg in 1713 and that he 'produced more tones than an organ but with less mathematical precision'. This report indicates the possibility of hand-stopping as early as 1713, and hints that there may have been solo horn concertos for this player to perform at this date.

Trombone

It: *trombone*
Fr: *trombone*
Ger: *Posaune*

1. In 14th-century Spain and England, developed from the Roman *buccina* (a trumpet with a slide). The word 'trombone' is an augmentation of the name *tromba* (Italian for 'trumpet'). The Old English word 'sackbut' for trombone comes from the 15th-century French *sacqueboute* = 'pull-push'.
2. Used in the 17th century as part of the bass line, especially in Church music.
3. Wagenseil's Concerto in E flat (*c* 1760?).
4. The symphonies of Torelli come into the category described in 2, above. Beethoven's famous use of the trombone in the finale of his Fifth Symphony (1805) is antedated by the symphony-like overtures to Dalayrac's operas *Adèle et Dorsan* (1793) and *Alexis, ou l'Erreur d'un Bon Père* (1798).
5. Anton Adam Bachschmidt (1705/9–*c* 1780) was a trombone virtuoso who lived in Eichstädt. He may have been the earliest instrumentalist to specialise in the trombone. The instrument is still receiving attention as a solo instrument, as a recent concerto by Ian Parrott testifies. Nielsen's Flute Concerto (1926) has an important part for bass trombone.

Tuba

It: *tuba*
Fr: *tuba*
Ger: *Tuba* or *Basstuba*

1. Developed about 1829 and patented in 1835 in Berlin. The word comes from the Roman name for the long, straight trumpet.
2. Berlioz's *Symphonie Fantastique* (1830), in which it takes the part of the obsolescent ophicleide.
3. Vaughan Williams' concerto (1954).
4. As 2, above.
5. The English composer John White (b 1937) has written a symphony for organ and six tubas, and a work lasting three and a half hours entitled *Cello and Tuba Machine.* In the Hoffnung Music Festival Concert held in the Royal Festival Hall, London, on 13 November 1956, Chopin's A minor Mazurka Op 68/2 was played by Gerard Hoffnung himself and members of the Morley College Symphony Orchestra in an arrangement by Daniel Abrams for four tubas.

STRINGS

Violin

It: *violino*
Fr: *violon*
Ger: *Violine; Geige* (the old German name for 'rebec')

1. The Welsh *crwth* developed from the lyre in the 1st century BC, and in turn evolved gradually into the viol family. Successive

modifications, through the *lyra da braccio,* brought the violin to its modern form in Lombardy in about 1545. The word 'violin' comes ultimately from Lat: *vitulari* ('to be joyful', 'to skip like a calf'), through Lat: *vitula* (the root of 'fiddle'), Middle English 'viel', and 'viol', thence 'viola', the diminutive of which is 'violin' = a small viola.
2. Since its introduction in the mid 16th century, the violin, after an uncertain half-century of competition with the older viols, has been the stand-by of the orchestra.
3. Torelli: Op 8, Nos 7–12, published in Bologna in 1709, but written perhaps a few years earlier. Torelli's Op 8 also contains the earliest concertos for two violins (Nos 1–6).
4. See 2, above.
5. The best-known violin-maker was Antonio Stradivari (*c* 1644–1737), pupil of Amati and teacher of Bergonzi, Guarneri, and others. The first great composer/virtuoso of the violin was Arcangelo Corelli (1653–1713).

Viola

It: *viola*
Fr: *alto*
Ger: *Bratsche*

1. Similar to the development of the violin.
2. As for violin.
3. Giranek or Telemann, each of whom wrote a viola concerto 'before 1762'; Telemann also contributed a concerto for two viole at about the same time.
4. As for violin, but solo parts were included in Mozart's Sinfonia Concertante in E flat, K 364 (1779), and in Berlioz' symphony *Harold in Italy,* Op 16 (1834).
5. Benjamin James Dale wrote an Introduction and Andante for six viole in 1911.

Cello

(This is the accepted English abbreviation for 'violoncello')

It: *violoncello*
Fr: *violoncelle*
Ger: *Violoncell*

1. Developed alongside the other members of the violin group. The name 'violoncello' means literally 'small violone': see Double bass, below.
2. As for violin.
3. Corelli: in his concerti grossi, Op 6, published in 1715 but written many years earlier, the solo cello supports two solo violins. Jacchini wrote the first solo cello concerti in 1701.
4. As for violin.

Double bass

It: *contrabasso*
Fr: *contre basse*
Ger: *Kontrabass*

1. The development of the double bass followed the rest of the violin family, but stopped short, failing to oust the slope-shouldered configuration of the bass viol, known as the 'violone'. The name 'double bass' is functional: the instrument 'doubles' the 'bass' (ie cello) line.
2. As for violin.
3. Vaňhal's Concerto in E (*c* 1770?).
4. As for violin, but note also Dittersdorf's Sinfonia Concertante in D for viola and double bass, Kr 127 (*c* 1775), in reality a four-movement symphony with prominent solo parts for the string instruments.
5. Probably the earliest double bass virtuoso was Caspar Bohrer (1744–1809) who was also a trumpeter, but the most famous was undoubtedly Domenico Dragonetti (1763–1846), the Venetian-born player and composer for the instrument. The most spectacular work for the instrument is a fugue for four double basses written in 1939 by Arcady Dubensky. Franz Anton Hoffmeister wrote a quartet for double bass with string trio early in the 19th century, while this century has seen several works for the instrument, including sonatas by Ferenc Farcas and István Kardos, and a duo for two double basses by William Sydeman.

Key

1. Origin (with name derivation if known).
2. First use in the orchestra.
3. First true concerto.
4. First use in the symphony.
5. Additional facts.

Welsh triple harp, early 19th century (Horniman Museum, London)

Harp

It: *arpa*
Fr: *harpe*
Ger: *Harfe*

1. Possibly prehistoric and certainly pre-Egyptian in origin, it was well established in the Middle East by about 1200 BC and reached its present form by 1792. The word 'harp' probably derives from the plucking action of the fingers; compare Lat: *carpere* which is connected with harvest-time, the 'picking season'.
2. Incorporated from the earliest times in instrumental groups.
3. Handel's Organ Concerto in B flat, Op 4/6 (published in 1738), originally for the harp.
4. Berlioz' *Symphonie Fantastique*, Op 14 (1830).
5. Czerny wrote a *Konzertstück* for eight pianos and twelve harps.

PERCUSSION

Triangle

It: *triangolo*
Fr: *triangle*
Ger: *Triangel*

1. From Turkish military bands of antiquity. The name of the instrument, of course, describes the shape.
2. M Haydn's incidental music to *Zaire*, Per 13, (1777). However, orchestral inventories list the instrument in Hamburg in 1710 and in Dresden in 1717.
3. Mention should be made, in the absence of a concerto designed specifically for the triangle, of Liszt's Piano Concerto No 1 in E flat (1849) which includes a part for solo triangle of a complexity almost equalling that of the solo piano.
4. M Haydn's incidental music to *Zaire* (see 2, above) is counted as a symphony in Perger's list,

Key

1. Origin (with name derivation if known).
2. First use in the orchestra.
3. First true concerto.
4. First use in the symphony.
5. Additional facts.

but the first true symphony to incorporate the instrument was F J Haydn's Symphony No 100 in G, 'Military' (1794).

Cymbals

It: *piatti; cinelli*
Fr: *cymbales*
Ger: *Becken*

1. As for triangle. The name is derived possibly from the Gk: *kumbe*=cup.
2. Nicolaus Adam Strungk's opera *Esther* (1680).
4. M Haydn's symphony *Zaire,* Per 13 (1777).

Side drum (or snare drum)

It: *tamburo militaire*
Fr: *tambour militaire; caisse claire*
Ger: *kleine Trommel*

1. Descended from the earliest small drums of prehistory, via the military tabor of the Middle Ages. 'Side' refers to the fact that the drum is slung round the neck of the player on a strap and hangs against the hip; 'snares' are the wires running across the lower head of the drum.
2. Handel's *Musick for the Royal Fireworks* (1749).
3. Nielsen, in his Clarinet Concerto (1928) makes extensive use of a side drum as a solo instrument, as does Lopatnikov, the Estonian composer and pianist resident in the USA since 1939, in his Piano Sonata.
4. Grétry, in his multi-movement 'symphony' which acts as the overture to his opera *Le Magnifique* (1773).

Kettle-drums

It: *timpani*
Fr: *timbales*
Ger: *Pauken*

1. Originated in the ancient Orient. Originally the size of kettles, the instruments should nowadays perhaps be renamed 'cauldron drums'.
2. Monteverdi's *Orpheo* (1607).
3. The 19th century saw many works (by Berlioz, Lesueur, etc) in which timpani are given important and prominent parts to play, but the first true concertos for the instruments are the numerous percussion concertos of the present century, the first being by Milhaud (1929/30).
4. Torelli's Symphony in C, G 33 (before 1700).
5. The earliest timpani parts which have survived outside the opera-house are the two pairs in an anonymous Mass of 1682(?), formerly attributed to Orazio Benevoli.

Bass drum

It: *gran casa*
Fr: *grosse caisse*
Ger: *Grosse Trommel*

1. From Turkish military instrumental groups of antiquity.
2. Rameau's ballet héroïque *Zaïs* (1748).
4. M Haydn's Symphony in D, based on the incidental music to *Zaire,* Per 13 (1777), includes a 'tamburo turchese'.

OCCASIONAL VISITORS TO THE ORCHESTRA

Where known, the origin or date of invention is given, together with the instrument's first, or earliest important, use.

Woodwind

Alto flute. This appeared in the 18th century as an extension of the flute family. Paul Felix von Weingartner used it in his opera *Die Gefilde der Seligen* (1915), as did Hans Pfitzner in *Palestrina* (1917).

Bass clarinet. First made in 1772; Meyerbeer's *Les Huguenots* (1838).

Heckelphone, a baritone oboe invented in 1903 by Wilhelm Heckel (after whom it is named) of Bierbach-am-Rhein; Richard Strauss' *Salome* (1905).

Brass

Euphonium is a tenor tuba in B flat, invented about 1840, possibly by Sommer of Weimar. Used mainly in brass bands.

Flügelhorns, a group of instruments of varying sizes which appeared early in the 19th century. They feature extremely rarely in serious music, but Vaughan Williams employed one in his Symphony No 9 in E minor (1958).

Post-horn, a simple straight trumpet-horn which used to announce the arrival of the mail-coach in the 16th to 18th centuries. Johann Beer wrote a concerto for post-horn in B flat, hunting-horn in F, and orchestra (*c* 1695).

Wagner tuba, first built in 1870 to specifications laid down by Richard Wagner and employed in that composer's *Ring* cycle of music dramas (1869–76). Bruckner and Richard Strauss have also used the instrument, as has Felix Draeseke in his *Symphonica Tragica.*

Strings

Guitar, the national instrument of Spain, evolved in that country from the lute in the 16th century and has been used in serious music and folk-music from that time. The diminutive ukulele, which never appears in the orchestra, is of Portuguese origin.

Mandolin, a variety of lute which diverged substantially by the 18th century, when it became associated particularly with Naples. Vivaldi wrote a concerto for one mandolin (P 134) and another for two (P 133). Verdi used a mandolin in *Otello* (1887), and both Mahler and Schoenberg have scored for the instrument.

Percussion

Bells are more suited to the church belfry but have on occasion been used in the orchestra, eg: Dalayrac's opera *Camille* (1791), but their place is more commonly taken by **tubular bells,** which were first used by Sullivan and Stanford towards the end of the 19th century.

Castanets, from Sp: *castaña*='chestnut', the shells of which the instrument resembles in shape. Of Oriental origin, they came, via Africa, to Spain in the Middle Ages, where they settled as an instrument with which to accompany the dance; Bizet's *Carmen* (1875).

Celesta, invented in Paris about 1880 by August Mustel. Widor, in his ballet *Der Korrigane* (1880) was the first to employ the celesta, but by far the best-known use is in the 'Dance of the Sugar Plum Fairy' in Tchaikovsky's ballet *The Nutcracker* (1882).

Glockenspiel (Ger: meaning 'bell-play') in the 18th century meant a structure of real bells struck by hammers operated from a keyboard, a development of a Roman instrument of the 4th century. Handel used such a device in his oratorio *Saul* (1739). A later version of the glockenspiel emerged in the 19th century, minus the keyboard, in which metal plates were struck by hand-held hammers; the name is now given to an instrument with a keyboard, but the metal plates are replaced by tubes, giving rise to the alternative name 'tubophone'. Wagner and others have scored for the glockenspiel.

Gong (tam-tam). Originating in the Far East, the gong attained popularity in France at the time of the Revolution; Gossec's *Funeral March on the Death of Mirabeau* (1791).

Rattle. The Catholic Church replaced bells with rattles in the Late Middle Ages; their use in the orchestra dates from Beethoven's 'Battle of Vittoria' Symphony, Op 91 (1812), where they imitate musket-fire.

Tambourine, of extreme antiquity, used in the time of the Romans at festivities. Clementi's Twelve Waltzes for piano and tambourine, Op 38 (1798).

Temple blocks, a wooden instrument in the shape of a skull, hit with a stick; Walton's *Façade* (1923).

Xylophone (Gr: *xýlon* = 'wood'; *phon*= 'sound'), developed from the simple two-slab signalling instrument of primitive peoples. Lumbye was the first to use it in his *Traumbilder* (1873), but the best-known use dates from the following year: Saint-Saëns' *Danse Macabre.*

Marimba, a species of xylophone which developed in Africa, in which gourds act as resonators.

Wind machine, an invention of the early 20th century consisting of a rotating silk-covered cylinder rubbed by a pasteboard tongue; Richard Strauss' *Don Quixote* (1897).

Wood (or Chinese) Blocks, a series of hollow wooden blocks similar to temple blocks, above, struck with a stick; Gershwin's Piano Concerto in F (1925).

KEYBOARD

Organ

The principle of the organ–one pipe to each note–extends back to the panpipes of antiquity. In the pre-Christian era the instrument had divided into a species of portative (ie portable, to be played on the march) and positive (ie also portable up to a point, but much heavier and played in a stationary position). Experiments were made with different methods of note production (eg the Roman water-organ, or *hydraulis*), but the organ did not achieve multiple keyboards or pedals until its integration into church services in the Middle Ages. The first full-time organ-builder was Albert van Os, who worked in the Netherlands during the 12th century, and the earliest music to be written specifically for the organ dates from two centuries later. The peak of organ composition came with the music of J S Bach at the start of the 18th century. Apart from oratorio and other liturgical works, the organ is rarely heard in the orchestra today; when it is, as in Saint-Saëns' Third Symphony (1886), it makes an unforgettable impact.

Positive organ, 17th century

Pianoforte

The familiar pianoforte is a recent invention, reaching its modern perfection with the introduction of the iron frame in about 1859. Its origin, however, is found in the dulcimer of the Middle Ages, a levered mechanism replacing the dulcimer's manual hammers during the 14th century. Bartolomeo Cristofori (1655–1731) of Padua constructed the first true pianoforte in 1709, but the instrument achieved its earliest popularity far from Italy: in the British Isles, in fact. On 16 May 1767 at Covent Garden Theatre in London, Charles Dibdin accompanied Miss Brickler in 'a favourite song' from T A Arne's oratorio *Judith* (1764) on the pianoforte: this is the earliest known appearance of the instrument in public. The first public piano solo was played in Dublin the following year by Henry Walsh, and a fortnight later in London–on 2 June 1768–J C Bach performed on the instrument. This composer's *Sei Concerti per il Cembalo o Piano e Forte . . .*, Op VII, dating from about 1776, are the first piano concertos.

The first works in which two different types of keyboard instrument are set against each other, thus stressing the difference in tonal qualities, were composed in about 1780 by Heinrich Joseph Riegel (1741–99). Earlier, in 1740, C P E Bach had composed his Concerto in F, W 46, for two keyboard instruments and orchestra. This is often played today as a concerto for fortepiano and harpsichord but it was in fact written for two harpsichords and orchestra. The same composer's Concerto in E flat, W 47, actually written for fortepiano and harpsichord, was written in 1788.

MISCELLANEOUS

Accordion and Concertina. The accordion was invented in 1822 by Friedrich Buschmann of Berlin, who called it 'handaöline'. Larger instruments are equipped with a keyboard and are called 'piano accordions'. Pietro Deiro and Roy Ellsworth Harris, the American composers, have produced concertos for the accordion, and Roberto Gerhard included it in his Concerto for Eight Instruments without Orchestra.

The main difference between the accordion and the concertina, which was invented in 1829 by Sir Charles Wheatstone, is that, on the depression of one key, the accordion will produce two different notes as the instrument is drawn, then pressed, while the concertina produces only one note for both actions. Further, the concertina is never equipped with a keyboard. Serious compositions have been written for the concertina, including concertos by Giulio Regondi and Wilhelm Bernard Molique, and Tchaikovsky's Suite No 2, Op 53, of 1884 includes parts for four concertinas. Matyás Seiber wrote a work entitled *Spring* for accordion orchestra.

Ondes Martinot. Invented in 1928 by Maurice Martinot and originally known as 'ondes musicale'. The sound is produced by the movement of the hand in relation to a vibration-sensitive metal rod attached to amplifying equipment: the nearer the hand, the higher the note. The first work to incorporate the instrument was Dmitri Levidi's *Poème Symphonique* (1928). Concerts with as many as eight of the instruments have been given, and a concerto for ondes Martinot was composed by Jolivet in 1934; it is also given a part in Messiaen's *Turangalîla-Symphonie* of 1948.

Harmonium. The cheap and simple development of the organ has drawn only slight attention from serious composers. Dvořák included it in a handful of chamber works, and Mahler incorporated it in his Eighth Symphony (1907) (See p. 182). It was invented in Paris by G J Grenié (1756–1837) in the 1830s, when it was called 'orgue expressif'. Alexandre François Debain (1809–77) developed it into the harmonium we recognise today. Iain Stinson and John Whiteley set up a harmonium-playing marathon record of 72 hours on 6–9 January 1970 in Surrey, England.

Unconventional playing methods

There has always been an element of experimentation in instrumental techniques: the virtuoso violinist, for instance, might force an increase in the range of tone and effect available from his violin, creating new virtuoso boundaries and adding to the store of playing techniques for the benefit of future virtuosi. Not so legitimate, perhaps, are the weird uses to which some instruments have been put in order to create certain effects, uses which sometimes verge on abuses.

It is the violin which has been subject to much attention by experimenters. *Scordatura,* ie the deliberate mistuning of one or more of the strings, seems to have been specifically called for first by Biber about 1674 in his so-called 'Rosary Sonatas'. The effect has also been used by Vivaldi, Haydn, Mahler, etc, and has been extended to other members of the string group by Schumann and Kodály (cello), Wagner (double bass), and many others. *Col legno,* literally 'with the wood', directs that the bow should be played upside-down, with the wood in contact with the strings. Biber was the first to employ this effect also, in the first movement of his *Battalia,* a descriptive sonata (1673); Haydn also used it in the slow movement of his Symphony No 67 in F (*c* 1778), but the best-known example occurs in 'Mars', the first movement of Holst's *The Planets,* Op 32 (1914–16).

Among other unusual playing techniques is the strong pizzicato, in which the strings are plucked so violently that they rebound against the belly of the instrument with a snap. Once again Biber was responsible for inventing the effect to imitate musket-shot in *Battalia*; Bartók used the device tellingly in his String Quartet No 3 (1927), and other composers, among them Shostakovitch, have followed.

Yet again it is Biber who has the distinction of introducing another string effect, this time for the bass viol: he placed sheets of thick paper between the strings so that, when they were bowed normally, the instrument produced a dry, crackling sound, as of boots marching to a military drum, in *Battalia*. Much later, Richard Strauss directed that the double bass, the bass viol's successor, should be bowed *below* the bridge in *Salome* (1905) to represent the death-rattle of Jokanaan.

Rodion Shchedrin, the modern Russian composer, has brought a lively imagination to bear on orchestral technique: in his Concerto for Orchestra (1959) he requires the horn-players to 'pop' their instrument by slapping the mouth of the bell with the flat of the hand.

The same work calls for a piano in which paper is placed under the dampers to produce a nasal sound in imitation of a balalaika.

Chords from a solo horn have been asked for by a number of composers, the earliest possibly being Weber in his Horn Concertino in E minor, J 188 (1806). Four-part chords are produced in the following manner: the player blows one note conventionally but simultaneously hums another, usually lower, note, thus producing two tones. From the difference between these notes another tone emerges (the 'difference tone'), and a sum of the two basic frequencies produces a fourth tone at the top (the 'resultant tone').

Percussion has always been a favourite area for experimentation, the imaginations of Beethoven, Lesueur, Berlioz, Nielsen, and Stravinsky among many others bestowing upon the 'kitchen department' a rich supply of invention. Berlioz, for instance, required that the bass drum be laid flat so that percussionists might play it in the manner of timpani, and Nielsen called for the timpani to be struck with birch twigs in the slow movement of his Symphony No 2, *The Four Temperaments* (1902), a usage which calls to mind the effect produced by birch rods on the bass drum in the 'Janissary [Turkish] Music' in Mozart's *Il Seraglio* (1782). Other effects too numerous to detail in a general book of this nature include the placing of objects such as coins and chains on timpani heads and striking suspended cymbals with items as diverse as sponges and spanners.

Probably the most serious abuse has been reserved for the noble pianoforte. Many modern composers have directed that the strings should be played directly, bypassing the keyboard, by such objects as fingernails, nail-files, combs, hammers (presumably differing in weight and material from those with which the instrument was already equipped), spoons, brushes, etc, and by 'preparing' the piano in various ways in order to modify the tone. The habit is by now so commonplace among *avant-garde* composers that it is beginning to move out of the category of 'unusual use'. John Cage has written a full-scale concerto for prepared piano, and a list of music for the instrument thus modified is being compiled by the California State College.

3. INSTRUMENTS OF UNUSUAL INTEREST

At the end of the previous subsection (II. Orchestral Instruments Today) we discussed some of the many odd actions which players are directed to carry out in order to produce unusual effects from their instruments. Instrument-builders, too, have frequently allowed free rein to their imaginations. Results have been varied: to the inventors have been brought sometimes the unique effects they sought, sometimes merely a certain notoriety, and frequently a few polite smiles.

Firstly in this subsection are discussed the freak designs which often were built in quantity to satisfy some fashion or fad, and the closing part describes some of the unique instruments which have graced – and sometimes embarrassed – musical history. The order of each part is alphabetical since a grouping together of types would serve little purpose.

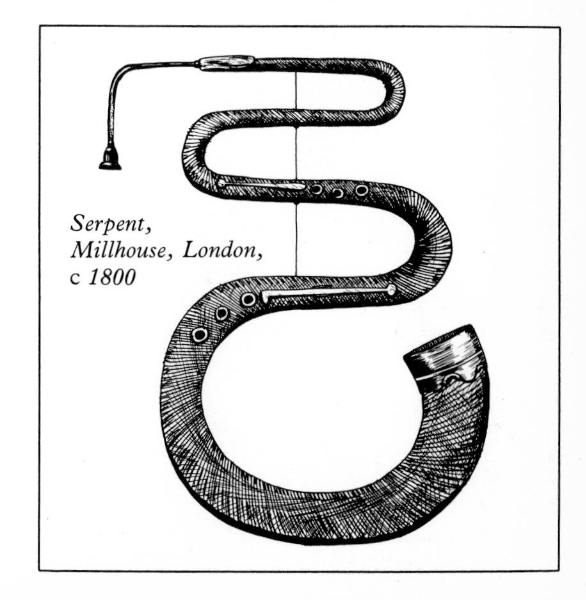

Serpent, Millhouse, London, c *1800*

Aeolian harp

Imagine a rectangular frame across which are stretched a number of strings all tuned to the same note. This device is then stood in a breeze and the strings vibrate in the passage of air. As the strength of the wind increases, overtones emerge from some of the strings to combine with the basic notes, producing a weird, unearthly, disembodied sound. This type of instrument, a mongrel somewhere between aerophones and chordophones, existed at the dawn of history: King David is said to have owned one. During the 19th century the instrument was fitted with a keyboard which controlled shutters to direct the wind on to certain strings at will, the strings by now being tuned to various notes, but the indefinite attack of the notes made the aeolian harp, the name of which commemorates Aeolius, the wind god, unsuitable for serious music, and it remains a curiosity but one of considerable charm.

Bagpipe

The bagpipe originated before the 1st century AD (Nero played one) as an 'external' version of the multiple-pipe aulos, the player's cheeks of the latter being replaced by a bag of air squeezed under the arm and the chanter and drone pipes equating with those of the aulos. The bag was originally made of the skin of a lamb or goat, minus the hindquarters; air is introduced into the bag via a pipe, either from the player's mouth or from bellows operated under the player's other arm. By the 13th century bagpipes of many different varieties were widespread in Europe and Asia, and soon they began to be made in different sizes.

Scottish Highland bagpipes (Popperfoto)

'The 'elbow pipes' (Ir: *uilleann,* later corrupted to 'union pipes') appeared in Ireland in the 16th century, and it is this type which found favour with the French in the *cornemuse* of that period.

The main modern difference between Irish and Scottish pipes is that the former has three drones, the latter two, in addition to chanter and 'breather'.

Although considered primarily as a pastoral instrument and as such often imitated in musical works dealing with the birth of Christ, the bagpipe also has connections with military endeavours in conjunction with drums; this use dates only from the 18th century. The Gurkha pipe bands of Nepal to this day strike terror into the hearts of friend and foe alike.

Alternative names for the bagpipe also indicate the extensive geographical range of the instrument in Europe, but species of bagpipe have existed for hundreds of years in India and China, where it may have originated.

askaulos	Greece
biniou	France (two players)
Blâterpfîfe	ancient Germany
cabrette	France
chorus	England
cornemuse	France
Dudelsack	Germany
dudy	Czechoslovakia
elbow pipes	Ireland
gaida	Bulgaria
gaita gallega	north-west Spain
koza	Poland
loure	France
masak	Hindustan
musette	France
piffero	Italy
piva	Italy
Platerspiel	Germany

Sackpfeife	Germany
Sacphîfe	ancient Germany
sruti	India
tibia utricularis	Roman Empire
uilleann pipe	Ireland
union pipe	Ireland
zampogna	Italy
zampoña	Spain
zampouna	Greece

Uses were made of the musette by Lully in some of his opera scores in the late 17th century, and Leopold Mozart wrote a concerto (1755) for bagpipe and hurdy-gurdy, with string orchestra. In 1773 Michael Haydn wrote a symphony in C, the scoring of which includes two 'pifferi' whose parts may be taken by two cors anglais or two bassoons (Perger 10)*. The 20th-century Yugoslavian composer Vlastimir Nikolovski has written a symphony (1970) in which a bagpipe is heard.

Baryton

Now obsolescent, this six-stringed bass gamba, sometimes with as many as 40 sympathetic strings which could be plucked with the left thumb, came into prominence in the mid 18th century when it was adopted by Prince Nicolaus Esterházy, the employer of Joseph Haydn. The composer produced numerous works for the instrument, including twelve divertimenti, 126 trios, 24 duos, and two concertos. However, Haydn was not the first composer to write for the instrument since Johann Georg Krause composed baryton music as early as 1704.

Chromomelodeon

An instrument invented and constructed by Harry Partch. In appearance it is like a harmonium, but it produces a 43-tone scale also invented by Partch. The contraption was constructed in Chicago in 1942.

Hardanger fiddle

A Norwegian folk-instrument named after the district from which it originated in the 16th century. The earliest surviving example (dated 1651) is preserved in the Bergen Museum. The instrument developed from early Norwegian fiddles such as the *gigja* and *fidla,* and from the viola d'amor.

Its four strings cross a bridge which is less arched than that of a normal violin, making the production of multiple stopping an easy task for the players who make a speciality of highly embellished and harmonised variants to the basic dances for which the instrument is mainly used. Among these dances are the *halling, springar,* and *gangar.* Four or five sympathetic strings of wire lie below the played strings.

There exists a concerto for the instrument by the Norwegian composer Geirr Tveitt.

Hurdy-gurdy

The 10th century saw the introduction of the coarse and complicated hurdy-gurdy, also known as *symphonia* and *organistrum.* The strings were set in vibration from below by a resined wheel which was cranked by hand, and the strings were stopped by tangents operated through a keyboard. Of course, all the strings were sounded together by this mechanism (*Symphonia*='sounding together'; this is also the Greek root of the musical form 'symphony': see Section IV) and no variation could be produced in the quality or amplitude of the sound. These limitations eventually outweighed the advantages of sheer volume which the hurdy-gurdy possessed at country-dance festivals, and during the Middle Ages the instrument, originally regarded as of high class, sank to the level of the street musician and the beggar. In the 18th century the tendency was for the instrument to improve its social standing since it had become associated with pastoral happenings, these being back in fashion among the aristocracy.

Leopold Mozart composed a concerto for the bagpipe and hurdy-gurdy (mentioned also above, under Bagpipe), written in such a way that the player, by changing instruments during pauses, could play both parts. The French composer Charles Baton was a virtuoso on the instrument, for which he also wrote chamber and concerted works. A later development of the hurdy-gurdy was the Italian *lyra-organizzata,* which incorporated a simple organ into the mechanism. Joseph Haydn wrote five concertos for two of these instruments, dedicated to King Ferdinand II of Naples, in 1790.

* See section on Thematic Catalogues, p. 219.

Nail violin

The name refers to the method of discovery (rather than invention) of the instrument. Hanging his bow on a nail in a ceiling beam at his home in St Petersburg, the German violinist Johann Wilde accidentally scraped the nail and was attracted by the resulting resonance. Subsequent experiment produced a cylinder of thick wood, the 'nails' or staples of which were driven in to different depths. The outermost bars of these staples are played with one or two violin bows.

Oliphant

This was a crescent-shaped horn originally made from the tusk of an elephant and imported into Europe from Byzantium during the 10th century. Also called the *huchet* or, in a tiny version only a few millimetres long, the *hifthorn* (Ger: *hief*='the sound of a hunting-horn or bugle'), it was used for hunting in England and was often made of solid gold, so highly did the Middle Ages regard their ceremonial and sporting instruments.

Ophicleide

By about 1850 the ophicleide had replaced the serpent as the bass instrument of the cornett family in French Church music and in military bands elsewhere. The name comes from Gk: *ophis*='snake'; *kleides*='keys', therefore 'a keyed serpent'. It achieved success during the mid 19th century but gradually fell from use as its range became covered by the bass tuba.

Serpent

Developed as a bass cornett during the 16th century and made of two shaped pieces of wood bound together, the serpent was able to produce a wide range of volume throughout its two and a half octaves but its tortuous shape may have combined with its unreliable tone production to put it out of fashion during the 19th century. Its use in France was primarily in the church, but Handel discovered the instrument in London and employed it in his *Water Music* (1717) and the *Musick for the Royal Fireworks* (1749). Mendelssohn, Berlioz, Rossini, and Wagner all utilised it. It was called the 'snake tube' in Germany, and the 'black pudding' in the north of England.

Tromba marina

The marine trumpet possibly originated in the Slav countries during the Middle Ages. It was known by the Greek term 'monochord', referring to its one main string, but the strange name 'marine trumpet' has a less obvious derivation. In form the instrument is long and slender, reaching a maximum of 2·2 m (7 ft 3 in) and tapering from 17·8 cm (7 in) to 5·1 cm (2 in), and it was roughly triangular in cross-section.

In its early days the thin end was placed against the chest while the other was held aloft at an angle away from the player. The outline of player and instrument from a distance might have resembled that of a herald trumpeter. Alternatively, or in addition, the sound may have suggested that of a trumpet: a single bowed string, lightly stopped to produce harmonics, passed over a bridge which was partly free to vibrate against the table thus producing a harsh, grating sound. Two other eventualities may account in turn for the components of the name: 'marine', by the resemblance to the naval megaphone ('speaking-trumpet') of the time; and 'trumpet' from the fact that the instrument was used in nunneries in place of the real trumpet (hence the German name *Nonnengeige* ='nun's violin'). Another German name for the instrument was the *Trummscheidt*= 'drum-log'.

The tromba marina died out about 1750, but not before Vivaldi had included it in a concerto, P 16.

Viola d'amor

Frequently called 'viola d'amore', supposedly referring to its seductive tone, the correct spelling omits the 'e'. The instrument, for many years thought to have been evolved in England in the 17th century, was in fact introduced into Europe, via Spain, by the Moors. Its resonant and characterful tone is produced by a series of sympathetic strings lying below the seven bowed strings. Vivaldi wrote a concerto for this instrument and the lute, accompanied by muted strings and muted harpsichord (a rare coloristic effect), P 266 in D minor, as well as several solo concertos, and J S Bach used it, for instance, in several cantatas. More recently, Meyerbeer included it in *Les Huguenots* (1836), Wilhelm Kienzl in *Der Kuhreigen* (1911), and Hindemith's Sonata for the Viola d'amor, Op 25, No 2, dates from 1929.

Viola pomposa

Said, without evidence, to have been invented by Johann Sebastian Bach. It is a five-stringed cross between the viola and violin; a concerto for the instrument was composed by Karl Heinrich Graun in about 1750, and another by Giovanni Battista Sammartini a few years later.

A COLLECTION OF UNIQUE INSTRUMENTS

The greatest number of musicians required to operate a single instrument was the six needed to play the gigantic orchestrion (or apollonicon) built in 1816. The orchestrion was one of the many types of harmonium built experimentally in the 19th century.

The largest stringed instrument ever constructed was a pantaleon with 270 strings operated by George Noel in 1767.

The longest single-word name of an instrument is 'hydrodaktulopsychic-harmonica', which is a variety of musical glasses.

Clavichord

The oldest surviving clavichord was built in 1543 by Domenico da Pesaro. It is to be seen in Leipzig University.

Drum

The largest drum ever constructed was built in 1961 by Remo Inc of North Hollywood, California, for Disneyland. In early days the size of drums was limited by the area of intact animal skin from which the heads were made, but with modern materials such as sheet plastic the size of a drum is theoretically unlimited: the Disneyland big bass drum has a diameter of 3·2 m (10 ft 6 in) and a weight of 204 kg (450 lb). There is a real danger with large drums that the concussion of beater on head could set up internal resonances which could cause the instrument to explode.

The world's largest playable guitar

Guitar

The largest playable guitar ever built was made in April 1970 by the Harmony Company of Chicago and was modelled after that Company's Sovereign No 1266. It stands 2·7 m (8 ft 10 in) tall, is 25·4 cm (10 in) deep, and weighs 36·3 kg (80 lb). The volume is 262 200 cm^3 (16 000 in^3) and the instrument cost an estimated $5000 to make. Today it is valued at $15 000. The 1·7 m (65 in) long neck is made of solid mahogany, the fingerboard is of rosewood, and the steel strings had to be specially made. It was built to test the capabilities of technicians and craftsmen, although, as its existence was not kept a secret, we may assume a certain element of advertising was intended.

The most expensive normal-sized guitar is the Gretsch White Falcon, valued in 1970 at £500.

Harmonica

The world's largest harmonica is 2·5 m (8 ft 2 in) in length and requires the combined efforts of six players at a time. It incorporates one bass, eleven chromatic, and one polyphonic mouth-organs, and was reported in 1963 by the Society for the Preservation and Advancement of the Harmonica.

The harmonica is the most popular of all musical instruments, at least among players: in 1965 an estimated 28 000 000 harmonicas were sold in the USA alone.

Harpsichord

The oldest harpsichord to which a date can be assigned with certainty is preserved in the Victoria and Albert Museum in London. It was built by Hieronymus of Bologna in 1521. The wording on the keyboard cover reads: ASPICITE VT TRAHITVR SVAVI MODVLAMINE VOCIS QVICQVID HABENT AER SIDERA TERRA FRETUN ('Behold how everything contained in air, heaven, earth, and sea is moved by the sweet sound of melody').

A construction plan for a harpsichord by Henricus Arnault of Zwolle is dated 1435 and is **the oldest known reference to the instrument.** It shows five sound-holes, and the instrument was built in the shape of a wing.

The most expensive harpsichord is a Flemish instrument of 1642, for which £9600 was paid by a private buyer at Sotheby's, London, on 27 November 1969.

Horn

The earliest surviving horn is a hartshorn in the Bernoulli Collection, dating from 1455.

The longest wooden horn is one constructed from a branch of a cypress tree with the 'knee' gouged out.

It is 8·1 m (26 ft 5 in) long and is owned by Horace Allison of the USA who made it. He uses no reeds or valves, but can produce numerous well-known airs by lip tension and air pressure.

An alphorn is reported from Aschau bei Kraiburg in Bavaria, as measuring 10 m (32 ft 9½ in) in length and requires the lung capacity of three men.

Kazoo

The kazoo is described in detail in Section VIII: The 20th Century Scene, where it takes its rightful place among the informal instruments which have been employed in jazz and popular music. Here it is necessary only to detail **the world's largest kazoo.** It is a monster instrument weighing 19·5 kg (43 lb) and measuring 2·1 m (7 ft) high by 1·3 m (4 ft 5 in) wide, and was reported by Barbara D Stewart, 'Manager and Kazoo Keeper' of the Kazoophony, Rochester, New York, in July 1975. The instrument is operated by four players simultaneously.

Octobass

A monster bass viol, 4 m (13 ft) high, invented in 1849 by J B Vuillaume of Paris. Its three strings were tuned from the lower end of the instrument, and stopping was effected either by hand (if the player had sufficient reach) or by pedals. Berlioz was said to have been enthusiastic, possibly more with the idea than with the instrument itself, and Karl Geiringer who heard it in the 1940s reports that the tone was unexpectedly weak.

In 1889, a John Goyers constructed his 'Grand Bass' which stood 4·6 m (15 ft) high.

Numerous reports of outsize double basses have appeared during the last two and a half centuries. The earliest is possibly that surrounding Joseph Kaempfer, a member of Haydn's orchestra at Esterháza. His instrument, known as 'Goliath' was 'unusually large'. For travelling (Kaempfer visited London) the instrument was dismantled by the unfastening of 25 screws.

Piano

Two of the earliest of Cristofori's instruments are still in existence. One, made in 1720 and heavily restored, is to be seen in the Metropolitan Museum in New York; another dated 1726, is preserved at Florence, in the Kraus Museum. This latter piano still possesses the original leather hammer-heads.

The world's ugliest piano was the one presented to Napoleon III by Queen Victoria on the occasion of his marriage. It is constructed in the shape of Napoleon's hat and, when it was sold in December 1971 for £220 to Tokyo University, a representative said that the instrument is 'unbelievably grotesque'.

The lightest baby grand piano weighed only 172 kg (379 lb). It was made by the Blüthner Piano Company, utilising aluminium for many of the parts, for use in the German zeppelin *Hindenburg*.

The most adventurous history of any musical instrument was experienced by the so-called 'Siena piano'. It was built in about 1798 by Marchesio of Turin and became a wedding-present to Rebecca Marchesio and Antonio Ferri upon the occasion of their wedding in about 1820, and was taken to the Ferri farmstead in Siena. Antonio Ferri, a grandson of this union, built the cabinet which survives today from wood reputed to be from the pillars of Solomon's Temple. The panels are some 12·7 cm (5 in) thick in places, and are carved to saturation-point with cherubs, drinking scenes, etc. In 1867 the instrument was shown at the Paris Exposition as the piano of which Liszt said that the tone was 'divine'. The following year it was made another wedding-gift, this time to Crown Prince Umberto from the city of Siena, and was taken to Rome by the Prince. Its following years were obscure and probably peaceful, but apparently the instrument was looted by the Germans during the Second World War and taken to North Africa to entertain the Nazi troops. Left behind during their retreat after the Battle of El Alamein, it was discovered by a salvage party and nearly blown up when suspected of being a booby trap. Somehow it had acquired a thick coating of plaster which hid its true identity even from specialists, and this and the sand-filled interior rendered the instrument useless for playing until repairs were carried out by the British Army. For the rest of the war it accompanied an English troup of forces entertainers, but on VE day it was in Tel Aviv, where it was left in the care of a scrap-dealer.

Its most ignominious period had arrived, during which it served as anything but a musical instrument: a meat-storage cabinet, a beehive, and a chicken incubator, among other things. It was at last rescued by Avner Carmi the piano-tuner and grandson of the piano virtuoso Mathis Yarmovsky. Carmi removed the plaster with the aid of 109 l (24 gal) of acetone and rebuilt the action and stringing. The only part of the workings to remain in original condition was the miraculously preserved sounding-board. Carmi worked from 1950 to 1953 before the instrument was brought back to playing condition, after which it was shipped to New York where a series of recordings of its 'period' but unremarkable sounds were made.

Trumpet

The earliest dated trumpet to survive was made in 1523 by Ubaldo Martini of Siena. It is preserved in the Berlin Musical Instrument Collection.

The smallest trumpet in the world was made in Berne, Switzerland by Karl Burri. It has three valves, and measures 12·7 cm (5 in) in length.

Tuba

The world's largest tuba is still in use in a South African circus. It stands 2·3 m (7 ft 6 in) high and measures 1 m (3 ft 4 in) across the bell. John Philip Sousa (1854–1932), the American 'March King', commissioned the instrument in 1896: it took two years to build and contains 12 m (39 ft) of piping.

The largest tuba in England is another which Sousa commissioned at the same time. Its weight is 45·4 kg (100 lb), and it measures 1·8 m (6 ft) high and 0·9 m (3 ft) across the bell. It is at present owned by a member of the Johnny Dankworth Band in London, having been reputedly left behind by Sousa after an English tour, when it came into the category of excess baggage. Both Gerard Hoffnung, the musician, comedian, and cartoonist, and 'Professor' Jimmy Edwards the comedian have played the instrument in public.

Violin

The most valuable violin in the world may be identified only indirectly since it has not been offered for sale. In 1972 an American buyer paid $250 000 (£104 166) for the Stradivarius 'Cassole' violin of 1716. On this scale, the famous 'Messie' Strad which is preserved in the Ashmolean Museum in Oxford would command a price in excess of £200 000, making it the most valuable violin in the world.

Antonio Stradivari (*c* 1644–1737), a pupil, along with Andrea Guarneri, of Nicolò Amati (1596–1684), was **the most famous violin-maker of all time.** Working all his life in Cremona, he produced violins, violas, and cellos, 712 examples of which are known to survive. His best instruments were produced during his so-called 'golden period' from 1700 to 1720.

BELLS

These instruments are often imitated in music, either by non-bell-like instruments playing carillon-like music (as for instance in Bizet's incidental music to *L'Arlesienne* of 1872) or by voices singing bell-like motives (Carl Orff's *Carmina Burana* of 1937). Alternatively, the actual sounds are reproduced by instruments such as the tubular bells or the glockenspiel. These latter uses are discussed on p 40. Here we are concerned with non-musical bells, mainly in places of worship.

The earliest known bell dates back to about 3000 BC; it was the 'Huang Chung' ('Yellow Bell') which established a standard musical tone for performances of Chinese temple music.

The earliest surviving bell dates from about 1000 BC. It is a handbell which may have been used for religious purposes, and was recovered from an archaeological site at the Babylonian Palace of Nimrod in 1849 by Mr (later Sir) Austen Henry Layard.

The oldest dated bell in England is to be found in Lissett Church, near Bridlington, Humberside, England. In October 1972 it was discovered to bear the date MCCLIIII (1254).

The world's largest bell was cast in Russia in 1733. Known as 'Tsar Kolokol' ('King of Bells'), it was designed to be hung in the Kremlin (completed in 1510), Moscow, but by mischance it was cracked in a fire in 1737 before it had been sounded. It rests today on a platform in the Kremlin, and stands 5·8 m (19 ft) high, measures 6·9 m (22 ft 6 in) in diameter, and weighs 196·1 tonnes (193 tons). In addition to this silent monument, Moscow holds the record for **the largest sounding bell** at a weight of 130 tonnes (128 tons).

Notable Bells of the World, by Countries

Country	*Location*	*Date cast*	*Weight in tonnes/(tons)*
Russia	Kremlin, Moscow	1733	196·1 (193)
Burma	Mandalay ('Mingun Bell')	*c* 1815	91·4 (90)
Japan	Honshu ('Choin-in')	?	75·2 (74)
China	Peking	?	53·9 (53)
Germany	Cologne Cathedral ('Petersglock')[1]	1923	25·4 (25)
Portugal	Lisbon Cathedral	14th century	24·4 (24)
Austria	St Stephen's Cathedral, Vienna ('Pummerin')	1957	23·9 (23·6)
France	Montmartre, Paris	1898	19·7 (19·4)
America	Riverside Drive Church, New York City[2]	1931	18·5 (18·25)
Czecho-slovakia	Olmutz, Moravia	1931	18·2 (17·9)
Spain	Toledo Cathedral ('Campaña gorda')	1753	17·3 (17)
Great Britain	St Paul's Cathedral, London ('Great Paul')[3]	1881	17 (16·76)
Canada	Montreal Cathedral ('Bourdon')	1847	11·2 (11·075)
Belgium	St Ramoldus Cathedral, Mechlin	*c* 1600	9·1 (9)
Poland	Danzig	1453	6·2 (6·05)
New Zealand	Wellington War Memorial	1929	5·1 (5)
Switzerland	Schafthausen ('Schillerglock')	1486	4·5 (4·42)

[1] The world's **heaviest** swinging bell.

[2] This bell was cast by the firm of Gillet and Johnston of Croydon, Surrey, England, and is the **heaviest tuned bell** in the world.

[3] This E flat bell in the south tower of the Cathedral is inscribed 'Vae mihi si non evangelizavere' ('Woe is unto me, if I preach not the gospel'), Corinthians 9:16.

The world's most famous bell is 'Big Ben', the hour bell in the Clock Tower of the House of Commons, London. It was cast in 1858, weighs 13·8 tonnes (13·575 tons), and has been broadcast daily by the British Broadcasting Corporation for many years.

The world's largest carillon is that of the 72-bell Laura Spelman Rockefeller Memorial Carillon in Riverside Drive Church, New York City, of which the 18·54 tonnes (18·25 ton) bell mentioned above is a part. The whole carillon was built by Gillet and Johnston, Croydon, a well-known and long-established firm of potters.

The heaviest carillon in the United Kingdom is in St Nicholas Church, Aberdeen, Scotland. Its 48 bells weigh a total of 25·8 tonnes (25·4 tons) and the range of the notes is nearly four octaves.

The world's highest belfry, in terms of distance from ground-level, is located 213·4 m (700 ft) up in Metropolitan Life Insurance Tower, New York City. The bells therein can be heard at a distance of 45 km (28 miles).

ORGANS

The largest and loudest musical instrument ever made is the Auditorium Organ, Atlantic City, New Jersey, USA. Built in 1930, the instrument has two consoles with a total of twelve manuals, 1477 stops, and 33112 pipes (from 0·5 cm ($\frac{3}{16}$ in) to 19·5 m (64 ft) in length). Its 'flat-out' volume generated by blower motors of 370 cv (365 hp) equalled that of 25 brass bands, but the instrument is today only partly functional. The ophicleide stop of the Grand Great is **the world's loudest organ stop.** Operated by a pressure of 254 cm (100 in) of water, its pure trumpet tone is six times greater than the loudest of locomotive whistles.

The world's largest church organ is in Passau Cathedral, Germany. Built in 1928 by D F Steinmeyer and Co, it has 16000 pipes and 5 manuals.

The largest cathedral organ in Britain is that completed in Liverpool Anglican Cathedral on 18 October 1926, with two five-manual consoles of which only one is now in use. The 9704 sounding pipes range from 9·75 m (32 ft) to 1·9 cm ($\frac{3}{4}$ in).

Europe's largest theatre organ is the Mighty Wurlitzer in the Odeon, Manchester. It is 15·2 m (50 ft) tall and weighs 5·1 tonnes (5 tons).

The 'highest' organ. In September 1971 an organ 'of considerable weight' was pushed to the top of Ben Nevis, 1343 m (4406 ft) high, by Kenneth Campbell of Sutherland. It is not recorded whether the instrument, once there, was actually played; nor, if it was, the size of the audience.

The biggest travelling organ is 8 m (26 ft) in length and 3 m (9 ft 9 in) high. It was built in the Black Forest, Bavaria, Germany, and its range is vaguely reported to be 'from super bass to super soprano'.

SUBMERGED INSTRUMENTS

In 1947 an Irish harp fitted with water-resistant nylon strings was played under water. Unfortunately, history has not recorded where, by whom, or why this exercise was carried out.

In March 1975 an underwater performance of Handel's *Water Music* (arranged by ?) was given on solo violin by Mark Gottlieb in the Evergreen State College swimming-pool in Olympia, Washington, USA. Mr Gottlieb reports that he is still perfecting his sub-aqua technique, concentrating especially on his bow speed and his detaché. Is it to be predicted that similarly appropriate venues may be chosen for future performances of Vaughan Williams' *Sinfonia Antartica,* Holst's *The Planets,* Haydn's 'Sun' Quartets, and Offenbach's *Orpheus in the Underworld*?

Mark Gottlieb, sub-aqua violinist

Section III

COMPOSERS

THE COMPOSER

In café, bus, and train you'll find
Him deep in thought with absent mind
Creating from a fund of fancies
Weird and woeful dissonances.

He works until the hour is late
Concocting rhythms intricate
For Sonatina, Fugue, and Suite,
(He never can spare time to eat).

He shrieks with joy and howls with pain
When from a sixteen-bar refrain
He builds a Symphony immense,
Cacophonous, and somewhat tense,

And from his mystic annotations
Destined to produce sensations
Comes eventually a mound
Of massive, overwhelming sound

He fills his sheet with marks and notes
On which he meditates and gloats,
Though sometimes others, in his scrawl,
Read harmonies not there at all.

With inky hands and shaggy locks
And tie for belt and gloves for socks,
Quite unaware of neighbours' curses
He sets to music reams of verses.

His daily output grows and grows,
There's nothing that he can't compose
From themes upon a cup and saucer
To choral episodes from Chaucer

He doesn't think to change his vest,
And never answers when addressed–
His mind is too engrossed for words
On semibreves, and tenths, and thirds.

In café, bus, and train you'll see
Him rapt away in ecstacy.
The critics greet his works with cheers,
But will they – in two dozen years?

Mary Kennard

THE FIRST COMPOSER

Consideration of this question brings the realisation that the description 'composer' is a relatively modern one. Firstly, it means one who composes, or orders, sounds, which he or she takes from a hypothetical chaos of an infinite number and type of sounds, into an intelligible sequence. Secondly, it has to be established that the composer has existed since the beginnings of music, but most of the time he was synonymous with the performer who composed the music spontaneously during performance, no attempt being made to write it down. When methods were eventually evolved for representing the played tone by the written character (see Section VII) it was done at first by composers whose names have not survived.

In the 12th century Richard Coeur de Lion (1157–99) composed simple ballads; no earlier personage who wrote down the music he composed can be established, so it seems that **the first composer** was a royal one. However, His Highness's ballads were by way of being folk-music–little more than popular songs of the time–and for so-called 'art music' we must turn to the composer Pérotin, known as 'Pérotin-Le-Grand' and 'Perotinus Magnus' (*c* 1160–*c* 1220) of Paris, who composed from 1180. Among his works are the first in the emerging art of polyphonic singing.

ROYAL COMPOSERS

The following list of reigning monarchs and their relatives who composed music should, perhaps, more correctly be added to the list of part-time composers (see below). Many royal personages attempted composing music during their leisure hours, often with only an elementary knowledge of the art, and even some whose output of music was tiny have been included.

Others met with fair success. Probably **the most musical of all monarchs** was Frederick the Great, whose four concertos for flute and 120 flute sonatas (*not* 121 as is usually given: Nos 8 and 60 in Spitta's list are identical) still receive occasional performances and recordings. In addition, his Symphony in D for two flutes, two horns, and strings stands beside similar works of the time (1742) as of at least equal quality.

The first royal composer was the well-known ballad-writer Richard Coeur de Lion. A composer of the more modern style of ballad is **the most recent royal composer:** King Phumiphon Adunet of Thailand (b. 1927) who wrote 'His Majesty's Blues', a tame and traditional 'pop' number. Between these extremes lies much regal talent. The list which follows is in chronological order within nations.

England

Richard Coeur de Lion (see above).

Henry VIII (1491–1547), writer of some popular court pieces.

Anne Boleyn (Bullen) (*c* 1507–36): her ballads included one entitled 'O Death Rocke Me On Slepe', which is said to have moved her husband.

Wilhelmina Caroline of Ansbach (1683–1737; wife of George II) wrote 'Church Call' which is still played before church parade in some army units.

Albert of Saxe-Coburg-Gotha, christened Francis Charles Augustus Albert Emmanuel (1819–61; consort of Queen Victoria) composer of the first work to be played in public in the Royal Albert Hall (see Section VI).

France

Marie-Antoinette (1755–93), a musical and cultured queen who regularly attended society concerts in Paris, and who composed light salon pieces.

Germany

Ernst Ludwig (1667–1739), Landgraf von Hessen, composer of instrumental music.

Wilhelmina (1709–58), Markgräfin von Bayreuth, and a favourite sister of Frederick the Great, wrote a harpsichord concerto in G minor which has achieved two recordings.

Frederick the Great (Friedrich der Grosse; Friedrich II, 1712–87), see above.

Anna Amelia (1723–87), Princess of Prussia, another sister of Frederick the Great and a pupil of Kirnberger. She wrote marches, chorales, etc.

Friedrich Wilhelm II (1744–97), composer of occasional court pieces and songs.

Friedrich Wilhelm III (1770–1840), composer of occasional court pieces and songs.

Louis Ferdinand (1772–1806), Prince of Hohenzollern and a nephew of Frederick the Great. Referred to by audiences who appreciated his joyful works as 'Beethoven with sunshine', he was respected by that composer and received the dedication of the Piano Concerto No 3 in C minor, Op 37.

Austria/Hungary

Ferdinand III (1608–57), Emperor of Austria and the composer of songs.

Paul Esterházy (1635–1713), Prince of the famous family later associated with Haydn, his compositions include music for the Church.

Leopold I (1640–1705), Emperor of Austria and the composer of instrumental pieces.

Joseph I (1678–1711), Emperor of Austria; he composed a number of vocal and instrumental works.

Rudolf (1788–1831), Archduke; later Archbishop of Olmütz. He was a pupil of Beethoven and the dedicatee of the 'Archduke' Trio, Op 97. As well as being a performer, Archduke Rudolf composed a number of works.

Denmark

Caroline Amelia of Augustenburg (1792–1866), wife of King Christian VIII, and a composer of salon pieces.

Ludwig Van Beethoven (1770–1827), the last of the truly classical composers (Mary Evans Picture Library)

Spain

Thibault IV (1201–53), King of Navarre and a composer of songs.

Alfonso X (1221–84), King of Castile and a song-writer.

Portugal

John IV (1604–56), King of Portugal and a motet-composer.

Pedro IV (d. 1831), King of Portugal and a former King of Brazil. He wrote the Portuguese National Anthem.

Thailand

Phumiphon Adunet, King of Thailand (see above).

MASTERS OF THE KING'S/QUEEN'S MUSICK

While composers in some countries are chosen to perform certain 'official' tasks in providing music for royal or State occasions, England is the only country to maintain an official court composer. He is known as 'The Master of the Queen's Musick', the archaic spelling of the last word indicating the antiquity of the post.

Today, the appointment is made by the ruling monarch in consultation with advisers and the duties are nominal. The composer thus chosen is likely to provide music for the most important of State occasions such as investitures, coronations, royal births, etc, but there is no binding compulsion to do so, and the Master of the Queen's Musick accepts the honour (always well deserved) without the drudgery which attended the post in its earlier history.

Evidence exists that James I employed a specific court composer, but the post was not officially recognised until 13 June 1626, when Charles I made provision for the position as part of the royal household. He awarded the title to the composer who had faithfully served his predecessor, and on 11 July 1626, Nicholas Lanier was appointed **the first Master of the King's Musick.** Lanier served that monarch until the latter's execution in 1649, and was reinstated to the post by Charles II after the Restoration.

The duties of the King's composer in the early days ranged from obtaining parts and copying them for performance, rehearsing and conducting, to being responsible for the behaviour of the court musicians both inside and outside the concert-room.

Of the nineteen Masters of the King's/Queen's Musick to date, only three (Nos 2, 6, and 12 in the list below) have retired from the post. In all other cases the composers were serving at the time of death.

Sir Edward Elgar, fifteenth Master of the King's Musick (Popperfoto)

MASTERS OF MONARCHS' MUSICK

	Composer	*Born*	*Appointed*	*Died*	*Served*
1.	Nicholas Lanier	1588	1626	1666	James I; Charles I; Charles II
2.	Louis Grabu	*c* 1638?	1666	1694? (ret 1674)	Charles II
3.	Nicholas Staggins	?	1674	1700	Charles II; James II; William and Mary; William III
4.	John Eccles	1668	1700	1735	Anne; George I; George II
5.	Maurice Greene	1695	1735	1755	George II
6.	William Boyce (Boyce took over duties unofficially in 1755 on the death of Greene; he retired on account of deafness in 1772)	1710	1757	1779	George II; George III
7.	John Stanley	1713	1772	1786	George III
8.	Sir William Parsons	1746	1786	1817	George III
9.	William Shield	1748	1817	1829	George III; George IV
10.	Christian Kramer	*c* 1788	1829	1834	George IV; William IV; Victoria
11.	François Cramer	1772	1834	1848	Victoria
12.	George Frederick Anderson	*c* 1801	1848	1876 (ret 1870)	Victoria
13.	Sir William George Cusins	1833	1870	1893	Victoria
14.	Sir Walter Parratt	1841	1893	1924	Victoria; Edward VII; George V
15.	Sir Edward Elgar	1857	1924	1934	George V
16.	Sir Henry Walford Davies	1869	1934	1941	George V; Edward VIII; George VI
17.	Sir Arnold Bax	1883	1941	1953	George VI; Elizabeth II
18.	Sir Arthur Bliss	1891	1953	1975	Elizabeth II
19.	Sir Malcolm Williamson	1931	1975		Elizabeth II

NONAGENARIAN COMPOSERS

Considerable sympathy and publicity are given to artists, especially composers, who retain their powers well into their old age. It is well known that Verdi wrote *Otello* during his 74th year, and that Vaughan Williams continued composing until shortly before his death at the age of 86; Stravinsky, too, remained remarkably active until the last of his 89 years, and Sibelius lived until 92 but apparently ceased composing at the early age of 60, living out the rest of his life in well-deserved retirement and comfortable semi-isolation in his beloved Finland. Many of the following composers are not so well known.

90 years old

Adam, Johann Ludwig (or Jean-Louis) (1758–1848).

Alcock, John (1715–1806), English Doctor of Music (Oxon), organist in London, composer and novelist.

Fischietti, Domenico, another who may not belong here since his dates are given alternatively as *c* 1720 to after 1810, and 1729–*c* 1810.

Goetschius, Percy (1853–1943), American composer and author.

Harris, Sir William (1883–1973), English organist and composer, mainly for his instrument.

Harwood, Basil (1859–1949), English Church composer.

Hill, Alfred (1870–1960), Australian composer who wrote *Overture of Welcome* in which the instrumentalists enter one after another, thereby reversing the procedure adopted in the last movement of Haydn's 'Farewell' Symphony.

Huë, Georges Adolph (1858–1948), French opera-composer.

Huygens, Sir Constantijn (1596–1687), Dutch musician, poet, politician, diplomatist, gymnast, artist, and playwright.

Mazzurana, Dr (1728–1818 or later), Italian composer and violinist; pupil of Tartini.

Ropartz (1865–1955), whose name is given as Joseph Guy-Ropartz and as Guy Marie Ropartz. He was a French composer and pupil of Massenet.

Smart, George Thomas (1676–1767), chorister and glee-composer of the Chapel Royal in London.

Spengel, Heinrich Ritter von (*c* 1775–1865), German composer.

91 years old

Baudron, Antoine Laurent (1743–1834), French symphonist.

Fioravanti, Valentino (1746–1837), Italian operatic composer.

Foerster, Joseph Bohuslav (1859–1951), Czech nationalist composer of many types of music.

Gretchaninov, Alexander Tikhonovitch (1864–1956), Russian composer of songs, piano music, and the once-popular 'Credo' from his Liturgy No 2, Op 29 (1908).

Huss, Henry Holden (1862–1953), American composer of many types of music and a teacher; he was a descendant of the Czech national hero John Huss.

Kaňka, Jan (1772–1863), Czech associate of Beethoven and a lawyer and amateur composer.

Malipiero, Gian Francesco (1882–1973), one of the most prominent of modern Italian composers, he was also a writer and musical editor concerned with ancient Italian music.

Perotti, Pater Giovanni Agostino (1764–1855), Italian composer whose birth date is sometimes given as 1769, thus depriving him of a position in this list.

Rieger, Gottfried (1764–1855), German composer who worked at Brünn.

Scott, Cyril (1879-1970), English symphonist, pianist, poet, and writer.

Siret, Nicholas (1663–1754), French composer and wind-player.

Tritto, Giacomo (1733–1824), Neapolitan opera-composer.

92 years old

Friml, Rudolf (1880–1972), Austrian composer of light operettas, for example *Rose Marie* (1924) and *The Vagabond Prince* (1925), etc.

Sibelius, Jan Julian Christian (1865–1957), symphonist, one of the greatest of 20th-century composers and the greatest to emerge from Finland.

93 years old

Widor, Charles (1844–1937), Parisian writer, organist, and composer of the popular Toccata from the Organ Symphony No 5, Op 42/1. He was in fact active in orchestral and chamber music, and a song-writer.

94 years old

Stolz, Robert (1881–1975), a pupil of Humperdinck and a composer of *The Merry Widow, The Count of Luxemburg, The Chocolate Soldier,* and other famous shows.

95 years old

Charpentier, Gustave (1860–1956), French composer famous for his opera *Louise* (1900).

Coward, Sir Henry (1849–1944), composer primarily of choral music in the north of England; knighted in 1926.

Creyghton (Creighton?), Robert (1639–1734), Church composer and Canon of Wells Cathedral, Somerset.

Gossec, François-Joseph (1734–1829), Belgian composer of operas and about 100 symphonies, one of which is now thought to be by another nonagenarian: Witzthumb (see below).

Lamoninary, Jacques-Philippe (1707–1802), French symphonist.

Perti, Giacomo Antonio (1661–1756), Bolognese opera-composer and writer of chamber works.

Ruggles, Carl (or Charles) (1876–1971), American painter and composer of deeply thought and uncompromising music.

96 years old

Abaco, Giuseppe Clemente Ferdinand (or Joseph Clemens Ferdinand) dall' (1709–1805), Brussels-born cellist and composer son of the more famous Felice.

Brian, Havergal (1876–1972), **the most prolific of all English symphonists,** having 32 to his credit. During an interview the composer, then well into his 90s, gave to Robert Simpson for a BBC programme, Brian left the room for a short time, returning to overhear Simpson asking the composer's wife about his health. 'Oh, I'm not going to die yet,' he said. 'I've just bought a new pair of trousers.'

Casals, Pablo (1876–1973), the world-famous expatriate cellist was also a skilful composer.

Dickinson, Clarence (1873–1969), American organist and composer for his instrument.

Mace, Thomas (*c* 1613–*c* 1709). Although the dates of this English Church composer and violinist are uncertain, there is little doubt that he was extraordinarily long-lived for his time.

Maschitti, Michele (Michel, Miquel, or Michelly) (*c* 1664–1760), Neapolitan violinist and composer.

Witzthumb, Ignace (1720–1816), symphonist (see Gossec, above), probably of Bohemian origin, who settled in Paris.

97 years old

Floyd, Alfred Ernest (1877–1974), English organist, conductor, composer, and broadcaster who spent most of his life in Australia.

Nivers, Guillaume (1617–1714), French composer, probably identical to Guillaume-Gabriel Nivers (1632–1714) and therefore not entitled to a place here.

98 years old

Berger, Francesco (1834–1933), Italian/German song-writer, piano composer and teacher in London.

99 years old

Reincken, Johann (or Jan Adam) (1623–1722), German organist and composer. It is said that the great Bach walked many miles to hear his improvisations in Hamburg.

The longest-lived composer is said to be le Comte de Saint-Germain who, according to confused reports, was born about 1660 and is still alive. If this seems incredible, what are we to make of his own report that he had discovered a potion which would prolong life indefinitely, as it had already prolonged his own for more than 2000 years? Among his other extravagant claims are that he can make gold and diamonds, that he could speak virtually all the European languages of the 18th century, and that he is the finest violinist and composer who ever lived. In respect of this last claim, examination of his thirteen sonatas in the British Museum (published by Walsh, 1750, and by Johnson, 1758) show them to be average works for their period.

A sober estimate of his dates is *c* 1710–*c*1780 *(Encyclopaedia Britannica)*, but this fails to take into account his reported conversation with Rameau in Venice in 1710 and a Paris appearance in 1789. In addition to being an alchemist, scientist, composer, and violinist, he was a singer in those days and travelled widely through Europe and the Middle East, from London (where he met Horace Walpole in 1743) to Persia, from Tunisia to St Petersburg (Leningrad); and herein perhaps lies part of the answer to the mystery. We are dealing with two Saint-Germains, father and son, both gifted in deception and proficient in music and the sciences, who each had the knack of leaving deep and lasting impressions wherever they went. The various reports from widely separated centres (there is even one from India, dated 1756), and the claims of the discovery of the elixir of life, would lend credence to the longevity story in those superstitious days, and there would be no one with the fortune to be in more than one place to coincide with Saint-Germain's visits in order to spot the discrepancies in age.

The truth of the matter may be guessed at as follows: a man born towards the end of the 17th century was self-assured and plausible enough to be taken at his word in the matter of his wild claims. He travelled all over Europe, making impressions and money, and was, for those days, exceptionally long-lived: perhaps a nonagenarian. Somewhere during his travels he sired a son who later saw the financial advantage of keeping the old man alive, but he was not so skilful in the deceptive arts, so the reports after the 1780s become fewer until a Viennese sighting in 1821. Thereafter the joke spent itself.

Until the sensation-seeking 1970s! As recently as 28 January 1972, a Richard Chamfrey appeared on French television claiming to be the real Comte de Saint-Germain. The audience witnessed him 'change lead into gold', which activity seems to have enabled him, during the last century and a half, to give up music as a means of making money. His trick, if it was one, was successful, but less success has met his latest claims: that he commutes between Earth and Mars, and that his age is now 17000 years. It is surprising that his modesty during the 18th century was so well developed as to permit him to deny 14800 years of his life; on the other hand it may be that for him Einstein's theory of time dilation works in reverse during his extra-terrestrial jaunts.

UNFORTUNATE COMPOSERS

Musical history is dotted with the sad figures of composers who had to fight severe disabilities, or who met their ends in tragic or unusual circumstances. Of all the misery catalogued below, most poignant must be that in **(b)**.

(a) Blind Composers

Bach, Johann Sebastian (1685–1750) went blind in later life.

Bériot, Charles Auguste de (1802–70), the Belgian violin composer and virtuoso who also built violins and was an artist, poet, and sculptor. He suffered from paralysis towards the end of his life in addition to blindness.

Cabezón, Antonio de (1510–66), Spanish keyboard composer who was blind from birth.

Delius, Frederick Fritz Albert Theodor (1862–1934), ended his life blind and partially paralysed. He was enabled to continue composing through the patient and selfless assistance of his amanuensis Eric William Fenby (b 1906).

Handel, George Frideric (1685–1759), went blind in 1753 but continued composing with the assistance of John Christopher Smith (1712–95), himself a noted London composer.

Hollins, Alfred (1865–1942), Scottish composer, organist, and pianist who received an Honorary D Mus at Edinburgh University, was blind from birth.

Landini, Francesco (*c* 1325–97), Florentine composer, organist, lutenist, and poet, blinded in an accident in early childhood.

Mercadante, Giuseppe Saverio Raffaele (1795–1870), Italian operatic composer, went blind in 1862.

Paradis, Maria Theresia (1759–1824), a blind Italian female composer who worked in Germany.

Paumann, Conrad (*c* 1410–73), a native of Nuremberg and blind from birth, he was organist at Frauenkirche, Munich, for the last 23 years of his life.

Rodrigo, Joaquin (b 1902), Spanish composer of the world-famous 'Aranjuez' Concerto, went blind in 1905.

Joaquin Rodrigo, the blind Spanish composer, with harpist Nicanor Zabaleta (EMI/Barahona)

Stanley, John (1713–86), English composer, blinded at the age of two by an accident.

Templeton, Alec Andrew (1909–63), Welsh composer famous for his *Bach Goes to Town*, was blind from birth.

Wolstenholme, William (1865–1931), English organist and composer, blind from birth.

(b) Deaf composers

Backer-Grøndahl, Agathe Ursula (1847–1907), Norwegian female pianist and composer.

Beethoven, Ludwig van (1770–1827), started to notice symptoms of deafness before he was

30, and the malady grew progressively worse until, towards the end of his life, silence closed in completely. In spite of this he continued composing right up to the end: the Choral Symphony and many of his greatest piano sonatas and string quartets were composed during the last ten years of total silence.

Boyce, William (1710–79), English author of 'Hearts of Oak' and Master of the King's Musick (George III). He went deaf in later life but put his years of silence to good use by collecting for posterity the works of earlier English Church composers.

Dupin, Paul (1865–1949), known as 'Louis Lothar'. He lost his hearing while still a youth but regained it about 1900.

Franz, Robert (1815–92), German song-writer who went deaf during his 30s due to a nervous disorder.

Knauth, Robert Franz–real name of Robert Franz, above.

May, Frederick (b 1911), Irish composer whose deafness began about 1940.

Smetana, Bedřich (1824–84), one of the best known of Bohemian nationalist composers, went deaf in 1874, succumbing also to mental illness.

Spontini, Gasparo Luigi Pacifico (1774–1851), Italian opera-composer; went deaf in 1848.

(c) Composers who went insane

Chabrier, Alexis Emmanuel (1841–94): melancholia led to paralysis and death.

Donizetti, Gaetano (1797–1848), famous Italian operatic composer, died insane.

Gurney, Ivor Bertie (1890–1937), English poet and song-writer, also a composer of orchestral music, etc, sustained injuries during the First World War which led to insanity and death.

Perosi, Lorenzo (1872–1956), Italian oratorio-writer and priest who died in a mental institution.

Schumann, Robert Alexander (1810–56), German writer and composer, suffered from a mental disorder which led him to attempt suicide. He died in a mental home.

Smetana, Bedřich (1824–84), Bohemian composer whose deafness (see above) led to his mental collapse.

Thomas, Arthur Goring (1850–92), English operatic composer who went insane shortly before death.

Vaňhal, Jan Křtitel (1739–1813), prolific Bohemian composer who worked mainly in Vienna but ended his days in a Paris asylum.

Wesley, Samuel (1766–1837), English composer of Church and concert music, received a head injury when young which ultimately led to insanity.

Wolf, Hugo (1860–1903), one of the world's greatest song-writers, suffered for many years from depression before finally going insane in 1897. He died in a Vienna asylum.

(d) Composers who were murdered

Cambert, Robert (1628–77), the composer of the first French opera, was murdered by his servant.

Caturla, Alejandro Garéra (1906–40), a Cuban composer who was assassinated.

Leclair, Jean-Marie (1697–1764), violinist, dancer, composer, and one of the greatest violin virtuosi of his day, was murdered on the steps of his Paris home, perhaps by a jealous rival.

Mozart, Wolfgang Amadeus (1756–91). The allegation, perpetuated in Rimsky-Korsakov's opera *Mozart and Salieri,* that Mozart was done to death by Salieri (because the former's operas were doing too well? Hardly! Even if they had been, this would have been a classic example of securing the stable door after the departure of the horse) has never been proved, although there is evidence to show that Mozart's demise was not due to natural causes but to some kind of poisoning.

Stradella, Alessandro (*c* 1642–82), one of the world's first symphonists, is said to have been assassinated by agents of the lover of a lady with whom Stradella had eloped. The story, whether true or not, has given rise to a novel by Marion Crawford and operas by Abraham Louis Niedermeyer (1846) and Flotow (1844), the composer of *Martha.*

Reversing the above, the tale goes that Carlo Gesualdo (*c* 1560–1615), the Italian Prince and composer, arranged for the murder of his wife and her lover.

(e) Composers who committed suicide

Beresowski, Maxim Sosonowitsch (1745–77), one of the first Russian symphonists.

Carey, Henry (1690–1743), English songwriter, and the composer of 'Sally in our Alley'.

Clarke, Jeremiah (*c* 1659–1707), English composer and organist at St Paul's Cathedral, London. He was the true composer of *Trumpet Voluntary*, for long attributed to Purcell. Being unlucky in love, Clarke shot himself.

Götzloff, Friedrich (18th century), German composer.

Guillemain, Gabriel (1705–70), French writer of mainly instrumental music.

Koczwara, František (?–1791), Czech composer, violinist, and double bass player, known in Germany as 'Franz Kotzwara', committed suicide in London.

Mewton-Wood, Noel (1923–53), Australian pianist and composer.

Paisible, Louis-Henri (*c* 1745–81), French composer and violinist.

Warlock, Peter (1894–1930), composing name of the Englishman Philip Heseltine, writer and editor of old English music. His best-known composition is probably the song cycle *The Curlew* (1922).

(f) Composers who met death due to war action

Alain, Jehan (1911–40), French composer and organist.

Browne, Denis (1885–1915), English composer and organist killed in action against the Turks.

Butterworth, George Sainton Kaye (1885–1916), English composer and collector of folk-music, killed in the Battle of the Somme.

Fleishman, Veniamin (1922–41), Russian pupil of Shostakovitch, died during the siege of Leningrad. His unfinished opera *Rothschild's Violin* was completed by Shostakovitch in 1968.

Granados, Enrique (1867–1916), travelling to England, he was drowned when HMS *Sussex* was torpedoed in the English Channel.

Heming, Michael Savage (1920–42), a London air-raid victim.

Karel, Rudolf (1880–1945), Czech composer who died in a Nazi concentration camp.

Koffler, Jozéf (1896–1942), Polish dodecaphonist, died in a Nazi Warsaw Ghetto massacre.

Laparra, Raoul (1876–1943), French composer, killed in an air raid.

Leigh, Walter (1905–42), English pupil of Hindemith, killed in action in Libya.

Magnard, Lucien Denis Gabriel Albéric (1865–1914), French composer, killed (or took his own life?) during the German invasion of France.

Schulhoff, Erwin (1894–1942), Czech composer, died in a Nazi concentration camp.

Webern, Anton (1883–1945), Austrian disciple of Schoenberg, killed by an American sentry in a tragic case of mistaken identity. The sentry, although not musically aware himself, is said to have suffered from acute guilt for the rest of his life, dying in the mid 1960s in a sanatorium.

(g) Composers who met death in unusual circumstances

In this list, natural causes are ignored unless they were contributed to by the unusual circumstances.

Chausson, Ernst (1855–99), **the only composer to have written a concerto for piano, violin, and string quartet,** died after crashing his bicycle at Linnay, France, on 10 June 1899.

Danby, John (1757–98), Yorkshire organist and glee-composer, spent the night in a damp inn bed. As a result he contracted paralysis of the arms which led to his death.

Delvincourt, Claude (1888–1954), was badly wounded during the First World War in spite of which he led a youth orchestra during the Second World War as a cover for subversive activities during the Nazi occupation of France, but he met his death in a road accident.

Dodd, Reverend Dr William (1729–77), English churchman and composer, was hanged for forgery.

Edelmann, Johann Friedrich (1749–94), German composer, guillotined in Paris.

Escurel, Jehannot de l' (?–1303), executed in Paris.

Ferroud, Pierre Octave (1900–36), French composer, died in a motor accident in Hungary.

Goudimel, Claude (*c* 1510–72), a French composer of Catholic music who made the mistake of turning Protestant. He was among the victims of the St Bartholomew's Day massacre of Protestants.

Linley, Thomas (1756–78), promising son of his like-named father, drowned in a boating accident.

Lully, Jean-Baptiste (originally Giovanni Battista Lulli, 1632–87), Italian, naturalised French in 1661. He was composer at the Court of Louis XIV and he kept his ensemble together by beating loudly on the floor with a heavy staff. Accidentally striking his foot one day, he developed a tumour which proved fatal.

Schobert, Johann (*c* 1720–67), German composer of instrumental music who lived in Paris. He and his family were wiped out after mistaking toadstools for mushrooms.

White (or Whyte), Robert (*c* 1530–74), English composer who fell victim to the Plague.

Wise, Michael (*c* 1648–87), organist, composer, and Master of the Choristers at St Paul's Cathedral, London. Losing an argument with his wife one evening in Salisbury, his home town, Wise rushed out and attacked the first person he saw. Unfortunately for him it was the nightwatchman who was armed with a billhook which he used on Wise with lethal effect. The report of the death, from *Notes for biographies of English musicians* by Antony à Wood reads: 'He was knock'd on the head and kill'd downright by the Night-watch at Salisbury for giving stubborn and refractory language to them on S. Bartholmews day at night, an. 1687.'

Readers who keep abreast of recent musical sensationalism may be surprised and disappointed not to find the name of Charles-Valentin Alkan (1813–88) included in the above list. After all, was he not supposed to have been an eccentric who changed his name from Morhange, avoided visitors to his Paris apartment, and who suffered the classic fate of a recluse: that of lying dead for days before anyone missed him? Alkan is also said to have distinguished himself in the method of his demise: an oaken bookcase fell on him as he clambered up to reach a volume of the Talmud.

There is not a jot of evidence for all this ballyhoo. That he died alone in his apartment is not in question, but there is no hint of foul play by a bookcase or any other object or person. It seems that, after all, his death at the age of 74 was due to dull old natural causes.

(h) Unlucky composers

Arne, Michael (1740–86), the composer of 'The Lass with the Delicate Air', was the bastard son of Thomas Arne; he spent some years in a debtors' prison.

Bainton, Edgar Leslie (1880–1959), English composer, spent the whole of the First World War in a German internment camp.

Cimarosa, Domenico (1749–1801), Italian operatic composer, died in a political prison.

Dale, Benjamin James (1885–1943), English composer, spent the First World War in a German PoW camp.

Duparc, Marie Eugène Henri Fouques (1848–1933), a pupil of César Franck, showed great promise as a song-writer but in 1885 his health collapsed completely and he spent the rest of his long life as an invalid.

Messiaen, Olivier Eugène Prosper Charles (b 1908), French composer and pianist, was held in a German PoW camp in Silesia in 1940–1. During this time he wrote his only major chamber work, *Quartet for the End of Time,* composed for himself and the only other proficient instrumentalists in the camp: a cellist, a clarinettist, and a violinist.

WOMEN COMPOSERS

A composer who also happens to be a female used to be considered a rare phenomenon, yet it has been an easy task to assemble a substantial collection of such phenomena from the last three centuries of musical history, at the same time knowing that another list of similar size would not present too great a problem. (See also Royal Composers, above.)

Arrieu, Claude (b 1903), French.

Arthur, Fanny (*c* 1820–79), pianist and composing wife of Joseph Robinson, the Dublin chorus master and singer.

Bacewicz, Grazyna (b 1913), Polish violinist and composer of orchestral and chamber works.

Backer-Grøndahl–see (b) Unfortunate composers, above.

Badarzewska, Thekla (1838–61), Polish song-composer who died very young.

Barnard, Mrs (1830–69), poet and song-writer who became famous for the song 'Come Back to Erin'.

Barraine, Elsa (b 1910), French pupil of Dukas.

Bauer, Marian (1887–1955), American composer, teacher, and author.

Beach, Amy Marcy (*née* Chaney, 1867–1944), **the first American female to write a symphony.**

Bosmans, Henriette (1895–1952), Dutch pupil of Pijper.

Boulanger sisters: Nadia (b 1887) (Juliette); Lili (1893–1918) (Juliette Marie Olga). These two French composers achieved their greatest fame for their teaching abilities.

Boyd, Anne (b 1940), Australian.

Branscombe, Gena (b 1881), Canadian pupil of Humperdinck; composer of piano and violin music and songs; resides in America.

Bright, Dora (1863–1952), English composer of three operas, piano concertos, etc, and as a pianist she was **the first to give a recital of wholly English music.**

Caccini, Francesca (18th century), Italian composer at a Florentine court; probably descended from the famous Giulio Caccini.

Carwithen, Doreen (b 1922), English orchestral and chamber composer.

Chaminade, Cecile (1857–1944), French pupil of Godard.

Charrière, Isabelle de (1740–1805), Swiss.

Coleman, Ellen (1893–1973), English composer of operas, chamber and vocal works.

Crawford, Ruth–see Seeger.

Daniels, Mabel Wheeler (1878–1960), American pupil of Chadwick; composer of orchestral and chamber music.

Danzi, Margarethe (18th century), pupil of Leopold Mozart and wife of Franz Danzi.

Demessieux, Jeanne-Marie-Madeleine (1921–68), French composer and famous as an organist; pupil of Dupré.

Diemer, Emma Lou (b 1927), American.

Doniach, Shula (b 1905), Russian-born pianist and composer, resident in England.

Dunlop, Isobel (1901–75), Scottish pupil of Tovey and a composer of vocal music.

Edelmann, Mlle (18th century), French; wife of J F Edelmann–see (g) Unfortunate composers, above.

ETPA = Ermelinda Talia Pastorella Arcadia, the Arcadian name of Antonia Amalia Walpurgia, Princess of Saxony (active *c* 1760–70), the composer of two operas preserved in the British Museum.

Gabashvili, Nana (b 1962), **the youngest female composer:** a student at Tbilisi Music School, she has written some 300 songs to date, sonatas, marches, and a children's operetta.

Gipps, Ruth (b 1921), English pianist, conductor, and composer; pupil of Vaughan Williams, she has composed vocal, chamber, and symphonic works.

Glanville-Hicks, Peggy (b 1912), Australian pupil of Vaughan Williams, now resident in America.

Grétry, Lucille (active in Paris *c* 1786), Belgian; sister of the famous composer A E M Grétry.

Guerre, Elizabeth Jacquet de la (1659–1729), **the earliest known woman composer:** French; author of keyboard pieces.

Hardelot, Guy d' (1858–1936), pseudonym of Helen Rhodes, the English composer of 'Because', etc. (Guy, from her maiden name; Hardelot from her birthplace in France.)

Harrison, Pamela (b 1915), English; pupil of Gordon Jacob.

Holmès, Augusta May Anne (1847–1903), of French/Irish parentage; pianist and composer and a pupil of César Franck. She used the pseudonym 'Hermann Zenta'.

Holst, Imogen (b 1907), composer, conductor, and promoter of the music of her father Gustav Holst.

Howell, Dorothy (b 1898), English composer of a piano concerto, etc.

LeFanu, Nicola (b 1947), English composer of vocal and instrumental music; started composing in 1969.

Lutyens, Elisabeth (b 1906), English twelve-tone composer.

Maconchy, Elizabeth (b 1907), English composer of a wide range of works; pupil of Vaughan Williams.

Martines (or Martinez), Marianna von (1744/5–1812). Italian; at the age of ten she

Imogen Holst, with Steuart Bedford (EMI/Anthony Lloyd-Parker)

was a pupil of Haydn, later of Porpora and G A Hasse; she lived and worked in Vienna.

Mendelssohn-Bartholdy, Fanny Cacilie (1805–47), German; sister of Felix and composer of songs and piano pieces, some of which were published under her brother's name.

Musgrave, Thea (b 1928), Scottish; pupil of Nadia Boulanger.

Oliveros, Pauline (b 1912), American *avant-gardiste.*

Pakhmutova, Alexandra Nikolayevna (b 1929), Russian; composer of orchestral, vocal, and chamber music.

Paradis – see (a) Unfortunate composers, above.

Pentland, Barbara (b 1912), Canadian twelve-tone composer.

Perry, Julia (b 1924), American.

Philidor, Anne Danican (1681–1728), a member of the French family which included the famous composer/chess-player F A Philidor.

Polin, Claire (b 1926), American.

Poston, Elizabeth (b 1905), English composer, pianist, and broadcaster.

Rainier, Priaulx (b 1903), South African composer and violinist; pupil of Nadia Boulanger, she has composed orchestral, chamber, and vocal music.

Rees, Cathrine Felicie van (mid 19th century), operetta-composer, and **the only female to write a national anthem** (see Transvaal).

Reichardt, Juliane (1752–83), originally from the Bohemian family of Benda; wife of J F Reichardt, and mother of the following:

Reichardt, Louise (1779–1826), daughter of the above, and composer of songs and piano works.

Rhodes, Helen – see Hardelot.

Savage, Jane (active *c* 1785–95), daughter of William Savage and author of keyboard and vocal music.
Schick, Philippine (1894–1970), German, based in Munich and mainly a choral composer. She founded the music section of the Society of German and Austrian Women Artists (GEDOK).
Schmelling, Elisabeth–see Schröter.
Schröter, Corona (1751–1802), pseudonym of Elisabeth Schmelling, actress, song-composer, and singer.
Schumann, Clara Josephine (*née* Wieck, 1819–96), German composer/pianist and wife of Robert Schumann.
Seeger, Ruth Crawford (1901–53), American; step-mother of Pete Seeger the folk-singer.
Sirmen (or Syrmen), Maddalena Laura Lombardini (*c* 1735–*c* 1798), Italian, but German by marriage to the composer Ludovico (Ludwig) Sirmen. She was a pupil of Tartini and worked in Paris and London.
Smyth, Dame Ethel Mary (1858–1944), English, but studied in Germany. Back in England she became a suffragette and was **the only woman composer to be jailed,** in 1911, for two years. She was made a Dame in 1922; wrote orchestral music and operas.
Tailleferre, Germaine (b 1892), French; composer/pianist and a member of Les Six (see Groups of Composers, below).
Talma, Louis (b 1906), American.
Tate, Phyllis Margaret Duncan (b 1911), English opera-composer; has also written orchestral music including a saxophone concerto, etc.
Taylor, Mrs Tom (*née* Laura W Barker, 1819–1905), English composer of stage, orchestral, vocal, and chamber music.
Trimble, Joan (b 1915), Irish composer; also a well-known piano duettist with her sister Valerie (b 1917).
Viardot, Michelle Pauline (1821–1910), daughter of Popolo Vicente Garcia the singer and composer; she was a pupil of Liszt.
White, Maude Valérie (1855–1937), English salon composer.
Wilkins, Margaret Lucy (b 1941), English composer and teacher, has written chamber, vocal, and choral music; started composing in 1970.
Williams, Grace (b 1906), English; pupil (but not a relation) of Vaughan Williams, and of Wellesz in Vienna.
Wolf, Maria Carolina (18th century), Bohemian, from the Benda family; married the German composer A F Wolf, himself a pupil of one of the Bendas.
Woodforde-Finden-Ward, Amy (Late Victorian), English. Famous for the *Indian Love Lyrics,* which she is reputed to have written in a mental asylum.
Zenta–see Holmès.

GROUPS OF COMPOSERS

There have been several instances of composers grouping themselves together in order to concentrate their aims, or who were grouped together by circumstances in a certain locality. These so-called 'schools' often represent important centres of musical activity. Some of the most prominent are given here, together with their members.

The Five

A term invented by the writer and critic Stasov; this group of composers was also known as 'The Mighty Handful'. All, apart from Rimsky-Korsakov, were 'spare-time composers' (see below), and even he began his career as a naval officer.

Balakirev, Mily Alexeyevich (1837–1910).
Borodin, Alexander Porphyrevich (1833–87).
Cui, César Antonovich (1853–1918).
Mussorgsky, Modest Petrovich (1839–81).
Rimsky-Korsakov, Nikolai Andreyevich (1844–1908).

Mannheim School

An influential group of composers centred upon the court of the friendly and approachable Karl Theodor, Elector of Mannheim, during the middle years of the 18th century. The Elector himself was a keen cellist and flautist, and he demanded from his players a concert or an opera every day. The founders of the 'School', whose aims were a previously unattained perfection of orchestral technique, the development of exciting orchestral effects, and the integration of wind instruments into the orchestral palette, were among the earliest composers of the homophonic symphony. (Where applicable, composers' names are given in the original after the better-known German forms.)

Stamitz, Johann Wenzel Anton (Stamič, Jan Václav Antonín) (1717–57).
Richter, Franz Xaver (. . . Frantísek . . .) (1709–89).
Holzbauer, Ignaz (1711–83).

The three composers built the new orchestra in 1742 out of the court musicians who had played at Mannheim since 1724, and before that in about 1710 at Düsseldorf. After the consolidation of the new Mannheim orchestra, the musical establishment was expanded by the arrival of other composers, most of them from Bohemia, among them being:

Cannabich, Christian (1731–89).
Filtz, Anton (Fils, Antonín) (?–1760).
Toeschi, Carl Joseph (an Italian, originally Carlo Giuseppe Toesca della Castellamonte) (1723/32–88).
Tzarth or Zart(h), Georg (Čart, Jiři) (1708–74).

During the second half of the century a second generation of composers influenced by, or working at, Mannheim appeared, among them:

Beck, Franz (František) (1723–1809).
Cannabich, Carl (1764–1806), son of Christian.
Danzi, Franz (1763–1826).
Eichner, Ernst (1740–77).
Erskine, Thomas Alexander (1732–81), the Scottish Earl of Kelly, who brought back to the British Isles the principles of the Mannheim School.
Fränzl, Ignaz (1736–1803).
Stamitz, Anton (1753–1820), son of Johann.
Stamitz, Carl (Karel) (1746–1801), son of Johann.

Viennese School

In the middle of the 18th century Vienna was an extremely active musical centre. The composers listed below did not necessarily work together; rather they gravitated to the Austrian capital while maintaining their independence, and it is only during the present century that the composers have been thought of as forming a group. A representative selection is given:

Albrechtsberger, Johann Georg (1736–1809).
Bonporti, Francesco Antonio (1672/78–1740/49).
Cimarosa, Domenico (1749–1801).
Dittersdorf, Carl Ditters von (1739–99).
Kozeluh, Leopold Antonín (1752–1818).
Monn, Georg Matthias (or MG) (1717–50).
Porpora, Nicolò Antonio (*c* 1686–*c* 1768).
Salieri, Antonio (1750–1825).
Vraničky, Pavel (1756–1808).
Wagenseil, Georg Christoph (1715–77).

It is, of course, to the first Viennese School that belong Haydn (although he worked outside Vienna until towards the end of his life) and Mozart, and later, Beethoven and Schubert.

Second Viennese School

Led by Schoenberg, the Second Viennese School became the centre of experiments into twelve-tone music, and the three main names (below) are regarded as the founders of the new method of composing. However, it is only fair to point out that the Austrian composer Josef Matthias Hauer (1883–1959) was developing along similar lines slightly before Schoenberg, in 1912.

Schoenberg, Arnold (1874–1951).
Berg, Alban (1885–1935).
Webern, Anton von (1883–1945).

North German School at the time of Frederick the Great

A vital and prolific centre of music pivoted round the Potsdam Court of the flute-playing King.

Bach, Carl Philipp Emanuel (1714–88).
Bach, Wilhelm Friedemann (1710–84).
Benda, Franz (František) (1709–86).
Benda, Georg (Jiří Antonín) (1722–95).
Graun, Johann Gottlieb (1699–1771).
Graun, Karl Heinrich (1701–59).
Kirnberger, Johann Philipp (1721–83).
Marpurg, Friedrich Wilhelm (1718–95).
Nichelmann, Christoph (1717–62).
Rodenwald, Carl Joseph (1735–1809).
Rolle, Johann Heinrich (1718–85).
Schaale, Christian Friedrich (1713–1800).
Schaffrath, Christoph (1709–63?).

Les Six

Music critic Henri Collet invented this name in 1920 for a group of five French and one Swiss (Honegger) composers:

Auric, Georges (b 1899).
Durey, Louis (b 1888).
Honegger, Arthur (1892–1955).
Milhaud, Darius (1892–1974).
Poulenc, Francis (1899–1963).
Tailleferre, Germaine (b 1892).

La Jeune France

A group of French composers who formed an association after the Second World War under the guiding influence of Messiaen, a pupil of Dukas and Dupré:

Baudrier, Yves (b 1906).
Jolivet, André (1905–74), a pupil of Varèse.
Lesur, Daniel (b 1908).
Messiaen, Olivier (b 1908).

Camerata

This was a group of Florentine dilettanti who met at the Palace of Count Giovanni Bardi, himself a musician, scientist, and writer, from about 1580 to 1608. The prime interest of the group was a revival of Greek drama, which they thought had had the accompaniment of music for much of the time. In the group were several poets, and it is probably due to their influence that the composers of the group sought to break away from the polyphonic singing of the time in order that the words of the songs might be understood the better in a homophonic setting. In this way, the Camerata was **the first to produce homophonic songs** which, because of the clarity of the words, began to take on a narrative function, leading gradually to a dramatic aspect. The stage was thus set for the first operas, which were produced by the composing members of the group:

Composers:

Peri, Jacopo (1561–1633), singer/composer.
Cavaliero, Emilio de' (1550–1602).
Caccini, Guilio (*c* 1546–1618), singer/composer.
Strozzi, P.
Malvezzi, C., (1547–97).

Poets:

Rinuccini, Ottavio (1562–1621), the first librettist (see Section V).
Marino, Giambattista (1569–1625).
Chiabrera, Gabriello (1552–1638).

Bolognese School

A group of composers based in and around the San Petronio Cathedral in Bologna towards the end of the 17th century. They included:

Alberti, Giuseppe Battista (or Matteo) (1685–1751).
Aldrovandini, Giuseppe (1672–1707).
Bononcini, Giovanni (1670–1755).
Grossi, Andrea (16? –17 ?).
Jaccini (or Iaccini), Giuseppe Maria (*c* 1670–*c* 1727).
Pasquini, Bernardo (1637–1710).
Perti, Giacomo (or Jacopo?) Antonio (1661–1756).
Torelli, Giuseppe (1658–1709).

The group, or 'school', was responsible for some of the first symphonies and instrumental concertos ever written (see Section IV).

The English School of Lutenist Song-Writers

This group of composers, all active in London at about the same time, forms a 'school' only in a loose sense. They were probably acquainted, and they all wrote songs or 'ayres' with lute accompaniment.

Attey, John (15?–1640), the first alphabetically, but the last to publish lute songs (in 1622).
Campian, Thomas (1567–1620).
Cavendish, Michael (1565–1628).
Corkine, William (15 ?–16 ?).
Dowland, John (1563–1626), the most famous and successful composer of his time.
Ford, Thomas (1580–1648).
Hume, Tobias (?–1645).
Jones, Robert (15 ?–*c* 1617).
Pilkington, Francis (*c* 1562–1638).
Rosseter, Philip (*c* 1575–1623).

FAMILIES OF COMPOSERS

The largest family of composers possessed the name Bach. Altogether 64 members of the

Johann Sebastian Bach (Popperfoto)

Johann Christian Bach, the Hillingdon portrait by Gainsborough

Bach family took up music as a profession in the two centuries between 1600 and 1800. Of those only a proportion were composers as distinct from performers: many of the earlier Bachs are described as simply 'town musician' or 'organist', which neither includes nor precludes the possibility that they wrote music which has not survived. Of the proved composers, the following is a list of the ten most important in chronological order of their birth dates. The nicknames attached to Johann Sebastian's four composing sons refer to the musical centres in which they mainly worked.

Bach

Johann Christoph (1642–1703), worked in Eisenach, brother of below.
Johann Michael (1648–94), worked in Gehren, brother of above.
Johann Bernard (1676–1749), worked in Eisenach; nephew of the brothers above.
Johann Ludwig (1677–1731), worked in Meiningen; distant cousin of Johann Sebastian.
Johann Sebastian (1685–1750), worked in Cöthen and Leipzig.
Wilhelm Friedemann (1710–84), the 'Halle' Bach; first child of J S.
Carl Philipp Emanuel (1714–88), the 'Berlin' or 'Hamburg' Bach; second child of J S.
Johann Christoph Friedrich (1732–93), the 'Bückeburg' Bach; sixth child of J S.
Johann Christian (1735–82), the 'Milan' or 'London' Bach; seventh child of J S; friend of Abel and Mozart.
Wilhelm Friedrich Ernst (1759–1845), worked in Berlin; the second child of J C F.

Other identification problems may occur in the following families:

Benda

1. František (1709–86), worked in Dresden in 1733; later with Frederick the Great in Potsdam from 1741; known as 'Franz.'
2. Friedrich Lud(e)wig (1746/52–92/94); son of 4; worked in Schwerin and Königsburg.
3. Friedrich Wilhelm Heinrich (1742–1812/14), eldest son of 1; pupil of Kirnberger, worked in Potsdam and Berlin.
4. Jiří Antonín (1722–95), worked with Frederick the Great from 1742; succeeded Stölzel at Gotha in 1749; held positions in Hamburg (1778) and Vienna (1779) before returning to Gotha in 1780. Probably the most prolific of the Benda family, Jiří wrote many symphonies, operas, and other music of all kinds. Because of his extended career in German centres, he was known as 'Georg'; references to 'G Benda' or 'J Benda' usually refer to Jiří Antonín even though the initials serve equally for other members of the family.
5. Jan (Giovanni) (1715–52), violinist/composer; died in Berlin.
6. Jan Jiří (1685–1757), one of the original Czech composers of the family and father of 1 and 4.
7. Johann Georg = 6.
8. Joseph (*c* 1724–1804), worked in Berlin from 1740; promoted to Konzertmeister in 1786.
9. Karl Hermann Heinrich (1748–1836), son of 1.

Two female members of the Benda family will be found in the article on woman composers, above, under the names of Reichardt and Wolf.

Haydn

Brothers Franz Joseph (1732–1809), worked in Esterházy and London, returning towards the end of his life to Vienna, and Johann Michael (1737–1806), worked in Salzburg. Both associated with Mozart.

Loeillet

One is likely to come across the following given names, indicating that there were four separate composers:

1. Jacob-Jean-Baptiste.
2. Jacques.
3. Jean-Baptiste.
4. John.

There are only two brothers involved here, in fact, each of whom changed his name. Both were born at Ghent and their original names were:

2. Jacques (1685–1746).
3. Jean-Baptiste (1680–1730).

For the last 25 years of his life, 3 Jean-Baptiste worked in London where, presumably for ease of use, he Anglicised his name to 4 John. 2 Jacques worked in Brussels, Munich, and Versailles and sometimes called himself 1 Jacob-Jean-Baptiste. It will be seen, therefore, that 3 Jean-Baptiste is identical with 4 John, and 2 Jacques is identical with 1 Jacob-Jean-Baptiste. Matters are further complicated by two other factors: both brothers wrote music for flute which to outward appearances seems similar, and the similarity to the name Lully, when pronounced in the French manner, has confused some publishers into presenting music by Loeillet as music by Lully, disregarding the wide difference in dates: Jean-Baptiste Lully (1632–87).

Martini

The following names are likely to be met in any study of 18th-century music. Only two brothers appear to be involved, but the similarity of their name to that of many other composers should be borne in mind. It is hoped that the following list will assist in identification:

1. Martigni, Gianbattista. Possibly a distorted version of 12 or 16a.
2. Martin, François (1727–57).
3. Martin, Philipp, a lutenist active *c* 1730–33.
4. Martin y Soler, Vicente (or Vicenzo) (1754–1806), not to be further confused with Antonio Soler (1729–83).
5. Martinelli, Antonio, active in Paris *c* 1750.
6. Martines (or Martinez), Marianne von (*c* 1744–1812), female pupil of Haydn and Porpora; worked in Vienna.
7. Martinetti. Probably a distorted version of Martinelli.
8. Martinez de la Roca, Joaquín (16 ?–17 ?), Spanish operatic composer.
9. Martini, Abbate Giovanni (18th century), worked in Venice.
10. Martini, SL (?).
11. Martini, Giuseppe (1703–79).
12. Martini, Giovanni Battista (or Giambattista) (1706–84), known as 'Padré Martini'; worked in Bologna.
13. Martini, il Tedesco (1741–1816) (ie 'Martini the German', whose real name was Johann Paul Aegidius Schwarzendorf). Alternative versions of his given names are Jean and Giovanni Paolo.
14. Martino, Filippo (=3 ?).
15. Martino, Johann Baptiste =16a.
16. Sammartini. Two brothers:
(a) Giovanni Battista (1698 or 1701 to 1775);
(b) Giuseppe (*c* 1693–*c* 1750/1).
Originally San Martini or San Martino, the names of these two composers have undergone considerable confusion and distortion. By convention rather than logic the names are given usually as follows in order to aid differentiation:
(a) Giovanni Battista Sammartini, worked in Milan.
(b) Giuseppe San Martini, worked in London.
There exist early editions of sonatas by 'Giuseppe San Martino di Milano' etc, the correct attributions of which may never be resolved.
17. San Martino–see 16.

Mozart

A clear father-son-grandson case. It is probably true to say that, had not the son been so overwhelmingly great, his father's and his son's music, attractive though it is, might never be heard today.

Franz Joseph Haydn (1732–1809) (Royal College of Music)

1. Johann Georg Leopold (1719–87).
2. Wolfgang Amadeus (Christened Johannes Chrysostomus Wolfgangus Theophilus–both Amadeus and Theophilus mean 'loved by God') (1756–91).
3. Wolfgang Amadeus II (1791–1844), a pupil of Albrechtsberger and Salieri, and the composer of over 50 works. Unfortunately his fate has been to fall too completely into the eclipsing shadow of his father.

Schmidt, Schmitt, and Smith

A German case similar to the Italian Martinii. Traces of the lives and works of the following musicians have been found in reference books:
1. Schmid, Fr X (=Franz Xaver?).
2. Schmidt, Antoni.
3. Schmid(t), Ferd(inand?).
4. Schmidt, Johann Christoph (1644–1720/28?), Kapellmeister in Dresden.
5. Schmidt or Schmitt, Joseph (or Giuseppe) (*c* 1750?–1808/15?), a prolific composer of symphonies and chamber works.
6. Schmidt, Leopold.
7. Schmiedt, Siegfried, a keyboard composer active *c* 1780–90.
8. Schmitt, F (=1?).
9. Schmitt, Johann Christian (1712–95)=John Christopher Smith, Handel's amanuensis.
10. Schmitt, Joseph (1734–91), like his near-namesake, 5, a composer of many symphonies and chamber works.
11. Schmitte, may refer to any of the above when given without further identification.
12. Smith, John Christopher, of German origin–see 9.
13. Smith, John Stafford (1750–1836), composer, conductor, and organist in London who collaborated with Sir John Hawkins in the preparation of the latter's *General History of the Science and Practice of Music* (1776).
14. Smith, Theodor, an English (?) composer of keyboard music, active *c* 1780.

NICKNAMES

Composers, as well as their works (see Section IV), have been given nicknames. They range from the flippant, through the physically descriptive, to attempts to identify the recipient's place in the history of music. Also included in this selection are some of the florid Arcadian names with which some of the early Italian composers wished to be known.

COMPOSER NICKNAMES

Nickname	*Composer*	*Remarks*
Anfione Eteoclide	Jommelli, Nicolo	Arcadian name
Arrigo il Tedesco–see Harry the German		
Bassetto	Grassi, Francesco	Roman composer, *c* 1701
Belgian Orpheus, The	Lassus, Roland de	
Berlin Bach, The	Bach, C P E	
Bückeburg Bach, The	Bach, J C F	
Buranello, Il	Galuppi, Baldasare	Born on the Venetian island of Burano
Caro Sassone, il	Hasse, J A	Known thus in Italy
Cielo, il	Landino, Francesco	*Cielo*='blind'; also called Francesco degli organi ('of the organs')
Clemens non Papa	Clemens, Jacob	Name given to prevent confusion with Clemens Papa, the Flemish poet
Divino Boemo, il	Mysliveček, Josef	Also known as Josef Venatorini–anything, it seems, to relieve the Austrians with whom he worked from wrestling with his real name
English Bach, The	Bach, J C	The only member of the illustrious family to make his living as a composer in England
Father of Orchestration, The	Gabrieli, Giovanni	

Nickname	*Composer*	*Remarks*
Father of the Symphony, The	Haydn, F J	A misleading epithet since the symphony had reached an advanced form before Haydn entered the field. 'Godfather of the Symphony' would be more accurate
Father of Swedish Music, The	Roman, J H	
Hamburg Bach, The	Bach, C P E	
Harry the German (Arrigo il Tedesco)	Isaac, Heinrich	
Hunchback of Arras, The	Hale, Adam de la	French trouvère
London Bach, The	Bach, J C	Worked in London from 1763
Milan Bach, The	Bach J C	Worked in Milan before going to England
Monopoli, il	Insanguino, Giacomo	
Music's Prophet	Monteverdi, Claudio	From him sprang the roots of opera and other vital forms
Napoleon of Music, The	Rossini, G A	He is said to have conquered Europe with his music
Papa Haydn	Haydn, F J	Refers to his alleged paternity of the symphony; see Father of the Symphony, above
Old Nosey	Bas(s)evi, Giacomo (Cervetto)	Perhaps a reference to a physiognomical characteristic
Prince of Music, The	Palestrina, G P de	This name was engraved upon the lid of his coffin
Red Priest, The	Vivaldi, A L	He is said to have had startlingly red hair
Rovettino	Volpe, Giambattista	
Signor Crescendo	Rossini, G A	Certainly not the inventor of this device (see Section VII), but certainly one of the most demanding employers of it
Strauss of Italy, The	Respighi, O	So-called perhaps by jealous Italians
Vecchio, il	Sirazi, G	
Wife of Haydn, The	Boccherini, L	An unkind name, given to indicate that, although of the same family as Haydn's, Boccherini's music has an effeminate weakness and insubstantiality
Wundermann, Des	Saint-Germain	See the Longest-lived Composer, above, for the alleged reasons for the name

PSEUDONYMOUS COMPOSERS

Throughout musical history composers, for a variety of reasons, have chosen to write under pseudonyms. Southern Europe in the 18th century saw a rash of alternative Arcadian names, a few of which assumed the role of nicknames, and in the same century there was a craze for anagrams and back-spellings. Of more practical use are those names chosen to render their owners pronouncable and recognisable in the foreign countries in which they were working; sometimes these names are 'translations' of the meanings of the originals, while others are apparently arbitrarily adopted local names. In most cases simplification seems to have been the aim.

Pseudonym	*Real Name*	*Remarks*
Accademico Formato	Marcheselli, D	Arcadian form
Adams, Stephen	Maybrick, Michael	Composer of 'The Holy City'
Agricola, Alexander	Ackermann, Alexander	Dutch motet-writer who adopted the Latin name when working in Spain

Pseudonym	Real Name	Remarks
Albicastro, Henrico	Weyssenburg, Heinrich, or Weissenburg von Biswang, Hainz	Swiss composer who adopted an Italian name
Alkan, Charles	Morhange, Charles Henri Valentin	See Composers who met death in unusual circumstances, above
Arcimelo	Corelli, Arcangelo	Arcadian form
Berlin, Irving	Baline, Israel	American composer of Russian origin who wrote 'I'm Dreaming of a White Christmas', etc
Chagrin, Francis	Paucker, Alexander	Romanian-born English composer
Claribel	Mrs Barnard	English composer of 'Come Back to Erin'.
Coperario, Giovanni	Cooper, John	English composer, dissatisfied with his mundane name
Copland, Aaron	Kaplan, A	American composer of east European origin
Creston, Paul	Guttoveggio, Joseph	American, of Italian origin
Duke, Vernon	Dukelsky, Vladimir	Russian composer resident in New York since 1929
Ellerton, John Lodge	Lodge, John	Prolific English composer
Fedele	Treu, Daniel Gottlieb	
Foss, Lukas	Fuchs, Lukas	German-born American pianist/composer
Franz, Robert	Knauth, Robert Franz	German song-writer
German, Edward	Jones, Edward German	English composer of *Tom Jones, Merrie England,* etc
Glebov, Igor	Asafiev, Boris	Russian composer who wrote as a music critic under the assumed name
Halévy, J F F E	Lévy, Jacques François Fromental Élie	French operatic composer
Hammer, F X	Marteau, Franz Xaver	Cellist/composer at Pressburg in 1783
Hardelot, Guy d'	Rhodes, Helen	See Women composers, above
Hopkins, Antony	Reynolds, Antony	Composer; also a well-known broadcaster
Idalviv	Vivaldi, A L	Back-spelling
Ille Cram, or Illecram	Marcelli, Vincenzo	Back-spelling of a possibly Rimini-based Italian composer
Jacob Polak; Jacob le Polonais; Jacob le Reys	? Polak, Jacob	Polish composer and lutenist who lived in Paris
Keler-Béla	Keler, Adalbert von	Hungarian march- and dance-composer
Lara, Isidore de	Cohen, Isidore	English opera-composer
Lothar, Louis	Dupin, Paul	French composer; see Deaf composers, above.
Mathis, G S	Seiber, Matyás	He used the pseudonym when writing for the accordion
Melante	Telemann, G P	Near-anagram
Moondog	Hardin, Louis Thomas	American composer
Mosonyi	Brandt, Michael	Hungarian nationalist composer
O'Byrne, Dermot	Bax, Arnold Edward Trevor	Used the pseudonym only for his literary works
Offenbach, Jacques	Eberst, Jacques	Born at Offenbach
Ozzaniugnas, Olocin	Sanguinazzo, Nicolo	Back-spelling of this Italian string-player and composer
Palestrina, Pierguigi	Pierluigi, Giovanni	Took his name from his birthplace
Punto, Giovanni	Stich, Jan Václav	A much-travelled Czech composer, known also in Germany as 'Johann Wenzel Stich'

Pseudonym	*Real Name*	*Remarks*
Regnal, Frédéric	Erlanger, Frédéric d'	Composer of German/American parentage, naturalised English
Reyer, Ernest	Rey, Louis Étienne Ernst	French writer of mainly vocal music
Roland-Manuel	Lévy, Roland Alexis Manuel	French
Rudhyar, Dane	Chennevière, Daniel	French composer who lived in America from 1917
Sauguet, Henri	Poupard, Jean-Pierre	French
Schröter, Corona	Schmelling, Elisabeth	See Women composers, above
Senez, Camille de	Wayditch von Verhovac, Count Gabriel	German composer of fourteen operas
Sharm	Marsh, John	Anagram
Strinfalico, Eterio	Marcello, Alessandro	Arcadian form
Stuart, Leslie	Barrett, Thomas A	English musical-comedy writer
Suppé, Franz von	Suppe-Demelli, Francesco Ermenegildo Ezechiele	Operetta-writer of Belgian origin
Tal, Joseph	Gruenthal, Joseph	Polish-born Israeli composer
Talbot, Howard	Munkittrick, Richard Lansdale	English operetta and musical-comedy writer
Toeschi, Carlo Giuseppe	Toesca della Castellamonte, Carlo Giuseppe	Italian composer active in Germany
Urtica	Kopřiva, Václav Jan	Composer and schoolmaster in the tiny Czech village of Citoliby
Venatorini, Josef	Mysliveček, Josef	See also il Divino Boemo
Viadana, Lodovici	Grossi, Lodovico	
Warlock, Peter	Heseltine, Philip	English composer who committed suicide
Zenta, Hermann	Holmès, Augusta May Anne	See Women composers, above

The composer with the most pseudonyms was the Late Victorian writer of ballads and salon pieces Charles Arthur Rawlings. The following is a list, hopefully complete, of his aliases:

Haydon Augarde
Jean Augarde
Jeanne Bartelet
Otto Bonheur
Emile Bonte
Faulkner Brandon
Louis Brandon
Henri Clermont
Auguste Cons
Eugene Delacassa
Leo Delcasse
Eileen Dore
Jean Douste
Denis Dupre
Leon Du Terrail
Seymour Ellis
Robert Graham
John Gresham
Maxime Heller
Emerson James
Harrington Leigh
François Lemara
Gilbert Loewe
Angelo Martino
Alphonse Menier
Nita
Paul Perrier
Maxime Pontin
Wellington Rawlings
Vernon Rey
Carl Ritz
Carl Rubins
Emile Sachs
Hans Sachs
Ralph Seymour
Herman Straus
Maurice Telma
Gordon Temple
Paul Terrier
Thomas Thome
Claude de Vere
Oscar Verne
Beryl Vincent
Christine Williams
Sydney West

Sharp-eyed readers spotting Wellington Rawlings in the above list, and then coming across the name Alfred Rawlings may be forgiven for thinking that they have found yet another pseudonym to add to the list. In fact, Alfred William Rawlings really existed–as brother of Charles Arthur, the composer of the hymn 'All Things Bright and Beautiful', and, depressingly, as the possessor of a string of his own pseudonyms:

Leslie Conyers
Max Dressler
Gustave Dumas
Florence Fare
Edith Fortescue
Stanley Gordon
Felix Lemoine
Guy Morris
Edward St Quentin
Ivan Stephonoff
Ivan Tchakoff
Jules Therese
Lionel Tree
Constance V White
Sydney L Wyman
John William Tomlinson

The American hymn-composer Philipp Paul Bliss is said to have disguised his works under more than 60 pseudonyms.

LITTLE-KNOWN COMPOSERS WITH WELL-KNOWN NAMES

The most frequently encountered name in composer lists is, perhaps surprisingly, Weber (not including, of course, Bach and Benda and other family groups, see above). There are seven Webers in addition to the well-known one; and several other famous composers have shared their names with composers of less renown:

Arnold, John (1720–92), publisher and composer of Church music, songs, catches, etc.
Arnold, Samuel (1740–1802), London organist and the composer of several operas.
Berg, Nathaniel (1879–1951), Swedish Army veterinarian who composed in his spare time.
Clementi, Aldo (b 1925), Italian.
Franck, Eduard (1817–93), French instrumental and orchestral writer.
Ives, Simon (1600–62), English composer and organist.
Nielsen, Riccardo (b 1908), Italian, of Scandinavian origin.
Schubert, Franz Anton (1768–1827), worked in Dresden.
Schubert, Johann Friedrich (1770–1811), worked in Stettin, Glozau, and Ballenstedt.
Schubert, Joseph (1757–1833), worked in Dresden.
Schumann, Friedrich Theodor (active *c* 1770–80).
Tchaikovsky, Boris (b 1925), Russian.
Wagner, Anton (18th century).
Wagner, Carl Jakob (1772–1822), worked as a Kapellmeister in Darmstadt.
Wagner, Georg Gottfried (1698–1757), German, a pupil of Kuhnau and J S Bach.
Wagner, Gotthard (1678–1738), German, worked in Bavaria.
Wagner, Joseph Frederick (b 1900), American.
Weber, Ben (b 1916), American.
Weber, Aloys.
Weber, Bernard Anselm (1766–1821), German; successor to Reichardt in Berlin in 1794.
Weber, Friedrich (Bedřich) Dionys (1766–1842), Czech composer and Director of the Prague Conservatory.
Weber, Gottfried (17 ?–18 ?), German composer, mainly of Church music.
Weber, Gustav (1845–87), Swiss.
Weber, Jacob Gottfried (1779–1839), German (identical to Gottfried Weber, above ?).

ADJECTIVISED COMPOSERS

As a labour- and word-saving device, writers occasionally describe music of one composer by reference to another, turning the latter's name into an adjective by the use of a suffix: '-ish', '-ian', or '-esque'. It is possible to carry this habit too far; the 'feel' of a composer's name thus distorted can be altered, clouding the meaning which the writer has sought to clarify.

For instance, Haydn, treated to adjectivisation, becomes **Haydnish, Haydnian,** or **Haydnesque.** The first two are clumsy while the third conveys the impression of an effeminate, Dresden China figurine completely removed from the tough spirit of the composer. Schumann suffers similarly in **Schumannesque.** On the other hand, Beethoven gains from **Beethovenian,** with its appropriate solidity and sonority, and from **Beethovenish,** which, being akin to 'tigerish', has a strength and tenacity in keeping with the character of the composer. **Coplandish,** with its affinity to 'outlandish', seems less than fair.

Similar games may be played with **Bachian, Vivaldian, Straussian, Corellian, Brahmsian,** etc, which fulfil their functions innocuously, but slightly suspect are those adjectives which alter the natural stress of the name to accommodate the suffix: **Mozartean** (the preferred form, for some reason; 'Mozartian', with an 'i', is less common), **Schubertian** (the composer, some authors would have us believe, of **Schubertesque Schubertisms;** and in his analysis of Schubert's Fifth Symphony, Tovey even refers to '**Schubertised** Mozart'–*Essays in Musical Analysis,* Vol I, 1935), **Dvořákian, Mendelssohnian, Elgarian,** and **Gershwinian.** Worse are those adjectives which change the last vowel sound: **Beethovenian** ('Beethoveenian', which has other qualities, however–see above), **Handelian** ('Handeelian'), **Wagnerian** ('Wagneerian'), and **Honeggerian** ('Honeggairian'?).

Worse still are the adjectives which alter the actual spelling of the name: **Tchaikovskian, Sibelian, Delian;** but the ultimate contempt must be reserved for the writer who forces names against all sense of euphony into an adjectival mould. Consider the undulating vowel sounds of **Berliozian, Rameauian,** and **Prokofievian,** the Greek and Scottish associations of **Orffian** and **Spohrian,** the description **Chopinesque** which, with its French 'in' sound, will work only on paper, and **Gounodian,** which refuses to do even that, and it will be realised that these composers should join the group which includes Rimsky-Korsakov, Vaughan Williams, and Smetana, as having unadjectivisible names.

COMPOSERS: FACTS AND FEATS

The most ingratiating composer could be said to be Luigi Boccherini (1743–1805). In a period of musical history when the tendency was to think of music in black and white, with half-tones and subtle statements the exception rather than the rule, Boccherini went to considerable trouble to present the reverse image. The direction 'sotto voce' ('in an undertone') abounds in his music to such an extent as to become almost a mannerism, and mild-mannered rhythms and sweet, gently curling melodies put his style apart from the more conventional 18th-century composer. An examination of his works reveals that, in nearly 600 works, almost all of them for instrumental groups or orchestra, amounting to some 1400 movements, the following directions appear:

Affettuoso ('effectionately')	20 times
Grazioso ('gracefully') or con grazia ('with grace')	25 times
Amoroso ('lovingly')	37 times
Soave ('agreeably', 'sweetly', 'delicately', 'gently', 'caressingly', 'lightly'), also soave assai ('extremely . . .) and soavita, and once even soave e con grazia	54 times
Dolce ('sweetly') or Dolcissimo ('very sweetly and gently')	148 times

Also to be found are Armonico ('harmoniously'), con innocenza ('with innocence'), piacere ('pleasingly'), and allegretto gentile ('not too fast, lightly and cheerfully', 'pleasingly', 'elegantly', 'gracefully'), together with hundreds of directions calling for very quiet playing (*pp* and *pp sempre*).

Contrast the above with his use of forceful indications, and his essentially gentle and pleasing nature becomes clear:

Appassionato ('passionately')	8 times
con brio ('with fire')	6 times
con forza ('with force')	once

The most 'wronged' composer was Franz Xaver Pokorny (1728–94) of Bohemian origin who wrote a large number of orchestral works, mainly for the Regensburg Court of Thurn und Taxis. Of his more than 160 symphonies, concertos, serenades, and divertimentos many were 'reattributed' after his death to other composers, likely and unlikely, living and dead. The probable culprit was Freiherr Theodor von Schacht, a composer himself and Pokorny's associate and social superior who, it is thought, was jealous of Pokorny's large output when compared with his own. Schacht took half of Pokorny's music and systematically removed the correct composer's name, inserting instead the names of any composer whom he happened to think might not find out. That there was some sort of intention to proceed right through the works of his social inferior and eradicate his name entirely is indicated by the fact that the names he chose as lucky recipients for Pokorny's music are largely in the group bearing the initial letters 'A' and 'B'. Eventually, perhaps, composers further down the alphabet would have stood host to the rest of the pieces.

This unique case has set researchers wondering ever since. Again and again the over-all conception of a composer's music has been thrown awry by one or two items from the Regensburg collection which bear no resemblance at all to the rest, and it was not until the work of Jan la Rue and J Murray Barbour in the early 1960s that light was shed on this strange crime and the intruding works removed from dozens of composers' lists to reconstitute Pokorny's life's work and reputation.

It might be suggested in passing that this exercise in musicology is not entirely valueless musically. Pokorny's music, what little of it has been performed since his death, seems to be of high value and is overripe for rediscovery.

The most tortuous distortion of a composer's name surrounds the Flute Concerto in D by Pokorny, which was attributed to, and has been recorded as by, Boccherini. This particular misattribution seems to have had nothing to do with Schacht: it came about as a result of a misreading of the name on the autograph:

Other distortions occurred during the 18th century, which may be fairily termed 'the Age of Inaccuracy' where music is concerned: Schmidtbauer became Bauerschmitt or Baurschmidt, etc, Holzbauer became Olxburg, and Wagenseil became Vagausell. There are countless other examples.

The most arrogant composer was Richard Wagner (1813–83). Many stories circulate to illustrate his high-handed attitude with his associates; one which typifies his overt disdain of the Jewish race is the report of his habit of conducting the music of Mendelssohn only while wearing gloves. At the end of the performance he would remove the garments and throw them to the floor, to be removed by the cleaners.

It was due to this anti-Semitic attitude that the Third Reich 'adopted' the music of Wagner and the spirit of Wagnerism, at the same time banning the performance of Mendelssohn's, and all Jews', music.

Gloves were also worn by Louis Antoine Jullien (1812–60) when he conducted Beethoven in London, but the gloves were pure white, were brought to him on a silver tray, and were intended as a mark of deep respect.

Richard Wagner (Popperfoto)

The fastest composer? This question has often been asked, but the answer cannot be clear since the question is imprecise. The *consistently* fastest composer must be Schubert who, as we see below, composed over 1000 works (each of his operas, cycles of songs numbering up to 24 individual items, suites of dances for piano or orchestra, and other groups of compositions counting as *one* each) in eighteen years, five months (May 1810 to October 1828). There are many instances in which Schubert would start and finish a work during the course of a single day.

Even this pace of composing may be surpassed by other men working *in spurts*. Vivaldi is said to have been able to compose a concerto in all its parts faster than his copyists could copy it; likewise Telemann (see below). Rossini is supposed to have been so laggardly for much of the time that he had to work fast on occasion to meet theatrical deadlines. A story, probably apocryphal, relates that an irate impresario, faced with an overture-less opera, locked Rossini in a room with manuscript paper and pen until he had written the overture. The composer is said to have passed the completed pages out through a window one by one to the waiting copyists. The story, attractive though it is, does not explain why that impresario found this course easier than the one usually adopted in such circumstances of borrowing an overture from another opera: the Overture to *The Barber of Seville* (1816) had already served for *Elisabetta, Regina d'Inghilterra* in 1815, and for *Aureliano in Palmira* two years earlier.

In modern times rapid composing is less common, due perhaps to the less demanding conditions in which present-day composers are required to conceive their music. Hindemith, however, on Tuesday, 20 January 1936, composed a *Meditation* for viola (his own instrument) and string orchestra in just over five hours in memory of the death of King George V which had occurred that day. The composer took the solo part at the rehearsals the following morning and the work was broadcast by the BBC that evening. *Meditation* is a work in four sections, lasting a total of fifteen minutes.

The most self-critical composer is probably Alan Hovhaness, the modern American composer of Scottish/Armenian parentage. During his early career he was much influenced by the style of Sibelius, and he produced many works which could be said to lie under the shadow of the great Finn. In the early 1930s, however, Hovhaness rethought his position and struck out on a strongly independent line of composition. His previous style was now anathema to him, and he destroyed over 1000 of his compositions, including seven symphonies (see Section IV), many vocal works, songs and cantatas, three operas, about five violin sonatas, several piano sonatas, fantasias and other chamber works. While deploring an action which robbed the world of a chance to hear this music and to judge it, we may be grateful that Alan Hovhaness has since that time been an extremely prolific composer, with a vast amount of music available for study.

Alan Hovhaness (courtesy, Alan Hovhaness)

A similar fate overcame the bulk of the music of Paul Dukas who, shortly before the First World War, ceased to allow his music to be published even though he continued to compose. He was responsible for destroying an unknown quantity of music during the 1930s, leaving a bare handful for the benefit of posterity. Among his few surviving pieces is one of the most popular concert works in the repertoire: *The Sorcerer's Apprentice.*

Working slowly and self-critically, the American composer Carl Ruggles (see Nonagenarians, above) must have suppressed countless hours of composing endeavour: his strongly self-searching personality allowed him to release only a small amount of his music to the world: just nine works, which are listed here:

Toys, for soprano and orchestra (1919).
Men and Angels, originally for six trumpets (1920) but rearranged for orchestra (1938).
Men and Mountains, for chamber orchestra (1924).
Portals, for string orchestra (1926, revised 1952/54).
Sun Treader, for orchestra (1931, but not performed in America until 1966).
Evocations–Four Chants for piano (1937–43, revised 1954).
Organus, for orchestra (1945).
The Sunken Bell, opera (in MS).
Vox Clamans in Deserto, for solo voice, chorus, and chamber orchestra (in MS).

The youngest composer of music which is still available for performance is Wolfgang Amadeus Mozart, whose earliest work was a Minuet and Trio in G, K 1, dated 1761, when the composer was four years old. Several more pieces appeared the following year, and thereafter his output accelerated until, by the time he was 20 he had written his first 30 numbered symphonies (and several unnumbered ones) including the great Nos 25 in G minor and 29 in A, twelve Masses and numerous other Church works, eight operas and other stage works, more than a dozen sonatas for various instruments, thirteen string quartets, the B flat String Quintet, K 174, and countless divertimentos, cassations, serenades, dances, marches, keyboard pieces, vocal works, and concertos. In the last category are five for keyboard (mostly based on the sonata movements of acquaintances), five for violin, one for bassoon, and the Concertone (='large concerto') for two violins and orchestra.

At his death at the age of 35, Mozart's total of works stood at or about the 1000 mark.

Despite their extraordinary fecundity, both Franz Peter Schubert and Jakob Ludwig Felix Mendelssohn-Bartholdy were comparatively late starters. Mendelssohn's earliest works date from his early teens, and works of true genius from his seventeenth year (the Octet in E flat and the Overture to *A Midsummer Night's Dream*); Schubert's earliest work is a Fantasia in G for piano duet, completed on 1 May 1810, when he was thirteen. He went on to compose over 1000 works in all forms then current, many of them not performed until many years after his death at the age of 31. Schubert is unique among composers for his astonishing productivity, especially since every one of his works must be regarded as 'early'.

It should be mentioned that Camille Saint-Saëns is said to have composed music at the age of three years, but none has survived from this period.

The most prolific composer of all time was Georg Philipp Telemann (1681–1767). His works are in process of being catalogued by a group of German scholars to be published as the *Telemann-Werk-Verzeichnis* by Bärenreiter in Kassel, Germany. This project was begun in 1950 and is still not complete; therefore it is too soon to attempt to give an accurate list of his compositions.

It is known, however, that he composed 40 operas, 40 passions, over 100 cantatas, and countless (as yet) orchestral suites and overtures (some estimates make it nearly 600, although a published thematic catalogue–see Hoffmann in Section VII–lists only 135, of which one is a doubtful attribution), concertos for virtually every melody instrument in existence at that time, hundreds of keyboard works and chamber pieces, etc. No other composer covered so wide a field so prolifically.

The composer who inspired most imitation and who provided the basis for most later works was Gioacchino Rossini, whose highly personal and spirited style serves as inspiration for many composers. Apart from the unacknowledged compositions which lie in the wake of Rossini's successful formulae, the following openly admit the Italian's influence:

Benjamin Britten: *Soirées Musicales* (1936); *Matinées Musicales* (1941)–based on themes by Rossini.

Eric William Fenby: *Rossini on Ilkla Moor* (1948), an overture in which the well-known Yorkshire song is subjected to Rossinian orchestration and development.

Fritz Geissler: *Italian Comedy Overture after Rossini* (1958). Rossini-like fragments are set into modern harmonic language and built into a work in buffo-overture form.

Mauro Giuliani: *Rossiniana,* Suites Opp 119 and 121.

Gordon Jacob: Overture: *The Barber of Seville Goes to the Devil.* A mock-Rossini work of great wit and charm.

Ottorino Respighi: *La Boutique Fantasque* (1919); *Rossiniana* (1925). In both these works Respighi, by adapting some of the lesser-known music of Rossini to ballet

Georg Philipp Telemann (Radio Times Hulton Picture Library)

presentation, has popularised music which might otherwise have been known only to specialists.

Franz Schoberlechner: *Fantasia and Variations on a Theme of Rossini,* Op 38 (1823). Schoberlechner was a pupil of Hummel.

Franz Peter Schubert: Overtures in the Italian Style: in C, D 591 (1817); in D, D 590 (1817). Written at the height of Rossini's popularity, Schubert is said to have set out to prove that writing a Rossini overture is a facile achievement.

Dmitri Shostakovitch: Symphony No 15 in A, Op 141 (1971). The first movement contains several references to the famous 'galop' from Rossini's *William Tell* Overture.

SPARE-TIME COMPOSERS

There are many composers for whom the activity of composing occupied only a fraction of their time, part, or indeed the majority, of their energies being channelled elsewhere. The list below omits the many priests and cantors who also composed, since the dispensing of music was in many instances an integral part of their duties.

Anthiel, George (1900–59), American novelist and thriller-writer who also conducted a newspaper agony column.

Atterberg, Kurt (1887–1974), Swedish composer who was an engineer until 1930.

Badings, Henk (b 1907), Dutch composer who was an engineer until 1937.

Balakirev, Mily Alexeyevich (1837–1910), worked for five years (1871–76) as an official in the expanding Russian railway system.

Berg, Nathaniel (1879–1951), Swedish composer who was an Army veterinary surgeon.

Billings, William (1746–1800), one of the earliest American composers; a song-writer and lyricist, he was by trade a tanner.

Borodin, Alexander Porphyrevich (1833–97), world renowned because of his 'Polovtsian Dances' from the opera *Prince Igor* (1890) and other delightfully tuneful works, he was in fact an amateur musician, his time being absorbed largely by research into chemistry for a Russian university.

Burian, Emil František (b 1904), a Czech singer and composer who is also a playwright, author, and producer.

Cage, John (b 1912), American *avant-garde* composer who has so many other activities that he may be regarded as an all-rounder: he is commercial artist, critic, teacher, poet, writer, lecturer, etc.

Carpenter, John Alden (1876–1951), American businessman.

Cras, Jean (1879–1932), a Rear-Admiral in the French Navy.

Cui, César Antonovich (1853–1918), a General in the Russian Army.

Diepenbrock, Alphonse (1862–1921), self-taught Dutch composer, primarily a school-teacher.

Herschel, Wilhelm Friedrich (1738–1822), the famous German astronomer who discovered the Martian polar caps and the existence of the planet Uranus (which he called 'Georgium Sidus'), and who postulated the theory that some so-called 'variable' stars were in fact double stars with a common centre of gravity (a theory since proved to be correct), was also a talented composer and organist.

Hoffmann, Ernst Theodor Wilhelm (1776–1822), the German writer immortalised in Offenbach's opera *The Tales of Hoffman* (1881), was a theatrical manager, lawyer, artist, and municipal official. He revered Mozart, adopting the name Amadeus to replace Wilhelm, and he composed instrumental music, an opera, etc.

Hopkinson, Francis (1737–91), an American statesman and writer, he was also the composer of the first American music to reach publication.

Hume, Tobias (?–1645), an Army Captain who composed for viols and voices during off-duty hours.

Lvov, Alexei Fedorovich (1799–1870), a Russian composer of operas and orchestral music; a Major-General and Adjutant in the Army of Emperor Nicholas I; he was conductor of the Imperial Court Choir 1836–55.

Mussorgsky, Modest Petrovich (1839–81), composer of *Boris Godounov* and *Pictures from an Exhibition* (both 1874), he was an Army officer and later a civil servant.

Rousseau, Jean-Jacques (1712–78), the Swiss author, philosopher, religious and political thinker (he wrote *The Social Contract* in 1762), was an active composer in France.

Susato, Tylman (Thilman, etc) (*c*1511–*c* 1561)

was an Italian composer and trumpeter, but he is remembered also as the first important music-publisher in Antwerp.

Teplov, Grigorii Nikolayevich (1719–89), the composer of the first Russian 'art-songs', he was also a prominent politician.

Titov, Aleksei Nikolayevich (1769–1827), the composer of eight operas, was also a Major-General in the Russian Army.

Trnka, Václav Jan (1739–82/91), an amateur composer, practiced as a Doctor of Medicine in Pesth.

Ulbricht, Maximillian (1752–1814), Viennese composer and land official.

The most exclusively pianistic composer was Fryderyk Franciszek Chopin, (1810–49), a piano virtuoso himself. He was born near Warsaw, but later settled in Paris, and never returned to his native country despite widespread tours. Not a single work of his composition excludes the piano. His output of nocturnes, waltzes, mazurkas, polonaises, etc, is well known, as are his two piano concertos. In addition there are many songs, a cello sonata, all accompanied by piano, and a piano trio in G minor, Op 8. The purely orchestral ballet *Les Sylphides* is merely a selection of arrangements from his piano works orchestrated by various musicians, the most widely known being Roy Douglas. Various other orchestral pieces (under such titles as *Chopiniana, La Nuit ensorcelée, Chopinata,* etc, come into the same category of arrangements from piano originals.

The most married composer was Eugene Francis Charles d'Albert (1864–1932), the composer of the opera *Tiefland* (1903), who had six successive wives.

The earliest composer to be awarded a Doctorate of Music at Cambridge was Robert Fayrfax (1464–1521), who was thus honoured in 1511.

The only composer without a nose was Josef Mysliveček (1737–81), known as 'il Divino Boemo.' He was the victim of a quack surgeon who decided that the only way of

Fryderyk Franciszek Chopin (Popperfoto)

Josef Mysliveček before his operation

curing 'the divine Bohemian's' venereal disease was to cut off his nose.

The first composer to be knighted by an English monarch was Henry Rowley Bishop (1786–1855), honoured by Queen Victoria in 1842. Bishop wrote the timeless song 'Home Sweet Home'.

An expert composer who was also noted for his proficiency in swordsmanship was le Chevalier Joseph Boulogne Saint-George (1839–99), a French mulatto who held a prominent position at the Court of Le Comte d'Ogny in Paris in the 1780s.

The composer of the noisiest symphonies was reputedly the Abbé Giovanni Pietro Maria Crispi (1737–97), who wrote sixteen symphonies in the bright, martial key of D major (his two others are in G major). He was said by Sir Charles Burney to have composed symphonies 'too furious and noisy for a room or, indeed, for any other place'. It should be borne in mind that this opinion is based on 18th-century premises and does not take into account the symphonic extravagancies of the 19th and 20th centuries.

MUSICAL FORGERIES

Henri Casadesus (1879–1947) composed music in imitation of 18th-century style. Works said to be by Johann Christian Bach and Carl Philipp Emanuel Bach are still current. Unlike Kreisler (below), Casadesus never admitted his forgeries.

Fritz Kreisler (1875–1962), the world-renowned violinist and composer, frequently introduced into his programmes items by ancient composers, such as Vivaldi, Pugnani, and Dittersdorf. In 1935 he announced to the world that these items (which were henceforth titled '. . . in the style of . . .') were of his own composition.

Charles Zulehner (1770–1830) worked in Mainz (where many of his compositions are still preserved in the Schott Archives). He passed off his music as by Mozart, evidently many years after the latter's death, since, if Mozart himself found difficulty in maintaining a financial balance with the real thing, what chance would a forger have?

A most exciting life was led by Giovanni Giuseppe Cambini (1746–1825), an Italian composer of a vast amount of chamber and orchestral music. He is reputed to have abducted a young girl in Naples and, sailing with her to Leghorn, they were waylaid by pirates. Their future was to be a life of slavery. Romantic writers would have us believe that Cambini was bound and manacled by the pirates, who then set about violating his young companion, of whom nothing further is heard. Later, while in slavery, his master allowed him to practice the violin and, impressed by his playing, he allowed the musician his freedom.

Perhaps more reliance may be placed on the rest of the story: to Paris in 1779, subsequently to be involved musically and politically in the French Revolution, after which he is said to have forged (or 'ghosted'?) quartets for publication under the name of Boccherini. 'Riotous living' accounted for his poverty during the last years, and his life ended sadly in total obscurity.

THE GREATEST COMPOSER

In a study of the facts and feats of music, perhaps this category has no place, yet it represents a question often asked and often answered with an assurance way above the ability of the facts to substantiate. Let us tackle the question by asking how one may arrive at a definition of the term 'greatness'. To be great, a piece of music must possess several qualities: (1) an ability to resist the natural selectiveness of time and remain in the repertoire of a majority of orchestras and artists without suffering from the frequent cycles of fashion which dictate that ears which enjoy certain sounds in, say, 1960, have ceased to do so today; (2) an ability to stir the listener afresh no matter how frequently performed; (3) an ability to attract new listeners, who help to maintain the piece in the limelight by their continuing demand; (4) the ability to stand up to analysis and dissection by experts without revealing damning faults in technique or design; and finally (5) a quality of melodiousness without which (1) to (4) would be undermined but which is also of prime importance in itself.

It must be admitted that, even among the so-called 'standard' classics, there are few works which fulfil all the above requirements, and it is our job to discover which do so and who wrote the majority of them. Examination of record catalogues, concert programmes, and writers' critiques of the past and present show that one composer, Ludwig van Beethoven, wrote the highest proportion of 'great' works when defined by the above method. Among his concertos, symphonies, sonatas, string quartets, overtures, and choral works may be found the most enriching music of all time, and his one opera, *Fidelio,* must be counted among the finest works ever staged. Indeed, it would be strange if it were otherwise, since the composer took endless pains to choose what was, for him, the ideal libretto, and having once selected his story of a woman's utterly selfless loyalty to a man, it follows that Beethoven, a severely self-critical artist, would provide the best music he could muster in which to clothe it.

Beethoven had unique opportunities to reach the peak of his chosen vocation, but some of these opportunities must have seemed the very opposite of benevolent to him at the time. To start with, a thorough training in technique was administered in a brutal, selfish manner by a father who set out to make of young Ludwig another child prodigy in the mould of Mozart some years earlier. The boy's age was even falsified by two years so that, later in life, even Beethoven himself was unsure of his correct year of birth. The groundwork of impeccable though hard-won technique provided Beethoven with the means to convey his intensely musical thoughts to his public. His thoughts were then systematically enriched, deepened, matured, and intensified by the cruellest stroke which fate has ever inflicted upon a composer: in his late twenties he began to notice the first signs of a deafness which grew progressively worse despite all attempts at a cure, until his last years were spent in total silence. The effect on a sensitive musician may be imagined, and he cannot be blamed for contemplating suicide: only an unquestioning religious faith prevented an act of self-destruction and this would certainly have deprived the world of countless works of highest genius.

Beethoven's opera has already been mentioned, but it is in the symphonic field that he is most widely known. His odd-numbered symphonies include the 'Eroica' and Choral, together with the world-famous Fifth and Seventh, and the 'Pastoral' Symphony (No 6), is also widely loved. So, too, are his only Violin Concerto of 1806, and his Fourth and Fifth Piano Concertos (the latter known as the 'Emperor'), together with several overtures: *Egmont, Coriolan, Prometheus,* and the four written for *Fidelio: Leonora* No 1, No 2, and No 3, and the *Fidelio* Overture itself.

Beethoven's greatest thoughts, however, may be said to lie in the late piano sonatas and more particularly in the five string quartets which were his last works. No composer has surpassed these extraordinary works in inwardness of feeling and perfection. The composer himself is said to have remarked that they may be difficult for his contemporaries but that they were written for the listener of 50 years ahead. In fact, some 150 years after Beethoven's death, the works still retain many of their mysteries; rare is the listener even today who can claim wholly to understand their contents. Perhaps only a sensitive artist who has experienced the same soundless torture as did Beethoven in his mid 50s can truly perceive all that this music has to offer.

In addition to the five standards to which it is submitted that Beethoven's greatest works reach, there is a sixth quality possessed by Beethoven alone: single-handed he transformed music. His influence was crushingly all-embracing. After Beethoven, music could never be the same again. His appearance in musical history at that time was a remarkable force by which the direction of music was wrenched out of one channel and placed firmly into another. Beethoven knew the rules but no one ever broke them more decisively or permanently.

Section IV

ORCHESTRAL AND INSTRUMENTAL REPERTOIRE

'There are three kinds of music: first, the music of the universe; second, human music; third, instrumental music.'

These words were written in the year AD 515 by the Roman philosopher Anicus Manlius Severinus Boëthius under the heading 'De Institutione Musica'. It is not clear precisely what he meant by 'music of the universe', unless he was referring in some vague way to a mysterious harmony of space and/or natural phenomena, but by 'human music' it is obvious that he meant music which is sung. Last, and by implication the least important in his list, comes 'instrumental music'. It is understandable that he should have thought little of music produced solely through instruments because the capabilities and variety of instruments available at that time were very much narrower than is the case today. In fact, the 'human music' of that time was produced by an instrument–the voice –which has remained unchanged during the intervening 1500 years, while instruments have changed, multiplied, and evolved to an extent which would have been beyond the craziest dreams of the later Romans.

This Section attempts to outline the basic forms of instrumental music which composers have developed since it first began to have an identity of its own during the 17th century.

Firstly, let us look briefly at one of the foundations of the whole art of music: tonality.

THE CONCEPT OF TONALITY

For more than three centuries, from the latter half of the 16th to the beginning of the 20th, the concept of key or tonality ruled the composition of music. Developed out of the ancient 'modes', the key system we are familiar with today was well established by the Baroque period, at which time it was, however, a purely technical feature of composition. Early in the 18th century, with the development of music of strongly contrasting characters, and with the gradual increase in the size of performing groups, 'key' began to have some meaning to composers outside the purely technical necessity of having to write 'in' one in order to be harmonically grammatical. Minor keys indicated a strength and muscularity in the character of the music while music written in the major was of a 'positive', or optimistic, mood. Key in music, therefore, became analogus to colour in painting.

It was also found that certain instruments sounded better in certain keys. Woodwind, for instance, favoured the 'soft' keys with flat signatures: F major, B flat major, E flat major, and their relative minors: D minor, G minor, and C minor. Violins, on the other hand, sounded out well in the sharp keys: G major, D major, and A major, since these keys encouraged the use of 'open' strings. Further, some instruments could be played *only* in the keys in which they were constructed: trumpets were usually made in C or D, horns in D and F, etc, and in other keys only the occasional note was playable by them. Logically, then, if a composer wished to write a work which was to make a brilliant effect at a ceremony or festivity, he would choose a key in which the violins would be at their most brilliant and trumpets could be used, together with their ubiquitous companions the timpani: D major. Therein, also, the brazen sound of hunting-horns could be employed if required.

It is for that reason that at least half of the many thousands of concert symphonies, curtain-raising overtures, and ceremonial serenades written during the 18th century are in D major.

The Baroque strength of minor-keyed works changed to a feeling of pathos and tragedy during the central years of the 18th century. At this time the novelist Friedrich Maximillian von Klinger was leading a literary movement in which deep passions and tragic drama were foremost. His novel *Sturm und Drang* ('Storm and Stress') supplied the term for the movement, and composers seized the style for their own ends. It became the fashion for composers to write serious, tragic, even belligerent, works in minor keys.

During the years surrounding the turn of the century (ie the years of Beethoven's ascendancy), another change came about in the use and choice of keys. For one thing, brass instruments were being evolved that could play chromatically and were thus no longer partly restricted to the keys of C, D, and F with which they were by now traditionally associated, and a similar change was coming about in respect of woodwind instruments. These were the years, too, during which the brilliance of the violins could be enhanced by sheer numbers so that the necessity of accommodating the music mainly, or predominantly, to their open strings for brilliance of effect was losing its force. The choice of key was becoming a subjective choice to be made by the composers, and they did not hesitate to exploit their new freedom of coloration. Major keys were in the main used for extrovert works in the 19th century while minor keys became the bringers of soft subtle shades and deeper emotions of a romantic nature.

Unless he has perfect pitch, the listener is unlikely to be able to recognise the key of a work simply by hearing it even if he might readily detect key changes within a piece, yet the characteristic aura of a key is a definite if mysterious phenomenon. In the list which follows many of the points raised above are illustrated: the prominence of festive and occasional works in C and D, and the Baroque strength, classical anger, and romantic fervour of the works in minor keys. But the reader may find, in going through the list, that a number of pieces in, for instance, G major, are among his particular favourites. No explanation is offered for this, but the reader is invited to draw his own conclusions about it after mentally comparing the works under each key heading.

Before we go on to the list, an explanation about the word 'in', in titles such as 'Concerto *in* A major.'

The convention of identifying musical works by keys grew out of practical considerations. Court orchestras of the 17th and 18th centuries, faced with a large and ever-growing library of music from their composers' production lines, might be asked to prepare, for instance, 'the A major Concerto' for performance, and the musicians would thus identify the required work simply by turning to the opening pages of their parts until arriving at a work with three sharps in the key signature. They were not concerned at that time that the work was not *wholly* in A major, the slow movement being in A minor, E major, or whatever. The work commenced in A major, and that, as far as identification problems were concerned, was the end of the matter.

This convention continues to this day. It encounters obstacles, however, where accuracy is concerned (see comments below, under 'D flat major'), and it should be realised that usage demands clarity: 'Brahms' Symphony No 1 in C minor', but pedantic punctiliousness demands accuracy: 'Brahms's Symphony No 1 commencing in C minor', since the work ends in a blaze of C major.

LIST OF KEYS

The list is in chronological order within each key, and mainly only works of popular prominence and significance have been included. Also given are the key 'signature' (ie the clue given to the performer at the head of a piece to direct him to sharpen or flatten the right notes for the key), and the related key in the opposite mode.

Although the subject of key in relation to colour has been alluded to above, it is fruitless to draw the analogies further than personal impressions will take them, since there is no technical or scientific basis for the supposed connections. Nevertheless, two composers, Rimsky-Korsakov and Scriabin, both masters of orchestral 'colour', have given their opinions about some key and colour relationships. Their impressions are noted against the keys concerned merely so that the reader may compare them with each other and with his own. Also given for some of the keys are the impressions of the German composer Johann Mattheson and some other authorities. Mattheson's impressions were listed in his *Das neu eröffnete Orchester* (Hamburg, 1713) and show that his favourite keys were G minor, C major, F major, G major, and A minor, while he showed a positive antipathy towards E flat major, B major, E major, F minor, F sharp minor, and B minor.

C major

An 'open' key, ie no sharps or flats in the signature. Relative minor: A minor.
One of the 'trumpet and drum keys'. This is the key of optimistic obviousness which can also embrace deep feelings. Rimsky-Korsakov saw this key as white; Scriabin as red. Mattheson described it as rough, bold, suitable for joyful situations but also, in the right hands, for tenderness.

18th century

Vivaldi: Violin Concerto, Op 8/6, 'Pleasure' (*c* 1725).
Mozart: 'Coronation' Mass, K 317 (1779); Symphony No 36, K 425, 'Linz' (1783); String Quartet, K 465, 'Dissonant' (1785); Piano Concerto, K 503, (1786); Symphony No 41, K 551, 'Jupiter' (1788).
Beethoven: Piano Concerto No 1, Op 15 (1797).
Haydn: String Quartet Op 76/3, 'Emperor' (1799) (note however that the 'Emperor's Hymn' movement itself is in G major).

19th century

Beethoven: Symphony No 1, Op 21 (1800); Overture *Leonora* No 2 (1805); Overture *Leonora* No 3 (1806); String Quartet, Op 59/3 (1806).
Rossini: *La Scala di Seta* Overture (1812).
Schubert: Symphony No 6, D 589 (1818); 'Wanderer' Fantasy, D 790 (1822).
Weber: *Der Freischütz* Overture, J 277 (1822).
Schubert: *Rosamunde* Overture, D 797 (1823); Symphony No 9, D 944 (1828); String Quintet, D 956 (1828).
Berlioz: *Symphonie Fantastique,* Op 14 (1830).
Schumann: Symphony No 2, Op 61 (1846).
Tchaikovsky: Serenade for Strings, Op 48 (1880).

20th century

Sibelius: Symphony No 3, Op 52 (1904–7).
Vaughan Williams: *A Sea Symphony* (No 1) (1912).
Sibelius: Symphony No 7, Op 105 (1925).
Shostakovitch: Symphony No 7, Op 60, 'Leningrad' (1941).
Vaughan Williams: *Sinfonia Antartica* (No 7) (1953).

C minor

Three flats: b, e, a. Relative major: E flat.
Often chosen for its dark and dramatic quality (particularly in that, by modulating to its tonic major, C major, it brings a victorious brightening of the music in the peroration). Quantz regarded this key, among others, as suitable for music of audacity, rage, and despair, Mattheson as sweet, sad, and useful for depicting sleep.

18th century

Vivaldi: Concerto for Strings, P 441, 'Al Santo Sepolcro'.
Haydn: Keyboard Sonata No 33, Hob XVI:20 (1771).
Mozart: Mass, K 427 (1782–83); Piano Concerto, K 491 (1786).
Beethoven: Piano Sonata, Op 13, 'Pathètique' (1798).

19th century

Beethoven: Piano Concerto No 3, Op 37 (1800); *Coriolan* Overture, Op 62 (1807); Symphony No 5, Op 67 (1807).

Weber: Concertino for clarinet and orchestra, J 109 (1811).
Schubert: Symphony No 4, D 417, 'Tragic' (1816); Quartet movement, D 803 (1820).
Beethoven: Piano Sonata, Op 111 (1822).
Brahms: Symphony No 1, Op 68 (1877).
Bruckner: Symphony No 8 (1885).
Saint-Saëns: Symphony No 3, 'Organ Symphony' (1886).

20th century

Rakhmaninoff: Piano Concerto No 2 (1901).
Shostakovitch: Symphony No 8 (1943).

C sharp minor

Four sharps: f, c, g, d. Relative major: E.

18th century

Haydn: Piano Sonata No 49, Hob XVI:36 (*c* 1777/79?).

19th century

Beethoven: Piano Sonata, Op 27/2, 'Moonlight' (1801); String Quartet, Op 131 (1826).

D flat major

Five flats: b, e, a, d, g. Relative minor: B flat minor.
An extremely rare key for a major work. Rimsky-Korsakov saw it as dusky warm; Scriabin as violet. A number of short works employ the key but the only major work known to the author to be listed as in D flat major is:
Robert Farnon: Symphony No 1 (1941).

It should be mentioned that Mahler's Symphony No 9, although usually listed as being in D major or D minor, is an example of this composer's 'progressive tonality' technique: it starts in D major but the final Adagio is in D flat. Taking the precedents of Beethoven's Symphony No 5 in C minor, his Choral Symphony in D minor, and Mendelssohn's Symphony in A minor, 'Scots', all of which end in their respective tonic major keys, Mahler's Ninth Symphony should be listed as being in D major; however, its important use of D flat in the finale, tonally remote from the key of the opening, should lead us, perhaps, to describe the work as being 'in D major–D flat major'. This, unfortunately, then ignores the prominent use of E major, D minor, G minor, and other keys in the work.

D major

Two sharps: f, c. Relative minor: B minor.
A martial, military key suitable for festive occasions in which instrumental brilliance is required. This description is borne out by both Rimsky-Korsakov and Scriabin, who described the key as yellow, sunny; and as yellow, brilliant respectively. Mattheson saw it as forthright, arrogant, warlike, and animated.

18th century

Handel: *Water Music* (the section with trumpets) (1717).
Bach: Orchestral Suites Nos 3 and 4 (*c* 1720); *Magnificat*, BWV 243 (*c* 1723); Brandenburg Concerto No 5, BWV 1050 (*c* 1723).
Handel: *Musick for the Royal Fireworks* (1749).
Mozart: Violin Concerto, K 218 (1775); 'Haffner' Serenade, K 250 (1776); Post-horn Serenade, K 320 (1778); Symphony No 31, K 297, 'Paris' (1778); Horn Concerto No 1, K 412 (1782); Symphony No 35, K 385 'Haffner' (1783); Symphony No 38, K 504, 'Prague' (1786); Piano Concerto, K 537, 'Coronation' (1788); String Quintet, K 593 (1790).
Haydn: Symphony No 101, 'Clock' (1794); Symphony No 104, 'London' (1795).

19th century

Beethoven: Symphony No 2, Op 36 (1802); Violin Concerto, Op 61 (1806).
Rossini: *Semiramide* Overture (1823).
Weber: *Oberon* Overture, J 306 (1826).
Mendelssohn: *Fingal's Cave* Overture, Op 26 (1830) (also partly in B minor, the relative minor key).
Brahms: Symphony No 2, Op 73 (1878); Violin Concerto, Op 77 (1878).

20th century

Sibelius: Symphony No 2, Op 42 (1901).
Shostakovitch: Symphony No 5, Op 47 (1937/38).
Vaughan Williams: Symphony No 5 (1943).

Elgar: *Pomp and Circumstance March No 1* (1901) ('Land of Hope and Glory').

D minor

One flat: b. Relative major: F.
A brooding and passionate key, sometimes chosen for its semi-religious feeling. It has the advantage that trumpets and drums may be used to give added emphasis at cardinal points. Mattheson: devotional, tranquil, but at the same time noble.

18th century

Vivaldi: Concerto Grosso, Op 3/11 (1712).
Marcello, A: Oboe Concerto (*c* 1716).
Bach: Harpsichord Concerto No 1 (1732?).
Haydn: Symphony No 26, 'Lamentatione' (*c* 1768).
Mozart: Piano Concerto, K 466 (1785); Requiem Mass, K 626 (1791).
Haydn: Mass No 9, 'Nelson' (1798); String Quartet Op 76/2, 'Fifths' (1799).

19th century

Beethoven: Piano Sonata, Op 31/2, 'Tempest' (1802); Symphony No 9, Op 125, Choral (1823).
Schubert: String Quartet, D 810, 'Death and the Maiden' (1826).
Schumann: Symphony No 4, Op 120 (1841, revised 1851).
Brahms: Piano Concerto No 1, Op 15 (1858).
Mussorgsky (arr Rimsky-Korsakov): *Night on a Bare Mountain* (1867) (ends in D major).
Brahms: *Tragic Overture,* Op 81 (1880).
Dvořák: Symphony No 7, Op 70 (1885).
Bruckner: Symphony No 9 (1894).

20th century

Sibelius: Violin Concerto, Op 47 (1903/5); Symphony No 6, Op 104 (1923).
Vaughan Williams: Violin Concerto (1925).

E flat major

Three flats: b, e, a. Relative minor: C minor.
This is Beethoven's 'heroic' key, but it has not been seen in this light by many other composers. Usually it is adopted for music of a mellow beauty in which melodic grace plays a large part. Rimsky-Korsakov thought of the key as dark, gloomy, bluish grey, and Scriabin as steel colour with a metallic lustre. For Mattheson this key represented pathos, earnestness, and sorrow, and is absolutely devoid of sensuality.

18th century

Vivaldi: Violin Concerto, Op 8/5, 'Storm at Sea' (*c* 1725).
Mozart: Sinfonia Concertante, K 364 (1779); Horn Concertos Nos 2, 3, and 4, K 417, 447, and 495 (1783–86); Piano Concerto, K 482 (1786); Piano Quartet, K 493 (1786); Symphony No 39, K 543 (1788); String Quartet, K 614 (1791).
Haydn: Piano Sonata No 62, Hob XVI:52 (1794); Symphony No 103, 'Drum Roll' (1795); Trumpet Concerto (1796).

19th century

Beethoven: Symphony No 3, Op 55, 'Eroica' (1804); Piano Concerto No 5, Op 73, 'Emperor' (1809).
Weber: Clarinet Concerto No 2, J 118 (1811); *Euryanthe* Overture, J 291 (1823).
Schubert: Piano Trio, D 929 (1828).
Schumann: Piano Quintet, Op 44 (1842).
Liszt: Piano Concerto No 1 (1849).
Schumann: Symphony No 3, Op 97, 'Rhenish' (1850).
Bruckner: Symphony No 4, 'Romantic' (1874).
Tchaikovsky: *1812* Overture, Op 49 (1881).

20th century

Elgar: Symphony No 2 (1911).
Sibelius: Symphony No 5, Op 82 (1914/15).
Shostakovitch: Cello Concerto No 1, Op 107 (1959).

E major

Four sharps: f, c, g, d. Relative minor: C sharp minor.
Despite the apparent brilliancy imparted to the key by the use of four sharps, this comparatively rare key seems, except for Mattheson, to attract friendly, self-confident music. Rimsky-Korsakov: blue, sapphire, sparkling; Scriabin: bluish white. Mattheson: fatal sadness and despair; pain akin to death.

Two costume designs for Haydn's opera Armida *(1784)*

18th century

Vivaldi: Violin Concerto, Op 8/1, 'Spring' (*c* 1725).
Bach: Violin Concerto No 2.
Scarlatti, D: Harpsichord Sonata, L 23, Kk 380, 'Cortège'.

19th century

Rossini: *Barber of Seville* Overture (1816).
Weber: *Jubel* Overture, J 245 (1818).
Rossini: *William Tell* Overture (1829) (the storm music, etc, is in E minor).
Dvořák: Serenade for Strings, Op 22 (1875).

E minor

One sharp: f. Relative major: G.
A certain exotic grandeur attaches to this key. It has its dark side but also a brilliant and full-blooded confidence. Quantz linked this key with C minor as suitable for music of audacity, rage, and despair; Mattheson heard it as thoughtful, profound, and sad: fast music in E minor will never be happy.

18th century

Haydn: Symphony No 44, 'Mourning' (1771).

19th century

Weber: Horn Concertino, J 188 (1806).
Rossini: *William Tell* Overture (1829) (see also E major).
Chopin: Piano Concerto No 1 (1830).
Mendelssohn: Violin Concerto No 2, Op 64 (1844).
Brahms: Symphony No 4, Op 98 (1884).
Tchaikovsky: Symphony No 5, Op 64 (1889).
Dvořák: Symphony No 9, Op 95, 'From the New World' (1898).
Sibelius: Symphony No 1, Op 39 (1899).

20th century

Vaughan Williams: Symphony No 6 (1947).

F major

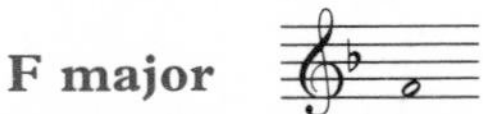

One flat: b. Relative minor: D minor.
The traditional 'pastoral' key, and the key of hunting-horns (as also is D major). Being a 'flat' key, it is particularly suitable for woodwind soloists. Rimsky-Korsakov: green; Scriabin: red. For Mattheson it expresses beautiful sentiments, generosity, love, and other virtuous feelings. It is like a proud, handsome, and wholly good person.

18th century

Handel: *Water Music* (the section with horns) (1717).
Bach: Brandenburg Concertos Nos 1 and 2 BWV 1046–7 (1723).
Vivaldi: Violin Concerto, Op 8/3, 'Autumn' (*c* 1725).
Bach: *Italian Concerto* for solo harpsichord, BWV 971 (1735).
Mozart: Oboe Quartet, K 370 (1781).

19th century

Beethoven: Violin Sonata, Op 24, 'Spring' (1801); Symphony No 6, Op 68, 'Pastoral' (1806); *Egmont* Overture, Op 84 (1810); Symphony No 8, Op 93 (1812).
Schubert: Octet, D 803 (1823).
Beethoven: String Quartet, Op 135 (1826).

F minor

Four flats: b, e, a, d. Relative major: A flat.
One of the darkest of the commonly used keys, F minor has drawn from some composers their bitterest music. Mattheson regarded it as tranquil, tender, but with a depth and power close to anxiety and despair: black melancholy, provoking horror in the listener.

18th century

Vivaldi: Violin Concerto, Op 8/4, 'Winter' (*c* 1725).
Haydn: Symphony No 49, 'Passione' (1768).

19th century

Beethoven: Piano Sonata, Op 57, 'Appassionata' (1806); String Quartet, Op 95 (1810).
Weber: Clarinet Concerto No 1, J 114 (1811).
Chopin: Piano Concerto No 2 (1829).
Tchaikovsky: Symphony No 4, Op 36 (1878).

20th century

Shostakovitch: Symphony No 1, Op 10 (1925).
Vaughan Williams: Symphony No 4 (1935).

F sharp minor

Three sharps: f, c, g. Relative major: A.
A rare and exotic key. It appears that the symphony mentioned below is the only one to be written in this key before 1800. Mattheson: 'here is the sadness of love, unrestrained and outlandish'.

18th century

Haydn: Symphony No 45, 'Farewell' (1772).

G major

One sharp: f. Relative minor: E minor.
An open and optimistic key, in some ways more so even than C major, since G rarely embraces deeper music. Rimsky-Korsakov's impression was: brownish gold, bright; Scriabin's: orange-rose; Mattheson's: rhetorical–an all-purpose key at once earnest and gay.

18th century

Handel: *Water Music* (the sections without brass instruments) (1717).
Bach: Brandenburg Concertos Nos 3 and 4, BWV 1048–9 (1723).
Mozart: Violin Concerto, K 216 (1775); Serenade in G, K 525, *Eine Kleine Nachtmusik* (1787).
Haydn: Symphony No 92, 'Oxford' (1789); Symphony No 94, 'Surprise' (1791); Symphony No 100, 'Military' (1794).

19th century

Beethoven: Piano Concerto No 4, Op 58 (1805/6).
Dvořák: Symphony No 8, Op 88 (1889).

20th century

Vaughan Williams: *A London Symphony* (No 2) (1914).
Elgar: *Pomp and Circumstance March No 4* (1907) ('All men must be free').

G minor

Two flats: b, e. Relative major: B flat.
Mozart's 'tragic' key, this has been used also by other composers to express deep emotion, but Mattheson, as so often out of step with other authorities, described it as perhaps the most beautiful key, combining earnestness, sweetness, liveliness, grace, and tenderness.

18th century

Corelli: Concerto Grosso, Op 6/8, 'Christmas' (*c* 1700).
Vivaldi: Violin Concerto, Op 8/2, 'Summer' (*c* 1725).
Albinoni (arr Giazotto): Adagio for strings and organ.
Haydn: Symphony No 39 (*c* 1768).
Mozart: Symphony No 25, K 183 (1773).
Haydn: Symphony No 83, 'Hen' (1785).
Mozart: Piano Quartet, K 478 (1785); String Quintet, K 516 (1787); Symphony No 40, K 550 (1788).
Haydn: String Quartet, Op 74/3, 'Horseman' (1793).

19th century

Brahms: Piano Quartet No 1, Op 25 (1861).
Bruckner: Overture (1863).

20th century

Moeran: Symphony (1937).

A flat major

Four flats: b, e, a, d. Relative minor: F minor.
Another rarely used key. Elgar's symphony mentioned below, is not the only symphony to have been written in the key: there are several examples from the 18th century by Vaňhal and Gassmann. Rimsky-Korsakov and Scriabin very nearly agreed as to the colour suggested by A flat, the former giving greyish violet, the latter purple violet.

18th century

Haydn: Piano Sonata No 31, Hob XVI:46 (*c* 1767).

19th century

Sibelius: *Finlandia,* tone poem, Op 26 (1899).

20th century

Elgar: Symphony No 1 (1908).

A major

Three sharps: f, c, g. Relative minor: F sharp minor.
The brilliance associated with the early Romantic symphonies listed below is due partly to the fierce and raw tone of horns in A. The key has also attracted composers for the solo clarinet. Rimsky-Korsakov saw the key as rosy and clear; Scriabin as green; Mattheson as affecting but brilliant; suited to sad feelings and violin music.

18th century

Mozart: Symphony No 29, K 201 (1774); Violin Concerto, K 219, 'Turkish' (1775); Piano Concerto, K 488 (1786); Clarinet Quintet, K 581 (1789); Clarinet Concerto, K 622 (1791).

19th century

Beethoven: Violin Sonata, Op 47, 'Kreutzer' (1803); Symphony No 7, Op 92 (1812).
Schubert: Piano Quintet, D 667, 'Trout' (1819).
Mendelssohn: Symphony No 4, Op 90, 'Italian' (1833).
Liszt: Piano Concerto No 2 (1839).
Bruckner: Symphony No 6 (1881).

20th century

Scriabin: Piano Sonata No 8, Op 66 (1913).

A minor

'Open', ie no sharps or flats. Relative major: C.
Music of strength and seriousness, with a misty, undefined sadness. Mattheson: somnolent, in a plaintive, refined way, and suitable for keyboard music.

18th century

Bach: Violin Concerto No 1, BWV 1041.

19th century

Weber: *Abu Hassan* Overture, J 106 (1810); *Preciosa* Overture, J 279 (1821).
Schubert: String Quartet, D 804 (1824).
Beethoven: String Quartet, Op 132 (1824–25).
Mendelssohn: Symphony No 3, Op 56, 'Scots' (1829).
Grieg: Piano Concerto (1868).
Brahms: Concerto for violin and cello, Op 102 (1887).

20th century

Sibelius: Symphony No 4, Op 63 (1911).

B flat major

Two flats: b, e. Relative minor: G minor.
A happy, self-confident key, to which composers often turned in later life as a vehicle for their most mature thoughts. Scriabin saw it as steely, with a metallic lustre, but Rimsky-Korsakov did not commit himself. Mattheson described the key as magnificent but also delicate.

18th century

Bach: Brandenburg Concerto No 6, BWV 1051 (1723).
Vivaldi: Violin Concerto, Op 8/10, 'Hunt' (*c* 1725).
Mozart: Bassoon Concerto, K 191 (1774); String Quartet, K 458, 'Hunt' (1784); Piano Concerto, K 595 (1791).
Haydn: Symphony No 98 (1792); Symphony No 102 (1794/95).
Beethoven: Piano Concerto No 2, Op 19 (1794/95).
Haydn: 'Heilig' Mass (1796); 'Theresia' Mass (1799).

19th century

Haydn: 'Creation' Mass (1801); 'Harmonie' Mass (1802); String Quartet, Op 103 (unfinished) (1803).
Beethoven: Symphony No 4, Op 60 (1805).
Schubert: Symphony No 5, D 485 (1816).
Beethoven: Piano Sonata, Op 106, 'Hammerklavier' (1818); String Quartet, Op 130 (1825).
Schubert: Piano Trio, D 898 (1827).
Schumann: Symphony No 1, 'Spring' (1841).
Brahms: Piano Concerto No 2, Op 83 (1881).

B flat minor

Five flats: b, e, a, d, g. Relative major: D flat.
An emotion-filled and sometimes angry key.

19th century

Chopin: Piano Sonata No 2 (1839).
Tchaikovsky: Piano Concerto No 1, Op 23 (1875).

20th century

Walton: Symphony No 1 (1935). Shostakovitch: Symphony No 13, 'Babi Yar' (1962).

B major

Five sharps: f, c, g, d, a. Relative minor: G sharp minor.
Rimsky-Korsakov described this rare-used key as sombre and dark blue, shot with steel, and Scriabin regarded it as bluish white. Very few major works have been centred in B, the large number of sharps in the signature presenting intonation difficulties. Mattheson heard the key as aggressive, hard, ill-mannered, and desperate.

18th century

Haydn: Symphony No 46 (1772).

19th century

Brahms: Piano Trio No 1, Op 8 (1854).

B minor

Two sharps: f, c. Relative major: D.
Tchaikovsky's 'black despair' key, and used also for music of religious strength and forceful tragic drama. Bach's use of it in the B minor Mass enabled him to brighten to the key's relative major for the introduction of trumpets and drums. On one occasion Beethoven described the key as 'black'; Mattheson, as moody, glum, and bizarre.

18th century

Bach: Suite No 2 for flute and strings, BWV 1067; High Mass, BWV 232 (1733).
Vivaldi: Symphony, P 21, 'Al Santo Sepolcro'.

19th century

Schubert: Symphony No 8, D 759, 'Unfinished' (1822).
Chopin: Piano Sonata No 3, Op 58 (1844).
Liszt: Piano Sonata (1853).
Borodin: Symphony No 2 (1876).
Brahms: Clarinet Quintet, Op 115 (1891).
Tchaikovsky: Symphony No 6, Op 74, 'Pathètique' (1893).
Dvořák: Cello Concerto (1895).

20th century

Shostakovitch: Symphony No 6, Op 54 (1939).

ORCHESTRAL MUSIC

The orchestra evolved in the theatre in the role of accompanist to stage action, but as it developed it gradually took on a separate identity until it began to be listened to for its own sake. Once this step had been taken it became necessary for composers to write independent music for orchestra. The various types of composition which have appeared since that time are discussed here.

Symphony

Probably the most 'important' form for a modern composer to approach, since a new symphony is expected to contain the greatest and most profound thoughts of the artist, presented skilfully and, so to speak, in evening dress.

The word 'symphony' has been used during the last 300 years for four different musical concepts:

1. A work for full orchestra usually in more than one movement, in which one or more of the movements is based on sonata form.
2. An orchestral work, in either one or three movements (occasionally more), used as an introduction to an opera. In this meaning, the words 'overture' and 'symphony' become identical.
3. A work for orchestra or small instrumental group which shows a marked tendency on the part of the composer towards what later came to be known as 'symphonic thought', but which was written before the development of sonata form (such works are often little more than extended fanfares). These early symphonies might be termed 'proto-symphonies'.
4. An instrumental introduction to a song or aria; sometimes also an instrumental interlude within an aria.

Today the word 'symphony' has come to mean almost exclusively the type of work described under 1, above. A short description of 'sonata form', therefore, becomes necessary so that the principles and endeavours behind a composer's thought processes when producing such a major work may be appreciated. In its simplest layout, a movement in sonata form will fall into four sections:

(a) **Exposition:** a presentation of a theme (A), a linking passage raising the basic key five full steps to the 'dominant key', wherein a second theme is presented (B). Another short linking passage called 'codetta' = 'little coda'.
(b) **Development:** a discussion, sometimes blending the two themes (A) and (B) and sometimes exploiting their contrasts.
(c) **Recapitulation:** a re-presentation of (A) and (B), but both in the main (tonic) key, sometimes modified thematically and dramatically in the light of what has taken place in the Development.
(d) **Coda:** an 'ending' or 'tail-piece' to tie loose ends and to round off the movement.

The importance of sonata form cannot be overstressed, either in the discussion of how composers treat it, or in the necessity of the listener grasping its principles in order to appreciate what a composer is trying to do in his sonata-form movements. Therefore, at the risk of seeming to dwell unnecessarily on this basic and elementary subject, we shall discuss further the possibilities behind sonata form in the hope that the listener, coming fresh to a work using this form as its main foundation, will understand and enjoy the composer's thoughts the more completely.

But first a word of warning. Having read a programme note in which a movement is described as being in sonata form, the listener should not expect the first sound he hears to be the start of (A). It is true that it *might* be so, but it is more likely that the movement will commence with a slow introduction, or at least will have a few bars to prepare the way, analogous to an after-dinner speaker rising to his feet, clearing his throat, and saying: 'Well now, unaccustomed as I am . . .'. Let us take a few moments to examine the first movement openings of Beethoven's symphonies in this light.

Symphony No 1: a slow introduction which establishes the main key with apparent difficulty.
Symphony No 2: a long slow introduction rich in thematic fragments.
Symphony No 3: two sharp chords, then immediately into the first theme (A) on cellos.
Symphony No 4: long slow introduction in mysterious mood to heighten the bright optimism of the first theme (A) of the Allegro vivace. Note the method by which the introduction is linked to the first theme: a hard crescendo and a rushing upward figure repeated eight times, giving the effect of an accelerando. The Allegro vivace actually starts at the top of the second upward rush, but the first theme does not appear until the last of these preparatory flourishes. It is as if the first theme has been 'rescued' from the clouds of the introduction, an idea greatly extended at the start of the recapitulation.
Symphony No 5: no introduction whatever. The first theme (A) is flung at the audience immediately.
Symphony No 6: the first note to be heard is the start of a drone-like support on violas and cellos; the first theme (A) starts immediately on a weak beat in the first bar.
Symphony No 7: an enormous slow introduction of more than 60 bars. The lead into the Vivace again features a quasi accelerando on hopping woodwind.
Symphony No 8: no introduction. Theme (A) starts immediately.
Symphony No 9: an extremely quiet throb or murmur of strings and horns from which crystallises the titanic first theme (A).

With these many possible ways of launching a symphony, Beethoven gave to future composers ideas which have been copied, modified, extended–and even ignored in favour of completely new concepts.

With the introduction out of the way, the **Exposition** may start in earnest. The basic plan of two contrasting themes may be modified in countless ways: one theme only may appear, perhaps in two guises, in which case the movement might be described as 'monothematic'. More likely in 19th- and 20th-century symphonies, however, is a profusion of themes or 'ideas' or 'motifs' which ideally should contrast each with the other. Often it is difficult on first hearing to sort out how many themes there are and where they begin and end.

In the **Development** these themes are discussed. It is up to the composer to decide whether both, or all, themes will appear for treatment, or whether he will extract from one of the themes as much mileage as possible. Alternatively, of course, he may decide to introduce an altogether new theme, either on its own or in conjunction with previously heard material. Beethoven, in the 'Eroica' Symphony (No 3), brings his development section to a huge climax, and then immediately introduces a completely new theme in a completely new key, thus leading to another area of development. Whichever subjects the composer chooses for his development section, this is usually the part of the movement in which most of the drama takes place, the opportunities for free-ranging thought being virtually limitless.

Recapitulation. After the drama of the **Development,** the themes heard in the exposition are played again, but their characters are often transformed in the light of what has happened to them in the **Development.** In some works, the **Recapitulation** will be 'regular', ie the themes will appear much as they did before, with the important exception that the second theme (B) is now in the main key of the piece. In other works the material of the **Exposition** may be so altered that it becomes only vaguely recognisable. The original order of the themes may be reversed; some of the material may be omitted entirely; new material may be added. Once again, the composer has the entire say as to what happens in the **Recapitulation** without a violation of the principles of sonata form taking place.

Coda. This is the tail-piece which brings the movement to an end. In earlier symphonies it was sometimes little more than a pair of 'that's that' chords (and occasionally not even that), but as the symphony as a form developed the **Coda** gained importance until, again in the case of Beethoven, it assumed the proportions of a 'second development'. The most extreme example is that of the finale of Beethoven's Symphony No 8 in F, the proportions of which are:

Exposition: theme (A) starting at bar 1; theme (B) starting at bar 48; theme (C) starting at bar 68.
Development: starting at bar 91.
Recapitulation: starting at bar 151 (A), with (B) at 224, and (C) at 243.
Coda: starting at bar 267 and lasting until bar 502 (with a new theme introduced at bar 286).

Therefore, the formally complete section of the movement lasts 266 bars, while the **Coda** takes 235 bars, almost as long again.

The above description of usual sonata form may be condensed to a diagram (1 below), with which we may compare a diagram of the finale of Beethoven's Eighth Symphony (2 below) to illustrate how far a composer may deviate from the plan while still producing a formally viable piece of music.

No 1

SLOW INTRODUCTION	EXPOSITION (A) (B)	DEVELOPMENT	RECAPITULATION (A) (B)	CODA

No 2

bar 1	bar 91	bar 151	bar 267 – bar 502
EXPOSITION (A) (B) (C)	DEVELOPMENT	RECAPITULATION (A) (B) (C)	CODA (incorporating D)

Sonata form is usually used for the first movement of a symphony; it may be used also for the slow movement and the finale, and it may even influence the construction of the Minuet or Scherzo which shares with the slow movement the central part of a standard symphony. However, a number of other forms are also commonly found in the symphony such as 'variation' and 'rondo' or derivations of them, and the Minuet or Scherzo movement is almost invariably in A–B–A form; ie the main movement leading into a contrasting central section (called by the old-fashioned term 'trio' since at this point the convention was to reduce the music to three voices or parts) and then a repeat of the main part. Beethoven instituted a modification of this plan: A–B–A–B–A, in which the trio appears twice, and a coda hinting at B closes the movement, and some composers have followed this idea with or without modifications.

The above outline of symphonic form, lengthy though it is, does not exhaust the possibilities open to composers, some of whom have created their own forms with greater or lesser success. Sonata form, which was developed gradually by a multitude of composers working together or separately, each one learning from his predecessors and including ideas which worked while rejecting others which did not, is not easily bettered by one composer working independently. There have been successful new forms created during the present century however, by such independently minded composers as Sibelius, Mahler, and Nielsen. Their handling of symphonic form requires patience and deep study on the part of the listener to reveal the composer's inner intentions.

Once the listener has mastered the basic outline of sonata form, he will find that many of the types of music he is likely to hear will conform in greater or lesser degree to its principles: the principles, that is, of contrast developing into conflict and thence into final resolution. Composers have employed sonata form for their overtures, sonatas (of course), string quartets, piano trios, and virtually every other field of music, including even opera and Mass. Almost it would be true to say that an understanding of sonata form leads to the understanding of most music which is written in what we have come to know as the standard tonal concept.

The first symphony, by which, of course, we mean a symphony in the third sense (see above) was written by Giuseppe Torelli (1658–1709), an Italian composer who worked in Bologna and was required to produce music for the festivals held in the San Petronio Cathedral in that city. By extending his fanfares and interspersing solos and string-band 'padding' between them, Torelli, certainly without realising it, was moving towards the kind of concerted instrumental work with contrasting timbres and thematic fragments which was later to play such an important part in symphonic evolution. Unfortunately, it is not possible precisely to say which of Torelli's works was composed first since, at the time, they were not considered historically important enough to date, or even to catalogue. Indeed, it is doubtful whether the composer would have expected his music to be remembered for longer than a week or so, by which time he would have produced more pieces to satisfy the demand for new ceremonial music. It was amid this atmosphere of rapid production, and the necessity for providing new music to be played by constantly altering groups of instrumentalists, that Torelli wrote many differently scored works within the same basic framework of the three-movement proto-symphony in fast-slow-fast design. In addition, the perennial problem of terminology enters into this discussion: there is no basic difference between a Torelli sonata for trumpet(s) and strings and a sinfonia or a concerto for the same forces, although, when the composer took advantage of the opposing galleries in the San Petronio Cathedral to write for two orchestras, one in each, answering and echoing phrases across the high-vaulted body of the building, he appears to have adhered to the descriptions 'sinfonia' and 'concerto' only, reserving 'sonata' for more modest works.

Before leaving the subject of the earliest symphony, let us examine one of Torelli's works, his Symphony in C, No 33 in Giegling's Catalogue. It is scored for an orchestra which, at the end of the 17th century, must have seemed excessively noisy, but which would have made a thrilling impression in the great cathedral hall:

Soloists	*Orchestra*
4 trumpets	2 oboes
2 oboes	bassoon
2 violins	violins 1 and 2
1 bassoon	violas
1 cello	cellos 1 and 2
	double basses 1 and 2
	timpani
	basso-continuo (comprising 2 organs and trombone)

Its three movements are in the form later used by Vivaldi for the majority of his concertos: first and third movements in ritornello-rondo form (ie a main idea repeated over and over again with modifications, separated by contrasting material), between which comes a slow contrasting section.

Torelli's first movement ritornello is a stunning rhythmic fanfare employing the full force of four trumpets and timpani. This is continued over violin figuration which is then extended alone. With the return of the fanfare, the trumpets imitate the violins' virtuoso passage-work, and then hand it over to the lower strings and the bassoon. More fanfares lead to a section for solo oboes, but these are brushed aside by yet more fanfares which close what in a later symphony we would call the 'exposition'. A new and quieter idea appears in which the figurations of the violins are extended (or developed), giving contrast to a trumpet-dominated movement, but once again the trumpets enter with their original idea (re-capitulation), and a number of solo oboe and solo violin passages lead to a final fanfare, as heard at the very beginning, bringing the movement to a half-close.

The Adagio is merely a short linking passage for full string band without brass or wind. The gigue-like finale is less martial than the first movement, and in the middle of the movement the trumpets lead a new and more melodic idea which is taken up by the other instruments. Oboes, bassoon, cello, and violins all have their solo opportunities, before Torelli springs upon us perhaps his greatest surpise: a quiet ending.

This feast of jubilant trumpeting and drumming, even if it cannot be proved to occur in the *very* first symphony, at least shows that Torelli was a worthy composer to instigate one of the most influential and important musical forms of the last 300 years, a form in which the composer is expected to reveal his deepest thoughts.

A recording of this remarkable work was made by the Zagreb Soloists' Ensemble conducted by Antonio Janigro, although unfortunately, excellent though the performance is, the conductor has chosen to present the work with reduced forces. Did he feel, perhaps, that the world was not yet ready for the onslaught of sound which Torelli unleashed in one of the first symphonies ever written?

So-called 'sinfonias' by Alessandro Stradella (1642–82), written for string band for concert use at unspecified dates may also be considered to be among the earliest to contain the first vestiges of symphonic feeling.

The earliest four-movement symphony was long thought to have been by the Austrian composer Georg Matthias Monn (1717–50), whose Symphony in D, dated 24 May 1740, has the following movement order: 1. Allegro; 2. Aria: Andante un poco; 3. Menuetto; 4. Allegro. This symphony is scored for two flutes, two horns, bassoon, and strings, and is No 1 in Wilhelm Fischer's Thematic Catalogue.

However, a date of 1724 is given for a 'sinfonia' for two violins, cello, and violone by the Venetian composer Alberto Gallo, whose dates are unknown. His symphony is laid out on the following plan: 1. Allegro; 2. Menuet (:) Allegro; 3. Adagio; 4. Presto.

An even earlier possible contender was broadcast by the BBC in about 1952. It was announced as a Symphony in D minor by Gioseffo Placuzzi, for lute, two violins, and harpsichord, the lute taking a semi-solo part. Its movements were: 1. fast; 2. slow and aria-like; 3. of moderate speed, in 3/4 time; 4. fast. The announcer stated that 'this is probably the earliest work in this form to be called a symphony', and he gave its date as 1692.

The most prolific symphonist was Johann Melchior Molter (*c* 1695–1765) who worked as Kapellmeister in Karlsruhe from 1722 to 1733, and then again from 1743 until his death. The total usually given is 169 symphonies, but the thematic catalogue of his works in the Karlsruhe Landesbibliothek includes four duplicates, thus reducing this total to 165. Furthermore, some of these works are in fragmentary form, others are not true symphonies (there is a suite, a cello concerto, a wind quartet, and other chamber works), but even so Molter has a clear lead over his nearest rivals in symphonic proliferation: Johann Gottlieb Graun (1703–71) with 117; Johann Christoph Graupner (1683–1760) with 113; and Karl Ditters von Dittersdorf (1739–99) with 107, of which several are lost, and Franz Joseph Haydn with 109.

The composer of the greatest number of extant symphonies in the 20th century was Havergal Brian, who died in 1972 aged 96. He was the author of 32 symphonies plus a vast amount of other music. His case is, in fact, one of the strangest in music, since, although one may believe it is possible to churn out symphonies (regardless of quality) at regular intervals throughout a life of exceptional length, this simply does not correspond to the fact of Havergal Brian's creative existence.

He was born in 1876 in Dresden, Staffordshire, and for much of his life seemed to treat music seriously but with little hope of fame. It was not until the last decade and a half of his life that his creative powers underwent a phenomenal acceleration, and no less than 22 of his total of 32 symphonies were written after the age of 80. Again, it might be assumed that these products of extreme old age are no more than the ramblings of a senile mind, yet the reverse is true. His style, during the latter half of his life always somewhat granitic and unyielding, actually tightened in the latest works. They show powerful, uncompromising musical language which revealed a clear-thinking, original mind which was apparently still developing and hardening at the time of his death.

Much of his music is still unknown but when this astonishing literature of 32 symphonies has been truly opened up we may yet find that the depth of his musical activity matched the expanse.

Two other modern composers should be mentioned as writers of numerous symphonies:

Nikolai Yakovlevich Miaskovsky (1881–1950), who composed 27 symphonies between 1908 and his death. His art was ultra-traditional, owing a great deal to the main-stream of 19th-century Russian music which was among the few things not altered in public esteem by the Revolution. The first work to come to notice was the Piano Sonata in F sharp minor in 1908 which was considered a fine example of the way in which traditional concepts might be modernised, but it was evidently too radical for the emerging Bolshevik tastes of the early 1920s, and Miaskovsky prudently moderated his language so that the greater part of his music, even that written towards the end of his life, is little more than excellently-written but out-of-date romanticism.

Alan Hovhaness (b 1911), an American composer of Scottish/Armenian descent (see Section III: the most self-critical composer). He is an enormously prolific composer who has written 28 symphonies, many of which are based on Armenian and other Eastern subjects. His First Symphony (ie that now known as Symphony No 1, 'Exile'), was first performed in Birmingham in 1938 under the baton of Leslie Heward; a version revised by the composer is published by Peters. However, owing to his change of creative direction in the 1930s, Hovhaness felt compelled to renounce his earlier Sibelius-influenced music, and at the time he destroyed seven of his symphonies. If that total is added to the number of still-existing symphonies, we find that Hovhaness has surpassed Havergal Brian in symphonic proliferation.

The first symphony to include parts for the human voice was Beethoven's Symphony No 9 in D minor, Op 125, Choral (1823). After three purely orchestral movements and an instrumental introduction to the fourth, this finale introduces a baritone solo (declaiming words by Beethoven) introducing an extended setting for soprano, contralto, tenor, and baritone with mixed chorus of Schiller's *Ode to Joy*.

The first Russian symphony is usually considered to be Rimsky-Korsakov's No 1 of 1865, written while the 21-year-old composer was serving as an officer in the Russian Navy. There is, however, an anonymous *Symphony on Ukranian Themes* which dates from about 1800, but strictly the earliest Russian symphonies were written by Maxim Sosonowitsch Berezovsky (1745–77) who was sent to Bologna by Catherine the Great to study with Padré

Martini in 1765. As yet, Berezovsky's, and possibly many other composers', symphonies lie unheard in Russian archives because that country is notably laggardly in excavating 18th-century musical treasures when compared with the outstanding work being done in Czechoslovakia, Hungary, and Poland.

The first Negro to write a symphony was William Grant Still (b 1895), whose *Afro-American Symphony* was composed in 1931.

The first American woman composer to write a symphony was Mrs Amy Marcy Beach (1867–1944), whose *Gaelic Symphony* was written in 1895.

Unusual Symphonies

Robert J Farnon (b 1917), the Canadian composer known primarily for his excellent light music pieces, the most famous of which is *Portrait of a Flirt,* wrote his first Symphony in 1941 in the unusual key of D flat major.

Georg Glantz (active during the years 1763–75), a Kapellmeister in Pressburg, Germany, wrote a symphony in 1774 for Turkish instruments alone, without strings. The scoring was for flutes, oboes, clarinets, trumpets, horns, bassoons, cymbals, triangle, and bass drum.

Charles Koechlin (1867–1950) was a French composer of Alsatian descent. He wrote a symphony entitled *Seven,* each of the four movements of which are based on the character of a film-star. Thus treated are the actresses Greta Garbo and Marlene Dietrich, the tragedian Emil Jannings, and the comedian Charlie Chaplin.

Antonín Reicha (1770–1836), the Czech composer who made his home in Paris, wrote a four-movement symphony in D, the full title of which is *Musique pour célébrer des grandes hommes qui se sont illustres du service de la nation française*. This work was designed to be performed in the open air, the audience to be placed at a position 50 paces from the orchestras, behind which, at a distance of a further 100 paces, were the drums. Two orchestras were to take part, these being separated by at least 30 paces, and also included in the scoring were parts for cannon and infantry march past. Among Reicha's pupils were Berlioz, Franck, Gounod, and Liszt.

Overture

There are four distinct types of overture:

1. The single-movement, symphonic, sonata-form piece in which the development section is either abbreviated or omitted altogether. Mozart's *Marriage of Figaro* Overture is a good example; others will be found in the overtures of Beethoven, Mendelssohn, Weber and Wagner.
2. As above, followed by a slow movement and a quick finale. The 18th century abounds with examples by Vivaldi, Galuppi, D and G Scarlatti, F J Haydn, and virtually every other operatic composer, Mozart provides perfect examples of this **Italian Overture** form in his so-called 'Symphonies' Nos 23 and 24 (K 181) and 182). In many cases the finale is constructed from greatly shortened material from the first movement. This form is also known as the 'Italian Overture', and Mozart's Symphony No 32 in G, K 319 (actually titled *Overture in the Italian Style)* illustrates the type precisely. A mongrel type is found in the same composer's *Magic Flute* Overture, in which a slow introduction leads to a rapid main movement. In central position is the 'slow movement'–merely three groups of developing chords–and this is followed by a development of the rapid material and a full recapitulation. The whole is capped by a short coda.
3. The so-called **French Ouverture** (note the spelling), consisting of a declamatory slow introduction, often in strongly dotted rhythm, followed by a fast movement, usually of fugal character. In some cases several French-style dances follow. Telemann wrote very many of this type of overture, as did Fasch and Hartwig and many other Germans, in whose country the French style in all forms of art was in vogue for much of the first half of the 18th century. But the originator of the style was Lully, the French composer of Italian birth who was imitated by countless French followers.
4. The **Concert Overture.** In form it may be similar to 1, often with a slow introduction, but it is not associated with a stage work and is often descriptive in character. Mendelssohn's *Fingal's Cave* Overture is the archetypal example; the two overtures of Brahms also fall into this category.

Overture types 1, 2, and 3 are usually used as

Franz Liszt, a prominent composer of symphonic poems (Popperfoto)

introductions to operas or other stage works, although type 3 merges imperceptibly with the multi-movement ouverture-suite for concert use, of which the best-known examples are the four by J S Bach. See Suite, below.

The first overture in which the mood of the music was meant to prepare the audience for the drama to follow in the opera was that written by Gluck for *Alceste* in 1767. It is an overture of type 1, but it is unusual in maintaining a slow tempo throughout. The composer explained: 'I feel that the overture should acquaint the audience with the mood of the opera.'

The first overture designed to be played after the rise of the curtain on the First Act of the opera is Grétry's *Le Jugement de Midas* of 1778. It is a hybrid overture which refuses to fall into any of the above categories. Its descriptive programme dictates its form: a slow introduction depicting dawn, a gentle Andantino in which a shepherd's pipe is heard, storm, and a return to the shepherd music.

The first overture of type 2 to be written by an Englishman was that to the opera *Peleus and Thetis* (*c* 1738) by William Boyce.

Symphonic Poem and Tone Poem

This is a large-scale orchestral work of descriptive character, the limits of which shade off into three other forms: *(a)* the concerto (Richard Strauss's *Don Quixote* is a symphonic poem for cello solo and orchestra, while Berlioz's *Harold in Italy* is a symphony for viola solo and orchestra of a strongly descriptive nature); *(b)* the symphony (Berlioz's *Symphonie Fantastique* is a descriptive symphony, and Debussy's *La Mer* is a tone poem in a form and layout close to the symphony); and *(c)* the overture (Beethoven's *Egmont* and *Coriolan* overtures, and Dvořák's *Hussites* Overture are concert overtures with symphonic poem intentions). The symphonic poem is a direct descendant of the mood-setting overtures of Gluck, Cherubini, Méhul, Weber, and Mendelssohn.

Suite, Divertimento, Serenade, etc.

Of these, the **suite** is the oldest form, being a string of dance movements which gradually evolved into a cogent and contrasting order, often including bourrée, courante, sarabande, menuet, gigue, etc, but with endless variations in the sequence. J S Bach wrote four magnificent orchestral suites, still called **Ouvertüren** in Germany. (A fifth Suite, in G minor, for strings and continuo, has not been proved to be a work of this composer; it is nevertheless an excellent piece in Late Baroque/Early Classical style).

Later in the 18th century, out of the suite and the lighter type of symphony, grew the **divertimento** and **serenade** (also cassation, *Finalmusiken*, etc), bright and entertaining pieces of many movements, liberally sprinkled with minuets (the one dance form which survived from the old suite) and usually ending with an extended rondo. The biggest compositions in this form were the serenades, and these often contained concerto-like elements in one or more movements. Taking Mozart again as an example, his output contains many such works, of which the Serenade in D, K 203, is an eight-movement work, buried in the midst of which is a three-movement violin concerto. The Divertimento in D, K 251, has six movements in which the solo oboe is given a part of concertante proportions.

Concerto

The word covers a multitude of forms which may be dealt with in four groups:

1. The **vocal concerto** of the 17th century, wherein the term is used in its purest meaning of a group of voices joining together in concerted effort.
2. In the early 18th century, Italian composers used the word for a string sonata when no one instrument was given soloistic importance. These works are in the direct line of musical evolution to the concert symphony.
3. A work in several (usually three or four) movements in which one instrument is given the position of highest prominence. In the 18th century the soloist was expected to contribute as much to the musical argument of the piece as to his or her own technical reputation, but as the century progressed the display aspect of the concerto became more and more important. This trend continued through the early 19th century, the orchestra taking a decreasingly important role, but the second half of the century saw the orchestra becoming a more active participant in the discussion. The present century has gone even further in this direction, some concertos being more in the nature of a duel between soloist and orchestra.
4. An early form of concerto, the **concerto grosso** = 'great concerto' is a work in which, at first, a string trio of two violins and cello, and later any number or description of instruments, were supported by a string band. The form was obsolete by the middle of the 18th century but was reborn a few years later in the **sinfonia concertante.** This was a two- or three-movement work in which a group of instruments was displayed against an orchestra. Gradually the rather meaningless word 'sinfonia' was dropped from the generic title, and the surviving component is still used to describe showy works for several instruments with orchestra, although the description 'concerto for orchestra' is also used.

Examples of the above groups were written by:

1. Adriano Banchieri; Andrea Gabrieli; Giovanni Gabrieli.
2. Torelli; Vivaldi; Albinoni; Manfredini.
3. Torelli; Vivaldi; Locatelli; Tartini; Mozart; Beethoven; Mendelssohn; Chopin; Brahms; Tchaikovsky; Dvořák; Grieg; Rakhmaninoff; Sibelius; Walton, etc.
4. Concerto grosso: Stradella; Corelli; Vivaldi; Albinoni; Bonporti; Leo; Avison; Stanley, etc. (Sinfonia) Concertante: Viotti; Pleyel; J C Bach; Sarti; Mozart; Haydn; Cambini; and in the present century: Bartók; Blacher; Martinu; Bloch; Hanuš; Ridout; Holmboe (eight of them); Frank Martin; Barraud; Lutoslawsky, etc.

'Concerto' is not the only word used by composers to indicate a work for soloist(s) and orchestra. In the 18th century **Concertone** was occasionally employed, meaning a large concerto; Mozart's K 190 in C, basically for two violins with prominent parts also for cello and oboe, is the best-known example. Giuseppe Sarti also wrote a Concertone in E flat, in which the soloists are two clarinets, two horns, two violins, viola, and cello, supported by a string orchestra.

Konzertstücke = 'concert studies', have been written by Weber (for clarinet, and for horn), Busoni, and others; concert rondos (in effect or in fact these are isolated concerto movements) by Mozart; Beethoven, etc, and Rodrigo wrote a concert serenade for harp and orchestra. Khachaturian has written a concert rhapsody for cello and orchestra.

Also to be found are Elegie, Poeme, Romance (or Romanza), Lyric Movement, Fantasie, Theme and Variations (see also the purely orchestral species, below), Ballade, etc, and of course the Symphonic Variations by Franck, Bax, and Bentzon.

Concertos for Unusual Instruments

By far the most usual instruments chosen for spotlighting in the concerto form are the piano, the violin, and the cello (see below for the first of each), but display works for other instruments are by no means uncommon. The reader is referred to the details given in Section II under specific instruments, to which may be added the following:

Accordion: Jindrich Feld (1975).

Flute with female chorus: John Fernstrøm (Op 52).

Flute and orchestra: *Concerto Lugubre* (1801) by Luigi Gianella.

Basset clarinet: Concerto in A, K 622 (1791) by Mozart–the well-known Clarinet Concerto in its original form.

Basset-horn: Concerto in F by Alessendro Rolla.

Trumpet: Alexander Arutyunyan (1950).
Raymond Hanson, Australian composer: Concerto in B flat (1952).
William Lovelock, Australian composer: Concerto in C.
Alexandra Nikolayevna Pakhmutova, Russian composer: Concerto in B flat minor (1955).

Post-horn and hunting-horn: Johann Beer: Concerto in B flat.

In the 18th century the orchestral and solo horn was still referred to as a 'hunting-horn' (or 'cor de chasse' etc); therefore, solo concertos by Haydn, Mozart, Rosetti, etc, were in fact concertos for hunting-horn.

Trombone: Johann Georg Albrechtsberger: Concerto in B flat (1769).

Viola: Ivan Evstafeivich Handoshkin: Concerto in C (1801).

Double bass and saxophone: *Ka,* by H J Hespos.

Double Bass: F J Haydn: Concerto in D (lost).
Dittersdorf: two concertos in E flat, Kr 171 and 172.
Dragonetti: Concerto in A.
Kussevitzky: Concerto (1905).
Franz Herf: Concerto.
Ivan Wiener: Fantasia Concerto.

Harp: Krumpholz: Concertos, Op 7.
Boïeldieu: Concerto in C.
Reinecke: Concerto in E minor, Op 182.
Glière: Concerto, Op 74 (1938).
Pierne: Concertstück, Op 39 (1901).

Guitar: By far the most popular is the 'Aranjuez' Concerto (1939) by the blind Spanish composer Rodrigo. Other concertos have been written, often for a specific guitar virtuoso, by Malcolm Arnold, Maurice Ohana, Maria Castelnuovo Tedesco, Richard Rodney Bennett, Salvador Bacarisse, and Stephen Dodgson, among others.

Mandolin: Vivaldi: one for mandolin (P 134) and another for two mandolins (P 133).
Johann (Giovanni?) Hoffmann: Concerto in D.

Sitar: Ravi Shankar: Concerto for sitar and orchestra (1968).

String groups: Following on from the early-18th-century concerto grosso for a group of (usually) three string soloists and string orchestra, **the ultimate in massed string soloists** comes with a work entitled *Constellations,* Op 22 (1958) for twelve string groups, composed by Per Nørgård, the modern Danish composer.

Harmonica: Arthur Benjamin: Concerto for mouth-organ (1955).
Malcolm Arnold: Concerto, Op 46 (1954).
Darius Milhaud: Suite for harmonica and orchestra (1943).

Organ, harp, and timpani: Jan Hanuš: Sinfonia Concertante, Op 31 (1954).

Percussion: Darius Milhaud: Concerto for percussion and small orchestra (1930).
Leonard Salzedo: Percussion Concerto.

Many other works featuring percussion alone or with other instruments have been written by, for instance, Carlos Chavez, George Anthiel, Roland LoPresti, Alan Hovhaness, David Bedford, Robert Moran, and Edwin Roxburgh.

Seven wind instruments, timpani, percussion, and strings: A concerto for this combination was written in 1949 by the Swiss composer Frank Martin.

Harp, harpsichord, piano, and double string orchestra: Frank Martin: *Petite Symphonie Concertante* (1945).

Voice: Glière: Concerto for coloratura voice (soprano), Op 82 (1943).
Zsolt Durko: *Dartmouth Concerto* for mezzo and orchestra. This work is a setting of a Masefield poem about the death march of the lemmings.
Bliss: Concerto for piano, tenor, strings, and percussion (1921).
Busoni: Concerto for piano, chorus, and orchestra.
See also Fernstrøm under Flute, above.

Benjamin Frankel's *Concerto for Youth, Audience, and Orchestra* was written in 1968 in response to a commission from the town of Unna in north Germany. For a successful performance, the audience should bring in any type of musical instrument which they happen to possess, failing which they should clap, whistle, stamp, etc.

The concerto for the most unusual instrument is probably that (or, rather, *those*, since there are several) written by J G Albrechtsberger to include the trombula. The works involved are, according to the catalogue of Lászlo Somfai:

No 7: Concertino in D for trombula, mandora, and strings (1769).
No 8: Concerto in F, à 5, for mandora, crembalum, and strings (1770).
No 9: Concertino in E flat, à 5, for trombula, harpsichord, and strings (1771).
No 10: Concerto in E for crembalum, mandora, and strings (1771).

Of the three unfamiliar instruments named in this list, 'Mandora' may be disposed of immediately: it is simply a species of lute as noted in the list in Section II. According to Somfai's catalogue, in a footnote on p 184, 'crembalum' is another name for 'trombula': 'Trombula, oder Crembalum: Maultrommel (guimbarde).' The only problem, then, is to identify the trombula.

The Concertino in E flat (No 9 in the list above) was identified by Albrechtsberger as 'Concertino in Eb. a cinque Stromenti (for) Tromb, Cemb Del Sig: G: A:', and the score gives the parts as for 'violins I and II, Bass, Tromb, and Cembalo'. The two references to 'Tromb' have led musicologists to believe that the solo instrument should be a trumpet ('tromba'), but examination reveals the solo part to be chromatic. Hitherto, music history has taught that the 18th-century trumpet, like the horn of the same period, was a non-chromatic instrument (ie the available notes were restricted to the harmonic series of the basic tone of the instrument), and that chromaticism did not become possible on the trumpet until the invention of the keyed trumpet by the Viennese trumpeter Anton Weidinger about 1796. It was for Weidinger's 'keyed trumpet', incidentally, that Joseph Haydn wrote his Trumpet Concerto in E flat, the first to be written for the keyed trumpet (1796), and the most famous of all trumpet concertos. To find a concertino in the same key dating from a quarter of a century earlier, and including a chromatic part for what was apparently a trumpet, makes nonsense of this particular piece of musical history, and has led some writers, among them the American musicologist Mary Rasmussen, to put forward the theory that an unidentified inventor known to Albrechtsberger, or perhaps that composer himself, developed a chromatic trumpet, later imparting the intelligence of its existence to Haydn (who knew Albrechtsberger in Vienna in the 1790s). Haydn then is thought to have brought this information to Weidinger, who developed the idea into the keyed trumpet for which Haydn wrote.

However, a further doubt is thrown on the credibility of the trumpet as the soloist in this particular work (Somfai No 9) by the composer's demand for only *five* instruments (ie the violin parts were not meant to be multiplied). The balance between two violins, a double bass, a keyboard instrument, and a trumpet, bearing in mind that the average volume of sound from one trumpet is approximately equal to the average volume from fourteen unison violins, would be ludicrously weighted in favour of the brass instrument, and this has been proved by recordings of the work in which a trumpet does in fact take the solo part.

Clearly, the indication 'tromb' cannot mean trumpet. What, then, does it mean?

One possible, and perhaps the only possible, alternative is 'trombula'. Two other suggestions have been the slide-trumpet (like a small trombone), and the trombone itself, but both these instruments would lead us again into balancing problems. Furthermore, for his Trombone Concerto (Somfai No 6), Albrechtsberger took the trouble to spell out the word in its entirety on the title-page: 'trombone'.

The 'trombula' remains to be examined. The word is a diminutive of tromba, which in turn shows relationships with Scot: *trump* and *tromp*, the Fr: *trombe de béarn* and *trombe de laquais* = 'servant's trumpet', and the Jew's trump of 16th-century England. The Ger: *Maultrommel* (literally 'mouth-drum') is possibly a distortion of an imported word in this family, although the 'drum' component is almost equally descriptive. All these terms point straight to one instrument: the Jew's harp.

If we accept that Albrechtsberger's four works were in fact written for the Jew's harp, two questions remain to be examined. First, why did the composer use two distinct terms ('trombula'; 'crembalum') for the same instrument? Secondly, the Jew's harp is a harmonic (ie non-chromatic) instrument just as much as is the mid-18th-century trumpet, which would appear to put us back to the beginning again.

In answer to the first question, we may assume that two different types of instrument were known to Albrechtsberger, although both of the Jew's harp family. Amplification of this supposition will be found in the possible solution to the second puzzle.

It was by no means unknown for travelling Jew's harp virtuosi to tour Europe in the 18th century, and for them to specialise in playing more than one of these instruments simultaneously. For a player to accommodate two instruments in his mouth was common; more than that would have required a device in which several Jew's harps were attached to a framework of wood. With a series of instruments each tuned to a different pitch, chromatic melodies would have been playable by proficient virtuosi. It is to be noted that such frames existed until well into the 19th century, some having provision for up to sixteen Jew's harps. Is it out of the question that a trombula virtuoso visited Vienna and that his playing impelled Albrechtsberger to compose some works for him; and that the said virtuoso had with him also a differently constructed frame of instruments which he called by the name of 'crembalum'?

Antonio Vivaldi, engraving from 1725

The composer of the most concertos is Antonio Vivaldi, who produced some 488 known examples (as listed by Pincherle, Kolneder, Fanna, Ryom, *et al*). However, this total may be regarded with suspicion for various reasons, some factors reducing, others expanding, the number.

Due to the lax terminology of the 18th century, the word 'concerto' was used indescriminately by Vivaldi and others so that works more accurately entitled 'sonata', or 'sinfonia', have been included, notwithstanding the fact that a separate section for sonatas exists in the various numbering systems. It has been found, also, that a number of works attributed to Vivaldi are alternatively ascribed in certain sources, and in many cases the correct author cannot yet be discovered.

Having reduced our total by the above means, we may now expand it by examination of external evidence. Vivaldi joined the Ospedale della Pietà di Venezia as composer in charge of musical activities in September 1703. In 1713 he was granted leave of absence for an unspecified period, which we may assume to have been about a year. From 1718 to 1722 he apparently commuted between his native Venice and Darmstadt, and in 1723, on his return to Venice, he was contracted to produce two concertos per month for the Ospedale. From 1725 to 1735 his movements are unknown in detail, but he evidently travelled in Europe for much of the time, putting in frequent appearances at Venice; his death occurred in Vienna in 1741.

It is probable that the contract of 1723 for two concertos per month was based on his known capacity: by then he had had published several sets of concertos and sonatas and had been astonishingly busy in the opera-house, so it was known that he was no laggard. In addition, he had accumulated a certain amount of fame at home and abroad, so the contract was likely to have been drafted well within his capabilities rather than it running any risk of stretching them. We may assume, then, that his production *up to 1723* had been in the order of, at the very least, two concertos per month; due to his other responsibilities his concerto-writing may have been halved during his busy years from 1718 to 1722, giving us twelve per year. The same reduction may be assumed during the vague years 1725–35, and we shall leave entirely out of account his final year of 1741, which we know was spent at least partly in Vienna, where he died.

With these speculations in mind, together with the certain knowledge that they may be faulted in many particulars if the true facts of Vivaldi's life and travels are ever incontrovertibly revealed, we may draw up the following table of *possible* concerto production:

Date	*Known or surmised circumstances*	*No of concertos?*
Sept 1703	Joined Ospedale della Pietà	6
1704–12	Relatively uninterrupted work	216
1713	Vacation	–
1714–17	Resumption of uninterrupted work	96
1718–22	Darmstadt/Venice alternation	60
1723–24	Contracted to write two concertos per month	48
1725–35	European travelling/Venice	132
1736–40	Relatively uninterrupted work	120
	Conjectural total	670

As intimated, these figures must be underestimates. In his early days he is said to have composed a concerto faster than his copyists could render it into parts for the instrumentalists, and it is within possibility that for some of his visits he produced a fresh batch of works to impress his hosts, thus putting his average higher for that period. In addition, as has been said, his operas were many and varied and his production of sacred vocal works and instrumental sonatas was also immense. From these somewhat computerised figures, however, we may feel entitled to expect that more concertos by Vivaldi are awaiting discovery. Meanwhile, his total of existing works in this form must stand, at 488, as far and away in excess of that of any other composer.

The first cello concertos were written by Jacchini and published in 1701.

The first violin concertos appeared in 1709 in the set of twelve concertos by Giuseppe Torelli, Op 8, but they may have been composed several years earlier.

The first concertos for piano were written by J C Bach and appeared about 1776.

(Amplificatory details about these pioneer works, and about other instrumental 'firsts' will be found in Section II.)

The composer of the most violin concertos is Vivaldi, who wrote 238 known examples.

The composer of the most flute concertos was Johann Joachim Quantz (1697–1773), whose total of 300 such works were mainly written for, and while in the service of, the flute-playing King Frederick the Great (see Royal Composers in Section III).

The concerto with the most soloists is by Vivaldi. Two concertos, in fact, both in C major (P 16 and P 87) are scored for eleven soloists:

P 87: violin, two violas, two flutes, oboe, cor anglais, two trumpets, two harpsichords, with strings.

P 16: two flutes, two salmoè, two violins in tromba marina, two mandolins, two theorbos, cello, with strings.

The first concerto to specify parts for clarinets. At least two works by Vivaldi were written for two clarinets, which play very much in the style of trumpets and, therefore, differ from the Mozartean use as mellow, seductive instruments. Vivaldi's concertos including clarinets were probably written in the last year or so of his life, and each is scored for two oboes,

Top A selection of best-selling BBC wildlife records (BBC)

Left Felix Mendelssohn (1809–47). Born in Hamburg the son of a banker and grandson of Moses Mendelssohn the philosopher (Royal College of Music) and two clarinets, with string orchestra (P 73 and P 74). Another concerto, P 84, with the subtitle 'Per la solennità di St Lorenzo', is scored for two flutes, two oboes, two clarinets, bassoon, two violins, and string orchestra.

VARIATIONS

Every one of the smaller forms has been transferred to the orchestra at one time or another, just as was the instrumental sonata, although unlike the sonata–which became the orchestral symphony–most of the other pieces retain their instrumental names. Possibly the most important and widest-used large orchestra form, apart from those mentioned in the foregoing sections, is the 'theme and variation' set. Important examples, among many others, of orchestral variations have been written by:

Bentzon: *Symphonic Variations,* Op 92 (1953).
Brahms: *Variations on St Anthony Chorale,* Op 56a (1873) (an arrangement for orchestra from a piece for two pianos).
Britten: *Variations on a Theme of Frank Bridge,* Op 10 (1938). *Variations and Fugue on a Theme by Purcell: The Young Person's Guide to the Orchestra,* Op 34 (1945).
Arensky: *Variations on a Theme by Tchaikovsky,* Op 35a.
Dvořák: *Symphonic Variations,* Op 78 (1877).
Elgar: *Enigma Variations,* Op 36 (1899).

In respect of this last named, perhaps one of the most popular works by any English composer, it is well known that Elgar never gave the clue to his enigma. The theme is not heard during the work, only its bass counterpoint being played, and it is upon this bass that the variations are constructed. All that the composer would ever say on the subject was that the melody was extremely well known; but every suggestion put to him as to its identity was warded off impatiently.

Roger Fiske, in *The Musical Times* for November 1969, convincingly suggests on harmonic grounds that the tune is 'Auld Lang Syne'. It would be neat to consider the case closed at this point since the choice of that tune is most appropriate to the nature of the work, dedicated as it is to 'my friends pictured within'.

Returning to the subject of variations in general, it should be remembered that some of the greatest sets occur in symphonies. Those that conclude Dvořák's Symphony No 8 and Beethoven's Symphony No 3, 'Eroica' are universally known, and the chaconne which comprises the finale of Brahms's Symphony No 4 is a close-knit and masterly set. Less well known are the numerous examples in the symphonies of Joseph Haydn (Nos 31, 72, 42, 47, 53, 55, 63, 70, 82, 85, 91, and 103, etc).

An interesting hybrid lying somewhere between the variation form and the symphony is the awkwardly titled *Symphonic Metamorphosis on Themes of Carl Maria von Weber,* by Hindemith. It is indeed symphonic in that it is in four contrasted movements, and it is metamorphic in that it takes a series of (little-known) themes by Weber and uses them as material upon which the whole work is constructed. It should be pointed out, however, that the word 'metamorphosis' is not an alternative for 'variations' since the themes of the older composer are taken merely as starting-points and are not subjected to variations in the usual way.

OTHER FORMS

Orchestral works have been written also with the following titles:

Ballade (Einem).
Canzona (G Gabrieli).
Capriccio(so) (Einem; Holst).
Dances: Bolero, Chaconne, Mazurka, Minuet, Polka, Waltz, etc, etc.
Essay (Barber).
Étude (Martin).
Fanfare (Mouret).
Idyll (Janáček; Martinů).
Legend (Dvořák; Svendsen–really a concerto movement).
March.
'Music' (Bartók; Jorgenssen).
Partita (Albrechtsberger; Walton).
Phantasy or Fantasy (Coates; Larsson).
Piece(s) (Schoenberg; Bartók).
Poème (Fibich).
Rhapsody (Alfvén; Bloch; Chabrier; Dvořák; Enescu; German; Liszt; Moeran).
Scherzo (Dukas; Dvořák).
Scherzo Capriccioso (Dvořák; Susskind).
Sinfonietta (Janáček; Martinů).

CHAMBER MUSIC

The dividing-line between orchestral and chamber music is not always clearly defined. Stravinsky wrote for a 'chamber group' of thirteen players (*Dumbarton Oaks* Concerto in E flat, 1938) and works such as Mendelssohn's Octet for two string quartets, and Spohr's Double Quartets for the same groups, have orchestra-like textures. On the other hand, some composers of full-scale symphonies seem to have in mind chamber sonorities for much of the time: Sibelius, Mahler, Shostakovitch, and Nielsen among them. The 18th- and early 19th-century octet for wind and strings is of approximately the same texture as the 18th-century symphony for two oboes, two horns, two violins, viola and cello/bass, but it is more correctly a chamber conception because each player has a semi-soloistic function in the octet whereas in the similarly scored symphony the wind instruments often merely support the harmonies, with a harmonic and rhythmic foundation provided by the lower strings, the violins carrying most of the melodic argument.

Jacqueline du Pré and Daniel Barenboim, expert chamber players (EMI/Clive Barda)

(This over simplification will stagger and perhaps collapse under too close a scrutiny because of the wide differences between composers' practices, but it will hold good for early symphonies and will serve to illustrate the historical foundation upon which composers built.)

Most chamber forms have the numbers of players implied in their titles: nonet (for nine players), octet, septet, sextet, quintet, quartet, trio, and duo (or duet). Some quintets and quartets are for a soloist and four or three, respectively, supporting string instruments. These are called 'piano quartets', or 'flute quartets', etc (which does *not* mean compositions for five pianos or four flutes. A flute quartet is for flute, violin, viola and cello, whereas a work for four flutes is called specifically, quartet for four flutes'), and are in effect smallscale concertos: Mozart, J C Bach, and other composers of their time wrote works entitled 'concerto' in which the accompanying string 'orchestra' could consist of one instrument to each string part. Occasionally ad lib wind and horn parts would be made available, and when these were used the string parts might be strengthened accordingly, making the work into a 'concert concerto' rather than a 'chamber concerto'. This fluidity was very much a matter of convenience in the 18th century: what use was there in writing a work which could be played only by a large (for the time) orchestra of 20 or so players, thus excluding the many 'societies' which had at their disposal only a few players? The orchestral trio and orchestral quartet of the composers of the Mannheim School (see Section III) similarly took into account pliable groups of players.

When there is no soloist the quintet, or more usually the quartet, would consist of strings only and would then become a small-scale symphony. Haydn is said to be the 'Father of the String Quartet', although the foundations upon which he built his paternity were ancient and widespread, stretching back into the consorts of viols of the 16th and 17th centuries. An even smaller symphony is formed by the string trio which, in some of the works of the 18th-century Mannheim School, were written in such a way that the parts may be multiplied. These were known as 'orchestral trios'; in the next generation of composers of the Mannheim

School the same principle was applied to 'orchestral quartets', the best-known examples of which were by Karel Stamič.

Duets may be for a wide variety of instrumental combinations. The true duet is one in which both protagonists have an equal share of the argument, as in those by Boccherini for two violins (Gér 56–62), or the same composer's fugues for two cellos or two bassoons (Gér 73); the so-called 'Eyeglass' Duo by Beethoven is for viola and cello, and other works exist by Telemann (two violins), Pleyel and Michael Haydn (violin and viola) in their Op 44 and Perger 127–130, respectively. Telemann is guilty of a 'Duett' in A for two bass gambas! Moving away from the string repertoire, we find sonatas for clarinet and bassoon by Beethoven, and for two keyboards by Mozart, Müthel, etc, but in mentioning these examples we are merely taking arbitrarily from an enormous repertoire.

Still technically in the realm of the duo or duet, but thought of more as accompanied solos for melody instrument and bass or keyboard, are the even larger quantities of sonatas for violin, cello, flute, oboe, or indeed any instrument whatever, with piano or other keyboard instrument. Paul Hindemith has shown in his didactic works a wide variety of accompanied solos within the lists of a single composer: there exist sonatas for flute, oboe, clarinet, bassoon, trumpet, trombone, violin, viola, viola d'amor, and cello, all accompanied by piano. Two hundred years earlier Telemann, in addition to producing pieces for most of these instruments, also added to the repertoire solos (accompanied by basso continuo) for recorder, oboe d'amore, viola da gamba, descant gamba, and even for bass gamba. One of his prettiest little items is a piece in E for panpipes and harpsichord.

But by far the largest number of works in this group are for violin and piano. Starting during the time of Mozart, when the keyboard was the dominant partner with the violin merely accompanying, the latter instrument gradually became more important with Beethoven and his contemporaries, until, with Schumann, Brahms, and many other 19th-century composers, the violin was the soloist proper, the piano simply providing an accompaniment, although often an important one. By the end of that century the so-called 'violin sonata' had turned into what was a duo for violin and piano in all but name, both instruments having equal say. A most odd example was written in 1922 by Bartók. His first sonata for violin and piano is written in such a way that the two players seem to be completely at odds. It is as if one were listening to two sonatas, one for piano, the other for violin, being performed simultaneously. In fact, Ernest Newman, in his notice of the first performance, after registering his disgust with the music, said as much: 'It was as as if two people were improvising against each other'.

Some chamber music facts

Vladimir Stcherbatchev, the modern Polish composer, wrote a nonet scored for string quartet, piano, harp, violin, dance, and light.

The first wind quintets (ie symphonic works for flute, oboe, clarinet, bassoon, and horn) were written by Cambini. His first examples date from about 1795.

The composer of the most string quintets is Luigi Boccherini. The standard string quartet is scored for two violins, two violas, and cello, but Boccherini favoured the alternative setting of two violins, viola, and two cellos (the scoring chosen by Schubert for his C major String Quartet, D 956 of 1828). Boccherini's totals are:

Quintets for two violins, two violas, and cello	24
Quintets for two violins, viola, and two cellos	113
Total	137

The first inventions, in the sense of suites for violin and bass, were written by A F Bonporti about 1715. The same term was used later by J S Bach for solo harpsichord music.

The composer of the most flute sonatas was King Frederick the Great (Friedrich II of Prussia) who wrote 120 for his own use.

SOLO INSTRUMENTAL MUSIC

Although it might be thought of as being part of the chamber music repertoire since it is ideally performed in a smallish room or chamber, solo instrumental music usually falls into a different category. Once again any instrument may be involved, but by far the most widely known and accepted solo music is for piano or some other keyboard instrument such as the harpsichord or organ. Strictly speaking, however, such music is duple in effect since the player has two hands with which to produce two distinct registers, the 'melody' register (right hand) and the accompanying 'bass' (left hand). In theory, keyboard music for two hands can exist in as many as ten lines, one for each finger and thumb, but in practice even the most complex rarely goes above four parts except for chords.

The forms such music might take are multifarious: sonata, suite, concerto (in this case without a supporting orchestra – see examples by J S Bach and Schumann), variations, prelude and fugue, chaconne, passacaglia, and many other types of dance (Chopin's piano compositions show a tremendous variety of stylised dance forms, none of which could be danced to), ballads and other forms 'borrowed' from vocal music, and arrangements from works for other combinations of instruments or full orchestra. Liszt, for instance, produced piano arrangements of Beethoven symphonies which, as examples of the arranger's art, deserve consideration as masterpieces in themselves.

It is the sonata which has attracted the most serious attention from composers for the solo keyboard instrument, and large numbers of keyboard sonatas were written by Domenico Scarlatti, C P E Bach, Haydn, Mozart, Beethoven, Clementi, and Schubert, to mention only the best known, up to the early 19th century, since when important sonatas have been produced by Chopin, Schumann, Brahms, Liszt, Rakhmaninoff, Scriabin, and others.

The organ, the so-called 'King of Instruments', also has a large repertoire of solo music. The first composer to come to mind in this context is J S Bach, but his huge and inclusive output of music for the instrument was preceded by works by John Bull, Sweelinck, Frescobaldi, Buxtehude, Pachelbel, and Bruhns, all of whom contributed to the organ literature which Bach used as a foundation and so easily capped.

After Bach (and indeed well before him), the literature for organ and harpsichord overlapped: what could be played on the one was usually equally suitable for performance on the other. With the possible exception of a few works for the pedal harpsichord, it is inconceivable that Bach's organ works should be played on the harpsichord. The loss in original textures and grandeur of the over-all effect would damage the works too seriously. Later in the 18th century, however, the dividing-line was not so hard and the works written for organ by many English composers, and by Haydn, Mozart, and Beethoven, are not so seriously affected by performance on a different instrument, simply because the works themselves are usually not of such consequence as those by Bach.

The 19th century saw the production of a small but important organ literature by Mendelssohn, Brahms, Liszt, Franck, Saint-Saëns, Reger, Widor, and Vierne. Since this late romantic flowering, the organ repertoire has been in the hands of a few specialist composers, only the occasional important work being produced by musicians of wider interests, among them Nielsen and Messiaen.

Solo works for instruments other than the piano or organ are much less common and are, owing to the danger of a single sound colour boring the ear, usually of much shorter duration. Often it will be found that such works are composed for instructional or practice use and are, therefore, enjoyable almost exclusively for the player. An exception may be made in the case of the masterly works of J S Bach for solo violin, solo cello, and solo flute. His lute works, too, exist within the realm of music designed to be enjoyed by the listener as well as by the performer.

The guitar repertoire is large but it has been developed mainly, and with one or two surprising exceptions, by composers who concentrated on the instrument, almost to the exclusion of other types of music. Fernando Sor was known as the 'Beethoven of the guitar' in the sense of being foremost a virtuoso and only secondly a composer (thus paralleling Beethoven's role in earlier life). As the national instrument of Spain, the guitar has naturally attracted composers of that country or who had origins or affinities with Iberia: Ponce, Turina, Halffter, Falla, and Villa-Lobos have also written for the instrument. The 'surprising exceptions' mentioned above are Berlioz, Weber, and Paganini, all of whom showed an interest in it, but of these only Paganini left music for solo guitar. Weber used it occasionally to accompany songs, while Berlioz included it in his treatise on instrumentation.

The guitar, like the other stringed and keyboard instruments discussed above, is a chord-producing as well as a melody-playing instrument. This accounts for its relatively wide popularity among composers, a popularity which cannot extend to most other instruments. Unaccompanied solos for oboe, horn, trumpet, clarinet, bassoon, etc, exist but are rare and of minor importance; percussion solos are slightly more common especially with young composers, and a number of solely percussion marches exist dating from the early-18th-century French courts.

SOME INSTRUMENTAL MUSIC FACTS

The piano nocturne was invented by John Field, who published the first in 1814, but it is evident that he had merely transferred to the keyboard a chamber type (and at times a vocal type; for Mozart and other composers wrote 'notturni' for voices and instruments) which was well established as a mood piece during the latter half of the 18th century. In addition, both Mozart and Haydn wrote multi-movement works of divertimento type with this title. At the time of Field's first set, Chopin, who adopted the form and made it distinctly his own, was four years old.

The impromptu was invented concurrently but separately by Heinrich August Marschner and Jan Hugo Voříšek, both of whom published pieces with this title in 1822. The name was taken up later by Schubert (in 1827), Schumann (1833), and Chopin (1836).

The inventor of variations is thought to have been Hugh Aston, who died in 1522. He was an English composer mainly of Church and keyboard music. An alternative English name for variations was 'divisions'.

The composer of the most sonatas for keyboard was Domenico Scarlatti who wrote 555 (according to Kirkpatrick). Recent research has attempted to add a few more to this total, but the question of authenticity arises, particularly as some of the additions are supposedly early works, and Domenico's father Alessandro wrote pieces in a style similar to his son's earliest attempts. Even more amazing when considering Domenico's output of harpsichord sonatas (the earliest works were called 'Essercisi' = 'exercises'), which were written mainly in Spain for the Royal Palace at Madrid, is that they come from the last 20 years or so of his long life.

Nearly all of his sonatas are single-movement works, although Kirkpatrick puts forward a strong case for many of them to be performed in pairs. A few early multi-movement sonatas exist for harpsichord and violin, but they are uncharacteristic and unremarkable. Many of the sonatas carry nicknames such as 'Pastorale', 'The Cat's Fugue' (the story being that the composer's cat suggested the theme while promenading on the keyboard), and 'Cortège'.

The 19th century saw a busy production of piano sonatas, among which Beethoven's 32 stand as a mighty testament to the range and subtlety obtainable from the newly established hammerklavier, or true 'hammered' piano. In the present century the output to date of 36 piano sonatas by the English composer John White represents **the modern record.**

The longest instrumental work. This question raises the subject: When does music cease to be music?

A few years ago it was reported that a 26-minute work entitled *In C,* in which the solo pianist plays only the note C for the entire performance, was given by the Norwegian pianist Siri Nome. It is further reported that the lights in the recital room were switched off to add atmosphere, and that when they were turned up at the end of the performance, Siri Nome was alone.

Erik Satie's aptly titled *Vexations* must come into a similar category. It consists of a 52-beat unbarred idea, with the indication 'Très lent,' played 840 times with as little variation as possible. The first performance, organised by John Cage at the Pocket Theatre, New York, in 1963, lasted 18 hr 12 min and was performed by a group of ten pianists in relay. Since then there have been many other performances: the second was in Berlin during August 1966 at which a relay of six pianists took part: for her second stint Charlotte Moorman introduced a novel way of breaking the monotony by appearing unclothed from the waist up. Her reasons were both musicological and financial: Satie, it is said, 'loved nudity', and John Cage bet her $100 she wouldn't do it. On this occasion the performance of the music took 18 hr 40 min.

The first *solo* performance of *Vexations* was given at the Arts Laboratory, Drury Lane, London, on 10–11 October 1967 by Richard Toop. According to reports he was sustained during the performance with cucumber sandwiches in black bread, and chocolate, but it is not recorded whether Satie's contribution to the proceedings also served to feed him up. Apparently not, since Mr Toop gave another performance, of a little over 24 hr duration in January 1968. The following year a performance was attempted in Australia but was not finished because the soloist was rushed to hospital in a coma after only 17 hr.

Vexations was published for the first time in England in the periodical *Music Review* in 1967.

Of similar effect but with rather more variety is a method of composing minuets according to the bar order dictated by the throw of dice. It consists of sixteen bars of 3/4 time attributed to F J Haydn. A performance utilising all 940 369 969 152 permutations would last in the region of 900 000 years without observing formal repeats. There has been no notice of a complete performance so far.

The longest non-repetitive work is a piece called *Sadist Factory* by Philip L Crevier of New York. It consists of all possible permutations of the scale of C major and occupies 1680 pages of computer print-out. Total playing time is calculated at 100 hr. If this piece were to prove successful there is nothing to prevent Mr Crevier from putting his computer to use in similar explorations of the other scales.

A work called *Solo for Double Bass*, written in 1969 by Malcolm Fox, is said to last, when played at the extremely fast tempo indicated, 73 000 000 000 years, but it may be assumed that a certain amount of repetition is involved.

WORKS WITH NICKNAMES AND SUBTITLES

A large number of works in and out of the current repertoire are identified only by key and perhaps an opus number (eg Symphony No 4 in

Franz Joseph Haydn (Popperfoto)

The skull of Joseph Haydn, which was separated from his body in a gruesome and ignoble episode in the history of music (Popperfoto)

B flat, Op 60 by Beethoven). For many music-lovers who are exasperated or perplexed by references to 'the Beethoven B flat' or 'Mozart G minor' (as if these were the only works written in these keys by these composers), the addition of a nickname or sub-title to a work is a useful mnemonic, and a large number of works have been given such titles. It is not our task here to decide which of these names are appropriate (as indeed some are) and which downright silly (a larger category!); there can be no doubt that such names are useful in identifying and memorising the works which bear them.

In preparing this list, the aim has been to include all the well-known names in the hope that it will be useful for those who can remember the name only and who need to find out the full and correct title and composition date of the work. In the 'Remarks' column a brief note is given as to the origin or cause of the name (where known), but in the cases of the Mendelssohn *Songs Without Words,* the Chopin Études, and some other groups, the meanings of the names are self-evident and are easily guessed from their romantic connections.

Also given are a selection of lesser-known titles. It is hoped that these titles, and the reasons for them, will prove of intrinsic interest even though much of the music is unlikely to be heard in a lifetime of listening.

In the matter of identification, the reader is referred to the list of thematic catalogues in Section VII.

NICKNAMES AND SUB-TITLES

Name or Sub-title	*Work*	*Composer*	*Remarks*
Accademica	Concerto in D minor for violin and strings (1925)	Vaughan Williams	The composer later rejected the title
Acteon Transformed into a Stag	Symphony in G, Kr 75 (*c* 1784)	Dittersdorf	No 3 of twelve symphonies based on Ovid's *Metamorphoses*
'Adélaïde'	Violin Concerto in D, K A 294a (*c* 1775?)	Mozart	Supposedly dedicated to the eldest daughter of Louis XV, Mme Adélaïde de France. It is now thought that the dedication has strayed from another work, and that the concerto itself may not be genuine Mozart
'Adieu, L''	Song Without Words in A minor, Op 85/2 (1845)	Mendelssohn	
Adieux, Les	Piano Sonata in E flat, Op 81a (1809)	Beethoven	In full: *Les Adieux, l'Absence, et le Retour.* Dedicated to the Archduke Rudolf, who was about to leave Vienna for a time
'Aeolian Harp'	Étude in A flat, Op 25/1 (1837)	Chopin	
Age of Anxiety, The	Symphony No 2 for piano and orchestra (1949)	Bernstein	Based on a poem of W H Auden
Airborne	Symphony (1946)	Blitzstein	A work for singers, orchestra, and narrator about the evolution of flying
'Alla Francese'	Concerto in C for strings, P 64	Vivaldi	Opens in declamatory style, in the manner of French works of the period
'Alla Rustica'	Concerto in G for strings, P 143	Vivaldi	Written in 'rustic' style throughout
'All' Inglese'	Concerto in A for violin, cello, and strings, P 238	Vivaldi	Said to have 'English' characteristics
All Men are Brothers	Symphony No 11, Op 186	Hovhaness	
Altitudes	Symphony No 4 (1964–66)	Martinon	The heights of mountains play an important part in the melodic construction
American, The	String Quartet in F, Op 96 (1893)	Dvořák	Written at Spillville, Iowa, and based partly on American (Negro) themes
'Amoroso, L''	Concerto in E for violin and strings, P 246	Vivaldi	Uses gentle and affectionate musical language
Ani	Symphony No 23 for large band and ad lib antiphonal brass choir, Op 249	Hovhaness	

Name or Sub-title	*Work*	*Composer*	*Remarks*
Antar	Symphony No 2, Op 9 (1868)	Rimsky-Korsakov	Antar was a 7th-century poet of Russian literature
Antartica	Symphony No 7 (1953)	Vaughan Williams	Based on the film music written by Vaughan Williams for *Scott of the Antarctic* (1951)
'Appassionata'	Piano Sonata in F minor, Op 57 (1806)	Beethoven	A title invented by the publisher; it refers to the passionate nature of the music
'Appassionata'	Song Without Words in A minor, Op 38/5 (1838)	Mendelssohn	
'Archduke'	Piano Trio in B flat, Op 97 (1811)	Beethoven	Dedicated to the Archduke Rudolf
Arevakal	Concerto for orchestra No 1, Op 88	Hovhaness	
Arjuna	Symphony No 8, Op 179	Hovhaness	
Arte del Violino, L'	12 Concerti and 24 Caprices for violin, Op 3 (1733)	Locatelli	A milestone in violin composition
'Assunzione di Maria Vergine'	Concerto in C for violin and two string orchestras, P 14	Vivaldi	Written for the Feast of the Assumption
	Concerto in D for violin and two string orchestras, P 164	Vivaldi	
Aviary, The	String Quintet in D, Gér 276 (1771)	Boccherini	Contains many imitation bird calls
Babi Yar	Symphony No 13 in B minor, Op 113 (1962)	Shostakovitch	Commemorates the Jewish cemetery at Babi Yar
'Bee's Wedding, The'	Song Without Words in C, Op 67/4 (1845)	Mendelssohn	Also known as 'Spinning Song'
'Belief'	Song Without Words in C, Op 102/6 (1845)	Mendelssohn	
Bell, The	Symphony No 2 (1943)	Khachaturian	The opening of the work is said to be bell-like
'Bell Anthem'	'Rejoice in the Lord Alway'	Purcell	
Bells of Zlonice, The	Symphony No 1 in C minor, Op 3 (1865)	Dvořák	The young composer lived at Zlonice and may have incorporated the motifs of the bells of the town into the work
'Berceuse'	Song Without Words in F, Op 53/4 (1841)	Mendelssohn	Also known as 'Sadness of Soul'
Berdlersgarn	Partita in D for wind and toy instruments (*c* 1800)	Družecký	
Bianchina, La	Sonata in D for trumpet and strings, Op 35 (1665)	Cazzati	
'Black Keys'	Étude in G flat, Op 10/5 (1833)	Chopin	
Bona Nova	Concerto No 1 in D minor for two instrumental groups (1689)	Muffat	
Boreale	Symphony No 8, Op 56 (1951–52)	Holmboe	Meant to indicate to the first audience, which was supposed to have been Viennese, the Nordic character of the work, the title proved useless since the first performance was after all given in Copenhagen
Brandenburg Concertos	Six Concerti Grossi, BWV 1046–51 (1717–21)	Bach	Written for the Markgrave of Brandenburg
'Brevis'	Symphony No 3 (1929)	Becker, J	
'Brevis'	Symphony (1953)	Bloch	
'Brevis'	Symphony No 22 (1965)	Brian	
Brotherhood	Symphony No 2, Op 25 (1968–69)	Carlstedt	
Burlesca	Symphony in G, DTB 3:22	Mozart, L	
Buscha, La	Sonata in C for two cornetti and strings	Legrenzi	
'Butterfly's Wings'	Étude in G flat, Op 25/9 (1837)	Chopin	
'Cacchia, La'	Concerto in B flat, for violin and strings, P 338, Op 8/10 (*c* 1725)	Vivaldi	One of several Vivaldi concertos depicting a hunting scene
Camp Meeting	Symphony No 3 (1904)	Ives	The meeting is a religious gathering
'Capricieuse'	Symphony No 3 in D (1842)	Berwald	An imaginative but appropriate title
Capriccio	Sonata in E, L 375, Kk 20	Scarlatti	
Capriola	Canzona, Book 1, No 1 (1584)	Maschera	The word means the same as 'Caprice'

Name or sub-title	*Work*	*Composer*	*Remarks*
Casa del Diavolo	Symphony in D minor, Gér 506 (1771)	Boccherini	An 'infernal' symphony whose last movement is based closely on Gluck's 'Dance of the Furies' from *Orfeo*
'Cat's Fugue'	Sonata in G minor, L 499, Kk 30	Scarlatti	The theme is supposed to have been suggested by a cat walking along the keyboard of the composer's harpsichord
'Cat Waltz'	Waltz in F, Op 34/3 (1838)	Chopin	The composer is supposed to have derived his inspiration in the same way as did Scarlatti (see above)
Celestial Gate	Symphony No 6, Op 173	Hovhaness	
'Cetra, La'	Six Concerti for oboes, flutes, bassoon, and strings (1738)	Marcello, A	An imaginative title for a series of inventive concertos
'Cetra, La'	Twelve Concerti for violin and strings, Op 9 (1728)	Vivaldi	
Champêtre	Concerto for harpsichord and orchestra (1929)	Poulenc	
Chasse, La—A frequently used title for a style of musical painting which was very popular during the 18th century and since (see also Cacchia, above, and Hunt, below). The following list is a selection only.			
	Sonata in D, Op 16(17) (*c* 1787)	Clementi	
	Trio in C, Op 22/3 (pub 1788)	Clementi	
	Sonata in B flat, for two oboi da caccia and bass	Fasch	
	Sonata No 12 for viola d'amor and guitar	Hrac(z)ek, A I	
	Symphony in G for four horns, shotgun, and strings, DTB 3:29	Mozart, L	
Choral	Symphony No 9 in D minor, Op 125	Beethoven	A chorus and vocal soloists are introduced in the finale
'Cimento dell' Armonia e dell' Inventione'	Twelve Concerti for violin and strings, Op 8 (*c* 1725)	Vivaldi	The title is an imaginative one which, translated, means 'The conflict between Harmony and Invention'
'Cinque Trombe'	Concerto in D minor, for two violins, two oboes, two flutes, bassoon, and strings, P 297	Vivaldi	A title given to several Vivaldi concertos (of which this is an example); it appears to mean merely that five blown instruments are included (two flutes, two oboes, and bassoon). No trumpets are involved
Circe	Symphony No 18, Op 204a	Hovhaness	A symphony based on material from the ballet *Circe*
Classical	Symphony No 1 in D, Op 25 1917)	Prokofiev	Written 'in the style of' the classical composers
'Colloredo'	Serenade in D, K 203 (1774)	Mozart	Used, but probably not written, for the name-day of Archbishop Colloredo
Colour	Symphony (1922)	Bliss	Points the heraldic significances of the colours purple, red, blue, and green
Communiqué 1943	Symphony No 1 (1952)	Finney, R L	
Concerto da Camera	String Quartet No 7 (1947)	Martinů	The over-all shape of the work is that of the classical concerto: fast–slow–fast
Concord, Mass, 1840–60	Sonata No 2 for piano with flute (1909–15)	Ives	Honours personalities who were prominent in that town: Emerson, Hawthorne, the Alcotts, and Thoreau
Conflict of Human Passions	Divertimento in D (*c* 1772), Kr 133 (also exists as a Symphony, Kr 46)	Dittersdorf	The seven movements are titled: 'Il Superbo'; 'L'Umile'; 'Il Matto'; 'Il Contento'; 'Il Constante'; 'Il Malinconico'; 'Il Vivace'
'Consecration of Sound'	Symphony No 4 in F, Op 86 (1832)	Spohr	
'Consolation'	Song Without Words in E, Op 30/3 (1834)	Mendelssohn	
Cornetto da Posta	Concerto in G for violin and strings, P 112	Vivaldi	Doubtful authorship: attributed to Somis, G B in an alternative source
	Concerto in B flat for violin and strings, P 350	Vivaldi	

Name or Sub-title	Work	Composer	Remarks
'Coronation'	Piano Concerto in D, K 537 (1788)	Mozart	Said to have been played during the festivities surrounding the coronation in Frankfurt of Leopold II
Cortège	Sonata in E, L 23, Kk 380	Scarlatti	The music suggests a procession
Cycle, The	Symphony No 4 (1948)	Mennin	
Dance	Symphony (1929)	Copland	Adapted from the ballet *Grohg*
'Death and the Maiden'	String Quartet in D minor, D 810 (1826)	Schubert	The second movement uses the theme of the song of that name, D 531
Deliciae Basiliensis	Symphony No 4 (1946)	Honegger	
Delirium Amoris	Concerto No 11 for strings (1689)	Muffat	
Didoni Abbandonata	Piano Sonata in G minor, Op 50/3 (1821)	Clementi	
	Violin Sonata in G minor, Op 6/10	Tartini	
Dispute of Ajax and Ulysses over the arms of Atreus	Symphony (LOST), Kr 84 (*c* 1784)	Dittersdorf	No 12 of twelve symphonies based on Ovid's *Metamorphoses*
Diran	Concerto for horn, trombone, and strings, Op 94	Hovhaness	
'Dissonance'	String Quartet in C, K 465 (1785)	Mozart	Remarkable for the harsh dissonances in the first movement
Di Tre re	Symphony No 5 (1951)	Honegger	A soft D (re) on basses and timpani ends each of the three movements
Divine Poem	Symphony No 3 in C, Op 43 (1903)	Scriabin	
'Dog Waltz'	Waltz in D flat, Op 64/1	Chopin	In which a dog is depicted chasing its tail. The piece is also known as the 'Minute Waltz'
Dolorosa	Symphony No 6	Saeverud	
Don Quichotte	Suite in G for strings (1761)	Telemann	The work describes events in the story
Dream Vision	Piano Sonata	Egge	
'Duetto'	Song Without Words in A flat, Op 38/6 (1838)	Mendelssohn	
'Dumky'	Piano Trio in E minor, Op 90 (1891)	Dvořák	Based on the Czech dance of that name
Easter	Symphony No 4 in C minor (1905)	Foerster	The movement titles are 'I: The Road to Calvary'; 'II: A Child's Good Friday'; 'III: The Charm of Solitude'; 'IV: Holy Saturday Victorious'
Ebony	Concerto for clarinet and orchestra (1945)	Stravinsky	Written for Woody Herman
Eco in Lontano	Concerto in A for two violins and strings, P 222 (1740)	Vivaldi	One of several 'Echo Concertos' by this composer
Edward	Ballade in D minor, Op 10/1	Brahms	
Eine Kleine Nachtmusik	Serenade in G for strings, K 525 (1788)	Mozart	Mozart's own name for his most popular work
Elebris (God of Dawn)	Concerto for flute and orchestra, Op 50	Hovhaness	
'Elegie'	Song Without Words in D, Op 85/4 (1845)	Mendelssohn	
Elegy	Trio for flute, viola, and harp (1916)	Bax	
Elegy	Symphony No 1 (1965)	McCabe	
'Emperor'	Piano Concerto No 5 in E flat, Op 73 (1809)	Beethoven	A title used in English-speaking countries only. There is no authority for the name
'Eroica'	Fifteen Variations and Fugue in E flat, Op 35 (1802)	Beethoven	The name was first attached to the symphony—'Written to the memory of a hero.' The contradanse theme in the finale was also used in the earlier Variations, leading to the name being inappropriately attached also to them
'Eroica'	Symphony No 3 in E flat, Op 55 (1804)	Beethoven	
Ertmannsonate I	Grande Sonate in F minor for piano, Denn 57a (1813)	Reichardt	Dedicated to Frau von Ertmann
Ertmannsonate II	Sonata in E minor for piano, Denn 57b (1813)	Reichardt	Dedicated to 'Mad. la Bar. de Ertmann'
Espaces	Symphony No 3	Landowski	

Name or Sub-title	*Work*	*Composer*	*Remarks*
'Espansiva'	Symphony No 3 in F–A, Op 27 (1910–11)	Nielsen	Indicates the expansive mood of the work
'Essay Sonatas and Sonatinas'	Six Sonatas (1753) and Six Sonatinas (1786) for keyboard instrument, W 63	Bach, C P E	Published as appendices to the composer's book *Essay on the True Art of Playing Keyboard Instruments*, which appeared in two editions, 1753; 1786
'Estray, The'	Song Without Words in B minor, Op 30/4 (1834)	Mendelssohn	
'Estro Armonico, L''	Twelve Concertos for string soloists and string orchestra, Op 3 (1712)	Vivaldi	The fanciful title means 'Harmonic Fantasy or Whim'
Etchmiadzin	Symphony No 21, Op 234	Hovhaness	Etchmiadzin is the central capital of Armenian religion
Etruscan	Concerto for piano and chamber orchestra (1955)	Glanville-Hicks	Reflects the atmosphere of the Etruscan tombs of Tarquinia
Exile	Symphony No 1, Op 17	Hovhaness	
'Eyeglass'	Duo in E flat, for viola and cello	Beethoven	In full: 'with the obligato for two eyeglasses'. It was written for Nicolaus Zmeskall, cello, and Beethoven himself, both of whom wore eyeglasses
Facets	Symphony No 3 (1950)	Blomdahl	
'Faithful Shepherd'	Six Sonatas for musette or viele or flute or oboe or violin, with bass, Op 13 (*c* 1737)	Vivaldi	More usually known by the Italian original title: *Il Pastor Fido.* Musette and veile, and to a lesser extent the flute and oboe, were known as pastoral instruments in the 18th century
Fall of Phaeton, The	Symphony in D, Kr 74 (*c* 1784)	Dittersdorf	No 2 of twelve symphonies based on Ovid's *Metamorphoses*
'Fall of Warsaw'	Etude in C minor, Op 10/12 (1833)	Chopin	
Fantastique	Symphony No 1, Op 14 (1830)	Berlioz	A descriptive and, in places, lurid, autobiographical fantasy
'Favorito, Il'	Concerto in E minor for violin and strings, P 106, Op 11/2 (*c* 1729–30)	Vivaldi	
'Feast of Saint Lawrence'	Concerto in C for two flutes, two oboes, two clarinets, bassoon, two violins, and strings, P 84	Vivaldi	In full: 'Per la solennità di S Lorenzo'
	Concerto in F for violin and strings, P 290	Vivaldi	
	Concerto in D, for violin, two oboes, two horns, timpani, and strings, P 444	Vivaldi	P 444 is the only known Vivaldi concerto in which timpani are required; the recent Ricordi publication, however, omits these instruments
Feast of the Assumption of the Virgin Mary	see 'Assunzione', above		
'Festive'	Symphony in E (1854)	Smetana	Smetana's only symphony is also known as 'Triumphal Symphony'. The finale closes with an extended and grandiose presentation of Haydn's 'Emperor's Hymn'
Fiery Angel	Symphony No 3 in C minor, Op 44 (1928)	Prokofiev	Based on material from the opera of that name
'Fileuse'	See 'Spinning Song', below		
Five	String Quintet (1969)	David Bedford	Refers simply to the number of players
'Fleecy Cloud'	Song Without Words in E flat, Op 53/2 (1841)	Mendelssohn	
Florilegium Primum	Ten Sonatas for strings	Muffat	
'Folk Song'	Song Without Words in A minor, Op 53/5 (1841)	Mendelssohn	Also known as 'Song of Triumph'
Four Ages of the World, The	Symphony in C, Kr 73 (*c* 1784)	Dittersdorf	No 1 of twelve symphonies based on Ovid's *Metamorphoses*

Name or sub-title	*Work*	*Composer*	*Remarks*
Four Temperaments	Theme and Variations for piano and orchestra (1946)	Hindemith	Both take as their theme the medieval description of the humours or temperaments of man: 'Four Humours reign within our bodies wholly, And these compared to four elements, The Sanguine, Choler, Flegeme, and Melancholy'
	Symphony No 2 in B minor–A, Op 16 (1902)	Nielsen	
Frei aber Einsam	Sonata for violin and piano (1855)	Brahms; Schumann; Dietrich	A 'joint' composition, each composer contributing one movement. The title translates as 'Free but lonely'.
Frescoes of Pompeii	Symphony No 7	Válek, J	The movements are named 'I: The Dead-living Town'; 'II: Villas of Mystery'; 'III: Destruction of Pompeii'
From my Life	String Quartet No 1 in E minor (1876)	Smetana	An autobiographical work
From the New Wolrd	Symphony No 9, in E minor, Op 95 (1893)	Dvořák	Written during rhe composer's visit to the American continent
Funèbre	Symphony in F minor for strings (1725)	Locatelli	Written after the death of the composer's wife
'Funèbre'	Concerto in B flat, for oboe, two salmoè, violin, two 'viole Inglese', and bass, P 385	Vivaldi	No specific occasion has been recorded to account for the dark mood of this work
Funèbre et Triomphale	Symphony No 2, Op 15 (1840)	Berlioz	Commemorating the July Revolution of 1830
Für Elise	Albumblatt in A minor (1810)	Beethoven	'Elise' has not been identified
Für Kënner und Liebhaber	Sonatas, Rondos, and Fantasias for keyboard, W 55, 56, 57, 58, 59, and 61	Bach, C P E	'For Professionals and Amateurs', a group of eighteen Sonatas, thirteen Rondos, and six Fantasias which were meant to be relatively easy to play while at the same time appealing to the professional musician
Gardellino	Concerto in D for flute, oboe, violin, bassoon, and bass, P 155	Vivaldi	Features the then fashionable bird-song imitations. The work was later published (*c* 1729–30) for flute and strings as Op 10/3
Gaspésienne	Symphony (1945)	Champagne	Inspired by the scenery of the Gaspé regions of East Quebec
'Gastein'	Symphony (1824) (LOST?)	Schubert	A symphony was composed at Gastein but was lost; some musicians believe that the Grand Duo in C, D 812, for piano duet is a reduced version of the symphony
Gesangszene	Violin Concerto No 8 in A minor, Op 47 (1816)	Spohr	In the style of a vocal scene
'Ghost'	Piano Trio in D, Op 70/1 (1808)	Beethoven	From the eerie character of the second movement
Giocosa	Symphony No 2	Egge	
'Golden'	Sonata in G minor for violin and bass (No 9 of *Ten Sonatas)*	Purcell	
Goldfinch	see 'Gardellino'		
Gothic	Symphony No 1 in D minor (1919–27)	Brian	The largest work ever written (see Section V)
Gothique	Symphony No 9 for organ solo, Op 70 (1935)	Widor	
Goûts Réunis, Les	Dixième Concert Royal in A minor (1722)	Couperin, F	
Grave	Symphony No 2 (1935)	Rosenberg	
'Great'	Symphony in E flat, Op 8 (*c* 1790)	Jírovec	
'Great'	Symphony No 9 in C, D 944 (1828)	Schubert	So named, it seems, not for any intrinsic greatness but merely to differentiate this work from the 'Little' (qv) Symphony in the same key. See also 'Heavenly Length'
'Grief'	Etude in E major, Op 10/3 (1833)	Chopin	

Name or sub-title	*Work*	*Composer*	*Remarks*
Gusto di cinque Nazioni, nel	Symphony in A, Kr 18 (1766)	Dittersdorf	
'Haffner'	Serenade in D, K 250 (1776) Symphony No 35 in D, K 385 (1782)	Mozart	Both works written for the Salzburg Haffner family
'Hallelujah'	Concerto in B flat for organ and strings, Op 7/3 (pub 1760)	Handel	Incorporates a motif from the famous chorus in *Messiah*
'Hammerklavier'	Piano Sonata in B flat, Op 106 (1818)	Beethoven	Written specifically to be played on the 'hammerklavier', the forerunner of the modern piano. All of Beethoven's last sonatas were designed to be so played. Correctly, therefore, the title should be appended to them all. (A similar case occurs with Haydn's 'London' Symphony)
'Hamburger Ebb und Fluth'	Suite in C (1723)	Telemann	Describes life on and beside the Alster. Also known as Telemann's Watermusic'
'Harmonious Blacksmith'	Harpsichord Suite No 5 in E (Air and Variations)	Handel	The famous story surrounding the Blacksmith at Stanmore who is supposed to have inspired Handel appears to have no foundation
Harold in Italy	Symphony No 3, Op 16 (1834)	Berlioz	Inspired by Byron's *Childe Harold*
'Harp'	Etude in A flat, Op 25/1 (1837)	Chopin	
'Harp'	String Quartet in E flat, Op 74 (1809)	Beethoven	The pizzicato passages in the first movement have attracted this name
'Heavenly Length'	Symphony No 9 in C, D 944 (1828)	Schubert	Schumann's name for the work. See 'Great' above
He Never Dies	Symphony No 1	Raichov, A	
Hercules transformed into a God	Symphony (LOST), Kr 81	Dittersdorf	No 9 of twelve symphonies based on Ovid's *metamorphoses*
Historical	Symphony No 6 in G, Op 116 (1839)	Spohr	The history of orchestral writing is illustrated by the four movements: I: Bach and Handel, *c* 1720; II: Haydn and Mozart, *c* 1780; III: Beethoven, *c* 1810; IV: Today, *c* 1840
'Hochzeit auf der Alm'	Divertimento (or Symphony) in G, Perger 7 (1768)	Haydn, J M	
'Hoffmeister'	String Quartet in D, K 499 (1786)	Mozart	Published by the Viennese publisher Hoffmeister; therefore, a meaningless title
'Hornpipe'	Concerto Grosso in B minor, Op 6/12 (1739)	Handel	The finale has a dance-like rhythm
'Hunt'	String Quartet in B flat, K 458 (1784)	Mozart	The finale suggests a hunting scene. See also 'Chasse' and 'Cacchia', above
'Hunting Song'	Song Without Words in A, Op 19a/3 (1830)	Mendelssohn	
Hymne de la Vie	Symphony No 2	Martinon	
'Hymn of Praise'	Symphony No 2 (14) in B flat, Op 52 (1840)	Mendelssohn	The choral finale is in the style of a hymn of praise
Hypochondriaca	Symphony in C, with trumpet solo (*c* 1780)	Schmidtbauer	Possibly adapted from music for a stage presentation
Ilya Murometz	Symphony No 3, Op 42 (1911)	Glière	Ilya Murometz was a hero of Russian folk-legend
Im Walde	Symphony No 3 in A, Op 153 (1869)	Raff	Inspired by woodland scenes
Incantation	Piano Concerto No 4 (1956)	Martinů	
Indissolubilis Amicita	Fasciculus No 8 in E for strings	Muffat	
Inextinguishable	Symphony No 4, Op 29 (1916)	Nielsen	Written during the First World War, this work expresses the indomitability of the human spirit
In Memoriam Dylan Thomas	Symphony No 4 (1954)	Jones, D	
'Inquietudine'	Concerto in D for violin and strings, P 208	Vivaldi	Possesses a restless mood

Name or Sub-title	Work	Composer	Remarks
Intimate Pages	String Quartet No 2 (1928)	Janáček	An autobiographical work dealing with the 74-year-old composer's feelings for a much younger woman, Kamila Stösslova
'Intimité L''	Etude, Op 10/3 (1833)	Chopin	
Invocation	Piano Sonata No 35 in F minor, Op 77 (1809)	Dusík, J L	In which the composer invokes the aid of benevolent powers in his struggle with fate
Irdisches und Gottliches in Menschenleben	Symphony No 7 in C for double orchestra, Op 121 (1841)	Spohr	'Mundane and Godly in the Lives of Men'. The work comprises a contest between childish innocence and worldly sophistication, the former overcoming the latter
Irene	Nonet for woodwind and strings	Holbrooke	
Irresolu, L'	Symphony in B flat, Post 11 (1780–90?)	Kozeluh, L	
Italian	Concerto in F for harpsichord solo, BWV 971 (1735)	Bach	A rare example of a concerto without orchestra; *Italian* refers to the fact that the work is in the traditional three movements of Italian invention: fast–slow–fast
Italian	Symphony No 4 (16) in A, Op 90 (1833)	Mendelssohn	A musical picture of the composer's impressions of Italy
Jason and the Golden Fleece	Symphony, Kr 79 (*c* 1784)	Dittersdorf	No 7 of twelve symphonies based on Ovid's *Metamorphoses*
Jaune	Symphony for tape	Boisselet	Based on the past and future history of the Chinese people
Jean de la Peur	Symphony No 1	Landowski	
'Jena'	Symphony in C (*c* 1797)	Witt	Published in Jena, and long thought to be an early work of Beethoven
Jephta	Symphony No 5 (1964)	Toch	
'Jeunehomme'	Piano Concerto in E flat, K 271 (1777)	Mozart	Perhaps written for Mlle Jeunehomme, who possibly visited Salzburg in 1776
Johannes Uppenbareles	Symphony No 4 (1944)	Rosenberg	
'Joyous Peasant'	Song Without Words in A, Op 102/5 (1845)	Mendelssohn	
'Jupiter'	Symphony No 41 in C, K 551 (1788)	Mozart	The earliest known use of the name was in 1819
Jeremiah	Symphony No 2 (1943)	Bernstein	
Kaddisch	Symphony No 3 (1963)	Bernstein	
'Kegelstadt'	Trio in E flat for piano, clarinet, and viola, K 498 (1786)	Mozart	'Skittle-alley' trio, said to have been planned out in the composer's head during a game of skittles
Khaldis	Concerto for piano, four trumpets, and percussion, Op 91	Hovhaness	
Kreutzer	Sonata in A for violin and piano, Op 47 (1803)	Beethoven	Dedicated to the French composer/violinist Rodolphe Kreutzer
Kreutzer Sonata	String Quartet No 1 (1923)	Janáček	An example of art begetting art begetting art. Beethoven's *Kreutzer Sonata* led to the writing of Tolstoy's book of the same name. Janáček wrote a piano trio on the subject in 1908, and much later dealt with it again in his first string quartet
Kullervo	Symphony, Op 7 (1891–92)	Sibelius	Kullervo is a hero of Finnish legend
Kurländische	Six Sonatas for keyboard, Op 3, Denn 40 (1782)	Reichardt	Dedicated to Herzogin von Kurland
Ladder, The	Symphony No 3	Tzvetanov, T	
Lamentatione d'Ariana	Concerto in E flat for violin and strings, Op 7/6 (1741)	Locatelli	
Leningrad	Symphony No 7 in C, Op 60 (1941)	Shostakovitch	Composed during the Siege of Leningrad, while the composer was trapped in the city
Leonore	Symphony No 5 in E (1873)	Raff	Inspired by a ballad written by G A Bürger

Name or sub-title	*Work*	*Composer*	*Remarks*
'Linz'	Symphony No 36 in C, K 425 (1783)	Mozart	Composed in Linz
'Little'	Symphony No 6 in C, D 589 (1818)	Schubert	So called simply to distinguish the work from the 'Great' Symphony, No 9, in the same key
'Little Russian'	Symphony No 2 in C minor, Op 17 (1872)	Tchaikovsky	The finale uses a folk-song, 'The Crane', from Little Russia (ie the Ukraine)
Liturgique	Symphony No 3 (1945–46)	Honegger	A work of religious character. The movement titles are: 'I: Dies irae'; 'II: De profundis clamavi'; 'III: Dona nobis pacem'
'Lost Happiness'	Song Without Words in C minor, Op 38/2 (1838)	Mendelssohn	
'Lost Illusions'	Song Without Words in F sharp minor, Op 67/2 (1845)	Mendelssohn	
'Madrigalesco'	Concerto in D minor for strings, P 86	Vivaldi	A religious title to indicate the seriousness of the piece
Maggia, La	Canzona No 5 in four parts (1584)	Maschera	
Maggot, A	Organ Concerto No 3: second movement	Arne	A 'Maggot' is an old English dance
Maniatico, Il	Symphony No 33 in C minor (1786)	Brunetti	There is a prominent solo cello part which runs wild and has to be calmed by the orchestra. One of Brunetti's great rivals in Madrid was Boccherini, who was famous as a cello-player
Maria Antonia	Concerto in G minor for harpsichord and strings, Denn 7 (1777)	Reichardt	Dedicated to Maria Antonia
Mars	Symphony in D	Pichl	The origin of the title is unknown, but since several other of his 88 symphonies were based on mythological subjects, possibly this martial work has some connection with the god of war
Matrimonial Tiff	Sonata in C for piano quintet (1796)	Vogler	A musical picture of a domestic incident
'May Breezes'	Song Without Words in G, Op 62/1 (1844)	Mendelssohn	
May Day	Symphony No 3 in E flat, Op 20 (1930)	Shostakovitch	Written to commemorate the national holiday of the working classes
Mélancolique	Sonata in F sharp minor, Op 49	Moscheles	
Meridional	Sonatina No 5 in D for guitar	Ponce	
Merry Ditties	Concerto for orchestra	Shchedrin	
Metamorfoser	Symphony No 4	Bentzon	
Midas Judges the Contest between Pan and Apollo	Symphony (LOST) Kr 83 (*c* 1784)	Dittersdorf	No 11 of twelve symphonies based on Ovid's *Metamorphoses*
Milanese, La	Canzona in eight parts, Op 18 (1639)	Viadana	
Military	Violin Concerto No 2 in D, Op 21	Lipinski, K	
'Minute Waltz'	Waltz in D flat, Op 64/1 (1847)	Chopin	Supposed to take only one minute to perform. Also called 'Dog Waltz'
Mondo al rovescio, Il	See *Proteo*		
Montevideo	Symphony No 2	Gottschalk	
'Moonlight'	Sonata in C sharp minor, Op 27/2 (1801)	Beethoven	Imaginative title without authority
'Morning Song'	Song Without Words in G, Op 62/4 (1844)	Mendelssohn	
Musica Notturna delle strade di Madrid, La	String Quartet in C, Gér 324 (1780)	Boccherini	'Night music in the streets of Madrid.' This wildly descriptive piece of merriment includes impressions of a little prayer bell, street singers, blind beggars, and a military retreat

Name or Sub-title	Work	Composer	Remarks
'Musikalische Spass'	Serenade in F, K 522 (1787)	Mozart	This musical joke is on everyone from Mozart's contemporaries to the modern listener
'Musique pour célébrer des grandes hommes . . .'	Symphony in D	Reicha, A	See p 100 for details and full title
Mysterious Mountain	Symphony No 2, Op 132	Hovhaness	
Nanga Parvat	Symphony No 7, Op 178	Hovhaness	
'New World'	See 'From the New World'		
Nightwatchman	Serenade in C for bass singer and strings	Biber	Also known as *Ronde de Nuit, La*
Noire	Symphony	Boisselet	A musico-political work discussing the future of the Negro
'Notte, La'	Concerto in B flat for bassoon and strings, P 401	Vivaldi	Descriptive works. P 342 was later published as Op 10/2 for flute and strings (*c* 1729–30)
	Concerto in G minor, for flute, bassoon, and strings, P 342	Vivaldi	
'Nullte'	Symphony in D minor (1864, revised 1869)	Bruckner	Symphony No '0', an unnumbered early work
'Ocean'	Symphony No 2 in C, Op 42 (1854)	Rubinstein	
October	Symphony No 2 in C, Op 14 (1927)	Shostakovitch	Commemorates the October Revolution. See also *1917*
On Sjølund's Fair Plains	Symphony No 1 in C minor, Op 5 (1842)	Gade	The first movement is based on the melody which the composer had used in 1840 in his setting of Ingemann's song of that name
'Organ'	Symphony No 3 in C minor, Op 78 (1886)	Saint-Saëns	An organ has a prominent part in the second half of the work
Orpheus and Euridice	Symphony (LOST), Kr 82	Dittersdorf	No 10 of twelve symphonies based on Ovid's *Metamorphoses*
'Overture in the Italian Style'	Symphony No 32 in G, K 318 (1779)	Mozart	A one-movement work with a slow section in central position. (See *Italian,* above)
'Overtures in the Italian Style'	Overture in C, D 591 (1817) Overture in D, D 590 (1817)	Schubert	Both works imitate the features of the typical Rossini overture popular at that time
Padovana, La	Canzona à eight for two instrumental choirs	Viadana	
Pantomima	Symphony in A (*c* 1768)	Vanhal	
'Paris'	Overture in B flat, K 311A (1778?)	Mozart	Doubtful. Supposed to have been written as a second 'Paris' Symphony during Mozart's visit there in 1778
'Paris'	Symphony No 31 in D, K 297 (1778)	Mozart	This is the symphony Mozart is known to have written for Paris (see above)
'Pastoral' or 'Pastorale'	For the 150 years from 1700 fashion demanded that every composer should produce at least one instrumental pastorale. During the first half of this period the pastorale had religious connotations, it being used as background music, so to speak, to Nativity scenes. Later, however (and earlier in the case of Vivaldi), the shepherds and shepherdesses were felt to have their own intrinsic musical value, so that a connection with events at Bethlehem became rare. In addition to the list below, there are well-known movements by Corelli, Torelli, Pez, and Locatelli, etc, usually in so-called 'Christmas' concertos.		
	Symphony No 6 in F, Op 68 (1806)	Beethoven	
	Piano Sonata in D, Op 28 (1801)	Beethoven	
	Symphony in F (*c* 1780)	Cannabich	
	Pastoral Symphony (1742)	Handel	'Symphony' used here in the sense of 'interlude for instruments'; this is No 13 in *Messiah*
	Symphony No 2	McPhee, C	
	Sonatas for harpsichord in D minor, L 413, Kk 9 in F, L 433, Kk 446 in C, L Supp 3, Kk 513	Scarlatti, D	Of the named sonatas which are, or could be, so called, we have chosen three of the best known
	Symphony in D, DTBIIIi: D4	Stamitz, J	
	Symphony in D minor	Tartini	

Name or sub-title	*Work*	*Composer*	*Remarks*
	Symphony No 3 (1922)	Vaughan Williams	
	Symphony in D (*c* 1750)	Werner	
'Pastorella'	Symphony in D, Op 5/3, BSB 27 (1761/62)	Gossec	
	Concerto in D for flute, oboe, violin, bassoon, and bass (or for two violins, bassoon, and bass) P 204	Vivaldi	
'Pastor Fido, Il'	See 'Faithful Shepherd', above		
Pastoritia	Symphony in G (*c* 1775)	Zimmermann	
På Sjølunds fagre Sletter	See *On Sjølund's Fair Plains,* above		
'Pathétique'	Piano Sonata in C minor, Op 13 (1798)	Beethoven	
	Symphony No 6 in B minor, Op 74 (1893)	Tchaikovsky	
Pauern Kirchfahrt genandt	Sonata in B flat for two violins, two violas, violone, and bass (late 17th century)	Biber	A country church-going, with imitations of the sounds of the Sabbath, ending up in the local tavern
Peasants Turned into Frogs, The	Symphony (LOST), Kr 78	Dittersdorf	No 6 of twelve symphonies based on Ovid's *Metamorphoses*
Perfidia	Keyboard Sonata No 28 in B flat	Cimarosa	
Phineus and his Followers are turned to Stone	Symphony (LOST), Kr 77	Dittersdorf	No 5 of twelve symphonies based on Ovid's *Metamorphoses*
'Piacere'	Concerto in C for violin and strings, P 7, Op 8/6 (*c* 1725)	Vivaldi	
'Piacevolezza'	String Quartet No 4 in F, Op 44 (originally Op 19) (1906)	Nielsen	Title discarded by the composer when the work was published
'Polish'	Symphony No 3 in D, Op 29 (1875)	Tchaikovsky	The main theme of the finale is in the rhythm of a polacca
'Post-horn'	Serenade in D, K 320 (1778)	Mozart	A solo post-horn figures in the second trio of the sixth movement
'Prague'	Symphony No 38 in D, K 504 (1786)	Mozart	Written for performance in that city
Prodigal Son	Symphony No 4 in C, Op 47 (1930) (revised 1947: Op 112)	Prokofiev	Based partly on music used in the ballet of that name
Prophéte, Le	Violin Concerto No 2 (1939)	Castelnuovo-Tedesco	
'Proteo, Il'	Concerto in F for violin, cello, and strings, P 308	Vivaldi	In full: 'Proteus, or the World Turned upside-down'. An 'Echo' concerto in which the composer indulges in fantasies suggested by the title
Prussian	String Quartets, K 575, 589, 590	Mozart	
Prussian Sonatas	Six keyboard Sonatas, W 48 (pub 1742)	Bach, C P E	The first works produced under the patronage of Frederick the Great, King of Prussia
	Six Sonatas for harpsichord, Denn 35 (pub 1775)	Reichardt	Dedicated to Frederike Luise von Preussen
Putain, La	Suite in G	Telemann(?)	*The Prostitute.* This introduces themes and ideas drawn from 'low life' in Hamburg. movement titles include: 'Die Schneckenpost' (Tavern song); 'Die Bauren Kirchweyh' (The Peasants' Church Dance) – compare *Pauern Kirchfahrt,* above – 'Der Hexen-Tantz' (Seductress's Dance); 'Die Baas Lisabeth' ('Cousin' Lizzie); and 'Der Vetter Michel Ziehbart' (Playboy cousin Goatbeard)
'Rage over a Lost Penny'	Rondo a Capriccio in G for piano, Op 129 (1803)	Beethoven	An early-19th-century nickname perhaps indicating that the work seemed to be a storm in a teacup
'Rain'	Violin Sonata No 1 in G, Op 78 (1879)	Brahms	

Name or Sub-title	Work	Composer	Remarks
'Raindrop'	Prelude in D flat, Op 28/15 (1839)	Chopin	The insistent patter of rain outside his study window is supposed to have given Chopin the idea for the repeated notes to be heard in this Prelude
'Razumovsky'	Three String Quartets, Op 59 (1806)	Beethoven	Dedicated to Count Razumovsky
Reformation	Symphony No 5 (17) in D minor, Op 107 (1830)	Mendelssohn	Written to commemorate the 300th Anniversary of the Augsburg Confession
'Regrets'	Song Without Words, Op 19b/2 in A minor (1830)	Mendelssohn	
'Reliquie'	Sonata in C, D 840 (1825)	Schubert	Refers to the fact that only the first two movements of this Sonata were completed. They were published in 1861 as *Last* [sic] *Sonata – Unfinished*
Representatio Avium	Sonata in A for violin and bass	Biber	The 'birds' of the title include: bat, cuckoo, frog, hen, cock, quail, cat, and a 'March of the Gnats'
Rescue of Andromeda by Perseus	Symphony (LOST), Kr 76	Dittersdorf	No 4 of twelve symphonies based on Ovid's *Metamorphoses*
'Restlessness'	Song Without Words in F sharp minor, Op 19b/5 (1830)	Mendelssohn	
Return and Build the Desolate Places	Concerto for Trumpet and Wind Orchestra, Op 213	Hovhaness	
Return to Paris	Piano Sonata No 13 in A flat, Op 70 (1807)	Dusík, J L	Reflects an event in the composers life, after the collapse of his publishing firm in London
'Revolutionary'	Etude in C minor, Op 10/12 (1833)	Chopin	
Rhenish	Symphony No 3 in E flat, Op 97	Schumann	Evokes the composer's feelings of life in the Rheinland
'Riposo, Il'	Concerto in E for violin and strings, P 208	Vivaldi	A relaxed and reposeful work
'Ritiro, Il'	Concerto in F for violin and strings, P 256	Vivaldi	
	Concerto in E flat for violin and strings, Fanna I:231	Vivaldi	Discovered after the completion of Pincherle's catalogue
Ritmico	Symphony (1932)	Jelinek	
'Romantic'	Symphony No 4 in E flat (1874, revised 1878 and 1880)	Bruckner	This work originally possessed a 'programme' in the Romantic manner which was later suppressed by the composer
'Romantic'	Piano Sonata in F sharp minor, Op 184	Rheinberger, J	
Romeo and Juliet	Symphony No 4, Op 17 (1839)	Berlioz	A programmatic 'Dramatic' symphony based on Shakespeare's play
Ronde de Nuit, Le	Serenade in C for bass voice and strings	Biber	Also known as *The Nightwatchman* Serenade. It features the call of the night patrol: 'All's Well'
'Rosary Sonatas'	Sixteen Sonatas for violin and bass	Biber	Based on the 'Mysteries of Joy' (Nos 1–5), 'of Sorrow' (6–10), and 'of Glory' (11–16)
Rouge	Symphony	Boisselet	A politico-musical composition
Rustica	Symphony No 1 (1949)	Panufnik	
Rustic Wedding	Symphony, Op 26 (1876)	Goldmark	(originally 'Landliche Holhzeit')
Sacra	Symphony No 3 (1963)	Panufnik	
'Sadness of Soul'	Song Without Words in F, Op 53/4 (1841)	Mendelssohn	Also known as 'Berceuse'
Saga of a Prarie School	Symphony No 7	Gillis	Programmatic work
'Saint Anne's Fugue'	Fugue in E flat for organ, BWV 552	Bach	The theme is similar to the first line of the hymn 'Saint Anne' by Croft
Saint Vartan	Symphony No 9, Op 80 (1950)	Hovhaness	Written to commemorate the 1500th Anniversary of the Death of Saint Vartan Marmikonian, the Armenian warrior, in 451

Carl Maria Friedrich Ernst Von Weber (1786–1826) (Royal College of Music)

Name or sub-title	Work	Composer	Remarks
Same Atnam	Symphony No 3	Petersen-Berger	
'Santa Lingua di Sant'Antonio'	Concerto in D for violin, two oboes, and strings, P 165	Vivaldi	An occasional work
'Santo Sepolcro, Al'	Sonata in E flat for strings, P 441	Vivaldi	Written for religious occasions
	Symphony in B minor for strings, P Sinf 21	Vivaldi	
'S.A.R. di Sassonia'	Concerto in G minor for three oboes, three violins, two flutes, two bassoons, two harpsichords, violas, and bass, P 359	Vivaldi	Written for the Elector of Saxony in Dresden: 'Per la Sua Altezza Reale di Sassonia'
Schluckenauer	Harpsichord Concerto in G, Denn 2 (1772)	Reichardt	Written at Schluckenau
Scottish'	Symphony No 3 (15) in A minor, Op 56 (1829–42)	Mendelssohn	Like the *Fingal's Cave* Overture, this work reflects the impressions the composer gained during his visit to Scotland
Seasons, The	Symphony No 9 in B flat, Op 143 (1849)	Spohr	A descriptive work which treats the seasons. Like Glazunov's ballet, the cycle starts with 'Winter'
	Four Violin Concertos, Op 8/1–4, P 241, 336, 257, 442 (*c* 1725)	Vivaldi	
Sea	Symphony No 1 in C for soprano, baritone, chorus, and orchestra (1912)	Vaughan Williams	Based on Walt Whitman's poems. The movement titles are: 'I: A Song for All Seas, All Ships'; 'II: On the Beach at Night, Alone'; 'III: The Waves'; 'IV: The Explorers'
Semplice	Symphony No 6 (1924–26)	Nielsen	
	Symphony No 6 (1951)	Rosenberg	
'Senza Cantin'	Concerto in D minor for violin and strings, P 310	Vivaldi	The E string ('cantin') is to be removed from the solo violin, thus rendering the concerto extremely difficult to play
'Serenade'	Song Without Words in E, Op 67/6 (1845)	Mendelssohn	
Serieuse	Symphony No 2 in G minor (1842)	Berwald	
Seven	Symphony	Koechlin	see Section IV
'Shepherd Boy'	Etude in A flat, Op 25/1 (1837)	Chopin	
'Shepherd's Complaint'	Song Without Words in B minor, Op 67/5 (1845)	Mendelssohn	Also known as 'Song of the Heather'
Short	Symphony No 2 (1931–33)	Copland	
Siege of Megare	Symphony (LOST), Kr 80	Dittersdorf	No 8 of twelve symphonies based on Ovid's *Metamorphoses*
Siegeslied	Symphony No 4 (1932–33) for soprano, chorus, and orchestra	Brian	'The Psalm of Victory', based on Luther's German text for Psalm 68
Silver Pilgrimage	Symphony No 15, Op 199	Hovhaness	
Simple	Symphony, Op 4 (1934)	Britten	Written for the young. The movement titles are: 'I: Boisterous Bourée'; 'II: Playful pizzicato'; 'III: Sentimental Sarabande'; 'IV: Frolicsome Finale'
Sinfonia da Requiem	Symphony, Op 20 (1940)	Britten	Written to the memory of the composer's parents
Singulière	Symphony No 4 in C (1845)	Berwald	
'Solennità di S. Lorenzo'	See 'Feast of Saint Lawrence'		
'Song of the Heather'	Song Without Words in B minor, Op 67/5 (1845)	Mendelssohn	Also known as 'Shepherd's Complaint'
Song of the Night	Symphony No 3	Szymanowsky	
'Song of Triumph'	Song Without Words in A minor, Op 53/5 (1841)	Mendelssohn	Also known as 'Folk Song'
'Sordino, Con'	Concerto in F for flute, muted strings, and muted harpsichord, P 262, Op 10/5 (*c* 1729–30)	Vivaldi	
'Sospetto, Il'	Concerto in C minor for violin and strings, P 419	Vivaldi	

Name or sub-title	*Work*	*Composer*	*Remarks*
Sperantis gardia	Suite in G minor for strings (1695–98?)	Muffat	
'Spinning Song'	Song Without Words in C, Op 67/4 (1845)	Mendelssohn	Also known as 'Bee's Wedding'
Spiritata, La	Canzona I, à four (1608)	Gabrieli, G	
'SS. Assunzione di Maria Vergine'	See 'Assunzione', above		
Study	Symphony in F minor (1863)	Bruckner	Originally meant by the composer to be an exercise in orchestration and composition, this work has established itself recently as a work in its own right
Steinkerque, La	Trio Sonata in B flat for flute, oboe, and bassoon (1692)	Couperin, F	
'Storm at Sea'	Concerto in E flat for violin and strings, P 415, Op 8/5 (*c* 1725)	Vivaldi	Both of Vivaldi's works depict the chaotic drama of a sea storm in their first movements; that of Zavateri does so in its last. However, it should be stated that such chaos, as depicted in the musical language of the early 18th century, is very mild indeed. See also *Tempesta del' Mar*
	Concerto in F for flute, oboe, violin, bassoon, and strings, P 261, (Op 10/1 for flute and strings, *c* 1729–30)	Vivaldi	
	Concerto for violin and strings, Op 1/12 (1735)	Zavateri	
'Stravaganza, La'	Twelve Concertos for violin and strings, Op 4 (*c* 1712/13)	Vivaldi	
Sultane, La	Sonata à four (*c* 1695)	Couperin, F	
'Sweet Remembrances'	Song Without Words in E, Op 19b/1 (1830)	Mendelssohn	
Symphonie Fantastique	See *Fantastique,* above		
'Symphony for Fun'	Symphony No 5½	Gillis	The movement titles are: 'I: Perpetual Emotion'; 'II: Spiritual?'; 'III: Scherzofrenia'; 'IV: Conclusion!'
'Symphony of a Thousand'	Symphony No 8 in E flat (1907)	Mahler	see Section V
'Tarantella'	Song Without Words in C, Op 102/3 (1845)	Mendelssohn	
'Tempest'	Sonata in D minor, Op 31/2 (1802)	Beethoven	
'Tempesta di Mare'	See 'Storm at sea'		
Tempesta del'Mar, La	Symphony in E flat, Op 4/3 (*c* 1760)	Holzbauer	
Three Journeys to a Holy Mountain	Symphony No 20 for full band, Op 223	Hovhaness	
Three Mysteries, The	Symphony No 3, Op 48 (1950)	Creston	The movements are entitled: 'I: The Nativity'; 'II: The Crucifixion'; 'III: The Resurrection'
Titan, The	Symphony No 1 in D (1888)	Mahler	Thus named by the composer, after the novel by Jean Paul
'Torrent, The'	Etude in C sharp minor, Op 10/4 (1833)	Chopin	
To the Memory of an Angel	Violin Concerto (1935)	Berg	The 'Angel' was Manon Gropius, the daughter of Mahler's widow
Tragic	Symphony No 4 in C minor, D 417 (1816)	Schubert	Title added later by Schubert himself
Tragica	Symphony No 6 in D minor (1948)	Brian	Originally written as the Overture (or Prelude) to a projected opera based on Synge's tragedy *Deirdre of the Sorrows*
'Tristesse'	Etude in E, Op 10/3 (1833)	Chopin	
'Trout, The'	Quintet in A for piano and strings, D 667 (1819)	Schubert	The fourth movement is a set of theme and variations on the composer's song 'Die Forelle' ('The Trout'), D 550
'Unfinished'	Symphony No 8 in B minor, D 759 (1822)	Schubert	Long thought to consist of only two movements, attempts have been made recently to complete the work from the remaining sketches and from some of the *Rosamunde* music

Name or Sub-title	Work	Composer	Remarks
Universe	Symphony	Ives	A planned but only partially sketched work first considered in 1915 but not complete at the composer's death in 1951. (See Section V: Biggest?)
'Venetian Gondola Song'	Songs Without Words: in G minor, Op 19b/6 (1830); in F sharp minor, Op 30/6 (1834); in A minor, Op 62/5 (1844)	Mendelssohn	
'Villanelle'	Etude in G flat, Op 25/9 (1837)	Chopin	
Vishnu	Symphony No 19, Op 217	Hovhaness	
Voces Intimae	String Quartet in D minor, Op 56 (1909)	Sibelius	An authentic title, suggested by the character of the slow (third) movement
'Wagner'	Symphony No 3 in D minor (1873, revised 1878, 1889, and 1890)	Bruckner	Dedicated to that composer
Wahrheit der Natur	Symphony in F, Perger 46 (1769?)	Haydn, J M	Taken from the music to a 'mythological operetta' of this title. The full title is: *Die Wahrheit der Natur in den drey irdischen Grazien, nämlich in der Dichtkunst, Musik, und Malerey.* ('The Truth of Nature, in the Three Earthly Graces, namely, Poetry, Music, and Painting')
'Waldstein'	Piano Sonata in C, Op 53 (1803–4)	Beethoven	Dedicated to Count Waldstein
'Wanderer, Der'	Fantasia in C for piano, D 760 (1822)	Schubert	The second movement is based on the song of this name, D 493
'Wedge'	Fugue in E minor, BVW 548	Bach, J S	So called from the ever-widening intervals of the theme
Weimarer	Six Sonatas for harpsichord, Denn 36 (1778)	Reichardt	Dedicated to Anna Amalia von Weimar
'Wellington's Victory'	See 'Battle of Vittoria', above		
White Mass	Sonata No 7 in F, Op 64 (1911)	Scriabin	
Wine of Summer, The	Symphony No 5 (1937)	Brian	Based on the poem by Lord Alfred Douglas
'Winter'	Concerto in F minor for violin and strings, P 442, Op 8/4 (*c* 1725)	Vivaldi	No 4 of four concertos descriptive of the four seasons
'Winter Daydreams'	Symphony No 1 in G minor, Op 13 (1866)	Tchaikovsky	Taken from the title of the first movement: 'Daydreams on a Wintry Road'
'Winter Wind'	Etude in A minor, Op 25/11 (1837)	Chopin	
Wratislaw	Six Concertos for keyboard and orchestra, Op 1, Denn 1 (1772)	Reichardt	
'Württemburg'	Six Sonatas for keyboard, W 49 (pub 1744)	Bach, C P E	
Zartik Parkim	Concerto for piano and chamber orchestra, Op 77	Hovhaness	
1905	Symphony No 11 in G minor, Op 103 (1957)	Shostakovitch	Written to commemorate the abortive revolution of that year
1917	Symphony No 12 in D minor, Op 112 (1961)	Shostakovitch	Celebrates the successful Bolshevik Revolution of 1917. See also *October*

The composer of the most works to which nicknames have been appended is Franz Joseph Haydn. As the author of many hundreds of works, he was not averse to the occasional nickname to assist his audiences' memories, but most of the titles which have become attached to his compositions are not authentic, often stemming from publishers' sales efforts after the composer's death. The names in the following list, therefore, may be regarded as unauthentic unless otherwise stated.

It is believed that this is the first time a 'complete' list of these nicknames, with remarks as to their origins, has been published all together. Doubtless the reader will know of some which have been overlooked unintentionally here; he may even be willing to supply some of his own invention. Letters connected with matters discussed in this book will be welcome, but those airing their writers' imaginations in the invention of mnemonic titles for Haydn's music will probably be ignored.

NICKNAMES AND SUB-TITLES OF WORKS BY HAYDN

Work and Title	*Date*	*Origin of name (where known)*
Symphonies		
No 1 in D, 'Lukaveč	1759?	The work was written at Lukaveč, the estate of Count Morzin for whom Haydn worked between 1759 and 1761. This Bohemian estate saw the production of several early Haydn symphonies, each of which has equal right to the title
No 6 in D, *Le Matin* No 7 in C, *Le Midi* No 8 in G, *Le Soir*	1761	Authentic titles referring to the programmatic nature of this set of works which Haydn produced for his new employer Prince Paul Anton Esterházy, whose service he joined in May 1761. Apart from the obvious effects such as the representation of the rising sun at the start of No 6 (cf the Quartet Op 76/4), a music lesson in the slow movement of the same work (cf the Divertimento in F, Hob XVIIa:1), and a mild thunderstorm, called 'la Tempestà', in the finale of No 8, the works are not rich in pictorial representation
No 13 in D, 'Jupiter'	1763	A recent (mid-20th-century) name adopted simply because the opening theme of the finale has a superficial resemblance to that of the finale of Mozart's 'Jupiter' Symphony. The retention of this name is not recommended lest further accidental similarities lead to yet more confusion
No 22 in E flat, 'The Philosopher'	1764	A late-18th-century (and therefore less unauthentic than others) invention referring to the deep and brooding character of the first movement
No 26 in D minor 'Lamentatione'	*c* 1768	Widely used in the 18th century, this appropriate name accurately describes the character of religious intensity behind the music
No 27 in G, 'Brukenthal' or 'Hermannstädter'	*c* 1760	Both titles refer to the curious circumstances surrounding what was thought to be the discovery of a 'new' Haydn symphony in 1946 in Baron Brukenthal's library at Hermannstadt in Transylvania (now Romania). The work was recorded and publicly performed as a newly discovered Haydn symphony before it was realised that other sources for the work had been known long enough for it to have been included in the standard numerical listing
No 30 in C, *Alleluja*	1765	A probably authentic title referring to the use of a Gregorian alleluja theme in the first movement
No 31 in D, 'Hornsignal'; also 'Auf dem Anstand'	1765	Nineteenth century descriptive titles referring to the hunting-horn fanfares in the first and last movements
No 38 in C, 'Echo'	*c* 1766/8	A modern title referring to the persistent use of the echo device in the slow movement (cf the Divertimento in E flat, Hob II:39)
No 39 in G minor, 'The Fist'	*c* 1768	A ludicrous apellation originating very recently (in the office of a sales-conscious record company executive?) which refers to the uncompromisingly severe nature of the music
No 43 in E flat, 'Mercury'	*c* 1771	A nickname of obscure and antique origin which may refer to the brilliant (mercurial) violin passagework in the outer movements
No 44 in E minor, 'Trauer'	*c* 1771	From the end of the 18th century. The feeling of the music is one of grief and mourning

Work and Title	*Date*	*Origin of name (where known)*
No 45 in F sharp minor, *Farewell*	1772	A probably authentic, and certainly appropriate, title. In the autumn of 1772, Haydn's band, who were expected to work hard for many months at Prince Nicholaus Esterházy's summer residence in rural Hungary, without the comforts of a proper home and family life, asked Haydn if he, as head of musical activities, could find a way to convince the Prince that it was time to leave for the winter. Haydn, the subtle and sensitive diplomat, took his latest symphony and modified the ending of the finale to which he added a long slow section in which the instrumentalists are directed, one by one, to stop playing, put out their candles, and quietly leave the platform. At last, only two players were left, Haydn himself and his leader Luigi Tomasini. It is reported that the Prince immediately saw the point of the joke against him and decided to leave the castle the very next day
No 48 in C, 'Maria Theresia'; also 'Sancta Theresia'	1769?	Originally thought to have been written for the visit to Esterháza of the Empress Maria Theresia in 1773, recent evidence indicates that the work involved was really Symphony No 50 in the same key. Reference to Saint Theresia comes from a partly misunderstood identification which became entered on a copy of the work at Frýdlant Castle in Czechoslovakia
No 49 in F minor, 'La Passione'	1768	A reference to the sombre nature of the work. It may be assumed, without evidence, that the work was involved in some way with the Easter activities at Esterháza
No 53 in D, 'Imperial'	*c* 1777	A general nickname referring to the ceremonial style of the opening movement
No 55 in E flat, 'Schoolmaster'	1774	The slow movement, 'Adagio, ma semplicemente', is written in a plodding rhythm which apparently suggested to 19th-century listeners an elderly schoolmaster, cane in hand, portentously patrolling his charges
No 59 in A, 'Fire'	*c* 1766/68	The movements were apparently used between or during the acts of the play *Die Feuersbrunst* ('The Burning House'), given at Esterháza in 1773/74
No 60 in C, *Il Distratto*	1774	A symphony reconstructed (in six movements!) from music for the play *Der Zerstreute (Le Distrait,* or *Il Distratto,* 'The Absent-Minded One'), performed at Pressburg (Bratislava) in 1774. Unlike that for No 59, the title of No 60 has unquestionable authenticity
No 63 in C, *La Roxelane*	1777?	Following the precedents for No 60, this work should be called either 'Il Mondo della Luna' ('The World of the Moon'), the Overture of which became the first movement, or 'Soliman II', since it was into the latter play, given at Esterháza in 1777, that Haydn injected a piece for the heroine, La Roselane. Her aria later became the basis for the variations in the slow movement of the symphony
No 64 in A, *Tempora mutantor*	*c* 1775	In full: *'Tempora mutantui, etc.'* For a fascinating solution to the hitherto obscure origin of this strange title, the authors are indebted to an article (see Bibliography) by Jonathan Foster of Liverpool University. He points out that the words open the epigram 'O Tempora' by John Owen: Tempora mutantur, nos et mutamur in illis: quomodo? fit semper tempore peior homo Thomas Harvey's 1677 translation gives: The Times are Chang'd, and in them Chang'd are we: How? Man, as Times grow worse, grows worse, we see. Jonathan Foster goes on to show that the opening Latin line, repeated, fits the music of the first twelve bars of the finale of Haydn's Symphony No 64
No 69 in C, *Laudon* [*sic*]	*c* 1778	A completely authentic title (apart from the spelling). Haydn recommended to his publisher in 1783 that the work be headed with the name of the most famous Austrian Field-Marshal of the day: Ernst Gideon, Freiherr von Loudon (1717–90)
No 73 in D, *La Chasse*	1781	An authentic title, taken from the character of the finale (presto). The movement was first written as the Overture to *La Fedeltà premiata* ('Fidelity rewarded'), performed at Esterháza in 1781, for which it sets the scene of sylvan blood-lust

Work and Title	*Date*	*Origin of name (where known)*
No 82 in C, 'The Bear'	1786	A title added by early French audiences ('L'Ours') to characterise the growling start of the finale
No 83 in G minor, 'The Hen'	1785	Another naïve name ('La Poule') referring to the clucking motive in the first movement and perhaps also to that in the Andante
No 85 in B flat, *La Reine de France*	1785/86	The first French edition carried the name. It is reported that the work was a favourite of Queen Marie-Antoinette (1755 – guillotined 1793); the title must have greatly assisted Haydn's popularity before the Queen's fall from grace a few years later
No 88 in G, 'Letter V'	*c* 1787	An unhelpful title which refers only to the designation given to the work in the catalogue of the old Philharmonic Society in London, which went on to identify No 89 in F as 'Letter W'. It is to be hoped that the title of No 88 will slip into the oblivion from which that for No 89 has never emerged
No 92 in G, 'Oxford'	1789	Played in that city on the occasion of the composer receiving his Honorary Doctorate of Music in 1791. The work was in fact dedicated to Le Comte d'Ogny, as were Nos 82–86, and was not specifically composed for Oxford
No 94 in G, *Surprise*	1791	Known as *Paukenschlag* ('Drum stroke') in Germany. Authentic titles, in that they were used during Haydn's London visits in 1791–95. In the Andante, after a quiet statement and then another statement, quieter still, of the melody, a sudden fortissimo chord from full orchestra (ie not from timpani alone) punctuated the proceedings. Haydn is said to have remarked: 'This will startle the ladies.'
No 96 in D, *Miracle*	1791	Another migrating nickname (see No 48). At the popular concerts Haydn gave in London the audiences were often anxious to catch a closer glimpse of the composer at his keyboard and would move forward, leaving an empty space at the rear of the hall. On one such occasion a chandelier fell from the ceiling on to the empty seats. No one was hurt and the excited audience is said to have proclaimed that a miracle had occurred, and the title was immediately given to the symphony which was playing at the time. Unfortunately, not only has it now been proved that the symphony in question was No 102 in B flat (No 96 had been given at a concert three years earlier), but that the whole episode seems to have been exaggerated: *The Morning Chronicle* of the following day said in part: 'The last movement [of symphony No 102] was encored; and notwithstanding an interruption by the accidental fall of one of the chandeliers, it was performed with no less effect.'
No 100 in G, *Military*	1794	A wholly authentic title, approved by Haydn for inclusion in programme announcements. It refers to the use, unique in Haydn's symphonies, of Turkish military instruments in the second and fourth movements: triangle, cymbals, and bass drum
No 101 in D, 'Clock'	1794	The slow movement has a persistent rhythmic accompaniment said, by 19th-century concertgoers, to resemble the ticking of a clock. It may be fancifully conjectured that Haydn was thinking along the same lines: why else would he insert a whole bar of silence, at slow tempo, if not for rewinding?
No 102 in B flat, 'Miracle'	1794/95	See No 96
No 103 in E flat, 'Drum Roll'	1795	Known in Germany as *Paukenwirbel* ('Drum roll'). An appropriate name referring to the arresting opening of the first movement by a solo drum
No 104 in D, 'London'	1795	Haydn's last symphony, and one which is no more entitled to the name than any or all of the immediately preceding eleven since all were written for the English capital
Toy Symphony in C	*c* 1788?	An unauthentic work written by Leopold Mozart (father of Wolfgang). It comprises three movements (Nos 3, 4, and 7) of a *Sinfonia Berchtoldgadensis* (or Cassation) in G for toy instruments and orchestra which became attached to Haydn's name late in the 18th century. There is no evidence that Haydn had any hand in the work or its arrangement, yet the tradition that it should be included in his canon is remarkably tenacious

Work and Title	*Date*	*Origin of name (where known)*
String Quartets		
Op 1, No 1 in B flat, 'La Chasse'	1755–60?	The opening phrase is reminiscent of a hunting-call (cf Symphony No 73)
Op 3, No 5 in F, 'Serenade'	*c* 1760	Refers to the meltingly beautiful character of the slow movement. Recent research suggests that the Op 3 set may have been written partly by Romanus Hofstetter (1742–1815)
Op 17, No 5 in G, 'Recitative'	1771	The third movement makes use of operatic recitative technique
Op 20, Nos 1–6, 'Sun Quartets' also 'Great Quartets'	1772	The first edition by André of Offenbach in 1784, bears a striking rising sun motif on its title-page. The name 'Great Quartets' was used by Haydn's contemporaries, referring perhaps to the depth of feeling which Haydn had, for the first time, poured into the quartet form
Op 33, Nos 1–6, 'Russian Quartets', also 'Gli Scherzi'	1781	The set was dedicated to the visiting Grand Duke Paul of Russia (later Tsar Paul II), who expressed admiration for Haydn's music. Each work contains a movement described as 'Scherzo' or 'Scherzando' ('joke' or 'jokingly'), thus giving rise to the alternative nickname
Op 33, No 2 in E flat, 'Joke'		The last movement closes with a tantalising joke of the kind at which Haydn was so expert
Op 33, No 3 in C, 'Bird'		A name deriving from the bird impressions of the first movement
Op 33, No 5 in G, 'How do you do?'		In England the opening phrase of the work is said to resemble this interrogatory greeting, but in its country of origin the phrase would be difficult to fit to 'Wie geht's?'
Op 50, No 5 in F, 'Dream'	1787	The second movement possesses a mysterious, dream-like quality
Op 50, No 6 in D, 'Frog'	1787	Haydn, in the finale, employs a device known as 'bariolage', in which the same note is played on two different strings, one open the other 'stopped'. In rapid alternation this gives a curious croaking effect
Op 55, No 2 in F minor, 'Razor'	1788	The story goes that Haydn was experiencing difficulty when shaving and exclaimed: 'My best quartet for a good razor.' His publisher Bland, with great presence of mind, rushed out to purchase a razor, thereby clinching one of the best bargains of his life
Op 64, No 5 in D, 'Lark'; also 'Hornpipe'	1790	At the beginning of the first movement the first violin soars aloft, suggesting the flight of a lark to 19th-century audiences. The finale, a kind of moto perpetuo, has the character of a hornpipe
Op 74, No 3 in G minor, 'Rider' or 'Horseman'	1793	Rhythmic emphasis in both the first and last movements suggests the jerky motion of a horse-rider
Op 76, No 2 in D minor, 'Fifths'	1799	The quartet opens with a powerful theme based on the interval of the falling fifth. In the third movement the composer uses a device of continuous two-part canon between the violins in octaves on the one hand and the viola and cello, also in octaves, on the other. The result is an eerie melody which has led to the movement being called 'Hexenmenuet' ('Witches' Minuet')
Op 76, No 3 in C, 'Emperor'	1799	The world-famous theme of the slow movement, Poco Adagio cantabile, is said to have been inspired by the English National Anthem which Haydn heard during his London visits (see National Anthems in Section V). Haydn felt that the Austrian people, too, were entitled to a melody of equal grandeur and solemnity, and he proceeded to write one of far greater quality. The tune was arranged for all manner of instruments and groups, including a choral version as 'Gott erhalte Franz den Kaiser', and it exists to this day as an English hymn starting with the words 'Glorious things of Thee are spoken'. The original title for the movement gave rise to that for the quartet as a whole
Op 76, No 4 in B flat, 'Sunrise'	1799	At the start of the first movement the first violin gradually emerges from the harmonies like the rising sun (cf Symphony No 6)
Op 76, No 6 in E flat, 'Fantasia'	1799	A mnemonic title drawing attention to the existence as a second movement of a Fantasia in B major, a most unusual feature in a most unusual key
Masses		
No 2 in E flat, *Great Organ Mass*	*c* 1766	So called from the highly developed concertante organ parts in the Kyrie and Benedictus
No 4 in G, *Six-four-time Mass*	1772	Referring merely to the Pastorale-like character of the Kyrie
No 5 in B flat, *Little Organ Mass*	*c* 1775	An organ solo appears in the Benedictus. The distinction between 'Great' and 'Little' (see No 2) refers to the size of the forces used in the respective works, and to their duration

Work and Title	*Date*	*Origin of name (where known)*
No 6 in C, *Mariazellermesse*	1782	Written for the Austrian Monastery of Mariazell. An authentic name
No 7 in C, *Drum Mass,* also *Mass in Time of War*	1796	Written as Napoleon approached Vienna with his invading army, there is a powerful part for timpani in the Dona Nobis Pacem. The name *Drum Mass* was used during Haydn's lifetime, but *Mass in Time of War* is even more authentic since Haydn used it as a heading for the work
No 8 in B flat, *Heiligmesse*	1796	A German mnemonic title referring to the use in the Sanctus of an old hymn set to the words 'Heilig, heilig, heilig' ('Holy, holy, holy')
No 9 in D minor, *Nelson Mass*	1798	Completed and first performed during a time of Austrian rejoicing at the news of Nelson's victory over Napoleon at Ab'ukir. Nelson visited Haydn at Eisenstadt two years later, when the two men from such different professions exchanged congratulations and gifts
No 10 in B flat, 'Theresia Mass'	1799	Thought to have been written for the Empress Marie Therese, wife of Emperor Franz II, but now known to have been composed for the name-day of Princess Maria Hermenegild, as were the other five last Masses. The work actually composed for the Empress was the Te Deum in C of 1799; ie the same year as the present Mass, hence the confusion
No 11 in B flat, 'Creation Mass'	1801	The Gloria introduces a theme already famous from the oratorio *The Creation* of 1798
No 12 in B flat, 'Harmonie Mass'	1802	In German-speaking countries the word *harmonie* refers to groups of wind instruments playing together. In this, his last large-scale work, Haydn employed a large band of wind instruments, giving them unusual freedom among the textures
Other works with nicknames		
Divertimento in C, Hob II:11, 'Man and Wife', also 'The Birthday'	*c* 1761	In the second movement and finale, duets between violins and bass suggest dialogues between a man and his wife. The origin of the title 'The Birthday' is unknown
Divertimento in E flat, Hob II:39 'Echo'	*c* 1761	A work constructed in echo between the string orchestra and a string trio (cf Symphony No 38)
Divertimento in B flat, Hob II:46 'St Anthony'	pub 1780	The second movement and finale are based on the old *St Anthony Chorale.* Probably not an authentic work of Haydn, the attribution was given weight by Brahms's use of the melody in his *Variations on a Theme of Haydn*
Marches in E flat and C, Hob VIII:1; 'Two Derbyshire Marches' March 'For the Prince of Wales', in E flat, Hob VIII:3; also 'For the Royal Society of Musicians' March in E flat, Hob VIII:4 Hungarian National March		The names of these marches merely indicate the occasions or regiments for which they were written. A number of other marches ('Napoleon's March'; 'Napoleons Siegesmarsch'; 'Marsch fur das k.k. Infantrie-Regiment Coloredo' and 'Marsch Brillande' [*sic*] de la 66 Brigad des Chasseurs' are of doubtful authenticity
'Ox Minuet' in C, Hob IX:27		The story goes that Haydn was paid for a minuet, written for a wedding, by a live ox. The anecdote was worked into a 'vaudeville' (1823) with music by Haydn's pupil Ignaz Xavier Ritter von Seyfried (1776–1841), but it seems that, although the stage play was based on many of Haydn's compositions, arranged for the occasion, the 'Ox Minuet' itself was an invention of Seyfried himself
Capriccio in G, Hob XVII:1 'Acht Sauschneider müssen seyn'	1765	An early work employing a rural theme which was adopted also by other composers. The origin of the song is not known
Sonata in F, 'La Bataille de Rossbach' Hob XVII:F3		One of numerous descriptive battle pieces of the 18th century. The sonata is not by Haydn; other composers suggested as the true author are J C Bach, C P E Bach, and Graun
Divertimento in F, Hob XVIIa:1 'Il Maestro e lo Scolare'	*c* 1765?	A duet for keyboard in which the master leads the pupil through a series of studies before they join together in the finale (cf Symphony No 6)
Pieces for flute-clock, Hob XIX:		
No 4 in C, 'Der Dudelsack'	1772	Includes an imitation of bagpies (*dudelsack)*
No 6 in F, 'Kaffeeklatsch'	1772	Thought to be suggestive of the gossiping customers in a coffee-shop.
No 8 in C, 'Wachtelschlag'	1772	An imitation of the call of a quail

The work with the longest title is arguably a symphony in C by Pavel Vraničky, a Czech composer who wrote a number of works in Hungary. In the original Hungarian the title is: *A' Magyar Nemzet Örōme Midőn annak Tōrvényei, s' Sdabadságai II. Jósef Tsászár és Király alatt, kis Karátson havának (Januárius) 28dik napján 1790-ik Esztendőben, vissza állittattak vala. Egy Nagy Szimfónia Három darabból álland. I. A' Nemzet' első vigassága, s' ennek el terjesztése. II. A' Rendek' kellemetes érzékenységei, és azok kőzt vissza tértt Egyvesség. III. A' Koszég Örōme a' Szent Korona' vissza érkezése alkalmatosságával.* Op 2.

An English translation of this name may be said to run: 'Joy of the Hungarian nation when her laws and freedoms were restored under Emperor and King Joseph II on the 28th day of the month of Circumcision (January) of the year 1790. A great symphony consisting of three pieces. I. The nation's first jollifications and its dissemination. II. The pleasant sensibilities of the states of the realm and the unity restored among them. III. The joy of the community on the occasion of the holy crown.' Op 2.

The symphony is scored for two flutes, two oboes, two bassoons, two horns, two clarini (trumpets), timpani, and strings, and was published by the firm of Imbault in Paris in 1791.

FAMILIAR TITLES TO UNFAMILIAR MUSIC

Certain titles are inseparably associated with certain composers. 'New World', for instance, always brings to mind Dvořák, *La Traviata* suggests Verdi, and *Elijah* Mendelssohn. It is only slightly disconcerting to find the uniqueness of title of Vaughan Williams's *A Sea Symphony* threatened by the *Ocean Symphony* of Anton Rubinstein, Beethoven's Ninth Symphony having to share its name with a work by Holst, and 'Emperor' identifying a string quartet by Haydn, a piano concerto by Beethoven, and a waltz by Strauss. Other connections will doubtless spring from a study of the foregoing list.

A dig in the basement of the musical archives produces a handful of forgotten works the titles of which are extremely well known.

Barber of Seville, The: opera by Rossini (1816); also an opera by Paisiello (1782).

Belshazzar's Feast: oratorio by Walton (1931); also incidental music by Sibelius (1906).

Bohème, La: opera by Puccini (1896); also an opera by Leoncavallo (1897).

Christmas Oratorio, The: by Bach (1734); and also one by Johann Schelle (1648–1710), who composed at St Thomas's School, Leipzig and whose oratorio was probably familiar to Bach.

Clemenza di Tito, La: opera by Mozart (1791); also a balletto by Caldara (*c* 1728).

Daphnis et Chloë: ballet by Ravel (1912); also ballet music by Boismortier (1747), and by Rousseau (*c* 1761).

Don Giovanni: opera by Mozart (1787); also an opera by Gazzaniga (1787).

Enigma Variations: orchestral work by Elgar (1899); also a solo piano work by Cipriani Potter (1858).

'Eroica': symphony (1803) and piano variations (1802) by Beethoven; also a solo violin sonata (in C, Op 29) by Tovey (1913).

Eugene Onegin: opera by Tchaikovsky (1879); also an opera by Prokofiev (1934, first performed in 1974).

Four Seasons, The: a series of four violin concertos by Vivaldi (*c* 1725); also a ballet by Glazunov (1913), an oratorio by Benedetto Marcello (1731), and a lost cantata by Bach.

Job: 'a Masque for Dancing' by Vaughan Williams (1930); also oratorios by Dittersdorf (1789) and by Parry, about which George Bernard Shaw, critic and executioner, said: 'I take *Job* to be, on the whole, the most utter failure ever achieved by a thoroughly respectworthy musician. There is not one bar in it that comes within fifty thousand miles of the tamest line in the poem.... This dreary ramble of Dr Parry's through the wastes of artistic error. . . . I hope he will burn the score, and throw *Judith* in when the blaze begins to flag.'

Masaniello: opera by Auber (1828); also an opera, *Masaniello furioso*, by Keiser (1706).

Mr Wu: song by George Formby (1933); also an opera by d'Albert (1932).

'Pathètique': sonata by Beethoven (1798); and a symphony by Tchaikovsky (1893); also an oratorio by Georgi Sviridov (20th century), and an overture by Kabalevsky.

Pelléas et Mélisande: opera by Debussy

(1902); and a suite by Sibelius (1905).

Prometheus: ballet by Beethoven (*c* 1801); also an opera by Fauré (1900).

Ré Pastore, Il: opera by Mozart (1775); also an opera by Uttini (1755).

Ruy Blas: overture by Mendelssohn (1839); also an opera by Glover (1861).

Tempest, The: Fantasy overture by Tchaikovsky (1873) and a sonata by Beethoven (1802); also operas by Halévy (1850) and Gatty (1920).

War Requiem: by Britten (1962); also *The Requiem for those who died in the war against Fascism* by Kabalevsky (1949).

ANIMALS AND MUSIC

A collection of music with zoological connections, omitting the more tenuous links with the animal kingdom such as operas entitled *Richard the Lionheart* or *Rip van Winkle*. Since the authors do not profess any knowledge of matters zoological, the grouping follows that adopted by Gerald L Wood, FZS, in *The Guinness Book of Animal Facts and Feats*.

Mammals

1. Ass

'Wild Asses' and 'Personages with Long Ears' (in *Carnival of the Animals*) – Saint-Saëns

Platero and I (1956) for solo guitar – Castelnuovo-Tedesco

2. Bat

Die Fledermaus (operetta, 1874) – J Strauss II

See also Nicknames and Sub-titles: *Representatio Avium*

3. Bear

'The Tame Bear' and 'The Wild Bears' (from *The Wand of Youth* Suite No 2, Op 1b) – Elgar

Bear Dance (No 10 of *Ten Simple Pieces for Piano*, 1908) – Bartók

The Bear (opera, 'Extravaganza', 1967) – Walton

See also Haydn list.

4. Cat

The Cat and the Bird (song cycle, 1872) – Mussorgsky

'The Owl and the Pussy Cat' (song, 1966) – Stravinsky

L'Enfant et les Sortilèges (opera, 1925) includes a cat as one of its characters – Ravel

See also Nicknames and Sub-titles

5. Cattle

Le Boeuf sur le toit (ballet, 1919) – Milhaud

The Wild Bull (electronic work) – Subotnik

6. Deer

The Enchanted Stag (cantata profana, 1930) – Bartók

Prélude à L'apres-midi d'un faune (1894) – Debussy

'Like at the Hart' (anthem) – Howells

Der Steyrische Hirt (capriccio, 1679) – Kerll

La Chasse du Cerf (suite, 1708) – Morin

See also Nicknames and Sub-titles: *Acteon Transformed into a Stag*

7. Dog

Variation XI: 'GRS' of the *Enigma Variations*, Op 36 (1899) begins with a musical picture of a dog leaping into a river – Elgar

'Will Ye Buy a Fine Dog' (song) – Morley

See also Nicknames and Sub-titles

8. Elephant

'Jumbo's Lullaby' (No 2 of *Childrens' Corner* Suite, 1908) – Debussy

'Barber le Petit Elephant' (*Children's Tale*, 1940)–Poulenc

Circus Polka for a Young Elephant (1942) – Stravinsky

9. Fox

The Cunning Little Vixen (opera, 1924) – Janáček

'Tomorrow the Fox will Come to Town' (part-song) – Ravenscroft

Rénard (Burlesque, 1922) – Stravinsky

'The Fox' (song, 1930) – Warlock

10. Goat

'Goat Paths' (song) – Howells

11. Horse

The Bronze Horse (opera, 1835) – Auber

Ritterballett (1790) – Beethoven

Rodeo (1942) – Copland

En habit de Cheval (two chorales and two fugues, 1911) – Satie

The Horses (three songs, Op 10, 1967) – Hugh Wood

My Horses (variations, *c* 1823) – Archduke Rudolf

12. Kangaroo
Kangaroo Hunt, for piano and percussion (1971) – Lumsdaine

13. Lion
'Now the Hungry Lion Roars' (song) – William Linley

14. Mouse
'Marriage of the Frog and the Mouse' (part-song) – Ravenscroft
Variations on Three Blind Mice (1973) – Tavener
L'Enfant et les Sortilèges (opera, 1925) includes a mouse as one of its characters – Ravel

15. Ox
'I Have Twelve Oxen (song, 1918) – Ireland
See also Haydn list: 'Ox Minuet'

16. Pig
See Haydn list: *Capriccio*

17. Seal
The Seal-Woman (opera, 1924) – Bantock

18. Sheep
'Sheep May Safely Graze' (from Cantata No 208, 1716) – J S Bach
Lie Strewn the White Flocks (pastoral) – Bliss

19. Squirrel
L'Enfant et les Sortilèges (opera, 1925) includes a squirrel as one of its characters – Ravel

20. Tiger
The Tigers (opera) – Havergal Brian

21. Whale
Leviathan (symphonic poem, 1974) – Cowie
Moby Dick (cantata) – Herrmann
The Whale (cantata, 1966) – Tavener

Birds

Birds (General)
'The Gipsy and the Bird' (ballad) – Benedict
The Aviary (String Quintet in D, Gér 276, 1771) – Boccherini
'The Birds' (song, 1929) – Britten
The White Bird (1927) – Carter
Uccellatori (opera, 1759) – Gassmann
Deux Avares (opera, 1770) – Grétry
'Little Bird' (No 4 of *Lyric Pieces,* Op 43, 1884) – Grieg
'St Francis of Assisi Preaching to the Birds' (No 1 of *Two Legends* for piano, 1886) – Liszt
Oiseaux exotiques (1965) – Messiaen
Reveil des Oiseaux (1953) – Messiaen
Catalogue d'Oiseaux – Messiaen
Les Oiseaux et les sources – Messiaen
The Cat and the Bird (song cycle, 1872) – Mussorgsky
'Little Chirping Birds' (song) – Pilkington
'Of All the Birds' (part-song) – Ravenscroft
The Birds (suite, 1927) – Respighi
'Dance of the Birds' (from *Snow Maiden,* opera, 1882) – Rimsky-Korsakov
'But My Bird is Long in Homing' (song, Op 36/6, 1899) – Sibelius
The Firebird (ballet, 1910) – Stravinsky
'As Wanton Birds' (madrigal for five voices, 1600) – Weelkes
See also Nicknames and Sub-titles: *Aviary, The; Representatio avium*
See also Haydn list

Birds (Specific)

22. Bluebird
Oiseau Bleu (opera, 1919) – Wolff
Bluebird (Pas de deux, after Tchaikovsky, 1941) – Stravinsky

23. Canary
Kanarienkantata – Telemann

24. Cocks and Hens
'Ballet of the Unhatched Chicks' (in *Pictures from an Exhibition,* 1874) – Mussorgsky
'When the Cock Begins to Crow' (catch) – Purcell
'Hens and Cocks' (in *Carnival of the Animals)* – Saint-Saëns
'Dance of the Cockerels' (from *Maskerade,* opera, 1906) – Nielsen
The Golden Cockerel (opera, 1909) – Rimsky-Korsakov
See also Haydn list

25. Cuckoo
'The Merry Cuckoo' (from *Spring Symphony,* Op 44, 1949) – Britten
Coucou (harpsichord piece) – Daquin
On Hearing the First Cuckoo in Spring (1912) – Delius
'Cucu, Cucu, Cucu' (song) – Encina
The Cuckoo and the Nightingale (Organ Concerto in F, Op 4 (set 2)/7) – Handel
'The Cuckoo Song' – Nicholson
'The Cuckoo in the Heart of the Wood' (in *Carnival of the Animals)* – Saint Saëns

'The Cuckoo Song' – Simpson
Cuckoo (Presto in C for harpsichord) – Gasparini
Cucu (capriccio, 1679) – Kerll
Sul Canto del Cucu (Toccata in A for harpsichord) – Pasquini
See also Nicknames and Sub-titles
The song of the cuckoo is heard often in children's works such as Leopold Mozart's Cassation in G for orchestra and toy instruments.

26. Curlew
Curlew River (opera, 1964) – Britten
The Curlew, (song cycle, 1922) – Warlock

27. Dove
The Wood Dove (symphonic poem, Op 110, 1896) – Dvořák
'The Dove' (Welsh part-song, 1931) – Holst

28. Duck
The Ugly Duckling (Op 18, 1914) – Prokofiev

29. Falcon
'The Falcon Flew High' (chorus from opera *The Coachman at the Way-Station)* – Fomin

30. Finch
A Charm of Finches – Cowie

31. Goldfinch
See Nicknames and Sub-titles

32. Goose
With the Wild Geese (1910) – Harty
The Golden Goose (choral ballet, 1926) – Holst
Mother Goose Suite (1908) – Ravel

33. Lark
'Lo, Hear the Gentle Lark' (song) – Bishop
'Horch, horch die Lerch' (Lied, D 889, 1826) – Schubert
Horch, horch die Lerch (paraphrase after Schubert) – Liszt
The Lark Ascending (1914) – Vaughan Williams
See also Haydn list

34. Magpie
'Magpie' (song, 1867) – Mussorgsky
The Thieving Magpie (opera, 1817) – Rossini

35. Nightingale
An die Nachtigal (Op 46/4, 1868) – Brahms
Nachtigalen Schwingen (Op 6/6, 1853) – Brahms
'Nightingales' (No 5 of *Seven Partsongs,* Op 17, 1937) – Finzi
'The Lover and the Nightingale' (No 4 of *Goyescas,* 1911) – Granados
The Cuckoo and the Nightingale (Organ Concerto in F, Op 4 (set 2)/7) – Handel
'En mai quant li rossignolet' (chanson) – Muset
'Le Rossignol et la Rose' (song) – Saint-Saëns
'An die Nachtigal' (Lied, D 196, 1815) – Schubert
Song of the Nightingale (ballet, 1917) – Stravinsky
'The Nightingale, the Organ of Delight' (madrigal in three parts, 1603) – Weelkes
'The Nightingale' (song, 1702) – Weldon
Nachtigal und Rabe (opera, 1818) – Weigl
*Rosignol (*opera, 1816) – Lebrun
'The Nightingale' (from *Sieben fruhe Lieder,* 1908) – Berg
The nightingale plays a character in Ravel's *L'Enfant et les Sortilèges,* and supplies a voice as one of the toy instruments in Leopold Mozart's Cassation in G for orchestra and toys

36. Owl
'Owls–an Epitaph' (part-song, Op 53/4, 1907) – Elgar
'The Owl and the Pussycat' (song, 1966) – Stravinsky
'Sweet Suffolk Owl' (madrigal in five parts, 1619) – Vautor

37. Peacock
The Peacock (variations, 1939) – Kodály

38. Phoenix
The Phoenix (Concerto in D for four bassoons, unaccompanied) – Corrette

39. Pigeon
Two Pigeons (ballet) – Messager

40. Quail
The quail is one of the toy musical instruments called for in Leopold Mozart's Cassation in G

41. Raven
'The Three Ravens' (part-song) – Ravenscroft
Nachtigal und Rabe (opera, 1818) – Weigl

42. Robin
Bonnie Sweet Robin (variations for harpsichord) – Bull
'Ah Robin' (madrigal) – Cornyshe
'Bonnie Sweet Robin' – Dowland
Bonny Sweet Robin (ricercare à four) – Simpson

43. Sparrow
Spatzenmesse in C (K 220, 1775) – Mozart
From the Book of Philip Sparrow (1971) – Orr

44. Stormbird
Stürmvogel (opera, 1926) – Schjelderup

45. Swallow
'The Swallow Leaves Her Nest' (part-song, 1910) – Holst
Village Swallows (waltz) – Josef Strauss
'The Swallow' (part-song) – Morley

46. Swan
'The Silver Swan' (madrigal, 1614) – Gibbons
'A Swan' (song, Op 25/2, 1876) – Grieg
Schwannengesang, (song cycle, D 957, 1828) – Schubert
'Swan of Tuonela' (No 3 of *Four Legends,* 1895) – Sibelius
Swan White (Op 54, 1908) – Sibelius
Swan Lake (ballet, Op 20, 1876) – Tchaikovsky

Reptiles

47. Serpent
'Serpent Dance' (in ballet *The Truth About Russian Dancers,* 1920) – Bax

48. Snake
'Ye Spotted Snakes' (song in incidental music for *A Midsummer Night's Dream,* Op, 61, 1842) – Mendelssohn
'You Spotted Snakes' (song, 1755) – J C Smith

Amphibians

49. Frog
*The Frog (*galliard) – Morley
'The Marriage of the Frog and the Mouse' (part-song) – Ravenscroft
The Frogs (a comedy overture, 1935) – Bantock
See also Nicknames and Sub-titles: *Peasants Turned into Frogs; Representatio Avium*
See also Haydn list

Fish

50. Fish
'Fish in the Unruffled Lakes' (song, 1937) – Britten

51. Goldfish
'Poissons d'or' (No 6 of *Images,* 1905) – Debussy

52. Trout
'Die Forelle' (Lied, D 550, 1817) – Schubert
'The Trout' (Piano Quintet in A, D 667, the second movement of which is based on the melody of the above Lied, 1819) – Schubert
Die Forelle (paraphrase after Schubert, 1846) – Liszt

Worms

'The Worm' (song) – Dargomizhky

Insects

53. Ant
The Ants, Comedy Overture, Op 7 – Joseph

54. Bee
'Where the Bee Sucks' (song) – Arne
'Where the Bee Sucks' (song) – Johnson
'Where the Bee Sucks' (song, 1963) – Tippett
'The Flight of the Bumblebee' (from the opera *Tsar Sultan,* 1900) – Rimsky-Korsakov
'Sweet Honey-Sucking Bees' (madrigal in five parts, 1609) – Wilbye
See also Nicknames and Sub-titles

55. Beetle
'The Beetle' (from *The Nursery* song cycle, 1872) – Mussorgsky

56. Butterfly
'Papillons' (song, Op 2) – Chausson
'Moths and Butterflies' (from *The Wand of Youth* Suite No 2, Op 1b, 1908) – Elgar
Papillons (for cello and violin, Op 77, 1898) – Fauré
'The Butterfly' (No 1 of *Lyric Pieces,* Op 43, 1884) – Grieg
Le Papillon (ballet, 1860) – Offenbach
Madame Butterfly (opera, 1904) – Puccini
Papillons (piano, Op 2, 1832) – Schumann
Les Papillons (ordre No 2) – Couperin
See also Nicknames and Sub-titles

57. Cricket
The Cricket on the Hearth (opera, 1914) – MacKenzie
Grillo del Focolare (opera, 1908) – Zandonai
Heimchen am Herd (opera, 1896) – Goldmark

58. Flea
'Song of the Flea' (1879) – Mussorgsky
'Herodiade's Flea' (discarded from *Façade,* 1923) – Walton

59. Fly
'The Fly' (song, 1966) – R R Bennett
'The Tale of the Small Fly' (from *Mikrokosmos,* vol 6) – Bartók

60. Gadfly
The Gadfly (suite of incidental music, Op 97, 1955) – Shostakovitch

61. Gnat
See Nicknames and Sub-titles: *Representatio* avium

62. Moth
'Moths and Butterflies' (from *The Wand of Youth* Suite No 2; Op 1b, 1908) – Elgar

63. Wasp
The Wasps (Aristophanic Suite, 1909) – Vaughan Williams

Animals in general are dealt with in several compositions:

Saint-Saëns: *Carnival of the Animals,* a Grand Zoological Fantasy for two pianos and orchestra (1886), originally conceived for chamber group, mainly for the composer's own amusement. The suite has the following movements: 'Introduction and Royal March of the Lions; 'Cocks and Hens'; 'Asses'; 'The Tortoise'; 'Elephant'; 'Kangaroos'; 'The Aquarium'; 'Personages With Long Ears'; 'The Cuckoo in the Heart of the Wood'; 'The Aviary'; 'Pianists'; 'Fossils'; 'The Swan'; 'Finale'.
F J Haydn: *The Creation* (oratorio, 1797/98) mentions eagle, lark, dove, nightingale, whale, leviathan, lion, tiger, stag, horse, cattle, sheep, insects, and worm.
F J Haydn: *The Seasons* (oratorio, 1798/99) mentions lambs, fish, bees, and birds.
Banchieri: *Contrapunto bestiale,* in which the 'words' take the form of animal imitations.
J Bennett: *All Creatures Now* (1700).
Poulenc: *Les Animaux Modèles* is an orchestral suite containing movements entitled 'The Amorous Lion', and 'The Two Cockerels'.
Janáček: *The Cunning Little Vixen* (opera, 1924) includes the characters of Owl, Gnat, Woodpecker, Badger, Cricket, Jay, Frog, Grasshopper, Hens, Dog, Fox, and of course the Vixen herself.
Sullivan and Stephenson wrote an opera entitled *The Zoo* (1875).
Prokofiev: *Peter and the Wolf,* a musical fairytale (1936) features the Bird, the Duck, the Cat, and the Wolf.

THE DEVIL AND MUSIC

The Devil and things diabolical have inspired composers for hundreds of years. The Orpheus legend of Greek mythology provided the material for many librettists and opera-composers: some of the fruits of these liasons are listed in Section V under The Most Popular Opera Stories. In the ballet theatre, Orpheus has been dealt with by:

Deller: *Orpheus und Eurydike* (1763);
Stravinsky: *Orpheus* (1947);

and in the concert hall by:

Liszt: *Orpheus* (tone poem, 1854).

The Faust story, which first appeared in Germany in 1587, has also produced many operas based on the original story or a derivation thereof, together with a number of stage works:

Berlioz: *The Damnation of Faust* (cantata, 1846)
Bertin: *Fausto* (opera, 1831).
Boïto: *Mefistofele* (opera, 1868).
Brüggemann: *Margherita* (opera, 1910).
Busoni: *Doktor Faust* (opera, 1925).
Gounod: *Faust* (opera, 1859).
Hervé: *Le Petit Faust* (opera, 1869).
Liszt: *A Faust Symphony* (1854).
Liszt: *Mephisto Waltz* (1881).
Moore: *The Devil and Daniel Webster* (opera, 1938).
Schumann: *Scenes from Goethe's 'Faust'* (1853).
Spohr: *Faust* (opera, 1816).
Wagner: *A Faust Overture* (1840, revised 1855).
Walter: *Doktor Faust* (opera, 1797).
Zöllner: *Faust* (opera, 1887).

Also concerned with the Devil and his works are the following pieces:

Boccherini: *La Casa del Diavolo* (Symphony, Gér 506, 1771): the finale is based on the 'Dance of the Furies' from Gluck's *Orfeo.*
Dvořák: *The Devil and Kate* (opera, 1899).
Mussorgsky: *A Night on a Bare Mountain* (symphonic poem, 1867).

Saint Saëns: *Danse Macabre* (symphonic poem, 1874).
Schubert: *Der Erlkönig* (Lied, D 325, 1815).
Stravinsky: *The Rake's Progress* (opera, 1951) and *The Soldier's Tale* (play with music, 1923) in which the Devil purchases the soldier's soul in the form of a violin.
Tartini: *The Devil's Trill* (Sonata in G minor, *c* 1735): Tartini is said to have dreamed of hearing the Devil playing a sonata and, upon waking, the composer tried to recall the music and set it down in a sonata of his own.
Weber: *Der Freischütz* (opera, 1821), in which the Devil has a speaking part.
Weinberger: *Schwanda the Bagpiper* (opera, 1927).

In the Saint-Saëns, Stravinsky, and Tartini works the Devil is identified with a fiddle. Both Tartini and Paganini, supreme violinists in their respective ages, did nothing to discourage the rumour that their phenomenal techniques were in some way due to diabolical bargaining. A violin actually called 'Le violin du Diable' was made in 1734 by Giuseppe Guarneri del Gesú of Cremona.

FOOD AND MUSIC

For potential food on the hoof, wing, fin, and paw, see Animals and Music, above.

1. Feasts and Banquets
Musical Banquet (1610) – Dowland
Tafelmusik (three 'Productions' of music to be played while the court was feasting, 1731) – Telemann
Belshazzar's Feast (oratorio, 1931) – Walton
Belshazzar's Feast (incidental music, Op 51, 1906) – Sibelius
Alexander's Feast (oratorio, and an associated concerto grosso, 1736) – Handel
The Spider's Banquet (ballet, 1912) – Roussel
See also Nicknames and Sub-titles: 'Feast'

A Musical Menu

2. Ale
'Bring us Good Ale' (No 2 of five part-songs, Op 34, 1916) – Holst
'I Gave Her Cakes and Ale' (catch) – Purcell
'He That Will an Alehouse Keep' (song) – Ravenscroft
'Good Ale' (song, 1922) – Warlock
He That Drinks is Immortal (cantata) – Purcell

3. Fruit
The Love of Three Oranges (film music, 1921) – Prokofiev
Three Pieces in the Shape of a Pear (1903) – Satie

4. Meat
'When Jesus Sat at Meat' (madrigal) – Nicholson

5. Pie
O Dame Get Up and Bake Your Pie (piece for piano, 1946) – Bax

6. Wine
Wine, Women, and Song (Op 333, 1869) – J Strauss II

7. Soufflé
Soufflé, for flute, piccolo, and alto flute – Petrassi

8. Cakes
'I Gave Her Cakes and Ale' (catch) – Purcell
The Wedding-Cake (caprice for piano and strings, Op 76) – Saint-Saëns

9. Coffee
'Coffee Cantata (cantata No 211, *c* 1732) – J S Bach
Kaffeeklatsch in F (for mechanical organ, 1772) – Haydn

20. Cream
Schlagobers ('Whipped Cream') (ballet, 1921) – R Strauss

11. Chocolate
The Chocolate Soldier (operetta) – J Strauss II

12. Champagne
The Champagne Galop (Op 8) – J Strauss I
The Champagne Polka (Op 211) – J Strauss II

GEOGRAPHY AND MUSIC

A musical tour round the world and beyond. In the main, works such as Scottish songs, Chinese dances, etc, and those describing the character of the composer's own country have been avoided.

The British Isles

1. Avon
'Thou Soft-Flowing Avon' (song) – T Arne

2. Canterbury
The Canterbury Pilgrims (opera, 1884) – Stanford
The Canterbury Pilgrims (opera, 1917) – Koven

3. Derbyshire
See Haydn list

4. Edinburgh
Prigione d'Edinburg (opera, 1838) – Ricci
Prison d'Edinbourg (opera, 1833) – Carafa

5. England
Elisabetta, regina d'Inghilterra (opera, 1815) – Rossini
Merrie England (operetta, 1904) – German
La Festa di Sporalizio della Regina d'Inghilterra (opera, 1761) – Hertel

6. Liverpool
Emelia di Liverpool (opera, 1824) – Donizetti

7. London
Italiana á Londra (opera, 1778) – Cimarosa
Ritorna di Londra (opera, 1756) – Fischietti
London Symphony, No 2 in G (1914, revised 1920) – Vaughan Williams
Cockaigne Overture (Op 40, 1901) – Elgar
Hammersmith Prelude (Op 52, 1930) – Holst
'The Lass of Richmond Hill' (song) – Hook
St Giles Cripplegate – Nitzsche
'West London' (song) – Ives
See also Haydn list

8. Oxford
See Haydn list

9. Padstow
The Padstow Lifeboat (Op 94) – Arnold

10. Penzance
The Pirates of Penzance (opera, 1879) – Sullivan

11. Portsmouth
Portsmouth Point Overture (1925) – Walton

12. Scotland
Celtic Requiem (1969) – Tavener
Celtic Symphony (1940) – Bantock
Fingal's Cave (The Hebrides) Overture, (Op 26, 1832) – Mendelssohn
Miracle in the Gorbals (ballet, 1944) – Bliss
Scottish Rhapsody – Walton

13. Stolham
Stolham River (piano piece, 1932) – Moeran

14. Shropshire
A Shropshire Lad (rhapsody, 1912) – Butterworth

15. Wales
See Haydn list: 'March for the Prince of Wales'

16. Windsor
Windsor Castle (opera, 1794) – Haydn
The Merry Wives of Windsor (opera, 1849) – Nicolai
In Windsor Forest (cantata, 1911) – Vaughan Williams

Windsor Castle, subject of an opera by Haydn (Popperfoto)

17. Yorkshire
'Yorkshire Feast Song' (Z 333, 1690) – Purcell

Europe

18. Austria
'Auf der Donau' (Lied, D 553, 1816) – Schubert
Donauweibchen (opera, 1798) – Kauer
Tiroler Wastel (opera, 1796) – Haibel
See also Nicknames and Sub-titles: 'Linz'

19. Czechoslovakia
Schwestern von Prag (opera, 1794) – Müller
In the Tatras (symphonic poem, 1902) – Novak
See also Nicknames and Sub-titles: *Bells of Zlonice;* 'Prague'

The Russian composer Peter Ilich Tchaikovsky (1840–93) who began life as a civil servant and died of cholera at a comparatively early age (Novisti)

20. Denmark
The Prince of Denmark's March – Clarke
A Phantasy Journey to the Pharoe Islands (rhapsody overture, 1927) – Nielsen
On the Fair Plains of Sjϕlund (Symphony No 1 in C minor, Op 5, 1842) – Gade

21. Finland
Finnish Rhapsody (Op 88) – Glazunov

22. France
A la Française (Symphony in A, Post 10, 1780–90?) – L Kozeluh
Amadis de Gaule (opera, 1779) – J C Bach
Dilettante d'Avignon (opera, 1829) – Halévy
Maries de la Tour Eiffel (ballet, 1921) – Auric, Honegger, Milhaud, Poulenc, and Tailleferre
Paris, Song of a Great City (1899) – Delius
Le Jongleur de Notre Dame (opera, 1902) Massenet
Pariser Polka (Op 382) – J Strauss II
Jour à Paris (opera, 1808) – Isouard
See also Nicknames and Sub-titles: 'Alla Francese'; 'Paris'

23. Germany
Roland von Berlin (opera, 1904) – Leoncavallo
Bavarian Dances (Op 27, 1896) – Elgar
From the Bavarian Highlands (choral songs, 1895) – Elgar
Schweriner (String Quartet in B flat, Denn 34, *c* 1774) – Reichardt
See also Nicknames and Sub-titles: 'Brandenburg'; 'Gastein'; 'Hamburg'; 'Jena'; 'Rhenish'; 'Saxony'; 'Weimar'
See also Haydn list: 'Hermannstadt'

24. Greece
La Bella Greca (opera, 1784) – Cimarosa
Amadis de Grèce (opera, 1699) – Destouches
The Ruins of Athens (incidental music, Op 113, 1811) – Beethoven
Timon of Athens, the Man-Hater (opera, Z 632, 1690) – Purcell
The Siege of Corinth (opera, 1826) – Rossini
Ariadne in Crete (opera, 1734) – Handel
Ariadne auf Naxos (opera, 1775) – J Benda
Ariadne auf Naxos (opera, 1912) – R Strauss
Ariane dans L'Isle de Naxos (opera, 1782) – Edelmann

25. Holland
Aleida von Holland (opera, 1866) – Thooft

26. Hungary
'Hungarian' (violin concerto, Op 11) – Joachim
See also Haydn list: 'Lukaveč'; 'March'

27. Iceland
'Icelandic' Symphony No 16 – Cowell

28. Italy
Italian Concerto in F (BWV 971) – J S Bach
Aus Italien (symphonic fantasy, Op 16, 1886) – R Strauss
Italian Serenade (1887) – Wolf
A Turk in Italy (opera, 1814) – Rossini
Italian Caprice (Op 45, 1880) – Tchaikovsky
In the South (overture, Op 50, 1903) – Elgar
Souvenir de Florence (sextet, Op 70, 1892) – Tchaikovsky
Valentine de Milan (opera, 1822) – Méhul
Carnaval Romain (overture Op 9, 1843) – Berlioz
Carnival in Rome (1873) – J Strauss II
Esule di Roma (opera, 1828) – Donizetti
Roma (Symphony (Suite) in C, 1868) – Bizet
Sicilian Vespers (opera, 1855) – Verdi
Festes Vénitiennes (opera, 1710) – Camprá
Nacht in Venedig (opera, 1883) – J Strauss II
See also Nicknames and Sub-titles: *Frescoes;* 'Italian'

29. Mediterranean
Mediterranean (a piano piece, also orchestrated by the composer, 1921) – Bax

30. North Sea
Nordseebilder Waltz (Op 380, 1890) – J Strauss II

31. Norway
Four Norwegian Moods (1942) – Stravinsky
Reminiscences from the Norwegian Mountains (symphonic poem, 1842) – Berwald

32. Poland
'Polish' (Symphony No 3 in D, Op 29, 1875) – Tchaikovsky
See also Nicknames and Sub-titles: 'Fall of Warsaw'

37. Russia
Russa (Symphony in A, *c* 1760) – dall'Oglio
Ciro in Armenia (opera, 1753) – Agnesi
St Petersburg Quadrille (Op 255) – J Strauss II
Siberia (opera, 1902) – Giordano
May Night in the Ukraine (piano piece, 1911) – Bax

An der Wolga Polka (Op 425) – J Strauss II
See also Nicknames and Sub-titles: *Leningrad;* 'Little Russian'

34. Scandinavia
See Nicknames and Sub-titles: *Boreale*

35. Spain
'Spanish Night' ('Noche Espagnole') (from *Façade* Suite No 2, 1938) – Walton
Spanish Caprice (Op 34, 1887) – Rimsky-Korsakov
The Rose of Castile (opera, 1857) – Balfe
Nachtlager von Granada (opera, 1834) – C Kreutzer
Memories of a Summer Night in Madrid – Glinka
The Barber of Seville (opera, 1816) – Rossini
Étoile de Séville (opera, 1845) – Balfe
Deux Avuegles de Tolède (opera, 1806) – Méhul
See also Nicknames and Sub-titles: *Musica Notturna*

36. Switzerland
'Swiss Yodelling Song' (from *Façade* Suite No 1, 1926) – Walton
Alpine Symphony (Op 64, 1915) – R Strauss

37. Turkey
Violin Concerto No 5 in A, K 219, 'Turkish' (1775) – Mozart
Symphony No 14, Op 194, 'Ararat' – Hovhaness

America

38. North America
Afro-American Symphony (1931) – Still
Indian Suite (Op 48, 1897) – McDowell
Appalachian Spring (1944) – Copland
Appalachia (1902) – Delius
Grand Canyon Suite (1931) – Grofé
Symphony No 3, *Louisville* – Egge
Three Places in New England (1914) – Ives
Central Park in the Dark (1907) – Ives
Transatlantic (for orchestra, 1938) – Anthiel
See also Nicknames and Sub-titles: *Concord, Mass.*

39. South America
Symphony No 2, *India* (1935) (ie the South American Indian people) – Chavez
Latin American Symphonette (1940) – Gould
Symphony No 1, *A Night in the Tropics* – Gottschalk
Perle du Brásil (opera, 1851) – David
Brazilian Impressions (1928) – Respighi
El Salon Mexico (1936) – Copland
Symphony No 2, *Montevideo* – Gottschalk

Asia

40. China
Voyage en Chine (opera, 1865) – Bazin
Chinese Galop (Op 97) – J Strauss I

41. India
The Indian Queen (opera, Z 630, 1695?) – Purcell
Alessandro nell'Indie (operas: 1738 Corselli, Galuppi; 1745 Pérez; 1762 J C Bach; 1763 Sacchini; 1774 Piccinni)

42. Japan
Japanese Suite (1915) – Holst

43. Pakistan
Le Roi de Lahore (opera, 1877) – Massenet

44. Persia
Rose of Persia (operetta, 1899) – Sullivan
Distressed Innocence, or the Princess of Persia (opera, Z 577, 1690) – Purcell

Asia Minor

45. Babylon
An Wasserflüssen Babylon (chorale prelude, BWV 653) – J S Bach

46. Baghdad
Barber of Baghdad (opera, 1858) – Cornelius
Caliph of Baghdad (opera, 1800) – Boïeldieu
Schiava in Baghdad (opera, 1820) – Pacini

47. Bethlehem
Les Enfants de Bethlehem (cantata, 1907) – Pierne

48. Jerusalem
'O Pray for the Peace of Jerusalem' (anthem) – Nichòlson
'Jerusalem' (Op 208, 1916) – Parry
Gerusalemme distrutto (opera, 1794) – Zingarelli
Gerusalemme liberata (opera, 1803) – Righini
Gierusalemme liberata (opera, 1687) – Pallavicino
Jérusalem délivrée (opera, 1812) – Persuis
See Nicknames and Sub-titles: *Etchmiadzin*

Africa

Afro-American Symphony (1931) – Still

49. Algiers
Italian Girl in Algiers (opera, 1816) – Rossini

50. Cairo
Caravane du Caire (opera, 1783) – Grétry

51. Egypt
Ballet Egyptien (Op 12) – Luigini
Thamos, King of Egypt (incidental music, K 345, 1779) – Mozart
Cesare in Egitto (opera, 1735) – Giacomelli
Israel in Egypt (oratorio, 1739) – Handel
Crociato in Egitto (opera, 1824) – Meyerbeer
Giulio Cesare in Egitto (opera, 1724) – Handel
Mosé in Egitto (opera, 1818) – Rossini

52. Johannesburg
Johannesburg Festival Overture – Walton

Antarctica

See Nicknames and Sub-titles

Miscellaneous

53. Terrestrial
Symphony No 22, Op 236, *City of Light* – Hovhaness
L'Isola disabitata (opera, 1779) – Haydn
Magic Island (symphonic prelude) – Alwyn
Utopia Ltd (operetta, 1893) – Sullivan
White Mountain (piano piece, 1927) – Moeran

54. Sun
See Haydn list

55. Moon
Silver Apples of the Moon (electronic composition, 1967) – Subotnik
The Excursions of Mr Bruček to the Moon (opera, 1920) – Janáček
The World of the Moon (opera, 1750) – Galuppi
The World of the Moon (opera, 1777) – Haydn

56. Space
Atlas Eclipticalis, for string trio, harp, piano, clarinet, and percussion (in which the shapes of the heavenly constellations are transcribed into musical shapes) – Cage
The Space Dragon of Galatar, an opera workshop project for voices, sound effects, and piano – Paynter
Aniara (space opera, 1959) – Blomdahl

MEDICINE AND MUSIC

The therapeutic power of music was discovered in 1942 by Mrs Cassandra Franklin, wife of Walter S Franklin, a retired President of the Pennsylvania Railroad. Mrs Franklin was a member of the 'Grey Ladies', an unpaid volunteer Red Cross organisation. During her work with patients at Tilton Army Hospital, near Fort Dix, New Jersey, she encouraged many of the war-wounded to remarkably quick and complete recoveries. Her methods are now widespread in America and are gradually gaining ground in Europe.

MONTHS AND SEASONS AND MUSIC

The Curious Musical Instrument Calendar (instrumental suite, 1748) – Werner
Jazz Calendar (composition for jazz ensemble) – Bennett
Morning and Evening (a series of twelve movements, one for each month, for mechanical organ, 1759): 'January', 'April', August', 'November', and 'December' by Eberlin; the rest by L Mozart
The Seasons (ballet, Op 67) – Glazunov; (oratorio, 1797/98) – Haydn; (suite for percussion) – Takemitsu
The Four Seasons: see Nicknames and Sub-titles

1. Spring

'Longing for Spring' (song) – Alnaes
'Now Spring in all the Crevasses' (song) – Alnaes
Sonata in F, Op 24, 'Spring' (1805) – Beethoven
'Frühling' (song, Op 6/2, 1853) – Brahms
'Frühlingslied (song, Op 85/5, 1882) – Brahms
Spring Symphony (Op 44, 1949) – Britten
Appalachian Spring (1944) – Copland
'Rondes de Printemps' (No 3 of *Images)* – Debussy
Printemps (1887) – Debussy
On Hearing the First Cuckoo in Spring (1908) – Delius
Journal de Printemps (ten orchestral suites, Op 1, 1695) – Fischer
'Spring Dance' (No 6 of *Lyric Pieces,* Op 47, 1888) – Grieg
'Spring' (song, Op 33/2) – Grieg
Fire of Sping (prelude for piano, 1915) – Ireland

'Song of the Spring Tides' (No 3 of *Sarnia* Suite for piano, 1941) – Ireland
Frühlingsnacht (paraphrase after Schumann for piano) – Liszt
Roman Spring (cantata, 1969) – Milner
Songs of Springtime (1934) – Moeran
'Spring Voices' (song, 1936) – Quilter
Ode to Spring (for piano and orchestra Op 76) – Raff
'Am Buch in Frühling' (Lied, D 361, 1816) – Schubert
'An den Frühling' (Lied, D 245, 1815) – Schubert
'Frühlingsglaube' (Lied, D 686, 1820) – Schubert
'Im Frühling' (Lied, D 882, 1826) – Schubert
'Frühlingslied' (Lied, D 398, 1816) – Schubert
'Frühlingsnacht' (No 12 of *Liederkreis,* Op 39, 1840) – Schumann
'O Primavera, pioventu de L'Anno' (madrigal) – Schütz
Spring (for accordion orchestra) – Seiber (writing under the name G S Mathis)
'Spring in the Park' (No 4 from *Pelléas and Mélisande,* Op 46) – Sibelius
'Flying is Spring' (song, Op 31/1, 1891) – Sibelius
'It Was in the Early Spring' (song, Op 38/2, 1878) – Tchaikovsky
'All the Flowers of Spring' (choral song, 1923) – Warlock
Spring of the Year (1925) – Warlock
'Im Frühling' (Lied, 1888) – Wolf
Frühlings Erwachen (opera, 1928) – Ettinger
Frühlingsnacht (opera, 1908) – Schjelderup
Last Spring (elegiac melody, Op 34) – Grieg
Spring Overture (Op 9, 1913) – Jeremiáš
Primavera Overture (Op 31, 1934) – Riisager
Rite of Spring (ballet, 1913) – Stravinsky
See also Nicknames and Sub-titles

2. April

'Chanson d'Avril' (song, 1866) – Bizet
April (piece for piano, 1925) – Ireland
'As dewe in Aprylle' (song, 1918) – Warlock

3. May

May Night in the Ukraine (piano piece, 1911) – Bax
'The Sorrows of May' (part-song) – Bennett
'Mainacht' (Lied, Op 43/2, 1866) – Brahms
'O Süsser Mai' (part-song, Op 93a/3, 1884) – Brahms
'May Song' – Elgar
'In a May Morning' (No 2 of *Sarnia* Suite for piano, 1941) – Ireland
On a May Morning (piano piece, 1921) – Moeran
'The Merry Month of May' (song, 1925) – Moeran
'In a Merry May Morn' (madrigal) – Nicholson
May Night (opera, 1880) – Rimsky-Korsakov
'In Pride of May' (madrigal in five parts, 1598) – Weelkes
See also Nicknames and Sub-titles

4. Easter

Easter Oratorio (BWV 249, 1735) – J S Bach
'Ostern' (No 5 of *Seven Pieces,* Op 145) – Reger
Sonata in C for four organs, *Per la Festa di Pasqua* (1772) – Müller
See also Nicknames and Sub-titles

5. Summer

'Summer Days' (from *Seven Fruhe Lieder,* 1908) – Berg
Nuits d'Été (song cycle, Op 7) – Berlioz
'Sommerabend' (Lied, Op 85/1, 1882) – Brahms
It Fell Upon a Summer Day (1601) – Campian
In a Summer Garden (1908) – Delius
A Summer of Song (1930) – Delius
Summer Night on the River (1914) – Delius
Before and After Summer (song cycle, Op 16) – Finzi
'It Never Looks Like Summer' (No 5 of *Till Earth Outwears,* Op 19, 1955) – Finzi
Pastorale d'été (1933) – Honegger
Summer Evening (1919) – Ireland
Summer Valley (piece for piano, 1925) – Moeran
Summer Day (orchestral suite, Op 65a) – Prokofiev
'Late Summer' (song, 1919) – Warlock
Songe d'une Nuit d'Été (opera, 1850) – Thomas
Songe d'une Nuit d'Été (opera, 1925) – Vreuls
Summer Night (opera, 1910) – Clutsam
A Midsummer Night's Dream (1826–43) – Mendelssohn
Concerto d'Été for violin and orchestra (1944) – Rodrigo
See also Nicknames and Sub-titles: Estate; Summer; Wine of Summer

6. July

'Fourth of July' (No 3 of *Holidays Symphony,* 1913) – Ives

7. Whitsun

'Pfingstern' (No 6 of *Seven Pieces,* Op 145) – Reger

Sonata in B flat for four organs, *Per la Pentecost* (1775) – Müller

8. Autumn

'Autumn. (song) – Berkeley

In Autumn (piano piece, 1924) – Bridge

'Automne' (song, Op 18/3, *c* 1880) – Fauré

'Autumn Storm' (song, Op 18/4) – Grieg

Autumn Music – Panufnik

'Autumn Night' (song, Op 38/1, 1904) – Sibelius

'Im Herbst' (Lied) – Wolf

See also Nicknames and Sub-titles

9. September

'Dans le fôret de Septembre' (song, Op 85/1, 1903) – Fauré

10. October

October Mountain (1942) – Hovhaness

11. Winter

Winter Pastorale (1927) – Bridge

Winter Words (songs, Op 53, 1953) – Britten

Winter is an Icy Guest – Praetorius

Winter Bonfire (suite, Op 122) – Prokofiev

Chant d'Hiver – Ysaÿe

Wintermärchen (opera, 1908) – Goldmark

Winternachtsdroom (opera, 1902) – Boeck

Der Winter, for bass gamba and continuo – Telemann

See also Nicknames and Sub-titles: 'Winter'; 'Winter Daydreams'; 'Winter Wind'

12. November

November Woods (symphonic poem, 1917) – Bax

November Steps (1967) – Takemitsu

13. Christmas

Christmas Oratorio (BWV 248, 1734) – J S Bach

Santa Claus Symphony (No 3, 1858) – Fry

'Weinachten' (No 3 from *Seven Pieces,* Op 145) – Reger

Christmas Eve (suite, 1895) – Rimsky-Korsakov

Weinachtsmusik – Schoenberg

Noel Suisse (harpsichord piece) – Daquin

Sonata in A for four organs, *Pastorale per il Santo Natale* (1772) – Müller

'Christmas' (song for chorus, 1846) – Tolhurst

See also Nicknames and Sub-titles: Christmas Pastorale

14. February

'February Morning at the Golf' (song) – Alnaes

'At Middlegate Field in February' (No 2 of *I Said to Love,* songs) – Finzi

February's Child (piano piece, 1929) – Ireland

POLITICS AND MUSIC

In the widest sense, politics have often entered into music. It was 'politic' for instance, for kapellmeisters to write precisely what their masters wanted and not necessarily what their inner compulsions would have led them to write. Much war music is at base politically motivated: it is written to stir the people and/or to appease tough political masters, but it is evident from some of the works thus produced that the composers concerned would rather ignore the doings of the politicians and get on with the more benign occupation of composing music.

An exception is Luigi Nono. In 1970 he wrote *Y Entonses comprendio,* a homage to Che Guevara. It employs electronic sounds, three

Edward Heath conducting the London Symphony Orchestra (Popperfoto)

sopranos, and three comediennes. Part of the electronic sound-track is of the voice of Fidel Castro reading his last letter from Guevara; elsewhere the performers, reading from passages by the revolutionary poet Carlos Franqui, shout their message at the audience. At the first performance in Brussels in 1970 the composer was to be found handing out political leaflets to the audience.

A composer who combined his interest with politics and virtuoso pianism, reaching high in all three spheres, was Ignacy Jan Paderewski (1866–1941). He studied the piano with Leschetizky, wrote concertos, chamber and instrumental works and a symphony, and was the first Prime Minister of Poland (1919–21). He was incidentally the highest-paid serious pianist, accumulating a fortune of some $5 000 000, of which $500 000 was earned in the 1920–23 season.

Nearer our own time is Edward Heath, British Prime Minister 1970–74, who is an enthusiastic organist, and choir conductor, and who has recorded with the London Symphony Orchestra as conductor.

Elsewhere we have discussed composers who have written very many works. Eastern politics seem to have dictated a strange opposite phenomenon: a work written by many composers, the *Yellow River Concerto*. It was apparently designed by a committee of six musicians, one of whom, Hsien Hsing-Hai, was chosen as the work's 'composer'. The concerto itself is a banal agglomeration of late-19th-century romanticism, shy acknowledgements of 'modern' style, and a tub-thumping vessel for the message of triumphant Chinese Communism.

RAILWAYS AND MUSIC

The idea for this listing was suggested by one of the many fascinating sections in the sister book *The Guinness Book of Rail Facts and Feats* by John Marshall (1975). The author lists a number of works which have been suggested by trains and railways (to which I have taken the liberty of adding two more), and he points out that other composers such as Dvořák, possessed an enthusiasm for trains equalling that of any schoolboy without actually writing any music in which that method of transport is depicted.

Berlioz: *Song of the Railroads* (1846).
Ellis: *Coronation Scot* (1937).
Honegger: *Pacific 231* (tone poem, 1923).
Lumbye: *Jerbane Polka* (*c* 1850).
Prokofiev: *Winter Bonfire* (suite, Op 122, 1949) (A delightful tale of a children's winter camping expedition. The journey to and from the site is made by rail.)
Rosenberg: 'Railway Fugue' from *Journey to America* (opera, 1932).
E Strauss: *Bahn Frei Polka* (Op 45, *c* 1900).
J. Strauss II: *Vergnugungzug* ('Excursion train') and *Polka Galop*, Op 281 (1864).
Villa-Lobos: *Bachiana Brasilieras* No 2 (1930) (the fourth movement is called Toccata: 'Little Train of the Caipira').

A number of railway stations have been named after operatic subjects:

Cecchina in Rome, after the heroine in Piccinni's *La Bouna Figliuola* (1760).
Swiss Cottage, London, after Adam's opera *Le Châlet* (1834).
Szép Ilona, in Budapest, after Offenbach's *La Belle Helène* (1864).

WARS AND MUSIC

The splendour of the uniforms, the excitement of the bugle calls, the thrill of the charge, and the rattle and boom of the guns have frequently inspired composers to write music depicting wars. Often the colourful stories of heroic deeds have drawn imaginative music from a composer who wished his audience to visualise the scene in lurid and harrowing detail: some even went as far as imitating the moans and cries of the wounded and dying at the end of the battle. Generally, however, the noble and exhilarating aspects were stressed, and the victories were occasions for jubilant music and the firing of yet more cannon.

Since 1945 it has been realised by composers that there is no honour or pride in battle: an atomic war is a war in which no one wins, and composers have often turned to the ultimate in pessimism, drawing the picture of a silent, dead, and futureless planet. The Sixth Symphony of Vaughan Williams, for example, leaves one with a feeling of post-atomic desolation. He has accurately foretold the future in the mood of his Fourth Symphony (1935) in which the appalling years of the Second World War were implied. In Symphony No 5, written at the height of that war (1943), a scene of sunny post-war peace seems to be conveyed, but the last movement of the grim, disturbing Sixth Symphony (1947) is a long section of barely mobile music, never rising above pianissimo. The composer was reluctant to specify any programme for these three symphonies, but seen in the context of world events, their message is unmistakeable.

The first composer to write war music was Claudio Monteverdi. His *Madrigali guerrieri* (1638) and the 'Sinfonia da Guerra' from the opera *Il Ritorna d'Ulisse in Patria* (1641), this latter of an authenticity which has not been finally established, are antedated by his *Il Combatto di Tancredi e Clorinda* (1624) which in form lies between a small opera and a cycle of descriptive madrigals.

A selection of other composers who have dealt with war or subjects concerning war is given below:

J C Bach: Sonata in F for harpsichord or fortepiano, *Qui Represente La Bataille de Rosbach.* This descriptive piece was published in London about 1782, but the accuracy of the attribution to J C Bach is doubtful.

Balfe: *The Siege of Rochelle* (opera, 1835).

Beethoven: 'Battle Symphony' in *Egmont* incidental music, Op 84 (1810).
'Battle of Vittoria' Symphony Op 91 (1813), also known as the 'Battle' Symphony.

Biber: Suite in D, for strings, *Battalia* (1673).

Britten: *War Requiem* (Op 66, 1962).

Byrd: *The Battell,* for solo virginals.

Coates: *The Dambusters' March.*

Dandrieu: Suite of symphonies *Les caractères de la Guerre* (1718), reputedly used in one of the composer's operas.

Guglielmi: The opera *Enea e Lavinia* (1786) required over 80 troops for each performance.

Haydn: *Mass in Time of War* (1796), also known as the *Drum Mass.*

Isaac: *A la Bataglia,* instrumental piece.

Janáček: Piano Sonata *From the Street 1. x.1905,* only a part of which survives, commemorates an incident on that date during a patriotic demonstration in Brno in which František Pavlík, an unarmed civilian, was assassinated by Austrian troops.

Khachaturian: *The Battle for Stalingrad* (1942).

Kodály: 'The Battle and Defeat of Napoleon'–from *Háry János* Suite (1926).

Liszt: *The Battle of the Huns* (tone poem, 1856).

Locke: *The Siege of Rhodes* (opera, 1656).

Martinů: *Memorial to Lidice* (1943) (see below).

Molchanov: *The Dawns are Quiet Here* (a 'front-line' opera, 1972).

Mozart: Contretanz in C, K 535, *La Bataille* (1788).
Contretanz in C, K 587, *The Siege of Helden Coburg* (1789).

Muffat: 'Fasciculus VIII', from *Indissolubilis Amicitia* (instrumental suite).

Muradeli: Symphony: *The War of Liberation* (1942–45).

Neubauer: Symphony in D, Op 11, *La Bataille de Martinestie oder Coburgs Sieg über die Türken* (1789).

Pedrotti: *Guerra in Quattro* (opera, 1861).

Prokofiev: 'The Battle on the Ice', from *Alexander Nevsky* (Cantata, Op 78, 1938).

Shostakovitch: Symphony No 7 in C, *Leningrad* (Op 60, 1942).
The Fall of Berlin (Op 82, 1949).
String Quartet No 8 in C minor (Op 110, 1960).

Storace: *The Siege of Belgrade* (opera, 1791).

Suk: *War Tryptich* (Op 35, 1914–20).

Susato: *La Bataille* (pavane for instruments).

Tchaikovsky: *1812* Overture (Op 49, 1880).

Verdi: *Battaglia di Legnano* (opera, 1849).

Vivaldi: *Juditha Triumphans* (oratorio, 1716).

Walton: *The Spitfire* (prelude and Fugue, 1942).

Of the numerous war scenes in operas of all ages, it is worth noting one in particular for its extraordinary tempo marking. The opera *Sofonisba* (1762) by Tommaso Traetta (or Trajetta) opens with a battle scene in which two oboes, two horns (pitched in C and D respectively), and a string band are instructed to play 'Allegrissimo e strepitosissimo', literally, 'very joyfully and with much animation and gaiety and extremely noisily and boisterously'.

The most famous rhythmic pattern is the group of three short notes and one long one with which Beethoven opened his Fifth Symphony. Speculation surrounds Beethoven's 'meaning': two popular theories are circulated, first the explanation attributed to Beethoven himself: 'Thus Fate comes knocking at the door', and secondly the notion that Beethoven, the nature-lover, was immortalising a bird call. The grim force with which the motif is projected in the first, third, and fourth movements of the symphony point more convincingly to fate than to a defenceless yellowhammer as being the true inspiration; that is, if any extra-musical explanation at all is required.

The symphony, and particularly the first four notes, was chosen to act as a rallying-call for the peoples of Nazi-occupied Europe during the Second World War. The 'dit dit dit dah' rhythm is identical to the international Morse signal for the letter 'V', which came to be regarded as the symbol of ultimate victory. The letter was chalked on walls and doors, and the 'V-sign', immortalised by the Prime Minister, Mr (later Sir) Winston Spencer Churchill in his salute (palm outward) of the two raised fingers, was surreptitiously practised throughout the war-darkened Continent, to the serious detriment of Nazi morale. Transferred to sound, the signal was utilised in knocking on doors and windows or anywhere else to attract attention, and even during idle rail- or window-tapping while waiting in food queues.

Music notation		Morse		letter		Roman numeral		number	
♪♪♪ ♩	=	···–	=	V	=	V	=	5	=

Beethoven's Fifth Symphony, the start of which may be set to the words 'Vic-tor-y V'

The most potent factor in the propagation of this rhythm was its use by the BBC as a time signal between news broadcasts to occupied territories. Heard at intervals as a dull, insistent drum-tap to assist the tuning of home-made radios, it seemed to typify the dark, ominous will of the underground movements eventually to arise and overcome the Nazi oppressors.

The signal was carefully chosen by the London planners. Once the rhythm itself had been chosen, it was essential for the actual sound to fulfil a number of requirements. It had to be absolutely distinctive; simple and easily remembered, and acoustically satisfactory. In short, the notes had to be heard clearly in poor receiving conditions, sometimes against atmospherics; it had to be of a tone quality to facilitate tuning, and above all it had to be audible at low-volume level but not carry outside the cramped hide-outs in which it was listened to by news-hungry groups.

In 1942 the German SS General Reinhard Heydrich was killed by patriots in Czechoslovakia. As a reprisal, the German authorities ordered the entire destruction of the mining village of Lidice. Every man was shot, along with 56 women; the rest of the women and the children were removed to concentration camps and every building in the village was levelled. The Nazis attempted to wipe out entirely the very existence and memory of the village. As a mark of protest a number of towns elsewhere took the name of Lidice (among them San Geronimo, Mexico, and a completely new village near Joliet, Illinois), and the tragic village is commemorated in music in a moving tone poem by Bohuslav Martinů entitled *Memorial to Lidice,* completed the following year. At the climax of this work the 'Victory V' motif from Beethoven's Fifth Symphony dominates the music like a grim warning of revenge.

At the collapse of the Nazi forces in Europe on 8 May 1945, the call-sign of the Overseas Service of the BBC underwent a dramatic transformation. James Blades, who had recorded the war-time rhythm on an African slit-drum, re-recorded it using modern orchestral timpani which thundered out the call in a thrilling affirmation of victory.

Section V

OPERA, CHORAL AND VOCAL

La Scala Theatre, Milan (Popperfoto)

(a) OPERA

'An *Opera* is a Poetical Tale, or fiction, represented by Vocal and Instrumental Musick, adorn'd with Scenes, Machines and Dancing. The suppos'd Persons of this Musical *Drama*, are generally Supernatural, as Gods and Goddesses, and Heroes, which at least are descended from them, and in due time are to be adopted into their number.' John Dryden

A CHRONOLOGICAL INTRODUCTION

Dryden's 17th-century view of opera goes on in its snobbish way grudgingly to admit 'meaner persons' such as shepherds only if they are essential to the action, but the common person was strictly excluded for most of the time. Opera's subjects were later to include all manners and classes of people, and we may assume that the earliest ancestors of opera were also a little less high-class conscious, as has been hinted in Setting the Scene. In that Section, the earliest roots of opera were guessed at; now it is time to give a more definite presentation of the known facts concerning the components which may have led to the establishment of opera as a form.

400 BC Euripides' play *Orestes* was performed with accompanying music, some of which may have been sung.

c **1283 AD** Adam de la Hale (*c* 1240–88), a French trouvère known as the 'Hunchback of Arras', wrote *La Jeu de Robin et de Marion,* which was performed in Naples at about this time. It is a kind of proto-opera in which a story is told in music. The title of this piece has led to the belief that the composer had some connection with the Sherwood Forest area of Nottinghamshire (Robin Hood; Maid Marian) and that he might even be identified with the Sherwood minstrel Alan-a-Dale, since a similarity of name is apparent. However, there is no evidence that Hale ever came to England (his connections with Italy are stronger: he accompanied his employer the Count of Artois, to Naples and Sicily, and he died in Italy), or that any part of the Robin Hood legend originated abroad. Neither does the story of *Le Jeu de Robin et de Marion* bear a resemblance to any of the Robin Hood tales.[1] Regretfully, we must conclude that the approximate similarities in dates and names are coincidental.

1472 Angelo Poliziano's play *Orfeo* was produced in Mantua. Edward J Dent suggests that its structure indicates that many of the poems were sung.

16th century The Italian composer Vincenzo Galilei, the father of the astronomer Galileo Galilei, produced songs and lute solos which may have assisted in the development of opera as a distinct art form. During the century, the setting of sacred texts and miracle plays to music gradually took three separate ways. These resulted in the following concepts which, despite elements from each which could be found in the others, had crystallised by about 1600 into:

1. **Masque**–a usually mythological play with poetry, music, and dancing, and other stage presentations, in which the actors wore masks.
2. **Oratorio**–a presentation of a liturgical story with music, so called because it would be performed in an oratory rather than in a church or theatre.
3. **Opera**–the Italian word for 'work' (compare *opus)*; the Italian word for opera is *Melodrama* = 'melody' + 'drama'). Its concern with stories of gods and heroes has already been described.

Opera was a virtually exclusively Italian possession for the first three-quarters of a century after its commonly accepted beginning, and it took a further 75 years before any serious attempt at opera in a different language was made. The important dates follow:

1597 The earliest true opera: *Daphne* by Jacopo Peri–lost. Although the music is lost, the libretto by Rinuccini survives together with some of the directions for the production. A big, terrifying serpent is required which is controlled by a man on all fours within. The creature is required to sway and undulate, to flap its wings and to breathe fire.

1600 The earliest surviving opera: *Eurydice* by Peri and Giulio Caccini (1546–1618). Caccini later that same year reset the same Eurydice story without assistance from any other composer. These works were performed at the house of Giovanni Bardi, Count of Vernio, in Florence.

1607 The earliest opera of which performances are still occasionally to be seen: Monteverdi's *Orfeo*. The instrumentation for this work was: two violini piccoli, first and second violins, violas, two viole da gamba, contrabass gamba, four recorders, two cornets, five trombones (alto, three tenor, bass), three trumpets. In addition a large complement of continuo instruments would have been required, including harpsichord, positive organ, lutes (harps?), viola da gamba, and bass gamba.

[1] However, the famous English outlaw has not been overlooked by opera-writers: William Shield dealt with the story in 1784, and Sir Henry Rowley Bishop wrote an opera entitled *Maid Marion* in 1822. In America, Reginald de Koven composed an opera *Robin Hood* in 1890.

1627 The first German opera was *Daphne* by Heinrich Schütz. It was produced at Torgau but it has since entirely disappeared.

1637 The first public opera-house at which an admission fee was charged was opened in Venice.

1656 The first English opera, and the first opera ever heard in England. Sir William Davenant, who later became Poet Laureate, wrote a libretto for an entertainment he described as *The First Dayes Entertainment at Rutland House by Declamation and Musick: After the Manner of the Ancients*. This was a series of speeches between which vocal and instrumental music was performed. The music is lost. Later the same year Davenant's libretto *The Siege of Rhodes* was set to music by Henry Lawes, Henry Cooke, Matthew Locke, Charles Coleman, and George Hudson. This is probably **the opera in which most composers had a hand.** The famous diarist John Evelyn entered the following comment after seeing the opera (5 May 1659): '. . . a new opera after the Italian way, in recitative music and scenes, much inferior to the Italian composure and magnificence.'

1671 The first French opera was *Pomone* by Robert Cambert.

1674 The first occasion in England upon which the opera orchestra was brought to its present position in the theatre was for a performance of Locke's *Tempest* at Dorset Gardens Theatre, London. Hitherto the band had played on a concealed platform above the stage; now it was brought down to a position just below the line of sight of the audience, immediately in front of the stage.

1674 The first foreign opera heard in England was *Ariane* by Louis Grabu (?–*c* 1694) with a libretto by Cambert. It was in fact given in an English translation, and was performed on the occasion of the wedding of the Duke of York and Mary of Modena.

c **1675 The beginnings of a breakaway form–Pantomine**–are to be found in the stage parodies of Thomas Duffett, whose operatic caricatures probably contained the origins of the conventions of the 'Principal Boy' being taken by a young actress, and the 'Dame' by a male comedian.

1692 The first opera to be based on a Shakespeare story was Purcell's *The Fairy Queen* adapted (by E Settle?) from *A Midsummer Night's Dream* and given at the Dorset Gardens Theatre, London, in April of that year.

1704 The first opera to be heard in Prague was Sartori's *La Rete di Vulcano*.

1710 The first opera in England to be performed entirely in Italian was *Almahide,* a pastiche by a group of composers led by Giovanni Bononcini. It was Italian opera in London which prompted Dr Johnson's famous description of 'an exotick and irrational entertainment'.

c **1750 The first comic operas** were written about this time; they were designed to be performed between the acts of opere seria.

1779 The first Russian opera was *Melnik, Koldun, Obmanschchik i Svat* by Evstignei Ipatovich Fomin (1761–1800), but Italian opera written by émigré composers had thrived, particularly in St Petersburg (now Leningrad) for many years. Franceso Araia wrote **the first opera in the Russian language:** *Cephal i Prokris,* libretto by Alexander Sumarokov, produced in St Petersburg on 10 March 1755.

1794 The first American opera was *Tammanny* by James Hewitt (1770–1827).

1819 The first Spanish opera was *Los Esclavos Felices* by Juan Crisostomo Antonio Arriaga y Balzola (1806–25).

1866 The first true Czech opera was *The Bartered Bride* by Smetana, one of eight operas by this composer.

1899 The first Portuguese opera was *Serrana* by Alfredo Keil (1850–1907), a German composer working in Portugal.

By the early 19th century a convention had grown up concerning terminology. **Grand opera** was defined as that in which all the words are set to music, from recitative, through aria, duet, trio, and other ensembles, to chorus.

The alternative term, **comic opera,** was reserved for opera in which some of the words were spoken.

If any differentiation is still necessary, it is time these old-fashioned terms were replaced.

As it stands, works such as Beethoven's *Fidelio* and many other serious operas are deprived of the description 'grand' and are lumped together with 'comic' operas.

OPERATIC PROLIFERATION

As in all other art forms, once opera had become an established practice with its own rules and ingredients, and the public was used to the form and clamoured for more, the creators answered the demand with what seems like over-production. It has been estimated that at least 25 000 operatic libretti were written before the year 1800, and many of these libretti were set to music more than once–some a great many times. This profusion began early in the history of opera and did not cease until the end of the last century, as the following table shows. Of course, it is not possible always to be accurate as to the numbers of operas written by a given composer (Albinoni claimed to have written over 200 operas, never spending more than a week on any one, but only about thirty five are known to us): often it is found that two or more composers share in the production of a single work, and sometimes it is difficult to draw a definite line between an opera and, say, an oratorio or a cantata. The totals below, therefore, are somewhat provisional, but there seems little doubt that the first (ie earliest) composer in the list has a clear lead over his rivals in operatic proliferation, judging by extant works.

Composer	*Number of operas*
Draghi, Antonio (1635–1700)	*c* 175
Scarlatti, Alessandro (1660–1725)	115
Keiser, Reinhard (1674–1739)	*c* 100
Hasse, Johann Adolf (1699–1783)	102, including 14 intermezzi and 23 pastiches
Galuppi, Baldassare (1706—85)	96, plus many pastiches
Gluck, Christoph Willibald von (1714–87)	107
Guglielmi, Pietro (1727–1804)	*c* 100
Piccinni, Nicolò (1728–1800)	*c* 120
Paisiello, Giovanni (1740–1816)	83, plus 16 cantatas, serenatas, etc
Müller, Wenzel (1767–1835)	100+
Bishop, Sir Henry Rowley (1786–1855)	69, plus arrangements and adaptations of other composers' operas; masques, ballets, etc.
Offenbach, Jacques (1819–80)	104 operas and operettas

OPERAS IN WHICH THE HERO AND/OR HEROINE DIES

Despite the natural human love of happy endings, by no means all operas end happily. In some instances, the closing death scene is of spectacular and gruesome violence, as when the heroine in Halévy's *La Juive* dives into a cauldron of boiling oil, or when Fenella in Auber's *Masaniello* hurls herself into the mouth of Vesuvius (from the Royal Palace in Naples–quite a leap); but in one way or another all the following characters pay the ultimate price for their pride, heroism, folly, or guilt.

Opera[1]	*Composer*	*Departing hero/heroine*
Acis, Galatea e Polifemo	Handel	Acis
Adriana Lecouvreur	Cilèa	Adriana
Africaine, L'	Meyerbeer	Selika and Neluski
Aïda	Verdi	Aïda and Radames
Aleko	Rakhmaninoff	Zemfira
Amore dei Tre Ri, L'	Montemezzi	Avito and Manfredo
André Chenier	Giordano	André Chenier and Madeleine
Arlesiana, L'	Cilèa	Federico

[1] In some cases the identical story has been set to music by one or more other composers. The best known only are given here.

Opera	Composer	Departing hero/heroine
Billy Budd	Britten	Billy Budd
Bohème, La	Puccini	Mimi
Boris Godunov	Mussorgsky	Boris
Bronwen	Holbrooke	Bronwen and Caradoe
(Part 3 of the Trilogy *The Cauldron of Anwyn)*		
Carmen	Bizet	Carmen
Cavalleria Rusticana	Mascagni	Turiddu
Combattimento di Tancredi e Clorinda, Il	Monteverdi	Clorinda
Consul, The	Menotti	Magda
Dalibor	Smetana	Milada and Dalibor (both versions)
Damnation of Faust	Berlioz	Faust

Boris Christoff, whose portrayal of Boris Godunov is world renowned (Popperfoto)

Opera	Composer	Departing hero/heroine
Dante and Beatrice	Philpot	Beatrice
Daphne	Strauss, R.	Leukippos
Death in Venice	Britten	Aschenbach
Debora e Joele	Pizzetti	Sisera
Demon, The	Rubinstein	Tamara
Devil Take Her, The	Benjamin	The Poet
Dido and Aeneas	Purcell	Dido
Doktor Faustus	Busoni	Faustus
Don Carlos	Verdi	Don Carlos
Don Giovanni	Mozart	Don Giovanni
Don Quichotte	Massenet	Don Quichotte
Ernani	Verdi	Ernani
Eugène Onégin	Tchaikovsky	Eugène Onégin
Favorita, La	Donizetti	Leonora
Faust	Gounod	Margarita
Fedora	Giordano	Fedora
Fête Galante	Smyth	Pierrot
Flying Dutchman, The	Wagner	Senta
Forest, The	Smyth	Heinrich and Röschen
Force of Destiny, The	Verdi	Leonore
Francesca da Rimini	Rakhmaninoff	Paolo and Francesca
Francesca da Rimini	Zandonai	Francesca
Giaconda, La	Ponchielli	Giaconda
Gloriana	Britten	Queen Elizabeth I
Goldsmith of Toledo, The	Offenbach	Magdalena
Götter-dämmerung	Wagner	Siegfried, Brünnhilde, and the inhabitants of Valhalla
Goyescas	Granados	Fernando
Huguenots, Les	Meyerbeer	Raoul and Valentine
Iernin	Lloyd	Iernin
Immortal Hour, The	Boughton	Eochaidh
Iris	Mascagni	Iris
Ivan the Terrible	Rimsky-Korsakov	Olga

Opera	*Composer*	*Departing hero/ heroine*
Jewels of the Madonna, The	Wolf-Ferrari	Gennario
Jongleur de Notre Dame, Le	Massenet	The Juggler
Juive, La	Halèvy	Rachel
Katerina Ismailova	Shostakovitch	Katerina Ismailova
Katya Kabanova	Janáček	Katya Kabanova
Königskinder	Humperdinck	The King's son and the Goose Girl
Lakmé	Delibes	Lakmé
Life for the Tsar, A	Glinka	Ivan Susanin
Lucia di Lammermoor	Donizetti	Lucia and Edgar
Lucrezia Borgia	Donizetti	Genarro and Lucrezia
Luisa Miller	Verdi	Luisa and Rodolfo
Lulu	Berg	Lulu and Geschwitz
Macbeth	Verdi	Macbeth and Lady Macbeth
Madame Butterfly	Puccini	Madame Butterfly
Maid of Pskov	Rimsky-Korsakov	Olga
Mam'selle Fifi	Cui	Lieutenant van Eyrik
Manon	Massenet	Manon
Manon Lescaut	Puccini	Manon
Masaniello	Auber	Fenella and Masaniello
Masked Ball, The	Verdi	Riccardo
May Night, A	Rimsky-Korsakov	Pannochka
Medium, The	Menotti	Toby
Mefistofele	Boïto	Faust
Mozart and Salieri	Rimsky-Korsakov	Mozart
Nabucco	Verdi	Abigaille
Nerone	Boïto	Rubria
Norma	Bellini	Norma
Oberst Chabert	Walterhausen	Chabert and Rosine
Oedipus Rex	Stravinsky	Jocasta
Otello	Verdi	Desdemona and Otello
Pagliacci, I	Leoncavallo	Nedda and Silvio
Pauvre Matelot, Le	Milhaud	The Sailor
Pelléas and Mèlisande	Debussy	Mèlisande
Prophète, Le	Meyerbeer	Bertha, Johan, and Fides
Queen of Cornwall, The	Boughton	Tristram and Iseult
Queen of Sheba, The	Goldmark	Assad
Queen of Spades, The	Tchaikovsky	Herman
Rake's Progress, The	Stravinsky	Adonis
Rape of Lucrecia	Britten	Lucrecia
Rigoletto	Verdi	Gilda
Roi de Lahore, Le	Massenet	Alim und Sita
Roi d'Ys, Le	Lalo	Margared
Roméo et Juliette	Gounod	Romeo and Juliet
Rusalka	Dvořák	The Prince
Salome	Strauss, R	Jokanaan and Salome
Samson and Delilah	Saint-Saëns	Samson and Delilah
Semiramide	Rossini	Semiramide
Simone Boccanegra	Verdi	Simone Boccanegra
Stone Guest, The	Dargomijsky	Don Juan
Suor Angelica	Puccini	Sister Angelica
Tabarro, Il	Puccini	Luigi
Tannhäuser	Wagner	Elisabeth and Tannhäuser
Thaïs	Massenet	Thaïs
Tosca, La	Puccini	Cavaradossi and Tosca
Travelling Companion, The	Stanford	The Travelling Companion
Traviata, La	Verdi	Violetta

Opera	*Composer*	*Departing hero/heroine*
Tristan und Isolde	Wagner	Tristan and Isolde
Trojans, The	Berlioz	Cassandra and Choroebus
Trovatore, Il	Verdi	Leonora, Manrico, and Azucena
Vida Breve, La	Falla	Salud
Village Romeo and Juliet, A	Delius	Vreli and Sali
Wally, La	Catalani	Wally and Hagenbach
Werther	Massenet	Werther
Wozzeck	Berg	Marie and Wozzeck
Wreckers, The	Smyth	Mark and Thirga

OPERAS SET IN UNUSUAL OR EXOTIC SURROUNDINGS

The majority of operatic stories are set in a fairly narrow range of areas and periods. In the early days of operatic growth, the favourite settings were mythological, but gradually, as the popularity of opera required more and more works, and these in turn demanded further stories, writers of libretti widened their range to include ancient Rome, ancient Gaul, Spain, ancient and contemporary Russia, Switzerland, etc, the time span stretched from the old world of heros and satyrs, through the Middle Ages, and right up to the then present day. Subjects, always somewhat lurid and improbable, included witchcraft and magic; in fact, magic is still a prime ingredient of opera. Political occurrences were also dealt with in operas from the 18th century onwards and were given an enormous boost in popularity by the French Revolution, during which composers in that torn country competed to prove their patriotism and loyalty to whichever side happened to be nearest–and heaven help them if they declared their allegiance to one side and then fell into the hands of the authorities on the other! Political operas were frequently taken seriously by audiences and authorities alike, the extreme example being the occasion in 1830 at which Auber's *Masaniello* was performed in Brussels. It is entirely due to the performance of this opera on 25 August of that year that patriotic feeling crystallised into revolution and Belgium won independence from Holland, a state which was finally ratified on 20 January 1831. Operas are meant to stir the emotions, but it is doubtful that even Auber expected such a violent and far-reaching reaction, and since he never attended performances of his own works, the news of it must have come as a considerable shock to him. *Masaniello,* then, is **the only opera so far to have sparked off a revolution.**

The first operatic treatment of domestic tragedy, as opposed to comedy, was in Verdi's *Luisa Miller* (Naples, 1849), based on Schiller's play *Kabale und Liebe.* This was followed in Trieste the next year by the same composer's *Stiffelio* (later to provide much of the music for *Aroldo,* Rimini, 1857). *La Traviata* (Venice, 1853) and Charpentier's *Louise,* the latter set in the Paris slums (1900), also followed this trend.

However, the real purpose of this Section is to list operas which are set in other than the usual mid and south European locales. The usual disclaimer is necessary: such a list can not–and need not–ever be complete, but the writer has so far been unable to trace any operas set in the Antipodes, a somewhat unjust state of affairs if true, now that Sydney has a spectacular opera-house.

Unusual setting	*Opera*	*Composer*
Baghdad	*The Barber of Baghdad* (1858)	Cornelius
Boston, Massachusetts	*A Masked Ball* (1859)	Verdi
Cairo and the Sahara Desert	*Marouf* (1914)	Rabaud
Californian Gold-rush	*The Girl of the Golden West* (1910)	Puccini

Unusual setting	*Opera*	*Composer*
China	*Turandot* (1926)	Puccini
	Turandot (1917)	Busoni
	The Nightingale (1914)	Stravinsky
	L'Eroe Cinese (1752)	Bonno
Egypt	*Aïda* (1871)	Verdi
	Djamileh (1872)	Bizet
	Thaïs (1894)	Massenet
	Zauberflöte (1791)	Mozart
Finland	*L'Etoile du Nord* (1854)	Meyerbeer
Gaza, Palestine	*Samson and Delilah* (1877)	Saint-Saëns
Heaven	*Mefistofele Prologue* (1868)	Boïto
Hell	*Francesca da Rimini* (1906)	Rakhmaninoff
Hell (part of the action)	*Orfeo* (1606)	Monteverdi
	Orfeo ed Euridice (1762)	Gluck
India	*Lakmé* (1883)	Delibes
	Savitri (1916)	Holst
Japan	*Iris* (1898)	Mascagni
	Madame Butterfly (1904)	Puccini
Lahore	*Le Roi de Lahore* (1877)	Massenet
Lima, Peru	*Le Carrosse du Saint-Sacrement* (1924)	Berners
Lisbon, on an ocean-going liner, and India	*L'Africaine* (1865)	Meyerbeer
Northern Norway	*Greysteel (The Bearsarks Come to Sirnadale)* (1906)	Gatty
Peru at the time of the Aztecs	*Opferung des Gefengenen* ('Sacrifice of the Prisoner') (1926)	Wellesz
Rhine, bed of the	*Das Rheingold* (1869)	Wagner
	Lurline (1860)	Wallace
	Lorelei (1863)	Bruch
	Elda (1880)	Catalani
Scotland: Northern Isles	*The Seal-Woman* (1924)	Bantock
On board HMS *Indomitable*	*Billy Budd* (1951)	Britten
On the moon (part of the action)	*Il Mondo della Luna* (1777)	Haydn
On a spaceship	*Aniara* (1959)	Blomdahl

GILBERT AND SULLIVAN

The most successful musical partnership of all time is also the most famous. When the composer Arthur Seymour **Sullivan** (1842–1900) formed an association with William Schwenk **Gilbert** (1836–1911) in 1871 they founded a style of opera (or operetta) production in which their respective talents were complemented to such a degree that the resulting series of stage works inhabit a special branch of genius: a sublime blend of melody, wit, and high spirits.

Their first opera was *Thespis*, produced at the Gaiety Theatre on 23 December 1871, and it was followed by a succession of operas which continued for a quarter of a century.

1875 *Trial by Jury*.
1877 *The Sorcerer*.
1878 *HMS Pinafore*.
1879 *The Pirates of Penzance*.
1881 *Patience*.

It was in 1881 that the Savoy Theatre, built specially for the presentation of Gilbert and Sullivan operas, was opened. The players who had been so successful, and who were to continue and increase this success for the next two decades at the theatre were known as 'the Savoyards'. The famous series of stage works continued:

1882 *Iolanthe*.
1884 *Princess Ida*.

1885 *The Mikado.*
1887 *Ruddigore.*
1888 *The Yeoman of the Guard.*
1889 *The Gondoliers.*
1893 *Utopia Limited.*
1896 *The Grand Duke.*

Sub-titles of Gilbert and Sullivan operas

All of the operas except *The Sorcerer* and *The Pirates of Penzance* carry sub-titles, as follows:

Bunthorne's Bride, Patience, or (1881).
Castle Adamant, Princess Ida, or (1884).
Flowers of Progress, Utopia Ltd, or the (1893).
Gods Grown Old, Thespis, or the (1871).
King of Barataria, The Gondoliers, or the (1889).
Lass that Loved a Sailor, HMS Pinafore, or the (1878).
Merryman and his Maid, The Yeoman of the Guard, or the (1888).
Novel and Original Cantata, A–Trial by Jury (1875).
Peer and the Peri, Iolanthe, or the (1882).
Statutory Duel, The Grand Duke, or the (1896).
Town of Titipu, The Mikado, or the (1885).
Witch's Curse, Ruddigore, or the (1887).

Although the success of the Savoy operas is unique in stage history because of the quality of the productions, and the delightful if uneven partnership between the providers of words and music, the concept itself was by no means new. Roots for the style can be traced in countless 'ballad' operas of the mid- and late-18th-century London theatres, and in comic opera from abroad.

A story circulates that, in a fit of spleen, and in an apparent attempt to belittle the mellow Sullivan and his music, Gilbert said: 'I know nothing about music. I merely know that there is composition and decomposition. That is what your song is–rot!' Perhaps because of such explosions, the famous partnership split up over a relatively trivial matter: the choice of a carpet for the Savoy Theatre.

Sullivan had by no means limited his associations with literary men to Gilbert; he tried hard to establish other connections both before and during his 'Gilbert days', but alas none had the popularity of the G and S productions. Here is a list of his other stage works, together with the names of the librettists:

Burnand (Francis Cowley) **and Sullivan:** *Cox and Box* (1867); *The Contrabandista, or The Lord of the Ladrones* (1867); *The Chieftan* (1894).
Carr and Sullivan–see Pinero and Sullivan.
Chorley (Henry Fothergill) **and Sullivan:** *The Sapphire Necklace* (1863–64, but never staged).
Grundy (Sidney) **and Sullivan:** *Haddon Hall* (1892).
Hood (Basil) **and Sullivan:** *The Rose of Persia* (1899); *The Emerald Isle* (1901, the music completed by Edward German after Sullivan's death).
Pinero (Arthur), **Carr** (Comyns), **and Sullivan:** *The Beauty Stone* (1898).
Stevenson (B C) **and Sullivan:** *The Zoo* (1875).

Sullivan's one excursion into grand opera was *Ivanhoe* (1891), with a libretto by Julian Sturgis after Walter Scott. In addition, Sullivan was a prolific hymn- and song-writer, the producer of incidental music for a number of plays including several by Shakespeare (*Henry VIII, Macbeth, The Merchant of Venice, The Merry Wives of Windsor,* and *The Tempest*), choral music, overtures, a Cello Concerto, and an 'Irish' Symphony in E major. There are also a few chamber and piano works.

THE LIBRETTO

One component of an opera which is sometimes overlooked, often disregarded, and frequently libelled, but without which there would be no opera, is the libretto. It is not generally realised that the great majority of the words are completed before the composer sets to work on the music. No matter how much it may seem that the reverse is true, it is simply not possible to set the words of a drama to music which already exists. No chicken-and-egg doubts here: the words always come first.

The word 'libretto' = 'little book' and comes from the time, near the beginning of operatic history, when the story and the music were bound separately. The earliest operatic singers were primarily actors who learnt their vocal parts by ear: to have the music *and* the words bound together would have made the book unnecessarily cumbersome.

Many famous writers have provided stores

upon which operas have been based, while other writers have even made a speciality of the operatic libretto.

The most successful librettist was Pietro Antonio Domenico Bonaventura Trepassi (1698–1782), the Italian poet who is better known by the name given to him by his adoptive father Vincento Gravina: Metastasio. The texts which he wrote, over 70 in number, were so popular during his lifetime that a list of his stories and the composers who set them would take on the appearance of a history of 18th-century opera. It is doubtful whether such a list could ever be completed (Grove says that some of his stories were set 60 or 70 times), but the following selection will indicate which of his libretti were the most frequently heard during the period of Metastasio's greatest popularity between 1724 and 1734. Alternative names were sometimes given for a substantially similar story, and these are given after the main entries to which they relate.

1724 *Didone Abbandonata,* set by Sarri, 1724; Porpora, 1725; Duni, 1739; Lampugnani, 1739; Galuppi, 1741; Hasse, 1742; Jommelli, 1747 and 1749; Terradellas, 1750; Manna, 1751; Fioroni, 1755; Bernasconi, 1756; Traetta, 1757; Zoppis, 1758; G Brunetti, 1759; Schwanenberg, *c* 1760; Jommelli, a third setting, 1763; Piccinni, 1770; Insanguine, 1772; Sacchini, 1775; Schuster, 1776; Holzbauer, 1779; Sarti, 1784; Cherubini, 1786; L Kozeluh, 1790; Paisiello, 1794; Paer, 1811; Reissiger, 1824.

1726 *Siroe (rè di Persia),* set by Sarri, 1726; Vinci, 1726; Porpora, 1727; Vivaldi, 1727; Handel, 1728; Hasse, 1733; Pérez, 1740; G Scarlatti, 1742; Manna, 1743; Conforto, 1752; Galuppi, 1754; Lampugnani, 1755; Errichelli, 1759; Piccinni, 1759; Latilla, *c* 1762; Giardini, 1763; Zoppis, 1765; Traetta, 1767; Sarti, 1779. Also set as a ballet by Raupach and Starzer, 1760.

1727 *Catone in Utica,* set by Vinci, 1727; Leo, 1729; Hasse, 1731; Handel, 1732; Vivaldi, 1737; Duni, 1740; K H Graun, 1744; Jommelli, 1749; Ferrandini, 1753; Höpken, 1753; Ciampi, 1757; J C Bach, 1761; Gassmann, 1761; Piccinni, 1770; Paisiello, 1789; Winter, 1791.

1728 *Ezio,* set by Porpora, 1728; Auletta, 1728; Vinci, 1728; Hasse, 1730; Handel, 1732; Lampugnani, 1736; Leo, 1739; Jommelli, 1741; G Scarlatti, 1744; Jommelli, second and third settings, 1748; 1749; Gluck, 1750; K H Graun, 1755; Hasse, second setting, 1755; Galuppi, 1757; Traetta, 1757; Jommelli, fourth setting, 1758; Brioschi, *c* 1760; Guglielmi, 1770; Mysliveček, 1777; Bertoni, 1781.

1729 *Alessandro nell' Indie,* set by Vinci, 1729; Duni, 1736; Hasse, 1736; Corselli, 1738; Galuppi, 1738; Brivio, 1739; Jommelli, 1744; Pérez, 1745; Wagenseil, 1748; G Scarlatti, 1753; Piccinni, 1758; Holzbauer, 1759; J C Bach, 1762; Traetta, 1762; Sacchini, 1763; G Cocchi, 1764; Fischietti, 1764; Naumann, 1767; Gatti, 1768; J A Kozeluh, 1769; Bertoni, 1770; Corri, 1774; Piccinni, second setting, 1774; Paisiello, 1775; Cimarosa, 1781; Cherubini, 1784; Bianchi, 1787; Neukomm, 1804.

Also set as *Alessandro e Poro* by K H Graun, 1744; as *Alexandre aux Indes* by Mereaux, 1783; as *Poro* by Handel, 1731; Porpora, 1731; Gluck, 1744; and as *Cleofilde* by Hasse, 1731. Vivaldi also set the story *c* 1736, but his opera is lost.

1729 *Semiramide riconosciuta,* set by Porpora, 1729; Vinci, 1729; Araia, 1737; Aliprandi, 1740; Jommelli, 1741; Lampugnani, 1741; Hasse, 1744; Terradellas, 1746; Hasse, second setting, 1747; Gluck, 1748; Galuppi, 1749; Pérez, 1750; K H Graun, 1754; Cocchi, 1757; Sacchini, 1763; Cocchi, second setting, 1771; Salieri, 1782; Meyerbeer, 1819.

1730 *Artaserse* set by Vinci, 1730; Brivio, 1740; Hasse, 1740; Gluck, 1741; Chiarini, 1742; K H Graun, 1743; Duni, 1744; Terradellas, 1744; G Scarlatti, 1747; Galuppi, 1749; Jommelli, 1749; Lampugnani, 1749; Gasparini, 1756; Hasse, second setting, 1760; J C Bach, 1761; Piccinni, 1762; Bernasconi, 1763; Paisiello, 1765; Giordani, 1772; Bertoni, 1776; V Manfredini, *c* 1780; Cimarosa, 1784; Cherubini, 1785; Isouard, 1794.

Also set as *Artaxerxes* by T Arne, 1762, and Salieri, 1780; as *Arsace* by Handel, 1738, and as *Mandane* by Hasse (his first setting of the story, 1730).

1731 *Adriano in Siria,* set by Caldara, 1731; Giai, ?1731; Giacomelli, 1733; Pergolesi, 1734;

Duni, 1735; Galuppi, 1740; Lampugnani, 1740; K H Graun, 1746; Hasse, 1752; G Scarlatti, 1752; Bernasconi, 1755; Ciampi, 1757; Schwanenberger, 1762; Colla, 1762; J C Bach, ?1765; Holzbauer, 1768; Insanguine, 1773; Sarti, 1778; Cherubini, 1782.

1732 *Demetrio,* set by Caldara, 1732; Pescetti, 1732; Giai, 1732; Hasse, 1732; Leo, two settings: 1735 and 1738; Pérez, 1741; Gluck, 1742; Wagenseil, 1746; Galuppi, 1748; Jommelli, 1749; G Scarlatti, 1752; Cocchi, 1757; Ferrandini, 1758; Paisiello, 1765; Piccinni, 1769; Bernasconi, 1772; Guglielmi, 1772; Paisiello, second setting, 1779; Cherubini, 1785.

Also set as *Cleonice* by Hasse, his second setting, 1740; Vivaldi also set the story but his opera is lost.

1733 *Démophon, Demophoon(te),* etc, set by Caldara, 1733; Leo/Sarro, 1735; Duni, 1737; Brivio, 1738; Lampugnani, 1738; Gluck, 1742; Jommelli, 1743; K H Graun, 1746; Hasse, 1748; Galuppi, 1749; Pérez, 1752; Manna, 1754; Hasse, second setting, 1758; Traetta, 1759; Ciampi, 1760; Boroni, 1761; Piccinni, 1761; Vento, 1765; Bernasconi, 1766; Jommelli, second setting, 1770; Vaňhal, *c* 1770; J Kozeluh, 1772; Paisiello, 1773; Bertoni, 1778; Gatti, 1787; Pugnani, 1787; Cherubini, 1788; Vogel, 1789; Portugal, 1794.

Also set as *L'Usurpatore innocente* by Federici in 1790, and as *Dirce* by Horn in 1821.

1733 *Olimpiade, Olympiade,* etc, set by Caldara, 1733; Vivaldi, 1734; Pergolesi, 1735; Brivio, 1737; Leo, 1737; Giacomelli, 1743; Fiorelli, 1745; G Scarlatti, 1745; Galuppi, 1747; Lampugnani, 1748; Wagenseil, 1749; Logroschino, 1753; Duni, 1755; Giardini, 1756; Hasse, 1756; Traetta, 1758; Jommelli, 1761; Fischietti, 1763; Sacchini, 1763; T Arne, 1764; Bernasconi, 1764; Gassmann, 1764; Brusa, 1767; Paisiello, 1767; Piccinni, 1768; Cafaro, 1769; Guglielmi, 1770; Piccinni, second setting, 1774; Gatti, 1775; V Manfredini, *c* 1777; Mysliveček, 1778; Sarti, 1778; Schwanenberger, 1782; Cimarosa, 1784; Paisiello, second setting, 1786; Minoia, 1787; Federici, 1789; Reichardt, 1790; Kraus, 1792; Donizetti, 1817.

Also set as *Wettkampf zu Olympia* by Poissl in 1815.

1734 *Il Clemenza di Tito,* set by Caldara, 1734; Leo, 1735; Veracini, 1737; Wagenseil, 1746; Grua, 1748; Pérez, 1749; Gluck, 1752; Adolfati, 1753; Jommelli, 1753; Ciampi, 1757; Holzbauer, 1757; Galuppi, 1760; G Scarlatti, 1760; Cocchi, 1765; Bernasconi, 1768; Naumann, 1769; Sarti, 1771; Mozart, 1791; Ottani, 1798.

Also set as *Tito Vespasiano* by Hasse in 1738.

Between 1734 and 1751 there were 26 stories which met with less acclaim; then came:

1751 *Il Ré Pastore,* set by Bonno, 1751; Höpken, 1752; Uttini, 1755; Hasse, 1755; Gluck, 1756; Galuppi, 1758; Lampugnani, 1758; Zoncha, 1760; Piccinni, 1760; Jommelli, 1764; Giardini, 1765; Guglielmi, 1774; Mozart, 1775; Giordani, 1778; Sarti, 1781.

Operas exist in manuscript by Agnesi and Nichelmann.

Also set as *The Royal Shepherd* by Rush in 1764.

There followed a score or so of libretti, some of which were set only once or twice, while a handful of others approached but did not attain the popularity of the earlier stories. With the settings, by Mozart in 1772 and by J C Bach in 1774, of his last story *Lucia Silla,* the long and influential reign of Metastasio came to an end.

Composers who wrote their own libretti

From early on in the history of opera, libretto-writing was an art distinct from the musical side of opera production. As we are shortly to see, the librettist built up for himself a reputation for producing stories mainly in poetic form–the more musical the words, the more successful the opera was likely to be. Unfortunately, the result of putting music and poetry first was often that the story had to go last: nowhere are there such ludicrous, involved, fatuous stories as those in operatic libretti.

Some composers have tried to avoid the complications inherent in the task of setting another's words to music by producing their own libretti. Wagner is the best-known example: not once did he trust the story of another man, and he thereby evaded the deep philosophical questing for 'the right story' which Beethoven suffered. In the list below are to be found: 1. Composers who always produced their own libretti; 2. Composers who sometimes produced their own libretti; and 3. Composers who also produced stories for others to set to music. This list is, of course, only a selection of the best-known composer/librettists.

1. Composers who always produced their own libretti

Berg, Alban (1885–1935).
Borodin, Alexander Porphyrievich (1833–87).
Busoni, Ferruccio (1866–1924).
Charpentier, Gustave (1860–1956) Although the libretto of *Louise* (1900) is credited to the composer, it was apparently contributed to by about a dozen writers, including Charpentier.
Chausson, Ernest (1855–99).
Delius, Frederick (1862–1934).
Indy, Vincent, d' (1851–1931).
Lortzing, Gustav Albert (1801–51).
Magnard, Albéric (1865–1914).
Schumann, Robert (1810–56).
Shostakovitch, Dmitri Dmitrevich (1906–75).
Wagner, Richard (1813–83).

2. Composers who sometimes produced their own libretti

Abert, Johann Joseph (1832–1915).
Albert, Eugen d' (1864–1932).
Anthiel, George (1900–1959).
Arne, Thomas Augustin (1710–78).
Atterberg, Kurt (1887–1974).
Bantock, Sir Granville (1868–1946).
Berlioz, Hector (1803–69).
Dittersdorf, Karl Ditters von (1739–99).
Donizetti, Gaetano (1797–1848).
Glinka, Mikhail Ivanovitch (1804–57).
Gounod, Charles François (1818–93).
Hindemith, Paul (1895–1963).
Holst, Gustav (1874–1934).
Janáček, Leoš (1854–1928).
Kienzl, Wilhelm (1857–1941).
Křenek, Ernst (b 1900).
Lalo, Edouard (1823–92).
Leoncavallo, Ruggiero (1858–1919).
Malipiero, Gian Francesco (1882–1973).
Menotti, Gian Carlo (b 1911).
Mussorgsky, Modest Petrovitch (1839–81).
Nono, Luigi (b 1924).
Pfitzner, Hans (1869–1949).
Pizzetti, Ildebrando (1880–1968).
Prokofiev, Serge Sergeivitch (1891–1953).
Rabaud, Henri (1873–1949).
Rezniček, Emil Nikolaus von (1860–1945).
Rimsky-Korsakov, Nikolai Andreyevich (1844–1908).
Saint-Saëns, Charles Camille (1835–1921).
Schmidt, Franz (1874–1939).
Schoeck, Othmar (1886–1957).
Schoenberg, Arnold (1874–1951).
Smyth, Dame Ethel Mary (1858–1944).
Spohr, Ludwig (1784–1859).
Strauss, Richard (1864–1949).
Stravinsky, Igor (1882–1971).
Tchaikovsky, Pyotr Ilyich (1840–93).
Telemann, Georg Philipp (1681–1767).
Vaughan Williams, Ralph (1872–1958).
Weinberger, Jaromir (1896–1967).
Wieniawski, Adam Tadeusz (1879–1950).

3. Composers who also produced stories for others to set to music

Boïto, Arrigo (1842–1918).
Rousseau, Jean-Jacques (1712–78).

A number of writers have concentrated largely or exclusively on opera libretti. A list of the most prominent is given below, together with some of their most important successes and other remarks.

Barbier, Jules (1822–1901), worked with Carré on *Les Noces de Jeanette* (Masse, 1853); *Faust* (Gounod, 1859); *Philemon et Baucis* (Gounod, 1860); *Mignon* (Thomas, 1866); *Roméo et Juliette* (Gounod, 1867); *Hamlet* (Thomas, 1868); *Tales of Hoffmann* (Offenbach, 1881).
Calzabigi (or Calsabigi), Raniero da (1714–95) was friendly with Gluck, with whom he worked to bring about various operatic reforms. He provided Gluck with a number of libretti including *Orfeo ed Euridice* (1762), *Alceste* (1767), and *Paride ed Elena* (1770). He also wrote libretti for other composers (eg *Opera Seria* by Gassmann, 1769).
Cammarano, Salvatore (1801–52), author and theatre manager. His stories include: *Lucia di Lammermoor* (Donizetti, 1835); *Don Pasquale* (Donizetti, 1843); *Il Trovatore* (Verdi, 1853).
Carré, Michel (1819–72)–see Barbier.
Forzano, Gioachino (or Giovacchino) (1883–1958), provided the libretto for two-

thirds of Puccini's *Il Trittico* (1819), ie *Suor Angelica,* and *Gianni Schicchi*. The story for the first part of the triptych, *Il Tabarro,* was written by Giuseppe Adami.

Ghislanzoni, Antonio (1824–93). His most famous story is *Aïda* (Verdi, 1870).

Gilbert, William Schwenk (1836–1911). The only librettist to be billed consistently above the composer. See above.

Goldoni, Carlo (1707–93), known as the 'Father of Opera Buffa', Goldoni wrote some 70 libretti, often using his pastoral name (Polisseno Feglio) or humorous anagrams (sometimes inexact) of his own name: Aldimiro Clog; Loran Glodici; Calindo Grolo; Sogol Cardoni. Galuppi was the best customer for Goldoni's libretti, setting about 20 stories, but as will be seen from the selection which follows, he was by no means the only composer to show an interest in these charming comedies: *La Generosità politica* (Marchi, 1736); *Il Negligante* (Ciampi, 1740; Paisiello, 1765); *La Contessina* (Maccari, 1743; Gassmann, 1770); *Il Mondo della Luna* (Galuppi, 1750; Haydn, 1777; Paisiello, 1783); *Arcifanfano* (Galuppi, 1750; Dittersdorf, 1777); *La Buona figliuola* (Duni, 1757; Piccinni, 1760); *La Pescatrice* (Paisiello, 1766; Piccinni, 1766; Haydn, 1770); *Lo Speziale* (Pallavicini, Act I, and Fischietti, Acts II and III, 1759; Haydn, 1768); *Il Ciarlatano,* (Scolari, 1759).

Halévy, Ludovic (1834–1908), Nephew of the composer Fromenthal Halévy. His collaboration with Henri Meilhac produced several Offenbach operettas, including *La Belle Hélène* (1864), *Barbe-Bleue* (1866), *La Vie Parisienne* (1866), and *La Périchole* (1868), and Bizet's opera *Carmen* (1875), and in association with H Crémieux, Offenbach's *Orphée aux enfers* (1858).

Illica, Luigi (1857–1919), best known for his partnership with Giuseppe Giacosa for Puccini's *La Bohème* (1896), *Tosca* (1900), and *Madame Butterfly* (1904). Illica was also responsible for many other less successful libretti: *Cristoforo Colombo* (Franchetti, 1892); *Andrea Chenier* (Giordano, 1896); *Iris* (Mascagni, 1898); *Germania* (Franchetti, 1902); *Siberia* (Giordano, 1903); *Tess* (Erlanger, 1909); *Isobeau* (Mascagni, 1911).

Piave, Francesco Maria (1810–76) wrote the libretti for Verdi's operas *Ernani* (1844), *Macbeth* (1847), *Rigoletto* (1851) and *La Traviata* (1853). He also collaborated with Boïto for Verdi's *Simone Boccanegra* (1857) but this was revised by Boïto in 1881.

Planché, James Robinson (1796–1880), best known for his *Oberon* (Weber, 1826).

Ponte, Lorenzo da (1749–1838), born Emanuele Conegliano, he worked as a writer in Dresden and Vienna until 1791, when he moved to London and opened a publishing house. From 1805 to his death he lived in Columbia, USA and became an American citizen. As Mozart's best-known librettist, he produced *Le Nozze di Figaro* (1786); *Don Giovanni* (1787), *Cosí fan Tutte* (1790), as well as books for Bianchi (*Antigona,* 1796; *Merope,* (1797), Martín y Soler (*Una cosa Rara,* 1786; *L'Arbore di Diana,* 1787; *La Scola de'maritati,* 1795), and Salieri (*Il Ricco d'un giorno,* 1784; *Axur, Ré d'Ormus,* 1788).

Romani, Felice (1788–1865), the author of some 80 libretti, ten of which were set by Donizetti and sixteen by Mercadente. Bellini also chose a number of stories: *Il Pirata* (1827); *Zaira* (1829); *La Straniera* (1829); *I Capuleti e i Montecchi* (1830); *Norma* (1831); *La Sonnambula* (1833) and *Beatrice di Tenda* (1833).

Romani's stories were also set by Carlo Conti, Carlo Coccia, Mayr, and Verdi (*Un Giorno di regno,* 1840).

Schikaneder, Emanuel (1751–1812), born Johann Schikeneder, he is best known for *Die Zauberflöte* (Mozart, 1791).

Scribe, Augustin Eugène (1791–1861), the so-called 'creator' of grand opera (see p 154). He wrote the following stories set to music by Auber: *La Muette de Portici* (also called *Masaniello*), 1828; *Fra Diavolo,* 1830; *Le Dieu et la bayadère,* 1830; *Le Philtre,* 1831; *Gustav III,* 1833; *Le Domino Noir,* 1837; *Le Lac des Fées,* 1839; *Crown Diamonds,* 1841; and *L'Enfante prodigu,* 1837.

He achieved considerable success with Boieldieu–*La Dame Blanche* (1825); with Halévy–*La Juive* (1835); *Guido et Ginevra* (1838); *Le Juif errant* (1852); with Meyerbeer–*Robert le Diable* (1831); *Les Huguenots* (1836); *Le Prophète* (1849); *L'Etoile du Nord* (1854); *L'Africaine* (1865).

Zeno, Apostolo (1669–1750) wrote a number of stories which were set to music by various Venetian composers. Among these libretti were: *Faramondo* (1699); *Temistocle* (1700); *Antioco* (1705); *Lucio Papiro* (1719); *Ormisda* (1721); *Alessandro in Sidone* (1721); *Ornospade* (1727).

The world's first librettist was Rinuccini, Ottavio (1562–1621). He provided the stories for the first operas: *Dafne* (1600); *Euridice* (1600); *Arriana* (1608).

The casual attitude towards plot and the sense of the story is typified by an experience related by Dr Burney during a visit to an opera in Milan in 1771. Unfortunately he does not give the title of the opera, so we are unable to see just how much or little damage was done to the plot in this instance, but it is evident from this story that the last thing to be considered at an 18th-century Italian opera was the sense of the libretto. 'After this I went to the opera, where the audience was very much disappointed: Garibaldi, the first tenor, and the only good singer in it, among the men, being ill. All his part was cut out, and the baritone, in the character of a blustering old father, who was to abuse his son violently in the first scene, finding he had no son there, gave a turn to the misfortune, which diverted the audience very much, and made them submit to their disappointment with a better grace than they would have done in England; for, instead of his son, he fell upon the prompter, who here, as at the opera in England, pops his head out of a little trap door on the stage. The audience were so delighted with this attack upon the prompter, who is ever regarded as an enemy to their pleasures, that they encored the song in which it was made.'

Interior view of London's Covent Garden Theatre on 8 April 1960, showing the Royal Box with the Queen and Royal party and President de Gaulle (Popperfoto)

One of the world's most popular opera-houses: Covent Garden, London (Popperfoto)

The most popular operatic stories are those based on *Armida, Orpheus,* and *Alceste.*

Armida is based on the poem *Gerusalemme liberata,* completed in 1575 by Torquato Tasso (1544–95) and has undoubtedly inspired more opera-composers and librettists than any other story. The following composers set the tale to music in greater or lesser accuracy, under different names:

Cherubini	1782	Persuis	1812
Dvořák	1904	Petri	1782
Ferrari	1639	Piccinni	1778
Gluck	1772	Pirasti	1785
Graun K H	1751	Righini	1803
Häffner	1801	Rossini	1817
Handel	1711	Sacchini	1772
Haydn F J	1784	Salieri	1771
Lully	1686	Traetta	1761
Mortellari	*c*1782	Vivaldi	1718
Mysliveček	1779	Wesström	*c*1770
Naumann	1773		

Orpheus, the legendary son of Apollo and the Muse Calliope, was written about by a number of classical writers, among them Ovid, Aristophanes, and Boëthius. His story has been set to music by numerous composers. Titles vary, but the basic story is the same:

Orfeo or Orpheus
Rossi (1647)
Sartori (1672)
Keiser (1698)
K H Graun (1752)
Barthélémon (1767)
J C Bach (1770)
F H W Benda (1787)

Orfeo ed Euridice or Orpheus und Euridike, etc
Gluck (1762)
Tozzi (1775)
Bertoni (1776)
Naumann (1786)
F J Haydn (1791)
Křenek (1926)

Euridice
Peri (1600)
Caccini (1602)

Miscellaneous
Favola d'Orfeo (1607): Monteverdi
Pianto d'Orfeo (1616): Belli
Morte d'Orfeo (1619): Landi
Orphée aux enfers (1858): Offenbach
L'Orfeide (1925): Malipiero
Malheure d'Orphée (1926): Milhaud
Favola d'Orfeo (1932): Casella

For non-operatic musical settings of the legend of Orpheus, and for works dealing with other diabolical subjects, see The Devil in Music in Section IV.

The tragedy *Alceste* was written in 432 BC by Euripides (*c* 485–407 BC), and, although apparently not as popular as *Armida* and *Orpheus,* has nevertheless attracted much attention for stage presentation under varying names such as *Admetus* and *Getreute Alceste,* etc:

Boughton	1922	Lully	1674
Edelmann	*c*1778	Schürmann	1719
Gluck	1767	Schweitzer	1773
Gresnick	*c*1781	Strungk	1693
Handel (*Admeto*)	1727	Wellesz	1924
Handel (*Alceste*)	1750		

Beethoven chose his opera libretto with the greatest care. When he wrote *Fidelio* in 1805 he felt that it alone reflected his own socialistic idea of the survival of the lowly in the face of authoritarianism, at the same time as representing Beethoven's ideal situation of love between a man and his wife. Such high ideals are rather reduced in value when one realises that the same story had been set before by Pierre Gaveaux in 1798, and by Ferdinando Paer in 1804. Later composers also set the story:

Anselm Hüttenbrenner (1794–1868) in 1835
Saverio Mercadante (1795–1870) in 1844
William Henry Fry (1813–64) in 1845.

The most frequent character to appear in English opera was Harlequin. English opera of the 18th century was a cross between continental comic opera, pantomime, and musical burlesque. It had its standard characters, such as the sailor home from the sea, the pompous gentleman who is almost invariably taken down a few pegs before the end of the evening's entertainment, and the young girl, often from the country, who usually manages to get her man. But the character who held most audiences was, ironically for an opera-player, the mute actor Harlequin himself, taken from the Arlecchino of the old Italian comedies.

The operas and pantomimes mentioned below are only those in which Harlequin, in various guises, figures in the title. Countless others exist in which the character appears for a greater or lesser part of the time, disporting himself most prominently in the section of the entertainment which came to be known as 'the Harlequinade'.

UNUSUAL NAMES

Many operas have unusual names in that they seem to have less weight than the operas themselves, or have mundane connotations which appear to be out of character with the concept of 'grand opera'. One such is Mozart's *Cosí fan tutte,* which may be translated as 'They all do it', or 'So do they all'. The names listed below go even further, in that they present odd combinations of syllables, or include strange words, or tell a whimsical tale in themselves.

'HARLEQUIN' OPERAS

Title	*Date*	*Composer*
Chaos, or Harlequin Phaeton	*c* 1800	Russell
Choice of Harlequin, The, or the Indian Chief	1782	M Arne
Friar Bacon, or Harlequin Rambler	1784	Shield
Harlequin and Faustus, or the Devil will have his own	1793	Shield
Harlequin and Oberon	1798	Reeve
Harlequin and Quixotte	1797	Reeve
Harlequin Free mason	*c* 1780	Dibdin
Harlequin Junior, or the Magic Cestus	1784	Shield
Harlequin Marriner, or the Witch of the Oaks (from which comes the popular imitation Scottish song 'Comin' Thru' the Rye')	1796	Sanderson
Harlequin Rambler, or the Convent in an Uproar	1784	Shield
Harlequin's Almanack	1801	Reeve
Harlequin's Invasion (from which comes 'Heart of Oak')	1759	Boyce
Harlequin's Museum, or Mother Shipton Triumphant	1792	Shield
Harlequin Sorcerer, with the Loves of Proserpine (later to be known as . . . *the Rape of Proserpine)*	1725	Galliard
Harlequin's Return	1798	Reeve
Harlequin Teague, or the Giant's Causway, Op 19	1782	Arnold
Hermit, The, or Harlequin at Rhodes	*c* 1770	Collett
Magic Oak, The, or Harlequin Woodcutter	1799	Attwood
Merry Sherwood, or Harlequin Forester	1795	Reeve
Mirror, The, or Harlequin Everywhere	1779	Dibdin
Necromancer, The, or Harlequin Dr Faustus	1723	Galliard
Triumph of Mirth, The, or Harlequin's Wedding	1782	Linley, Jr
Wizard's Wake, The, or Harlequin's Regeneration	1805	Russell

One opera, by Hubert Bath, not only has an odd name but was written by *just* the right composer!

Ali Hitsch Hatsch (1844), by Simon Sechter (1788–1867).
Allamistakeo, by the Italian composer Giulio Viozzi.
Bubbles (1923), by Hubert Bath.
Buz-Gloak Child, The, a Children's opera (1970) by Tim Higgs.
Emelia di Liverpool (1824), by Donizetti.
Genuis of Nonsense, An Original, Whimsical, Operatical, Pantomimical, Farcical, Electrical, Naval, and Military Extravaganza, Op 27 (1784), by Samuel Arnold (1740–1802).
Heironymus Knicker (1789) by Karl Ditters von Dittersdorf (1739–99).
Infidelio (1954), by Elizabeth Lutyens.
Inkle and Yarico (1787) by Samuel Arnold.
La Glu (1910), by Gabriel Dupont.
Love Laughs at Locksmiths (1803) by Henry Condell.
No Song, No Supper (1790) by Stephen Storace (1763–96).
Obi, or Three Finger'd Jack, Op 48, by Samuel Arnold.
Ol-Ol (1928), by Alexander Nikolaevich Tcherepnin (b 1899).
Time off? Not a Ghost of a Chance (1971) by Elizabeth Lutyens.
What a Blunder (1800) by John Davy.

OPERAS ABOUT COMPOSERS

A small group of works for which inspiration was drawn from the lives of earlier composers. The opera by Paul Graener takes a fact and exaggerates it; this, and the novel on the same subject by A E Brachvogel, has given posterity the completely wrong impression of the much-slandered son of J S Bach. Likewise, the opera by Rimsky-Korsakov takes a thread of supposition and turns it into a drama which might easily be believed by the gullible.

Chopin (1901) by Giacomo Orefice.
Friedemann Bach (1931), by Paul Graener.
Mozart and Salieri (1898), by Rimsky-Korsakov.
Palestrina (1917), by Hans Erich Pfitzner.
Rossini in Neapel (1936), by Bernard Paumgartner.
Alessandro Stradella (1844), by Friedrich von Flotow.
*Alessandro Stradella (*1846), by Abraham Louis Niedermeyer.
Taverner (1970), by Peter Maxwell Davies.
Trillo del Diavolo (1899) by Falchi, based on a supposed incident in the life of Tartini.
Ochsenmenuette (1823) by Seyfried, based on an incident in the life of Joseph Haydn. See nicknames in Section IV.
Richard Coeur-de-Lyon by Grétry (1784): although this monarch was possibly the very first recorded composer (see Royal Composers in Section III) Grétry's opera deals with his royal rather than his musical activity.

opera about an opera-singer

Maria Malibran (1925) by Robert Russell Bennett.

'NUMBERS'

The successive items (arias, choruses, ensembles, etc) in an opera are often referred to as 'numbers'. This practice dates back to the days when the first operas were emerging, yet it originated in a musical drama which is more in the nature of an oratorio than an opera: *La Rappresentazione dell' anima e del corpo,* by the Roman composer Emilio de' Cavalieri in 1600. The convention continued until the 19th century, when there was a move away from quartering the drama into parcels. The culmination, of course, came when Wagner conceived his music dramas as a whole, the music being virtually continuous from the first bars of the overture to the final curtain. This is one reason why it is artistically suspect to perform parts of a Wagner music drama out of context, a practice which gave rise to the expressive and accurate description of such excerpts as 'bleeding chunks'.

Since Wagner, several other composers have adopted the 'all-through' technique in opera, but a reaction has set in: Hindemith, in his opera *Cardillac* (1926), reverted to numbering the set pieces in the score, thus bringing the wheel full circle.

OPERAS EMPLOYING UNUSUAL EFFECTS OR 'PROPS'

Massenet's *Esclarmonde* (1889) called for a magic lantern for the projection of certain magic scenes.

Giordano's *Fedora* (1898) requires the use of bicycles on stage.

Křenek's *Jonny Spielt Auf* (1927) calls for a car on the stage.

Sousa's *The American Maid* (1909) was the first operetta to call for a film projector: the film that is shown is of scenes from the Battle of San Juan Hill.

Milhaud's *Christophe Colomb* (1930) was the first full-scale opera to use cinema techniques (showing tropical scenes while Christopher Columbus is reading of Marco Polo's adventures); the opera also calls for actors, narrator, an off-stage orchestra, and there are enormous double choruses and no fewer than 45 solo roles. The première took place on 5 May 1930 in Berlin under Erich Kleiber.

Boughton's *The Birth of Arthur* (1908/9) opens with 'human scenery'. As the curtain rises a castle comes into view, at the foot of which is the sea. Tenors and basses, grouped structurally, in fact comprise the castle while the waves of the sea are suggested by undulating movements of the women of the chorus.

The first opera to call for a church organ was Hérold's *Zampa,* given at the Paris Opèra-Comique on 3 May 1831. Just over six months later the same feature was required by Meyerbeer's *Robert le Diable,* at the Paris Académie on 21 November.

Hindemith's *Hin und Zuruck* is an operatic palindrome. It progresses normally from beginning to middle, then the music and action reverse, the opera ending when the beginning is once more reached.

Pietro Raimondi, an Italian composer who became Musical Director of St Peter's, Rome shortly before his death in 1853, wrote a number of serious and comic operas which, if performed simultaneously, make as much sense as when performed separately. This experimental design was extended also to three of the composer's oratorios.

The Swedish composer L J Werle's opera *Dreaming about Thérèse* is mounted in such a way that the audience becomes a kind of circular sandwich between the singers carrying the action in the centre, and the orchestra positioned round about the edges of the hall.

The first opera to make use of the leitmotif principle was not, as may be thought, by Wagner, who nevertheless made the technique his own, but appears as early as 1781 in Mozart's *Idomeneo.* It was also employed by Méhul in *Ariodant* (1799).

The longest opera ever written is the seven-act *The Life and Times of Joseph Stalin* by a Russian composer whose name is not given in the only references the authors have of the work. When given at the Brooklyn Academy of Music on 14–15 December 1973 the performance took nearly 13 hr 25 min.

The world's shortest opera is Milhaud's *The Deliverance of Theseus,* first performed in 1928 and lasting a mere 7 min 27 sec.

The first Western opera to be staged with the revolving-stage facility was Mozart's *Don Giovanni* at the Munich Residenz Theatre in 1896; the stage-builder was Karl Lautenschläger.

The idea of the revolving stage, upon which three sets were built and scene changes were effected quickly by a one-third revoltuion of a turntable, originated in Japan in the 18th century. Therefore, it is not unlikely that performances of Oriental operas were performed on such stages many years before the Munich occasion.

Many musicians have made their names in the concert-hall and opera-house and have then transferred their attentions to broadcasting.

A unique reversal is noted herewith:

The first TV personality to write a successful opera is Patrick Moore, widely famous for his long-running *The Sky at Night* programme in which astronomical subjects are explained in a way pleasing to scientist and layman alike. Mr Moore's opera *Perseus and Andromeda* was first performed at the Civic Centre, Shoreham, Sussex, on 2 October 1974 by the Shoreham Light Opera Company. In the composer's own words, 'Any music I write is of the 1875, not the 1975, type. Perseus, as you know, was an ill-tempered old bore who killed a gorgon years ago, by mistake, and has been living on his reputation ever since.

Patrick Moore, astronomer and musician extraordinary seen here as Tyndasus in the opera Perseus and Andromeda *which he himself wrote*

In 1975 Patrick Moore was 'working on the next one, which features Theseus. The Minotour, of course, is a very pleasant creature which likes biscuits, and the whole thing is a put-up-job by Minos and Ægeus, who have founded Minotours Ltd. Theseus, a pre-eminent dimwit, blunders into the plot; but the two villainous kings can't put him quietly out of the way. For one thing he is Ægeus' son; and–much more important–he is not insured.'

The first injunction taken out against an opera alleging damage of business potential was in respect of Hindemith's *Neues vom Tage* (1929). It was originated by the gas-heating company of Breslau in 1930 because of a scene in which the heroine takes a bath in water heated by electricity. She sings, in part:

Constant hot water,
No horrid smell,
No danger of explosion.

The first 'jazz opera' was *Porgy and Bess* (1935) with music by George Gershwin and libretto by his brother Ira and D Heyward. This work is also **the first Negro opera**–both hero and heroine are Negros–and it contains stylistic elements of blues and spirituals.

A purer jazz opera is *Sweeney Agonistes* by John Dankworth.

(b) NON-OPERATIC VOCAL MUSIC

The earliest origins of vocal music were outlined in conjectural form in Section I: Setting the Scene. The later history of the ever-fluid non-operatic vocal types of music may be sketched in here with a brevity and simplicity unworthy of the subject. Fuller details of the evolution and descriptive details of the various types will be found in more specialist works of reference. It should be borne in mind that throughout the history of vocal music the two distinct styles–sacred and secular–have often crossed and overlapped but, in order to clarify the lines, it has been necessary in the chart which follows to trace their development separately. It should also be noted that the dates given are the earliest for which we have

A CHRONOLOGICAL SURVEY

Century	*Technical Developments*	*Sacred music*	*Secular developments*
4th	Plainsong (four scales codified by Bishop Ambrose of Milan (*c* 333–397))	Ambrosian chant. Hymns	Accompanied and unaccompanied song in Latin. Folk song
6th	Four further scales added by Pope Gregory 'The Great' (ruled 590–604). Chants always sung in unison. Pope Gregory established music schools in Roman religious establishments	Gregorian chant	
9th	Organum: doubling of the unison parts by another part a fourth lower. Beginnings of polyphony		
10th		Liturgical drama	
11th	Appearance of three-part harmony		Troubadours of south France; songs sung in the vernacular
12th	The rise of polyphony dictates that rhythms be indicated in conjunction with words. Plainsong with upper parts reinforced above	Conductus	Trouvères of northern France; Minnesingers of Germany Pastoral plays with music (developed later to opera)
13th	Canon. Ten-part polyphony	Motets	Madrigals; Rondeaus; Part-songs
14th		Anthems	
15th		Passions	French chansons; Italian frottole in four parts
16th	Antiphonal polyphony; Homophony	Sacred concerti; Sacred symphonies	
17th	Voices with instruments	Oratorios	Masque (to opera)
18th		Symphonic Masses; National anthems	National songs; Lieder (German)
19th	General development of oratorio, Mass, song, lieder, etc, without formal innovations		
20th	Atonalism		

evidence. Musicological finds may at any time uncover facts which will put back any one of these dates.

The trouvères and Minnesänger of the 12th and 13th centuries were the first to secularise formal music. Important names among these artists are:

Trouvères:

Adam de la Hale (*c* 1230/40–*c* 87).
Guirant d'Espanha de Toloza (?–?).
Guillaume d'Amiens (?–?).

Minnesänger:

Walter von der Vogelweide (*c* 1165–*c* 1230).
Neidhart von Revental (?–1240).
Heinrich 'Frauenlob' (?–1318), the last of the Minnesänger.

The earliest composers to write non-polyphonic (ie homophonic) music were Giovanni Bardi (1534–1612), Giulio Caccini (*c* 1545–1618), and Jacopo Peri (1561–1633), all based in Florence.

The earliest antiphonal instrumental music probably dates from the early 16th century. Adriaan Willaert (*c* 1480–1562), the Flemish composer, was appointed to the position of Music Director at St Mark's Cathedral in Venice. It is known that he experimented with antiphonal choruses in the cathedral, and it is impossible not to conclude that he made similar experiments with instrumental groups. One of his pupils, Andrea Gabrieli (1510–86), also worked at St Mark's, and both he and his nephew Giovanni (1557–1612) exploited antiphonal effects in their instrumental as well as their choral music.

MASS

The High Mass (or Missa Solemnis) is a large-scale choral work, often with orchestra since the 17th century, divided into a number of sections, or movements. Vocal soloists usually take a prominent part in the presentation of the words,

The Italian Lilion Choir (300 singers), on the steps of St Paul's Cathedral, London (Popperfoto)

which are always the same. The sections of the Latin text of the Ordinary are as follows:

1. Kyrie eleison Christe eleison	Lord have mercy on us Christ have mercy on us
2. Gloria is excelsis Deo	Glory to God on High
3. Credo in unum Deum	I believe in one God
4. Sanctus Dominus Deus Sabaoth	Holy Lord God of Hosts
5. Benedictus qui venit in nomine Domini	Blessed is he that cometh in the name of the Lord
6. Agnus Dei	Lamb of God

Composers of Masses are very numerous, the post-plainsong main line descending from Palestrina, through J S Bach, Haydn, Mozart, and Beethoven, and on into the 19th century with Schubert, Weber, Liszt, Gounod, and Bruckner. A restrictive Papal Bull, issued in 1903 by Pius X, prevented the continuation of this line, forcing composers to put the meaning of the words on a higher priority than the musical treatment of them. This has had the effect of diversifying the forms that choral music has taken during the present century and a number of important works have appeared which fit awkwardly or not at all into the established forms and principles.

Among these will be found Masses in national tongues, cantatas called symphonies, and some works which even the composer hesitated to label too definitely. A selection only is given:

Samuel Coleridge Taylor: *Hiawatha's Wedding Feast* (Op 30/1, 1898).

Frederick Delius: *Mass of Life* (1905) and *Requiem* (1904–5) both to secular words. The Mass is a German setting of Nietzsche's *Zarathustra.*

Ralph Vaughan Williams: Symphony No 1, *A Sea Symphony* (1910).

Arnold Schoenberg: *Die Glückliche Hand* (1913).

Zoltan Kodály: *Psalmus Hungaricus* (1923).

Leoš Janáček: *Mša Glagolskaya* ('Glagolitic Mass') (1926).

Igor Stravinsky: *Symphony of Psalms* (1930).

Carl Orff: *Carmina Burana* (1936).

Dmitri Shostakovitch: Symphony No 13, *Babi Yar* (1962) and Symphony No 14, (1969).

The composer of the most Masses is Giovanni Pierluigi da Palestrina (*c* 1525–94), an Italian remembered as one of the greatest composers of the contrapuntal era. He set the Mass 93 times.

Dr Burney, on his visit to Italy, described Battista San Martini (whom we now call Giovanni Battista Sammartini, born in 1698 or 1701, died in 1775) as 'maestro di capella to half the churches in Milan, and the number of masses he has composed is almost infinite'.

On the continent of Europe *secular* Masses had a vogue in the late 15th and 16th centuries. They were usually based on words of a traditional nature, or on music from folk-sources.

The only English secular Masses of early days were written by John Taverner, Christopher Tye, and John Shepherd (or Shepheard). Each of these composers wrote a Mass with the title *Westron Wynde.*

Attempts to bring the principles of 'pop' music into the Church have been made by the Reverend Geoffrey Beaumont, whose *Twentieth Century Folk Mass* (1957) follows the Proper and Ordinary of the Mass but introduces most of the current elements of 'Tin Pan Alley': pop-jazz rhythms, rock 'n' roll, song-hymns in the modern idiom, etc. The Reverend Beaumont was also known for composing hymns in the 'straight' style for use on television.

In 1970, John(ny) Dankworth also wrote a *Folk Mass.*

MISSA BREVIS

This is an important sub-category of the mass. The Missa Brevis, (= 'Short Mass') is a setting of all the words of the Latin text in compressed form, usually running to less than half an hour. In order to obtain the maximum of constrast of tempi and texture, Mozart would deal with some parts of the text in a relaxed speed, compensating for the time thus 'lost' by running through other parts at high speed, often setting two or more vocal phrases in such a way that they were sung simultaneously. The reason for the rush, in Mozart's case, was that his employer, the Archbishop of Salzburg, demanded Masses to be over and done with in 30 minutes or less. He also stipulated that at the same time they had to feature the martial instruments of festivity: trumpets and drums. Perhaps he felt that what the music lacked in length and profundity would be made up in sheer concentrated noise. Of the several short Masses Mozart wrote, the best known is the so-called 'Coronation Mass' in C, K 317, of 1779.

Another definition of Missa Brevis is as a shortened version of the High Mass in which only the first two sections were performed.

REQUIEM

The Requiem, or Missa pro Defunctis (='Mass for the Dead') is a composition of mourning, once again set always to the same words. The sections of the text, which is a modified version of the High Mass, are as follows:

1.	Requiem aeternam dona eis	Eternal rest given unto them
2.	Kyrie eleison, Christe eleison	Lord have mercy on us, Christ have mercy on us
3.	Dies irae	Day of wrath
4.	Tuba mirum	Wondrous trumpet
5.	Rex tremendae majestatis	King of majesty tremendous
6.	Recordare, Jesu pie	Think, kind Jesus
7.	Confutatis maledictus	When the wicked are confounded
8.	Lacrimose dies illa	Day of mourning
9.	Domine Jesu Christe	Lord Jesus Christ
10.	Hostias et preces tibi, Domine	We offer Thee, Lord
11.	Sanctus	Holy
12.	Benedictus qui venit in nomine Domini	Blessed is he that cometh in the name of the Lord
13.	Agnus Dei	Lamb of God

Prominent in the line of settings of the Requiem text are those by Michael Haydn (1771); Mozart (1791), whose setting was left unfinished at his death and was completed by Franz Xaver Süssmayr, his pupil; Berlioz (Paris, 1837); Bruckner (1849, revised in 1854 and again in 1894); Verdi (St Mark's, Milan, 1874); Fauré (1887); and Benjamin Britten (*War Requiem,* 1962). Brahms's *German Requiem,* first heard in Bremen Cathedral in 1868, is not a true Requiem in the accepted sense since it is based on German words from the Bible. It should more correctly be called an oratorio.

ORATORIO

Oratorio had crystallised into a form distinct from masque and opera by about the year 1600, but in its treatment of a religious story in a semi-dramatic manner it ran alongside, and often almost collided with, opera itself.

Established in Rome in 1600, the oratorio has received the attention of many distinguished composers, from Cavalieri, through Schütz (*The Resurrection,* 1623; *Christmas Oratorio,* 1664), Pergolesi, J S Bach (*Christmas Oratorio,* 1734, in fact a collection of cantatas), Handel (*Messiah,* 1742, among many others), C P E Bach, Haydn (*The Seven Last Words,* 1785; *The Creation,* 1800; *The Seasons,* 1803), Beethoven (*Christ on the Mount of Olives,* Op 85, 1802), Rossini (*Moses in Egypt,* 1818), Spohr (*The Last Judgement,* 1825), Mendelssohn (*St Paul,* 1836; *Elijah,* 1847), Berlioz (*The Childhood of Christ,* 1854), Brahms (*German Requiem,* 1867, see above), Gounod (*Mors et Vita,* 1885), Elgar (*The Dream of Gerontius,* 1900; *The Apostles,* 1903), Honegger (*Le Roi David,* 1921), Vaughan Williams (*Sancta Civitas,* 1926), Walton (*Belshazzar's Feast,* 1931), and Tippett (*A Child of our Time,* 1940).

It will be seen that the type of text chosen for oratorio is most likely to be religious, but secular oratorios appear from time to time.

It should be noted that the usual method of distinguishing between opera and oratorio –that one has stage action and the other has not –is fallacious. In its earliest days, the oratorio was often accompanied by stage action; and even during the 19th century some of the more dramatic oratorios were sometimes presented as dramas. Perhaps the safest way to tell the two forms apart is to decide whether a performance of a given work will be less effective *without* stage presentation. If so, the work is an opera.

The composer of the first oratorio was Emilio di Cavalieri (*c* 1550–1602), whose oratorio *La Reppresentazione dell' anima e del corpo* ('The Representation of Soul and Body') was given in the oratory (hence Oratorio) of the Church of Santa Maria in Vallicella, Rome, in 1600.

The spread of oratorio, after its appearance in Italy, came about in the following way:

First German oratorio: *Historia der Auferstehung Jesu Christi* (1623) by Heinrich Schütz (1585–1672). This work, however, is an adaptation of a work by Antonius Scandellus (or Antonio Scandello) (1517–80): his *Resurrection,* of about 1573.

First French oratorio: *Le Reniement de St Pierre* by Marc-Antoine Charpentier (1634–1704), composed about 1690.

First oratorio heard in England: Handel's *Esther,* of 1720. The original title of the work was *Haman and Mordecai.*

First oratorio written in Russia: Giuseppe Sarti's *Oratorio for Catherine the Great* of about 1800.

First oratorio heard in America: an incomplete performance of Haydn's *Creation* was given in Bethlehem, Pennsylvania, in 1811. However, **the first oratorio to be composed by an American** was the *Hora Novissima* of 1893 by Horatio Parker (1863–1919).

The composer of the most oratorios was Antonio Draghi (1635–1700) who worked in Vienna. Between the years 1683 and 1700 he wrote 37 oratorios. This busy composer's name appears also under the heading Operatic Proliferation (p. 155).

The best known of all oratorios is *Messiah* by George Frideric Handel (1685–1759). *Messiah* is known and loved the world over by musicians and, inexplicably, by those with neither musical nor religious interest in the work and who would admit to listening to no other example of serious music. The reason for this may be the vast exposure which has been given to the work, hardly a year passing without it being given at Christmas-time, and also often again at Easter, in most of the English-speaking musical centres of the world.

Its first performance took place on 13 April 1742, at the Music Room, Fishamble Street, Dublin. From there, the work came to London, where it was given at Covent Garden Theatre on 23 March 1743, after which it spread throughout the country: Oxford, 1749, arranged by William Hayes; Salisbury, 1750, under the organist and conductor John Stephens; Bath, 1755, organised by Passerini; Bristol, 1756; Gloucester, 1757, arranged by William Hayes; Worcester, 1758; Hereford, 1759, under the organist Richard Clack.

A performance in London's Westminster Abbey on 26 May 1784, held to commemorate the 25th Anniversary of Handel's burial there was planned on a mammoth scale: 95 violins, 26 violas, 21 cellos, 15 double-basses, 26 oboes, 26 bassoons, 6 flutes, 12 trumpets, 4 sets of kettle-drums and, to enrich the lower line, a double bassoon, and specially made 'double-base [*sic*] kettle drums'. The chorus numbered 257 voices in addition to the soloists. Joah Bates directed the performance from a harpsichord specially designed with levers connecting it to the organ, 5·8 m (19 ft) away.

But it was not only in the British Isles that *Messiah* became popular. Translations into German were made by Friedrich Klopstok (1774), Johann Herder (1781), and Johann Adam Hiller (1786). The work was earlier performed in Hamburg in English on 15 April 1772 under the direction of Michael Arne (1740–86), its first performance in that country; it is reported that Gluck was present in the audience. Other German performances took place at Mannheim (1777), Schwerin (1780), Weimar (1780), Berlin (1786), and Leipzig (1786), these last two conducted by J A Hiller who controlled 200 performers.

Meanwhile, the tradition of excessively large performances of the work had not died in England. At the Handel Festivals at the Crystal Palace in 1857, and then annually from 1859 to 1926, the size of the choir frequently reached 4000.

PASSIONS

Although akin to the oratorio, the passion is of much greater antiquity. Its purpose is specifically to enact the Passion of Jesus Christ during Holy Week, and its roots lie in the old miracle and passion plays and in the very ancient Church convention of a semi-dramatic presentation of the Passion story in which the words of Christ (only) were chanted.

The earliest passions date from before 1440 and are by unknown English authors. They were designed for performance at Mass on Palm Sunday and other holy days. These examples approximately coincide with *Passions in a New Style* by the Belgian composer Gilles de Binchois (*c* 1400–60).

The earliest known polyphonic Passion settings are a *Luke Passion* and a *Matthew Passion* (the latter incomplete), both in Latin, dating from about 1450. The anonymous English composer(s?) set the choir parts only in polyphony: the solos are sung in plain song.

By the beginning of the 17th century passions were being written in both Latin and the local language of the composer, the first break having come about during the 1520s, when Johann Walther (1496–1570) wished to bring the Passion story to a wider audience.

Important among composers of Easter Passion music are the following composers: Lassus, Victoria, Byrd, Schütz, Keiser, Bach, Handel, C P E Bach (who composed 21 cantatas on Passion subjects), Stainer (*The Crucifixion,* 1887) and Penderecki (*St Luke Passion,* 1966).

TE DEUM

In full: Te Deum Laudamus ('To God we give Praise'). Just as a requiem is appropriate to a period of mourning, so is a Te Deum to a joyful occasion, such as a great victory. The Te Deum hymn is of extreme antiquity, as are most of the other sacred texts discussed in this Section, but the best-known settings date from the last 300 years or so. Famous examples have been composed by Purcell, Handel, Haydn, Berlioz, Bruckner, Verdi, Kodály, and Britten.

The joyful expression in the *Te Deum* of 1789 by Giuseppe Sarti (1729–1802), written to commemorate the victory of Prince Potemkin at Ochakov, extends to the use in the orchestra of bells, fireworks, and cannon.

CANTATAS

The word 'cantata', usually considered to represent the vocal equivalent of 'sonata,' nevertheless has a much wider application, so wide, in fact, that the word is merely one of convenience rather than, as with 'sonata', a fairly precise indication of the form and intention of the work concerned. The only certain feature to be expected of a cantata is that it will include at least one voice. Some cantatas are given above in the list of 20th-century choral works; these are among the largest and longest cantatas, but other examples might be much shorter, in several movements or in one continuous section, built along chamber lines or designed for pompous Church ceremonies, with or without instrumental accompaniment; and the text chosen by the composer may range from deeply devotional to permissive.

The earliest cantatas appeared near the start of the 17th century and were for a time considered to fulfil a function similar to that of early opera. In the late 18th and early 19th centuries an alternative name for cantata, again revealing operatic connections, was 'scena', often built along the lines of an operatic recitative and aria.

The composer of the most cantatas is Alessandro Scarlatti, who wrote over 700 examples ranging from chamber works for one voice and continuo to elaborate 'Serenatas' for several voices, chorus, and orchestra. A M Bononcini wrote some 375 cantatas, and J S Bach also produced a great many. His normally quoted total of 212 may be reduced to allow for some spurious works but is likely to be increased by the appearance of cantatas which are at present lost.

The oddest cantata was *Era la notte,* by an anonymous composer. It is in the Fitzwilliam Museum in Cambridge and was discussed in detail by Thurston Dart in an article in *The Musical Times,* April 1971. Written in about 1700, the cantata seems to present performance difficulties just for the sake of it. For instance, the work is in B major (five sharps) but there is no key signature at the start of the piece. This necessitates a bewildering display of accidentals. In addition, the time signature varies constantly: 9/6, 5/9, 7/8, 6/7, 5/6, 3/5, 8/3, and use is made of the duple diminution symbol

signifying that all notes and rests are to be given half their written value.

Dr Dart suggests that this is the work written in 1698 by Bononcini as a test for the young Handel during the latter's visit to Berlin.

SACRED CONCERTO AND SACRED SYMPHONY

Developed from the motet, the sacred concerto, or 'concerto ecclesiastici', has nothing to do with concerto in its later meaning of a soloist (or soloists) playing to orchestral support. Origi nally the word concerto meant a 'concerted' effort of several singers, players, etc, playing together. The old word 'symphony' (*sym*= together'; *phonia*='sound') has an identical meaning. A concerto ecclesiatica, therefore, merely meant a group of singers singing together in church.

This was, however, a richer form than the motet. Dramatic contrasts of mood and tone were introduced, and instruments were sometimes included. It will be seen that, with the use of instruments and contrasting timbres, the later meaning of concerto was already being heralded.

The earliest sacred concertos were written by the Gabrielis, Domenico and Giovanni, in about 1585. These were for voices unaccompanied. **The first accompanied concertos** were contained in *Kleine geistliche Concerten,* for voices and organ, written in 1636 by Heinrich Schütz. Before the style died out, other sacred concertos were written by Samuel Scheidt (1587–1654), etc.

CONDUCTUS, MOTET, AND MADRIGAL

The conductus was an ecclesiastical devotional melody the poetic text of which was sung simultaneously in several parts. Sometimes suitably secular tunes might be used in addition to the plainsong-based Church melodies. Its name may be taken from the fact that it was usually in processional march rhythm and was sung as the choir was 'conducted' to its place. The style began in the 12th century and gradually evolved during the next 100 years into the freer motet form until, by the middle of the 15th century, the conductus as such became obsolete. The motet developed into a contrapuntal work, sometimes with as many as ten independent parts, and strictly speaking is by definition an unaccompanied piece, the word 'motet' being a diminutive of the Old French *mot*='given word' (compare 'motto') or 'Scriptural saying'.

About the same time as the appearance of the motet, ie the mid 13th century, similarly contrapuntal unaccompanied pieces were being written for secular use, worldly affairs borrowing back from the Church the melodies which had been appropriated from folk-music for the sacred conductus. These secular compositions originated in Italy as *madrigale,* the word losing its *e* as the form gained popularity and spread throughout Europe, becoming particularly well established in the Netherlands and England.

The basic origins of motet and madrigal were, then, sacred and secular respectively, but as the popularity of the works grew the terms became confused with each other (and with alternative local descriptions) until, by the 16th century, not one of the above definitions was inviolable. There were sacred madrigals, secular motets, instrumental accompaniment might be attached to either, and the contrapuntal nature might disappear altogether in compositions for accompanied or unaccompanied solo voice. In some isolated instances, the term 'madrigal' might even be attached to an instrumental piece without voices at all.

The oldest canon, and the oldest six-part polyphonic work is the famous 'Sumer is icumen in', from England of the 13th century. The date often given as the origin of this 'round' or 'rota' is 1240, but argument is permissible among musicologists, the latest (firm) date found by the present writer being 1310. The text of this infinite round runs as follows:

Original	*Translation*
Sumer is icumen in,	Summer has arrived,
Lhude sing cuccu.	Loud sing the cuckoo.
Groweth sed and bloweth med	The seed is growing, the meadow flowering
And springeth the wde nu;	And the wood springs to life now;
Sing cuccu;	Sing cuckoo;
Awe bleteth after lomb,	Ewe bleats after the lamb,
Lhouth after calve cu;	The cow lows after the calf;
Bulloc sterteth, bucke verteth,	The bullock leaps, the buck stands high,
Murie sing cuccu.	Merry sings the cuckoo.
Cuccu, cuccu,	Cuckoo, cuckoo,
Wel singes thu cuccu.	Well sing you, cuckoo.
Ne swik thu naver nu.	Never stop now.

Evidence of earlier polyphony comes from a manuscript entitled *Musica Enchiriadis,* dating from the second half of the 9th century. This document is a treatise originally thought to have been written by the Monk Hucbald (*c* 849–930) in Belgium but now tentatively ascribed to one Otger, about whom little is known except that he probably died early in the 10th century.

The earliest motet is by an unknown English composer: *Ex semine Abrahae.* It was found in Worcester Cathedral and dates from the 12th century. This is, however, an isolated example, and for the first major flowering of the motet it is necessary to turn to the Flemish and Dutch composers who worked in Italy during the late 13th–mid 14th centuries: Heinrich Isaac (*c* 1450–1517), Jacob Obrecht (1453–1505), and Adriaan Willaert (*c* 1480–1562).

The composer of the greatest number of motets was Luigi Palestrina, who wrote some 600 examples.

The earliest madrigals were published in Rome in 1533 by a group of unknown composers. It is possible, but not certain, that among them were madrigals by Constanzo Festa (*c* 1490–1545), and perhaps some by the Flemish composer Philippe Verdelot (who worked early in the 16th century), both of whom lived in Rome. **The first madrigal composers,** therefore, are given tentatively as Festa and Verdelot, but another Flemish composer of madrigals was working in Venice at that time: Adriaan Willaert, see motets above. It was round Willaert and his followers such as the Flemish Jacob Arcadelt (*c* 1514–*c* 1567), that the madrigal achieved wide popularity.

The composer of the greatest number of madrigals was again (see motets, above) Luigi Palestrina, who wrote 200.

After the establishment of the madrigal style numerous composers took up the form in Italy, among them:

Cyprien van Rore (1516–65) another Flemish artist at Venice.
Roland de Lassus (*c* 1530–94).
Orazio Vecchi (1550–1605).
Luca Marenzio (1553–99).
Giovanni Croce (*c* 1558–1609).
Carlo Gesualdo (*c* 1560–1613).
Giovanni Gastoldi (? –1622).
Claudio Monteverdi (1567–1633).

The first madrigals published in England (which country could be called the madrigal's second home) was a collection entitled *Musica Transalpina,* thus neatly and memorably indicating its indebtedness to Italian originals, in 1588. This was a group collected by Nicholas Yonge (? –1619), a singer at St Paul's Cathedral, but the works therein were not actually called by the name 'madrigal'.

The first English publication of madrigals, called thus, was in 1595, when Thomas Morley (1557–1603), an organist at St Paul's Cathedral and, therefore, probably acquainted with Yonge, published *Madrigalls to Four Voyces* of his own composition. Just as the madrigal had become popular in Italy, so too did the English take to the new style, and many composers followed Morley's example:

John Milton (*c* 1563–1647) (not to be confused with the author of the same name, whose dates are 1608–74).
Michael Cavendish (*c* 1565–1628).
Robert Jones (? –*c* 1617).
John Bennett (*c* 1570–*c* 1620).
John Wilbye (1574–1638).
Thomas Weelkes (*c* 1575–1623).
John Farmer (? – ?).
Michael East (*c* 1580–1648).

The popularity of madrigals extended well into 18th-century England. In 1741 the Madrigal Society was formed in London by John Immyns, who practised law in the City. It proved so popular that there were not enough printed parts of the old madrigals to go round the gatherings; Immyns spent much time in copying out additional parts for these meetings. Existence of this and other societies has extended into the present century, and there is a ready market for gramophone records of madrigals. It is possible, therefore, to state that **the madrigal is the oldest form of music to have retained its popularity.**

HYMNS

There are over 500 000 hymns in existence. **The earliest** is 'Te Deum Laudamus': 5th or 6th century AD.

Choirboys of St Ann's Parish Church, Kew, London (Popperfoto)

The earliest exactly datable hymn is 'Jesus soit en ma teste et mon entendement' of 1490, translated into English ('God be in my head') in 1512.

The longest hymn is 'Hora novissima tempora pessima sunt; vigilemus', of 2966 lines, by Bernard de Cluny (12th century).

The longest English hymn is 'The sands of time are sinking', of 152 lines, by Mrs Anne Ross Cousins, *née* Cundell (1824–1906).

The shortest hymn is the anonymous (attributed to 'J Leland') one-verse 'Be present at our table, Lord'.

The most prolific hymn-writer is Mrs Frances Jane Van Alstyne (1850–1915), known by her maiden name Fanny Crosby, who was blinded at the age of six weeks. Despite this disability she wrote over 8000 hymns, 2000 more than the next most prolific: Charles Wesley (1707–88).

SONG

The oldest song in the world is also **the oldest performable piece of music of any sort** to have come down to us. It dates from about 1400 BC and is apparently a semi-sacred song relating the loves and activities of the gods. The story of the discovery of the song is worth relating in some detail.

In March 1928 a peasant was tilling the soil on the site of the ancient city of Râs Shamra on the Mediterranean coast of Syria at a point due east from Cape Andreas, the northernmost tip of Cyprus. He accidentally came across a cave containing evidence of an early civilisation –fragments of earthenware vases and the like–dating back to the 13th century BC. Further excavations by C A F Schaeffer and G Chenet were commenced in 1929. They revealed clay tablets upon which was inscribed a hitherto unknown cuneiform writing which was laboriously deciphered by Hans Bauer, Charles Virolleaud, and Edouard Dhorme, the alphabet being established by 1931. However, new finds at the Râs Sharmra site were to produce many

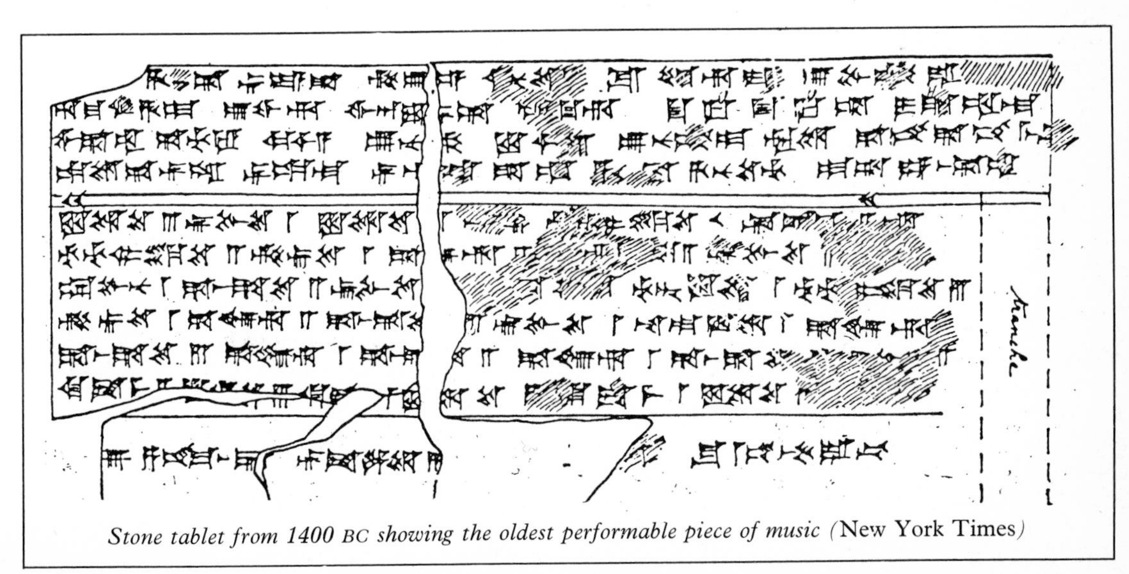

*Stone tablet from 1400 BC showing the oldest performable piece of music (*New York Times*)*

more linguistic problems, one in particular being a tablet containing ten lines of cuneiform characters which defied translation.

It was not until 1959 that this problem was tackled by Dr Anne D Kilmer, Professor of Assyriology at the Columbia University College of Letters and Science at Berkeley, California. Dr Kilmer was eventually able to determine that the upper four lines of script were the lyrics of a song, and that the rest of the tablet contained instructions for its performance. Unfortunately, further work is required to complete the translation of these instructions, some of which have been partly obliterated by time and the action of ancient fires on the site, but enough can be gleaned to enable musicologists to decide that the musical scale used at that time by the Ugaritic tribe is similar in form to that familiar to us today.

Due to the positon of Râs Shamra on the trade routes from the north and south areas of the Mediterranean to the East, the Ugarit peoples, a member of the Hebrew ethnic group, were subjected to a great many foreign influences from Egypt, Crete, and the Aegean countries. The Hurrian language, however, produced a cuneiform writing which is only vaguely related to other Near East scripts and seems to have maintained its individuality despite outside influences. Because of these factors it is at present impossible to decide whether the song, which begins 'Hamutu niyasa ziwe sinute', is a specifically Syrian (Ugaritic) creation, or an importation. At the present state of our knowledge, either possibility is equally likely.

Once Dr Kilmer had rendered the script into singable form in 1972, she arranged for Professor Robert Brown to construct an eleven-string lyre from birch and spruce, using as a pattern drawings preserved in the British Museum and made in the 1920s by Sir Leonard Woolley at an excavation site in Iraq.

The final step in the reconstruction was to bring the song to performance. On 6 March 1974, before an audience at Berkeley University, Richard L Crocker sang the song, accompanying himself on Professor Brown's reconstructed lyre. The performance was given in even crotchets because the clay tablets have not yet revealed the rhythm to which the words should be sung.

The first known French song was a translation into that language from the Latin text 'Cantica Virginis Eulalie Concine Suavissona Cithara'. Its subject was the martyrdom of St Eulalia and it was sung to the accompaniment of a cithara. The date is 882 AD.

The earliest composers of English art songs were Thomas Ravenscroft (*c* 1590–*c* 1633), whose first songs were published in 1609, and John Hilton (1599–1657). Ravenscroft's spirit, if not his name, lives on today in one of the most popular of all nursery songs: 'Three Blind Mice.'

The first song composed by an American was 'My Days Have Been So Wondrous Free' (1759) by the Philadelphian Francis Hopkinson (1737–91).

The only known example of a song sung in a court of law was when the Attorney John Brett sang 'Home Sweet Home' (from Bishop's opera *Clari*) to the jury in an attempt to get an aquittal on sentimental grounds for his client Lloyd Grable, a bank robber, in October 1935. The jury gave Mr Grable 'life' but Mr Brett was evidently allowed to go free.

The most frequently played and sung song is 'A Happy Birthday to You', written by Mildred and Patty Hill in 1893. Despite its popularity, the song did not achieve its first publication with the familiar words until 1935, it being sung previously to 'Good Morning to You'.

The most monotonous song is 'Ein Ton' (1859) by Peter Cornelius. The note B (the middle line of the treble clef) is repeated 80 times in 30 bars.

The composer of the most songs was James Hook (1746–1827), who composed over 2000, among them 'The Lass of Richmond Hill'.

The first sea-shanty to be included in an opera occurs in *Omai* (1785) by William Shield.

LIEDER

'Lieder' is often thought of simply as the German word for 'song', but in truth the form has rather more to it than that. The idea grew

Dietrich Fischer-Dieskau, world-famous baritone (EMI/Reg Wilson)

from the desire of serious-minded composers such as C P E Bach and Gluck to set poetry of high artistic distinction to a keyboard accompaniment. Both of these composers wrote 'Odes' and songs which are direct ancestors of the lied.

The composer of the first true lieder was Johann Rudolf Zumsteeg who worked for most of his life at Stuttgart. Claims for the distinction of the first lieder-composer have been put forward also on behalf of Karl Friedrich Zelter and Johann Friedrich Reichardt both of whom worked in Berlin, but Zumsteeg seems to have prior claim and is generally regarded as the composer who originated the style from Bach's and Gluck's models. Schubert is said to have regarded Zumsteeg very highly and he produced about 600 lieder of his own.

Other prominet composers of Lied were Loewe, with about 350; Schumann, with about 250; Brahms with about 200; and Wolf, with about 300.

WORKS OF MASSIVE PROPORTIONS

At the start of the 19th century there was a general impulse towards giganticism in music. Huge gatherings of instrumentalists and singers were assembled for the performance of existing works (see Section IV: Concerts), but alongside these appeared new compositions actually written for colossal forces, among them the *Grande Messe des Morts* ('Great Mass for The Dead', ie Requiem), Op 5 by Hector Berlioz (1803–69), which was composed in 1837 and first performed in Paris on 5 December of that year. The composer conceived the work on an enormous scale: to the large orchestra were added four brass bands (one at each corner of the group of performers) and a choir of 700 or 800, but Berlioz insisted that proportions between singers and orchestra should be maintained. In the event, the first performance was given by a mere 500 singers.

Other ambitious works were composed during the 1800s, but a further series of records was set early in the new century, culminating in **the largest work of all time** in 1927.

In 1907 Gustav Mahler completed his Symphony No 8, and when it was performed for the first time three years later it came to be known by the exaggerated title 'Symphony of a Thousand'. A representative performance might be regarded as that given in Liverpool Cathedral in 1965 when 700 performers took part: 180 instrumental players and 520 singers. However, Mahler's forces were exceeded by those requir-

Gustav Mahler (Radio Times Hulton Picture Library)

ed for *Gurre-lieder* of Arnold Schoenberg (1874–1951), which was completed in 1911: this calls for an extra choir and even more instruments. Then, after eight years of gestation in the composer's mind, came Havergal Brian's *Gothic Symphony* (at first known as Symphony No 2 but later renumbered as No 1) which was completed in 1927. In a radio interview, Brian admitted: 'It was never intended for performance: I expanded myself on something which might be regarded as impossible.' The 'impossibility' was removed in 1961, when Bryan Fairfax conducted a partly amateur first performance in the Westminster Hall, London. The first fully professional performance took place on 30 October 1966 under Sir Adrian Boult.

In this work 126 instruments are actually specified (Mahler: 62; Schoenberg: 69) *not including* the string band, which of course must be constituted in proportion with the rest of the forces.

In the chart which follows, the composers' requirements for these works are listed. Also shown for comparison are the instrumentation of the most ambitious of Bach's Brandenburg Concertos, of Beethoven's last and biggest symphony, and of Holst's most popular concert work.

	Mahler: Symphony No 8 (1907)	Schoenberg: Gurre-Lieder (1901)	Brian: 'Gothic' Symphony (1919–27)	Bach: Brandenburg Concerto No 1 (1723)	Beethoven: Choral Symphony No 9 (1823)	Holst: The Planets (1916)
Vocalists						
Vocal soloists	8	5	4	–	4	–
Choruses	2 large mixed choirs 1 choir of 400 children	3 four-part male choirs 1 eight-part mixed choir	2 large double choirs 1 children's choir	–	1 mixed choir	1 six-part female choir (hidden)
Woodwind						
Piccolos	1	4	2	–	1	2
Flutes	4	4	6	–	2	4
Alto flutes	–	–	1	–	–	1
Oboes	4	3	6	3	2	3
Oboe d'amore	–	–	1	–	–	–
Bass oboe	–	–	1	–	–	1
Cor anglais	1	2	2	–	–	1
Clarinets	3	3	5	–	2	3
High clarinets (E flat)	2	2	2	–	–	–
Bass clarinet	1	2 (A or B flat)	2	–	–	1
Bassett-horns	–	–	2	–	–	–
Bassoons	4	3	3	(1)	2	3
Contra Bassoons	1	2	2	–	1	1
Brass						
Horns	8	10	8 (+8*)	2	4	6
Trumpets	8	6	8 (+8*)	–	2	4
Bass trumpet	–	1	1	–	–	–
Cornets (E flat)	–	–	2	–	–	–
Alto Trombones	5	1	–	–	1	–
Tenor Trombones	2	4	3 (+8*)	–	1	2
Bass Trombone	–	1	1	–	1	1
Contrabass Trombone	–	1	2	–	–	–
Tenor Tuba	–	–	–	–	–	1
Tubas	1	1	2 (+8*)	–	–	1
Euphoniums	–	–	2	–	–	–
Keyboard						
Piano	1	–	–	–	–	–
Organ	1	–	1	–	–	1
Celesta	1	1	1	–	–	1
Glockenspiel	1	1	1	–	–	1
Harmonium	1	–	–	–	–	–
Harpsichord	–	–	–	1	–	–

	Mahler: Symphony No 8 (1907)	Schoenberg: Gurre-Lieder (1901)	Brian: 'Gothic' Symphony (1919–27)	Bach: Brandenburg Concerto No 1 (1723)	Beethoven: Choral Symphony No 9 (1823)	Holst: The Planets (1916)
Percussion						
Timpani	3 sets	6 sets	2 sets (+4 sets*)	–	1 set	2 sets
Side drums	–	1	2	–	–	1
Bass drums	1	1	2	–	1	1
Tenor drum	–	1	–	–	–	–
African long drum	–	–	1	–	–	–
Tambourines	–	–	2	–	–	1
Cymbals	1 pair	1 pair	6 large pairs	–	1 pair	1 pair
Triangles	1	1	2	–	1	1
Gong	1	1	1	–	–	1
Xylophone	–	1	1	–	–	1
Tubular bells	1 set	–	1 set	–	–	–
Thunder Machine	–	–	1	–	–	–
Chimes	1	–	1	–	–	–
Bird scare	–	–	1	–	–	–
Chains	–	large	small	–	–	–
Strings						
Harps	2	4	–	–	–	2
Mandolin	1	–	–	–	–	–
Violins I	√	√	√	1	√	√
Violins II	√	√	√	1	√	√
Violas	√	√	√	1	√	√
Cellos	√	√	√	1	√	√
Double Bass	√	√	√	(1)	√	√

*4 Bands each of 2 horns, 2 trumpets; 2 trombones; 2 tubas, and timpani.

BIGGEST?

As a supplement to the above, it should be mentioned that a potentially much larger work was conceived but has never been performed, nor is it likely to be.

In 1915 Charles Ives sketched out ideas for a work which was to be a musical equivalent of a scenic picture. It was to be in two halves, played simultaneously, the listener being meant to concentrate on the 'upper' half only, as if he were gazing at the sky and the tree-tops. Meanwhile, the 'lower' half of the music would be perceived subconsciously, as if it were the foreground of the scene. The work is then played through again, the listener focusing on the 'lower' music (the foreground) while the 'upper' (sky) music is taken in subconsciously. It appears that Ives's original conception involved enormous vocal and instrumental armies, and that it then grew in his mind until, in 1936/37 he put down a crystallised formula:

Plan for a Universe Symphony
1. Formation of the countries and mountains.
2. Evolution in nature and humanity.
3. The rise of all to the spiritual.

For this work there were to be crowds of people scattered in huge groups in valleys and on mountain-tops, forming multi-part choirs. These were to be supported by various orchestras, also spatially arranged, so that the physical aspect of the scenic picture is paralleled in music. The composer gave no limit to the number of performers to be employed; neither did he give a limit to the length of the *Universe Symphony:* he considered that the idea was beyond the scope of any individual to carry out. He invited other composers to contribute to the work, also on a posterity basis, therefore turning the work, which was meant never to be finished, into **the longest piece of music ever written and unwritten,** since its length and contents are infinite.

(c) NATIONAL ANTHEMS

The concept of the national anthem, or national hymn, is not as old as is generally thought. Two hundred years ago there existed a bare handful of anthems praising national sovereignty, and the popularity of anthems, started by that of England in the middle of the 18th century, was not fully launched until the patriotic fervour of the French Revolution gave the opportunity for the wide-spread acclaim of 'La Marseillaise' in 1795.

The first national anthem was 'Wilhelmus van Nassouwe' of the Netherlands, the music of which first appeared about 1572. The hymn was adopted as the Royal Anthem later in the 16th century. However, it should be noted that the *words* of the Japanese anthem originated amid the folklore of the 9th century.

The most widely known anthem melody is that to which are sung the words 'God Save our Gracious Queen'. This tune, the origin of which is buried in the volumes of keyboard dance music of the 16th century and may derive from vocal pieces of even earlier date, was chosen or, more correctly, seemed to choose itself, to crystallise patriotic sentiment among the London theatre-goers of the mid 18th century. Three almost simultaneous occurrences combined to rocket the tune to the heights of popular acclaim: it was published as a national song in the *Thesaurus Musicus* of 1744 **(its first appearance in print)**; it was arranged in grand fashion by Dr Thomas Arne and received performances in London's Drury Lane Theatre in 1745, while another arrangement was used similarly in the Covent Garden Theatre during the same year; and, also in 1745, the *Gentleman's Magazine* published words to fit the tune–words which are basically the same as those familiar today.

Once the qualities of grandeur and memorability became recognised by foreign authorities, the melody came to be adapted by them for local languages and requirements. **The first State to appropriate the tune** was Vienna in 1782 (subsequently to abandon it in favour of an even more striking melody–see below); Prussia followed in 1795, then Switzerland in 1811. Many German States took it up during the late 18th and 19th centuries (Baden; Bavaria; Mecklenberg; Schwerin, etc) and Liechtenstein followed about 1850. Meanwhile, America was using the tune for numerous word settings from 1832, the one most enduring being 'My Country, 'tis of Thee'. Sweden and Eire have taken the tune as a basis for unofficial national hymns in addition to their more thoroughly home-bred melodies.

The tune of 'God Save the King', therefore, has been the vehicle for words sung by England, her Commonwealth and Empire, America's millions, and many parts of Germany during the ages, in addition to Austria, Switzerland, and Sweden, among others. **No other national hymn is, and has been, so widely known.**

Composers have paid close attention to the tune since its earliest days. The following is a selection in chronological order of the most famous works in which it appears:

1746 Handel: *Occasional Oratorio.*
1763 J C Bach: Keyboard Concerto in D, Op 1/6.
1804 Beethoven: *Seven Variations on God Save the King.*
1812 Beethoven: 'Battle of Vittoria' Symphony.
1815 Weber: Cantata: *Kampf und Sieg,* J 190.
1818 Weber: *Jubel* Overture, J 245.
1870/1 Brahms: *Triumphlied,* for chorus and orchestra, Op 55.
1891 Ives: *Variations, etc, on a National Hymn* for organ.
1892 Dvořák: Cantata: *The American Flag.*
1960 Boisselet: *Symphonie rouge.*

Beethoven and Weber also made vocal arrangements of the melody. Both Ives and Dvořák based their works on 'God Save America'.

The most influential National Anthem: the simple nobility of 'God Save the King' immediately aroused the envy of other countries. First came the claims as to authorship of the tune, from Scotland, Germany, France, and even Moravia. Such claims are still made today–and listened to–in some quarters, but the fact is that the true composer of the melody is not known and will probably never be known. The nearest we can get to the truth is that several tunes bear a resemblance to it, and it may have been arranged by any one of the contenders (Purcell and John Bull being among them) from a number of dance tunes of a folk-character. It would be delightfully tidy if one day evidence were to be unearthed to prove beyond doubt that the melody was written by the appropriately named John Bull (1562–1628), but history and musicology are unlikely to be as kind as that.

After the authorship claims came the 'borrowings': other territories using the tune for their own words–see above. Following that came the imitations, the greatest being that by Haydn for Austria. If it had not been for the introduction of 'La Marseillaise' in 1795, showing prospective national-anthem writers that an aggressive march would do to arouse national feeling just as well as would a hymn tune, the British anthem would have had even more imitations than it has.

The national anthem with the most number of verses is that belonging to Greece. In 1823, Dionysios Solomós, the Greek poet, provided 158 four-line stanzas. For general use, however, the anthem is considerably shortened.

The longest anthem in the world is Argentina's 'Marcha de la Patria', composed by Blas Parera in 1813. It has an extended two-part Prelude, and a short instrumental link leading to a verse of 33 bars and a final chorus of seventeen bars.

The only national hymn to have been written by a ruling monarch is 'Himno da Carta' of Portugal, composed and written by Pedro I of Brazil in 1822 to commemorate that country's independence from Portugal. Four years later he followed his father John VI as King of Portugal, and he brought home with him the anthem, leaving Brazil to replace it with its own hymn nearly a hundred years later.

The 'Himno da Carta' is probably **the fastest composed in the world.** Legend has it that King Pedro I commenced writing it at 5.30 pm on 7 September 1822, and completed it, words and music, by nine o'clock that evening. It was sung in São Paulo that same night by the King himself (an accomplished musician with an opera to his credit) and a full chorus.

The most travelled national hymn tune is that known as the 'Polish Prayer', which migrated across Europe as follows: Composed by the French singer Jean-Pierre Solié as an aria 'Qu'on soit Jalouse' in his opera *Le Secret* (1796), which was performed in 1810, in Poland. Arranged by the Polish composer Karol Kurpiński in 1815 as the Polish National Hymn with the text beginning 'Bože coš Polske przez tak liezne wieki'. This anthem was forbidden in 1866 and replaced by the 'Hymn Polski' with words and music by J Wybicki. The descendant of the original Solié melody is heard today in Upper Silesia, and in Olomuč, Czechoslovakia, with a variant of the Polish words: 'Bože coš račil před tisice lety'. In Germany it is sung in public schools to more robust words, and was sung in the German Army as 'Zehntausen Mann, die zogen ins Manöver'. Finally, Italy has made of it a song beginning 'Vien qua, Dorina bella'.

The only anthem to have been composed by a woman was 'Kent gij dat volk vol heldenmoed' ('Know Ye This Race of Bravery'), written as the Transvaal Anthem in 1875 by Cathrine Felicie van Rees, who also composed operettas. This anthem has fallen out of use today, having been superseded by that for South Africa.

Anthems composed by famous composers. By far the best known, and also probably the greatest of all, is the 'Emperor's Hymn', by Franz Joseph Haydn. While he was in London, the ageing Austrian composer was repeatedly struck by the dignity of the British National Anthem, 'God Save the King', which was played on every occasion of even the most modest importance. Back in Vienna, he composed a melody of similar nobility, incorporating it as the second movement of his String Quartet in C, Op 76, No 3. In this form it is given a set of four variations. The melody quickly became adopted in Austria and Germany as the National Anthem or Hymn, and it still survives as the National Tune of the German Federal Republic (West Germany).

Charles Gounod (1818–93), the French composer, wrote his *Marcia Pontificale* in 1846 for the coronation of Pope Pius IX. This wordless march was adopted in 1949 as the official 'anthem' of the Vatican City. The tune used as a National Hymn by Egypt (United Arab Republic) was reputedly written by Giuseppe Verdi (1813–1901), but there is no evidence that this attribution is correct. Probably the word was put about by Egyptian officials that the Italian composer was responsible, since the opera *Aïda*, written to commemorate the opening of the Suez Canal in 1871, had made him the most popular composer in that rather musicless nation.

Austria's present National Anthem is an arrangement by V Kelerdorfer of Mozart's 'Brüder, reicht die Hand zum Bunde' from his *Masonic Cantata*, K 623, written in 1791. Appropriate words were written by Paula Preradović.

The country with the most national songs is, and was, Germany. Some of the anthems were unofficial, the dates given referring only to the time when they first became widely known.

1. Heil dir im Siegerkranz' (1794) — Words: H Harries (1790) and B Schumacher (1793); Music: ='God Save the King'

2. 'Prussian People's Song' (*c* 1816) — Words: J F L Duncker; Music: G L P Spontini

3. 'Ich bin ein Preusse' (1834) — Words: B Thiersch; Music: A H Neithardt

4. 'Was ist des Deutschen Vaterland?' (*c* 1845) — Words: E M Arndt (1813); Music: J Cotta (1813) (Alternative tune: G Reichardt (1826))

5. 'Die Wacht am Rhein' (1854) — Words: M Schneckenburger (1840); Music: K Wilhelm

6. 'Deutschland, Deutschland über Alles' (adopted 11 August 1922) — Words: A H H von Fallersleben (1841); Music: F J Haydn (1797)

(Although this anthem has been replaced by the entries below, it still endures as the Anthem of West Germany with the words 'Einigkeit und Recht und Freiheit' (adopted 1950). The melody is still as powerfully evocative as ever, but the original opening words lost a deal of credibility during the Second World War when cartoonists, depicting the American and English 1000-bomber raids on German cities, had their crews singing 'Allies, Allies über Deutschland').

7. 'Horst Wessel-Lied' (adopted by the Nazi Party in 1933) — Words and Music: H Wessel

8. 'Land des Glanens, deutsches land' (adopted in 1950 by West Germany, but almost immediately replaced with 6, with its new words) — Words: R A Schröder; Music: M H Reutter

9. 'Auferstanden aus Ruinen' ('From the Ruins') (adopted by the East German authorities in 1949) — Words: J R Becher; Music: H Eisler

In former days, some of the German *Länder* or States had their own anthems, many of them based on the music of 'God Save the King', with words adapted to local rulers.

Bavaria:

1. 'Heil unserm König, Heil!' (*c* 1805)	Words: ? Music: = 'God Save the King'
2. 'Bayern, O Heimatland' (1848)	Words: F Beck Music: F Lachner
3. 'Gott mit dir, du Land der Bayern (*c* 1856)	Words: M Öchsner Music: K M Kunz

Hesse:

'Heil, unserm Fürsten Heil' (*c* 1800)	Words: ? Music: = 'God Save the King'

Mecklenburg-Schwerin:

1. 'Gott segne Friedrich Franz' (*c* 1795)	Words: ? Music: = 'God Save the King'
2. 'Heil dir Paul Friedrich' (*c* 1825)	Words: ? Music: = 'God Save the King'

Saxony:

1. 'Den König segne Gott'	Words: G C A von Richter Music: = 'God Save the King'
2. 'Gott segne Sachsenland'	Words: A Mahlmann Music: = 'God Save the King'

Schleswig-Holstein:

'Schleswig-Holstein meerumschlungen'	Words: M F Chemnitz Music: C G Bellmann

Westphalia:

'Ihr mögt den Rhein den stolzen preisen' (1868)	Words: E Ritterhans Music: P J Peters

Württemburg:

1. 'Heil unserm König, Heil' (*c* 1800)	Words: ? Music: = 'God Save the King
2. 'Preisend mit viel Schönon Reden' (1826)	Words: J Kerner Music: trad

THE WORLD'S NATIONAL HYMNS, ANTHEMS, AND MARCHES

The following list includes also songs which have assumed the importance of national tunes without being officially accepted as such. Among these are some songs which are certainly prominent in the folk-cultures of their respective countries without necessarily having the solemnity or decorum which would be required at important national events: Australia's 'Waltzing Matilda', for instance, or America's 'Yankee Doodle Dandy'. However, these tunes are included because they have proved their value in times of war in rousing the spirits, and sometimes the anger, of soldiers of their nations.

The dates of adoption will be seen to differ considerably in some cases from the dates of composition but where there is only a short delay between the dates it has been felt unnecessary to include the earlier date.

In some cases where a country has more than one anthem or national song, whether official or unofficial, chronological order has been adopted.

With the politics of the world in a fluid state it is not possible to prevent a list of this sort going out of date before it reaches the printers. However, it is felt that the list will be of use historically, which is the reason that many anthems (for instance, those of eastern European countries) are included even though they have been submerged by political events.

Country		Title	Date of Adoption *=un-official	Words	Music	National/ Independence/ Saint Day(s)
Afghanistan		'Our Brave and Much-loved Ruler'	1930	M Makhtar	M Faruk	27 May
Africa (the whole continent)		'Nkosi Sikelel'i Africa'	?	E Sontonga (in Zulu)	E Sontonga (arr from trad)	
Albania		'Hymni i Flamurit'	1912	A Barseanu and A S Drenova	C Porumbescu	11 Jan 19 Nov
Algeria		'Par les foudres qui anéantissent'	?	M Zakaria	M Fawzi	
America	1.	'Yankee Doodle'	1782*	Trad (*c* 1758)	Anon English or Dutch	14 July 27 Nov
	2.	'Hail Columbia'	1798*	J Hopkinson	P Phile	
	3.	'My Country, 'Tis of Thee' (see p 184)	1832*	S F Smith	='God Save the King'	
	4.	'The Star-Spangled Banner'	1931 (3 Mar)	F S Key (1814)	J S Smith	
Andorra		'Himne Andorrà'	?	D J Benlloch i Vivó	E Marfany	8 Sept
Argentina		'Marcha de la Patria: Oid, mortales, el grito sa grado Libertad' (the longest National Anthem, see p 185)	1813	V Lopez y Planes	J B Parera	25 May 7 July
Australia	1.	'Waltzing Matilda'	*c* 1900*	A B Paterson	Marie Cowan (after a Scottish melody)	26 Jan 25 Apr
	2.	'Advance, Australia Fair'	?	P D McCormick	P D McCormick	
	3.	'Australia Will Be There'	?	W W Francis	W W Francis	
		In 1973 the Australian National Anthem Quest Committee mounted a competition to find an anthem to replace 'God Save the Queen' as the official anthem. Some 1300 entries were received from amateur and professional composers—all were rejected.				
Austria	1.	'Kaiserlied: Gott erhalte, Gott beschütze, unser Kaiser, unser Land' (see p 185)	1797 (12 Feb)	L L Haschka	F J Haydn	17 Apr 15 May
	2.	'Deutsch-Österreich, du herrliches Land'	1920	K Renner	W Kienzl	
	3.	Österreichische Bundeshymne: Sei gesegnet ohne Ende'	1929 (13 Dec)	O Kernstock	F J Haydn (=1)	
	4.	Austria was incorporated into Germany during the Nazi régime and was forced to adopt the words and music of Germany's anthem 6—see p 186				
	5.	'Land der Berge, Land am Strome'	1946 (22 Oct)	P Preradović	W A Mozart? (arr V Keldorfer) (see p 186)	
Belgium		'La Brabançonne: Après des siècles d'esclavage'	1830	H L A Dechet (known as 'Jenneval') and C Rogier	F van Campenhout (revised in Committee in 1951)	4 July
		(In 1951 this anthem replaced the original Flemish De Vlaamsche Leeuw' of 1845, which had words by H v Peene and music by K Miry)				
Bolivia		Himno Nacional: 'Bolivianos, el hado propicio'	1842	J I de Sanjinés	B Vincenti	9 Apr 6 Aug
Brazil	1.	=Portugal's Anthem, qv				
	2.	Himno Nacional: 'Ouviram do Ypiranga as margens plácidas'	1922	J O D Estrada	F M da Silva	7 Sept 11 Nov
Britain		'God Save the Queen' (see p 184)	1745	?	?	23 Apr
Bulgaria	1.	'Shumi Maritza okărwawena' ('Foaming Maritza')	1885	N Živkov	G Šebek	
	2.	'Bulgaria mila, zemya na gheroi'	1950 (30 Dec)	N Furnadziev; M Issaew; E Bagrjana	G Dimitrov; G Zlatev-Tscherkin; S Obretenov	

Country		Title	Date of Adoption *=un-official	Words	Music	National/ Independence/ Saint Day(s)
Burma		'Gba majay Bma pyay' ('Give Burma a Place in your Hearts')	1948	Trad	T K B Thoung	4 Jan 12 Feb
Burundi		'Cher Burundi, ô doux pays'	1961	J-B Ntabokaja	M Barengayabo	
Cambodia		'Nokoreach'	1941	Chuon-Nat	Trad (arr F Perruchot and J Jekyll)	11 Nov
Cameroon		'Chant de Ralliement'	1957	R J Afame	S M Bamba and M Nyate	1 Jan
Canada	1.	'The Maple Leaf Forever'	1867	A Muir	A Muir	1 July
	2.	'O, Canada!' 'Terre de vos aïeux'	*c* 1880	French: A B Routhier English: R S Weir (1908)	C Lavalée	
Central African Republic		'National Hymn'	1958	B Boganda (President)	H Peppert	
Chad		'Peuple Tschadien'	1958	P Villard	L Jidrolle	
Chile		Himno Nacional: 'Dulce patria, recibe los votos	*c* 1847	B de V y Pinato and E Lillo	R Carnicer	18 Sept
China	1.	'Tsung Kuoh hiung'	*c* 1912	Anon	Anon	10 Oct
Republic (Taiwan)	2.	''San min chu l'wu'	1929	Sun Yat-Sen	Ch'eng Mao-Yün	
People's Republic	3.	'Arise! We are Slaves No Longer'	1949	T'ien Han	Nie Eel	
Columbia		Himno Nacional: 'Oh! Gloria inmarcesible'	*c* 1905	R Núñez	O Sindici	20 July
Congo (formerly French Middle Congo)		'La Congolaise'	?	J Royer; J Spadilière; J Tandra	Trad	
Congo (formerly Belgian Congo)		'National Hymn'	?	S Boka	J Lutumba	
Costa Rica		Himno Nacional: 'Noble patria, tu hermosa bandera'	1853	J M Zeledón (1903, replacing anonymous words)	M M Gutiérrez	15 Sept
Cuba		'La Bayamesa: Al combate corred Bayameses'	1868	P Figueredo	P Figueredo	20 May
Czecho-slovakia		Kdi Domov Můj?' (This and the Slovak anthem were combined in 1919)	1919	J K Tyl	F Škroup (1834)	
Dahomey		'Enfants du Dahomey, debout'	1960	Committee	G Dagnon	
Denmark	1.	Royal Anthem: 'Kong Kristian'	*c* 1780*	J Ewald	D L Rogert	11 Mar 5 June
	2.	National Anthem: 'Der er et yndigt Land' ('There is a winsome land')	1844*	A Øhlenschläger	H E Krøyer	
	3.	'Den gang jeg drog afsted'	19th cent	F Faber	J O E Horneman	
Dominican Republic	1.	'Himmo de Capotillo'	*c* 1865	I M Calderón	I M Calderón	17 July
	2.	Himno Nacional de la Républica Dominicana. 'Quisqueyanos valientes, alcemas'	1900	E Prud'homme	J Reyes (1883)	
Ecuador		'Salve! O Patria!'	1866	J L Mera	A Neumann (1866)	11 Aug
Eire		Amhrón na bhFiann ('The Soldier's Song') ('We'll sing a song, a soldier's song')	1926 (July)	P Kearney	P Kearney and P Heaney (*c* 1917)	17 Mar
El Salvador		Himno Nacional: 'Saludemos la patria orgullosos'	1953	J J Cañas	J Aberle (*c* 1855)	15 Sept

Country	Title	Date of Adoption *=unofficial	Words	Music	National/ Independence/ Saint Day(s)
Estonia	Eesti Hümn: 'Mu isamaa' ('My Country')	*c* 1917	J W Jannsen (1865)	F Pacius (1848) (The same tune as that of the Finnish anthem)	
Ethiopia (Abyssinia)	Hymne National: 'Etiopia hoy, des yibalish'	1930	Trad (selected by Committee)	K Nalbandian (1925)	5 May 23 July
Faroe Islands	'Tú alfagra land mílt'	1907	S av Skardi	P Alberg	19 July
Finland	'Maamme laulu' ('Our Land')	1848	J L Runeberg	F Pacius (=The Estonian anthem)	6 Dec
France	1. 'La Marseillaise'	1795 (15 July)	R de L'Isle	R de L'Isle (1792)	
	2. 'Partent pour la Syrie'	1852	A de la Borde	L Drouet	
	(La Marseillaise returned as the National Anthem in 1873)				
Gabon	'La Concorde'	1960	G Damas	G Damas	
Germany	See above: **the country with the most National Anthems**, and the entry for Austria				
Ghana	'Lift High the Flag of Ghana'	1957	P Gbeho	P Gbeho	6 Mar
Greece	Hymn to Freedom: 'Se gnorizo apo tin Kopsi'	1863	D Solomós (1823–4) (158 stanzas, see p 185)	N Manzaros	25 Mar
Greenland	'Nangminek Erinalik' (The Danish Anthem is also used)	?	H Lund	J Petersen	
Guatemala	Himne Nacional: 'Guatemala feliz'	1887/1934	J J Palma	R Á Oraile	15 Sept
Guinea	'Liberté'	?	–	A' Yaya	2 Oct
Haiti	'La Dessaliniènne'	1903	J Lhérisson	N Geffrard	1 Jan
Honduras	Himno Nacional: 'Compatriotas, de Honduras los fueros'	1915	A C Coello	C Hartling	15 Mar 15 Sept
Hungary	1. *Rákóczy March*	18th cent*	–	Trad (arr V Ružičzka (1810) and J Bihari)	
	2. 'Szózat' ('The Appeal'): 'Hazádnak rendűletlenűl hégy hive óh magyar!'	1836	M Vörösmarty	B Egressy	
	3. Himnusz: 'Isten áldd még a magyart'	1842	F Kölczey (1823)	F Erkel	
Iceland	Lofsöngur: 'O Gud vors land'	1874*	M Jochumsson	S Sveinbjørnsson	17 June
India	1. 'Vande Mataram'	*c* 1896	B C Chatergee	R Tagore	16 Jan 15 Aug
	2. 'Jană-Gană-Mană'	1950 (24 Jan)	R Tagore	R Tagore (arr H Murrill; N Richardson)	
Indonesia	'Indonesia Raya' ('Indonesia, Fatherland')	1949	W R Supratman	W R Supratman	17 July
Iran	1. 'Salamati, Schah'	*c* 1873	Anon	P Lemaire	5 Aug
	2. Imperial Salute: 'Shahanshah i ma Zandah bada'	*c* 1934	H Afsar	D Nadjmi Moghaddam	26 Oct
Iraq	1. Iraq Royal Salute	1923	–	A Chaffon; A R Murray;	
	2. National Salute	1959	–	L Zambaka	
Isle of Man	Manx National Anthem	1907	W H Gill	Trad (arr W H Gill)	
Israel	'Hatikvah' ('Hope')				
	Zionist movement:	1897	N H Imber (in Hebrew)	Trad (arr S Cohen)	13 May
	Israel State:	1948	N Salaman (in English)		
Italy	1. *Marcia Reale*	1834*	–	A Gabelli	6 June
	2. 'Inno di Garibaldi' (previously: 'Inno, di guerra dei cacciatore delle Alpi' – 'Battle Hymn of the Alpine Hunters')	1860*	L Mercantini	A Olivieri	
	3. La Giovinezza: 'Su compagni in forte schiere'	1922	M Manni	G Blanc, arr G Castoldo	

Country	Title	Date of Adoption *=un-official	Words	Music	National/ Independence/ Saint Day(s)
4	'Inno di Mameli:' 'Fratelli d'Italia, l'Italia s' è desta'	1946 (2 June)	G Mameli	M Novaro (1847)	
Ivory Coast	'Abidjanaise'	1960	Committee	P M Pango	
Jahore	'Lago Bangsa Jahore'	1879	H M S B H Sulieman	M Galistan	
Japan	'Kimigayo' ('The Peaceful Reign')	1880*	Trad (9th cent)	H Hirokami (Revised F Eckert)	19Apr 3 May 3 Nov
Jordan	''A shaal Maleek'	1946	A I Ar-Rifaa'i	A At-Tauuir	22 Mar 15 Mar
Kenya	'Land of the Lion'	1963	C Ryan	C Ryan	
Korea (South)	'Tonghai Moolkura Paiktu Sani''	1945	Trad	An Ik Tae	15 Aug
Korea (North)	'Morning Sun, shine over the Rivers and Mountains'	1949	Pak se Jen	Kim won Gûn	
Kuwait	National Salute	?	–	Trad	
Latvia	Nacionata Himna: 'Dievs, sveti Latviju'	1873*	K Baumanis	K Baumanis	
Lebanon	Humne Nationale: 'Kullu na lil watan lil 'ula lil'alam'	1926	R Nakhlé	W Sabra; M El-Murr	
Liberia	L'Inno Nazionale: 'Salve, Libera, Salve!'	*c* 1864	D. B Warner	O Luca	16 July
Libya	'Ya Biladi'	1952	A B a Arebi	A Wahab	24 Dec
Liechtenstein	'Oberst am Jungen Rhein'	*c* 1850	H H Jauch	='God Save the King'	16 Aug
Lithuania	Lietuvos Himnas: 'Lietuva tévyné mūsu ('Lithuania, my Country')	1918	V Kudirka	V Kudirka	
Luxemburg	'Ons Hēmécht' ('Our Motherland')	1859	M Lentz	A Zinnen	23 Jan
Malagasi	'O bien-aimée terre de nos ancêtres'	1960	K Rabajaso	N Rabarsoa	
Malawi	'O God, bless our land Malawi'	1964	M F P Sanka	M F P Sanka	
Malaysia Malaya	'Negara Ku' ('My Country')	1957	M I A A Aziz	Trad	1 Feb 31 Aug
Mali	'A Ton Appel, Mali'	?	E Gambetta	E Gambetta	
Malta 1.	'Tifhîra lil Mâlta'('Malta's Song of Praise')	*c* 1910*	G A Vassallo (1870)	Trad	
2.	Innu Malti: 'Lil din l'art Helwa'	?	D K Psaila	R Samut	
Mauritania	Anthem	1958	–	Nikiprovetzki	
Mexico	Himno Nacional: 'Mexicanos, al grito de guerra'	1854 (16 Sep)	F G Bocanegra	J D Nunó, arr. B Beltrán	16 Sept
Monaco	'Hymne Monegasque'	1867	L Canis	B de Castro	19 Nov
Morocco	'Hymne Cherifien'	1956	–	L Morgan	7 Mar
Nepal	'Shri mân gumbhira Nèpâli'	?	Trad	Trad	18 Feb
Netherlands 1.	'Wilhelmus van Nassouwe' (The oldest National Anthem, see p. 184)	16th cent	P M van St Aldegonde (*c* 1590)	Trad (*c* 1572, first pub 1626)	30 Apr
2.	'Wien Neerlandsch bloed' ('When Netherland Blood)	*c* 1830*	H Tollens	J W Wilms (1815)	
Newfoundland	'When Sunrays Crown the Pine-clad Hills'	1901	C C Boyle	C H Parry	
New Zealand	'God Defend New Zealand'	1940	T Bracken	J J Woods (1876); R A Horne	6 Feb 25 Apr
Nicaragua	Himo Nacional: 'Salve a ti Nicaragua'	1939 (words)	S I Mayorga (1917)	A Castinove? (before 1821)	15 Sept
	'Hermosa Soberana' (This song is sometimes mistaken for the Nicaraguan Anthem)	–	B Villatas	A Cousin	
Niger	'La Nigérienne'	1961	?	?	
Nigeria	'Nigeria, We Hail Thee'	1960	L J Williams	Francis Benda	
Norway 1.	'Sønner af Norge' ('Children of Norway')	*c* 1850*	H Bjerregaard (1820)	C Blom (1820)	17 May
2.	'Ja, vi elsker dette landet' ('Truly do we love this Country')	1864	B Bjørnsson (1859)	R Nordraak	

Country		Title	Date of Adoption *=un-official	Words	Music	National/ Independence/ Saint Day(s)
Pakistan		'Pak sarzamin shabad' ('Pakistan, sacred country')	1953	A A H Jullunduri	A G Chagla	23 Mar 14 Aug
Panama		Himno Istmeño: 'Alcanzamos por fin la victoria'	1903 (4 Nov)	D J de la Ossa	D S Jorgea	3 Nov
Paraguay		Himno Nacional: 'Paraguayos, República ó muerte!'	1846	F A de Figueroa	E Dupuy, or L Cavedagnı	14 May 15 Nov
Peru		Himno Nacional: 'Samos libres, seámos lo siempre'	1821 (rev 1869)	J de la T Ugarte	J B Alzedo (rewritten 1912, by C Rebagliati)	28 July
Philipines		*Marcha Nacional Filipina*	1898	J Palma	J Felipe	4 July
Poland	1.	Hymn Polski: 'Bože, coš Polske przez tak liezne wieki' (The most migratory tune, see p 185)	1815	A Felinski	K Kurpinski (after J P Solié)	
	2.	'Z dyman pažarów z kurzem krwi bratniej'	*c* 1863	H Ujeski	J Nikorowicz	
	3.	'Jeszcze Polska nie zginęła'	1927	J Wybicki	?M K Oginski (*c* 1800)	
Portugal	1.	Himno da Carta: 'O Patria, O Rei, o Povo' (the only Anthem to have been composed by a reigning monarch, see p 185)	1822	King Pedro IV	King Pedro IV	10 June
	2.	Hino Nacional a Portuguesa: 'Herois do mar'	1910	H L de Mendonça (1890)	A Keil (1890)	
Prussia		'Heil dir im Siegerkranz' (see also Germany)	1795	B Schuhmacher	='God Save the King'	
Romania	1.	Trăiascǎ Regele' ('Long Live the King')	1861 (22 Jan)	V Alexandri	E A Huebsch	
	2.	'Zarobite čatuse im uromǎ vǎmǎn'	?	A Baranga	M Socor	
	3.	'Te Slavim, Români'	1953 (23 Aug)	E Frunza and D Desliu	M Socor	
Ruanda-Urindi (Rwanda)		'Rwanda, oh ma Patrie'	1962	M Habarurema	M Harbarurema	
Russia	1.	'Bože, Czarya khrani' ('God Save the Tsar') (Forbidden in 1917)	1833 (11 Dec)	V A Shukovski and A S Pushkin	A F Lvov (1833) (to replace the tune of 'God Save the King')	7 Nov
	2.	'The Internationale' (superseded in 1917, but still sung as the song of the Communist Party)	1917	E Pottier (1871) (translated to Russian by A Y Kots, and again (1932) by A Gapov)	A or P Degeyter	
	3.	Sóyus neroúshimyi respoublik svobodnyh' (once called 'The Song of Stalin')	1944 (15 Mar)	S Mikhalkov and E Registan	A V Alexandrov	
		Byelorussia 'A chto tam idzie?'	1910	J Kupala	L M Rogowski	
		(Armenia has its own anthem, with words by Sarmen and music by Khachaturian; it was approved in 1945)				
San Marino		'Onore a te'	?	G Carducci	F Consolo	9 Sept
Saudi Arabia		National Hymn	1947	–	A R Al-Latib	22 Mar 20 May
Senegal		Fibres do mon cœur vert	1960	L S Senghor (President)	H Peppert	
Sierre Leone		High we Exalt Thee	1961	C N Fyle	J Akar	
Slavia		(see Yugoslavia)				
Slovakia		'Nad Tatru sa blyska' (see also Czechoslovakia)	?	J Matůska (1844)	Trad	
Somalia		National Salute	1960	–	G Blanc	
South Africa		'Die Stem van Suid-Afrika' ('The Voice of South Africa')	1938	C J Langenhoven (1918)	M L de Villiers	31 May

Country		Title	Date of Adoption *=un-official	Words	Music	National/ Independence/ Saint Day(s)
Spain		*Marcha Real*	1770 (3 Sept) 1942	–	Anon (18th cent)	2 May 18 July
Sri Lanka		'Namō Namō Mathā	1952	A Samarakoon	A Samarakoon	4 Feb
Sudan		'Nahnu djundul' lâh'	1956	A M Salih	A Murgan	1 Jan
Surinam		'Het Surinaamse Volkslied	*c* 1893; 1954	C A Hoekstra	C de Puy (1876)	
Sweden	1.	'Bevare Gud vår Kung'	? *	?	=God Save the King	6 June
	2.	'Du Gamla, Du Frie'	1844*	R Dybeck	Trad (*c* 1810)	
	3.	'Ur Svenska hjertans djup en gang'	1844*	K W A Strandberg	J O Lindblad	
	4.	'Sverige, Sverige, Fosterland' ('Sweden, Sweden, My Fatherland')	1905	V v Heidenstam	W Stenhammar	
Switzerland	1.	'Rufst du, Mein Vaterland?' ('Callest thou, Fatherland') (see p 184)	1811	J R Wyss (German)	='God Save the King'	8 Aug
		'O Monts indépendants'		H Röhrich (French)		
		'Ci chiami, o Patria'		Trad (Italian)		
	2.	Swiss Psalm: 'Trittst im Morgenrot daher'	1841	L Widmar (German) C Chatelanet French) Trad (Italian)	A Zwyssig	
Syria		'Humát al-diyári 'alaikum salám'	1939	K Mardam Bey	Fulayfel brothers	22 Mar 17 Apr
Tanzania (formerly Tanganyika)		'God Bless Tanzania' (The old Tanganyikan anthem)	1961	E Sontonga	E Sontonga	
Thailand		'Sanrasoen Phra Barami'	1934	Prince Narisar-anufadtivongs and King Rama VI	P C Duriyanga	24 June
Togo (French)		'Salut à loi de nos aïeux'	1960	A C Dosseh	A C Dosseh	
Trinidad/ Tobago		'Forged From the Love of Liberty'	1962	P S Castagne	P S Castagne	
Tunisia	1.	March beylicale	*c* 1883*	–	Anon	25 July
	2.	'Älä khällidî Yä'	1958	J E Ennakache	S al Mahdi	25 July
Turkey		'Istiklâl Marsi' ('March of Independence'): 'Korkma! Sönmez bu safak larda yüzen al sancak'	1921 (12 Mar)	M Akif Ersoy	M Zeki Ungor	29 Oct
		(Before 1921, a different anthem was composed for each ruler)				
Uganda		'O Uganda, May God Uphold Thee!'	1962	G Kakoma and P Wingard	G Kakoma	
United Arab Republic	1.	Egyptian Royal Hymn (Served for the original UAR until Syria broke away in 1961)	1958	Committee (1940)	attrib G Verdi (*c* 1872) (see p 185)	1 Feb 22 Mar 18 June 23 July
	2.	'O Thou, my weapon' (Egypt only)	1960	S Shahien	K el Tawiel	
Upper Volta		'Fière Volta de mes aïeux'	1958	R Quedraogo	R Quedraogo	
Uruguay		Himno Nacional	1848 (27 July)	F A de Figueroa	F Quijano and F J Deballi	25 Aug
Vatican		*Marcia Pontificale*	1949	–	C Gounod (see p 185) (1846)	
Venezuela		'Gloria al bravo pueblo'	1881 (25 May)	V Salias (*c* 1810)	J J Landaeta (*c* 1810)	5 July

Ralph Vaughan Williams. Portrait by Sir Gerald Kelly in the possession of the Royal College of Music

Sir Malcolm Sargent, composer and conductor, who was knighted in 1947 (Royal College of Music)

Country	*Title*	*Date of Adoption *=unofficial*	*Words*	*Music*	*National/ Independence/ Saint Day(s)*
Vietnam (North)	The Vietnam Army Marches	1956	Van Cao	?	2 Sept
Vietnam (South)	'Quôc Thiêù Viêtnam' ('Youth of Vietnam) (Now presumably forbidden)	1948	L H Phuoc	L H Phuoc	
Wales	'Mae hen wlad fy nhadau' ('Land of My Fathers')	1858*	E James (English words by J Owen)	J James (Also used for the 'National Anthem' of Brittany with words by J Taldir)	1 Mar
Yemen	'Salimta Imaman Li' ar shilbi'	?	Trad	Trad	22 Mar
Yugoslavia	Serbs: 'Bože pravde' ('God of Justice')	1872	J Djordjewič	D Jenko	29 Nov
	Croats: 'Lijepa naša domovino' ('Our Fair Country')	1846	A Mihanovič	J Runjamin	
	Salvs: 'Naprey zastava Slave' ('Forward, Arise, Slav')	?	S Jenko	D Jenko	
1.	(In 1919 the three hymns were combined to form 'The King's Anthem')				
2.	'Hej Slavni' ('Ho, You Slavs!') (The so-called Pan-Slav Anthem)	1945	Anon	=Polish anthem	
	(In 1975 it was proposed by the Union of Yugoslav Composers that a new National Anthem be adopted. That nominated was 'Solemn Song' by Taki Hrisik)				

Section VI

ORCHESTRAS AND CONCERTS

THE CONDUCTOR

He makes the most alarming faces
When made aware of double-basses,
And urges with sardonic grins
The first (and second) violins.

He brings in clarinet and flute
With antics that are frankly cute
Whilst quashing with a careless yawn
The too-enthusiastic horn.

Bassoons and timps get equal shares
Of devastating frowns and glares,
Though, less impressed, the trombones sit
Oblivious to all but spit.

The harp and tuba would be flattered
If they felt he thought they mattered,
As it is they plink and boomph
With happy disregard for oomph.

He uses with commanding ease
His fingers, ears and nose and knees,
Though fails to note how critics' snores
Embroider the composers' scores.

He wags his baton and his eyebrows
To thrill the hearts of female highbrows
(Although it's probable he'd sooner
Have become a dance-band crooner).

Now what I want to know is this,
If not content with giving bliss
To women of uncertain years,
Would he excel in other spheres?

And if his passion were Meccano
Instead of cor anglais and piano
Would such women with such brains
Content themselves with building cranes?

Mary Kennard

These two vital factors in music-making are treated separately but it should be borne in mind that their histories are so closely dovetailed that any division must be arbitrary. Orchestras, in the loosest possible sense, gave rise to concerts; and in turn concerts have given rise to more orchestras. Time and again throughout musical history, a series of concerts has led to the establishment of a permanent orchestra to play them, the orchestra then taking the name of the series. A good example is to be found in the series of Philharmonic Society concerts begun in London in 1813. These led to the establishment of the Philharmonic Orchestra, later to be the Royal Philharmonic Orchestra which eventually led an autonomous existence. The name of the orchestra was revived when Sir Thomas Beecham founded a new organisation in 1946; therefore the present Royal Philharmonic Society and the Royal Philharmonic Orchestra have no connection with each other, the one existing as a concert *promoting*, the other as a concert *giving*, organisation.

DEFINITIONS

A few generally accepted words have unexpected origins:

Orchestra: A Greek word referring to the space (and not to those occupying it) between the auditorium and the stage in a playhouse, a space in which dancing sometimes took place, accompanied by instruments (Gk: *orkheomai* = 'dance').

Interior view of the Royal Festival Hall, London

Philharmonic: Gk: 'a lover of harmony' (therefore

Philomusica = 'a lover of music').

Symphony: As part of the name of an orchestra: taken from the primary concert work, perhaps to impute a seriousness of intention to the organisation. In America, **Symphony** has taken the place of **Orchestra** in popular usage. Therefore, for instance, Chicago Symphony is the complete and self-sufficient title for that concert-giving organisation.

MODERN ORCHESTRAS

The oldest orchestra still in existence is the Leipzig Gewandhaus Orchestra. It emerged from the Grosses Konzert, which began in 1743 and were known later as 'Liebhaber-Concerts' (1763) under Johann Adam Hiller. The name 'Gewandhaus Orchestra' dates from 1780, when a new room specially built for the activities of this group of players was built in the Gewandhaus ('Cloth-Merchants' House'). The Orchestra's most famous conductor was Mendelssohn, who took over in 1835. Until 1905 it was the convention that the orchestra should stand throughout the entire performance.

Concert hall of the Leipzig Gewandhaus

Since that time the conception of a permanently constituted body of players, whether municipally, corporately, or privately run, has given rise to a large number of orchestras. Among those still active are the following, listed in chronological order of their foundation.

1828 Société des Concerts du Conservatoire, Paris, founded by François Antoine Habeneck, the composer and violinist who gave French audiences their first opportunity to hear Beethoven's symphonies. The Orchestra gave its first concert on 9 March 1828 in the Conservatoire Théâtre, Habeneck conducting from the leaders' position.

1840 Liverpool Philharmonic. The first concert was given on 12 March 1840 under the direction of John Russell. Philharmonic Hall was built for the Orchestra in 1849, but this was destroyed by fire in 1933.

1842 Vienna Philharmonic. Its first concert was on 28 March, conducted by Karl Otto Nicolai, the composer of *Merry Wives of Windsor*.

1842 New York Philharmonic. At its first concert at the Apollo Rooms on 7 December, the conductor was Ureli Correlli Hill, co-founder with William Scharfenberg and Henry Christian Timm. The Orchestra joined with the New York Symphony in 1928, being known thereafter as the 'New York Philharmonic Symphony'.

Sir Charles Hallé (Popperfoto)

1858 Hallé Orchestra, Manchester, grew out of the Gentlemen's Concerts, Sir Charles Hallé taking them over on 1 January 1850. The first Hallé concerts were a subscription series started on 30 January 1858 at the Free Trade Hall, Manchester.

1864 Moscow Philharmonic, launched under the directorship of Nikolai Rubinstein.

1881 Boston Symphony, founded by Henry L Higginson. Symphony Hall was built in 1900.

1881 Lamoureux Orchestra, Paris, founded by Charles Lamoureux.

1882 Amsterdam Concertgebouw. The first concert in the newly built Concertgebouw ('Concert House') was held on 11 April 1888, at which the conductor was Henri Viotta. The last item in the programme was Beethoven's 'Choral' Symphony.

1882 Berlin Philharmonic, a corporate body formed out of an orchestra led by Benjamin Bilse. The first concert given by the new Orchestra was conducted by one von Brenner on 17 October 1882: a long programme in three parts, each beginning with an overture. Hans von Bülow was conductor of the Orchestra from 21 October 1887 to 13 March 1893, and he gave the Orchestra's first concert in Philharmonic Hall on 5 October 1888, at which he played the piano solo part of Beethoven's *Choral Fantasia*.

1886 Chicago Symphony.

1893 Cincinnati Symphony. First principal conductor was Frank van der Stucken.

1893 Munich Philharmonic. Established by Franz Kaim.

1894 Czech Philharmonic, formed as a society. The first concert was given on 4 January 1896: a programme of music by Dvořák, conducted by the composer.

1895 San Francisco Symphony.

1896 Los Angeles Symphony.

1899 Pittsburg Symphony.

1900 Philadelphia Orchestra, established by Fritz Scheel.

1901 Warsaw Philharmonic, founded under the protection of Prince Lubomirski and Count Zamoyski. The first principal conductor was Alexander Rajchman.

1903 Minneapolis Symphony.

1904 London Symphony, formed as a cooperative organisation.

1907 St Louis Symphony.

1913 Hague Residentie, founded by Henri Viotta.

1916 City of Birmingham Symphony.

1918 Cleveland Symphony. Principal conductor Nikolai Sokolov, the Russian composer and pupil of Rimsky-Korsakov.

1918 Orchestra de la Suisse Romande, founded by Ernest Ansermet, who remained its principal conductor until his death in 1968.

1919 Los Angeles Philharmonic.

1930 BBC Symphony, founded by its principal conductor Sir Adrian Boult.

1932 London Philharmonic, founded by Sir Thomas Beecham; the orchestra became autonomous in 1939.

1945 Philharmonia Orchestra, founded by Walter Legge.

1964 New Philharmonia, formed as a company out of the members of the Philharmonia Orchestra, which was wound up only a few days previously in March 1964.

1967 Orchestra de Paris, founded by its principal conductor Charles Munch.

In the foregoing list it will be noticed that a high proportion of the orchestras are American. The list is, however, by no means exhaustive for that country; in August 1970 it was estimated that there were 1436 orchestras active in that country, including 'community' orchestras. Among these were 30 major and 66 metropolitan orchestras. In addition there were 918 opera groups. In West Germany there are no fewer than 94 full-time professional orchestras.

CONCERTS

The earliest concerts, by which we mean music played together by a group of musicians and witnessed by passive listeners, must have taken place in the prehistory of music. Inevitably, music was listened to, as this has been part of its purpose from the start, so it follows that 'concerts' have existed ever since the day that two or three people grouped together to play their instruments simultaneously. In short, concerts have existed since the early days of humanity; it is merely references to them that have been lacking.

The earliest concert for which direct evidence exists took place in the 6th century BC. According to Daniel 3: 5, 7, 10, and 15, Nebuchadnezzar's orchestra in Babylon consisted of 'horn, pipe, lyre, trigon, harp, bagpipe, and every kind of music' (RV). The first reference to this court orchestra was set down in Aramaic in the 2nd century BC, and the standard translation given above appears to be only partly correct. Curt Sachs in his *The History of Musical Instruments* (1942) has returned to the original and retranslated the names:

Dr Sachs draws from this translation that the Biblical text describes not an ancient orchestra but nothing less than a musical performance of 2600 years ago, since it would not make sense to enumerate a series of instruments (trumpet or horn, pipe, lyre, harps) and then say that they sounded together (which is implied already), following this with the fact that they were accompanied by a rhythm group. He takes the final step by suggesting a new reading of the text: 'thus, a literal translation of the Aramaic text suggests the picture of a horn signal, followed by solos of oboe, lyre and harp [*sic*],

Original (in phonetic transliteration)	*Accepted translation (in RV)*	*Curt Sachs's retranslation*
Quarnā	horn	trumpet or horn (compare Lat: *cornu*='horn')
Mašroquītâ	pipe	pipe (from the verb *šriqâ*='whistling'; compare Middle English *scritch,* whence 'screech', 'shriek')
Qatros	lyre	lyre (from Gk: *kithara*)
Sabka	trigon	horizontal angular harp (an instrument similar in outline to a war machine of the time called *sabka*, which consisted of a boat with a vertical ladder at one end. The string pegs on the upright 'mast' of the instrument would have resembled the rungs of a ladder. The strings stretching from 'mast' to belly would account for the triangle suggested in 'trigon')
Psantrîn	harp	vertical angular harp (=Gk: *psalterion*)
Sūmponiah	bagpipe	a sounding together (=Gk: *symphonia;* 'the bagpipe', for which *symphonia* can be an alternative name, came much later)
Zmārâ	and every kind of music	rhythm and percussion group

and a full ensemble of these and some rhythmical instruments. It does not describe an orchestra, but an orchestral performance in the ancient Near East.'

The modern conception of 'concert' implies the kind of organisational control suggested by this Biblical text. There is another early reference to a concert in which the usual presence of such organisation is implied by a report of its exceptional absence: an instrumentalist in ancient Rome, a Greek by the name of Aristos, brought his players out on strike in about 309 BC over a dispute connected with meal-breaks. This is not only **the first musical stoppage due to strike action** but it is also the earliest of all labour disputes.

The subsequent history of concerts (originally given as 'consorts' in England) is unrecorded until the 15th century.

15th century Manuscripts of instrumental pieces to be performed as accompaniment to dances are held in libraries at Berlin and Munich.

1482 The first Accademia, set up primarily for musical instruction, discussion, *and* performance, were held in Bologna.

1484 A similar Accademia was set up in Milan.

1570 First French concerts: Académie Baïf set up by Jean Antoine de Baïf at the Court of Charles IX. Although clearly based on the Italian examples, these French meetings were less formal, consisting mainly of musical settings of poems written by members of the Académie.

1571 March 25. Waits sang and played shawms, recorders, sackbuts, violins, viols, and lutes from the turret of the Royal Exchange in London for the sole object of bringing pleasure to people living near by. This friendly practice was continued every Sunday (until stopped by Charles I in 1642) and holiday evenings from Lady Day to Michaelmas (until Pentecost in 1572).

c **1576** Orchestras of organs, lutes, viols, recorders, and pandoras, together with voices, would entertain the audience for an hour before and half an hour after a play at theatres such as that at Blackfriars, London. The practice had become widespread by the early 17th century.

1580–*c* 90 Nicholas Yonge gave private musical parties at his home in the City of London every day. Mostly these consisted of Italian (and English imitation) madrigals.

1672 September 30. Enter the demon finance for the first time: the musical performances at playhouses were not strictly what the audience had paid to see and hear; therefore, all musical performances up to that date had been free. **The first musical impresario** in the world was John Bannister or Banister. He was one of the 24 violinists of King Charles II's 'Musick', who saw a way to supplement his income. At Bannister's Music School, near the George Tavern, Whitefriars, every day at 4 pm were held concerts at which the performers, both instrumental and vocal, were placed out of sight behind a curtain. The public was allowed in to listen upon payment of 1s (5p) per head. These were **the world's first paid concerts.** In 1675 the organisation moved to Covent Garden, and later to Lincoln's Inn Fields, and finally to Essex Street, off the Strand.

1678 Thomas Britton, a coal-dealer, converted his Clerkenwell coal cellar into a concert-house and there, until his death, gave a series of concerts which started as diversions for his friends but quickly grew famous among the gentry. Visitors are said to have included Handel and other famous musicians. At first, entrance was free, but as numbers increased, Britton was compelled to limit them by imposing a fee of 1s (5p) per concert or 10s (50p) per year.

Having established itself squarely in the environs of London, the habit of concert-giving, both for fun and for reward, became common:

1710 Jean Loeillet gave concerts of Italian and other music mainly for the flute at his London home.

1714 Hickford, the Dancing Master, gave over his room to concert-giving, first at James Street, Piccadilly, and, from about 1738, in Brewer Street, Soho, until 1779.

1720 The Academy of Ancient Music was formed to give concerts at the Crown and Anchor Tavern in the Strand. These continued until 1792.

1724 The Castle Society, another organisation centred upon a local inn, did likewise at the Castle Tavern in Paternoster Row, and later elsewhere.

While these and many other organisations flourished in the English capital, the practice of concerts was developing in the courts and residences of Germany and other European countries, growing out of the schools of music, the Collegia Musicum, which themselves had evolved from the Italian Accademie, while in France another development of lasting importance was about to take place:

1725 Anne Philidor (Danican) founded the Concert Spirituels in Paris. These, the first true public concerts in France, were held in the Salle des Cent Suisses in the Château des Tuileries until 1784 and were extremely popular and influential, attracting the attention of composers from many other countries. For instance, to take the best-known example, Haydn wrote for the Concert Spirituels a fine set of six symphonies (Nos 82–87, 1783–85, known as 'Paris' Symphonies), and even after the series of concerts ceased in 1791 there were attempts to revive the name (1805; 1830).

1731 The earliest recorded concerts in America were given in Boston, Massachusetts and in Charleston, South Carolina.

1736 Earliest concerts in New York.

1743 The first modern symphony orchestra was established at the Court of the Elector Palatine, Duke Karl Theodor, at Mannheim. The orchestra was led by Jan Václav Antonín Stamič under whom it quickly became the finest band in the world. After a visit to Mannheim, Charles Burney was lost in admiration: 'An army of generals' was his description. After the death of Stamič the orchestra continued under a second generation of composer/player/conductors until 1778. See Groups of Composers in Section III.

Mannheim set an example for many royal households throughout Europe, among them the magnificent Esterházy Castle in rural Hungary at which Franz Joseph Haydn, who has fairly been called 'Father of the Modern Symphony Orchestra', composed for most of his working life until 1790.

A feature of 18th-century London which Haydn would have known during his visits (see below) was the gardens at which music was played. **The first** was at Marylebone (*c* 1650–1776) but **the most famous and longest established** (191 years) was at Vauxhall (1660-1859); another, at Ranelagh (1742–1803) should not be overlooked. These ornamental gardens supplemented the lively musical activities of the capital, which were mainly centred on the most famous concert-halls:

1760 Carlisle House in Soho Square (1760–80), run by Mrs Cornelys; **The Pantheon,** Oxford Street (1772–1814); **Hannover Square Rooms** (1775–1874), to which Johann Peter Salomon brought Haydn in 1791 for the start of his two highly successful London visits.

1768 What is thought to be the world's first annotated programme was for a concert of catches and glees put on at Drury Lane Theatre by Thomas Augustin Arne.

1776 The Concerts of Ancient Music commenced. They became known as the 'King's Concerts' from 1785 because of the regular attendance of King George III, and they continued until 1848.

1783 The professional concerts started, running until 1793.

By the end of the 18th century the concert principle was established throughout the musical world, but with the new century came new ideas, larger works of music and larger orchestras. Hitherto, the orchestra had been held together aurally by the leader sitting at a keyboard instrument and playing 'continuo', a device which had the dual purpose of giving the other players the tempo and beat, and filling in the missing middle harmonies of the work. As the 18th century progressed, however, this latter function became unnecessary, since the Mannheim composers had completed the harmonic structure with their imaginative use of wind and brass instruments, a technique which had been copied everywhere else.

The process of conducting with a stick seems to have grown out of three roots, and seeds of the practice appear to have been described as far back as the 13th century. In early 18th-century France it was the custom in the opera-house to beat out the rhythm loudly on the floor or a desk with a stick, a practice found as recently as 1895 in Pisa; in Mannheim Franz Xaver Richter would beat time inaudibly by waving a rolled-up music part in the air; and as the keyboard-conductor became less vital musically, the role of conductor devolved on to the leading violinist in some centres, and his lead with the bow would be followed by the other players. It was common for the conductor to face the audience until the mid 19th century.

Among the first to use a baton with any regularity was Johann Friedrich Reichardt, himself a violinist, harpsichordist, and composer in north Germany; it is known also that Mozart beat time soundlessly in Vienna, probably with expressive hand movements. Modern conducting, however, began with Berlioz, Spohr, and Wagner, and rapidly developed into an art form within itself.

With the larger music came the necessity for larger concert-halls:

1812 The Argyll Rooms, Regent Street, were opened in London, but were destroyed by fire in 1830.

1831 Exeter Hall, in use until 1880, replaced the Argyll Rooms.

1842 Crosby Hall, Bishopsgate Street, was built, to continue as a concert-hall until 1891.

1848 Holywell, in Oxford was opened, and it remains **the oldest concert-hall in Europe** still to be in use for music performances.

1855 The first Crystal Palace season opened. There were winter seasons for the first five years, but in 1860 a summer season was inaugurated and the series continued until 1901, mainly under the direction of August Manns.

At the opening of the first summer season of the Crystal Palace concerts on 4 May 1860 an orchestra of about 3000 was led by Michael Andrew Angus Costa. The concert was given in memory of Mendelssohn and consisted of a performance of *Elijah* (for which the number of singers is not recorded) and the Overture and Wedding March from *A Midsummer Night's Dream*. The Band of the Coldstream Guards also 'assisted', and a torchlight exhibition followed the concert.

1871, Royal Albert Hall opened. The first concert, on 29 March, presented the following programme:

Prince Albert: *L'Invocazione all 'Armonia.*
Handel: 'Lascia ch'io pianga'.
Curschmann: 'Ti Prego'.
Gounod: 'Salve dimora'.
Auber: 'Prayer' (from *Masaniello*).
Rossini: Overture: *The Thieving Magpie.*

The capacity of the Albert Hall is 7000–8000.

1893 Queen's Hall opened; it was destroyed in an air raid in 1941.

1901 Wigmore Hall opened.

1904 Aeolian Hall opened: it continued in use as a public concert-hall until 1941, when it was taken over by the BBC for use as a studio.

1951 Royal Festival Hall opened as part of the festivities surrounding the Festival of Britain. Its two smaller halls, in the same building complex: Elizabeth Hall for chamber performances and Purcell Room for recitals, were opened in March 1967.

For the future in London, the City authorities have an ambitious plan for an arts centre in The Barbican housing a concert-hall (see

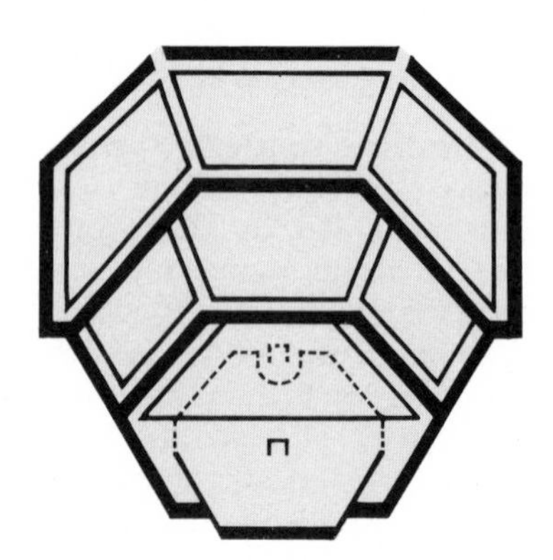

Seating plan of the new Barbican Concert Hall in the City of London. For normal concerts the audience capacity is 2000, but for larger works the orchestra is moved forward into the area outlined by dots, leaving room behind for a choir of 200. On these occasions the audience capacity is reduced to 1800.

seating plan) to be the permanent home of the London Symphony Orchestra, the Guildhall School of Music and Drama, a theatre, an art gallery, and a public library. In the same complex will be a students' hostel, restaurants and inns, shops, 2000 flats and maisonettes, and ample parking accommodation. Pedestrians will be confined to elevated walkways.

Similar plans have been carried out, or are in the active planning stage, for many of the world's art centres, illustrating that accommodation for musical performance is now a matter of course in urban planning. This has not always been the case: music has too often been regarded as a pastime for the rich and therefore outside the reach and understanding of the masses (see below).

The most recent major musical building complex, is the so-called 'Sydney Opera House', built on a point of land, Bennelong Point, projecting into Sydney Harbour. It may also hold the record for the slowest gestation of a concert building, since the period from inception of the idea to opening of the building was eighteen years.

1955: It was announced that a concert/opera-giving edifice was to be built at Bennelong Point and designs were invited in a competition.
1957: The Danish architect Joern Utzon won the competition for his startling and boldly revolutionary design.
1958: Foundations commenced.
1963: Foundations completed.
1967: Exterior completed.
1973: Interior completed.

Total cost of the project was $A 100 000 000, which was obtained mainly through public lotteries.

Although called the 'Sydney Opera House', opera takes only a small part of the available space and is, indeed, rather poorly catered for in the design: the stage is too shallow to allow ambitious presentations, and the wing area is severely restricted. Nevertheless, the name 'Opera House' is now established and is unlikely to be changed.

In all, there are some 900 rooms in the building, the major of which are:
Concert Hall, with seating for 2700.
Opera Theatre, with seating for 1550.

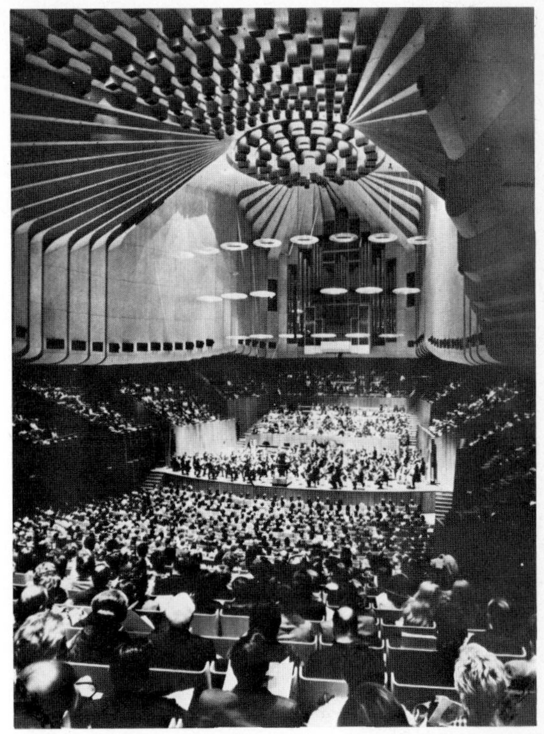

Concert hall of the Sydney Opera House (Sydney Opera House Trust)

Drama Theatre, with seating for 550.
Recital Room/Cinema, with seating for 420.
Fully equipped recording hall.
Rehearsal Rooms.
Exhibition Hall.

The first opera to be staged in the Opera Theatre was Prokofiev's *War and Peace*, by the Australian Opera conducted by Edward Downes in September 1973. The cast was:

Natasha	Eileen Hannan
Andrey	Tom McDonnell
Pierre	Ronald Dowd
Kuragin	Robert Gard
Kutuzov	Neil Warren-Smith
Napoleon	Raymond Myers

Production was by Sam Wanamaker and the Designer was Tom Lingwood.

Three weeks later, on 20 October 1973, the official opening was made by Queen Elizabeth II, and this was followed by a concert which concluded with a performance of Beethoven's Choral Symphony (No 9 in D minor, Op 125) conducted by Willem van Otterloo.

MUSIC FOR THE MASSES

Early attempts were made to popularise so-called 'serious' music, among them the concerts of open-air music in the Champs-Élysées, Paris, under Philippe Musard in the late 1830s. These led directly to the famous Promenade Concerts:

1837 Henri Justin Valentine conducted a series of promenade concerts in Paris, but they were not well attended and ceased after one short season.

1839 Promenade Concerts à la Valentine opened at the Crown and Anchor Tavern in the Strand, London. In the same year began the **Original Promenade Concerts à la Musard** at the English Opera House.

1840–1 During the winter season there were three separate promenade concert series running in London, all well attended, but after many years this splitting of effort became channelled by the appearance of a single driving force:

1895 August 8, the first of the Henry Wood Promenade Concerts opened with Wagner's *Rienzi* Overture. Sir Henry Wood was the manager and principal conductor of the concerts from that date until his death in 1944. His services to music were recognised by a knighthood in 1911. The Promenade Concerts, which still continue with unabated popularity, were held at the Queen's Hall until its destruction in 1941, after which they transferred to the Royal Albert Hall. During post-war years the name most closely associated with 'the Proms' was that of Sir Malcolm Sargent.

Sir Henry Wood conducting the Queen's Hall Symphony Orchestra at the Ealing Film Studios, November 1935 (Popperfoto)

Another successful operation in bringing music to a wider audience began in 1855 with the Crystal Palace Concerts which extended into the new century (see above). They were conducted throughout by August Manns in that spacious hall in spacious grounds, and furthered the 19th-century need for musical proletarianism in surroundings reminiscent of the 18th-century leisure and pleasure gardens.

In 1858 the optimistically titled 'Popular Concerts' began, being held every Monday and Saturday at St James's Hall. Being centred mainly on chamber music, their appeal was relatively limited, but they survived for 40 years, until 1898. Seventy years later (1968/69) the English Chamber Orchestra scored the distinction of being **the first chamber orchestra to make a world tour** (USA, Australia, New Zealand, Israel, Cyprus, Italy), giving a total of 28 concerts.

Popularity has always been the aim of those dedicated men and women who make music, of course, but the enthusiasm of the public can sometimes be carried to extremes:

The most encored work at one concert was the waltz *Sinngedicht* by Johann Strauss II: at the composer's first concert at Dommayer's Garden Restaurant in Vienna on Tuesday, 15 October 1844, this item, which had been designed to close the programme, did so with a vengeance, being encored nineteen times.

The popularity of certain items is paralleled by the popularity of music in general.

The largest 'hall' used for regular performances of serious music is Hollywood Bowl, opened in 1919 on a 20 hectare (50 acre) site in a natural depression, Beechwood Canyon, Hollywood. The summer series of 'Symphonies under the Stars' is held every year, and the seating capacity of 25000 is not excessive.

The first British orchestra to play at the Hollywood Bowl was the London Symphony Orchestra in September 1974.

Hollywood Bowl (Popperfoto)

The greatest attendance at any 'classical' concert was 130 000 for the New York Philharmonic Orchestra, conducted by Leonard Bernstein at Sheep Meadow in Central Park, New York City, on 6 August 1974.

MUSICAL GATHERINGS OF GIGANTIC PROPORTIONS

The conception of large forces in the performance of organised music-making came early in the history of music. The 40-part motet *Spem in alium* (for eight choirs of five separate voices each) of Thomas Tallis is an early example, and it is this kind of composition which led the Germans to accuse the English of being 'vastly fond of great noises that fill the ear'. However, the practice was not unknown on the Continent; the great *Festival Mass* originally thought to have been written by Orazio Benevoli for the consecration of Salzburg Cathedral in 1628, but now considered to be the work of an unknown composer working in Salzburg perhaps as late as 1682, was written for sixteen vocal soloists, four four-part choirs, six orchestras, and two organs; **53 parts** in all. (This work, incidentally, one of the grandest in the history of Church music, only narrowly escaped destruction and total oblivion when it was discovered behind the counter of a grocer's shop in Salzburg. But for the rapid, and probably rather startling, action of Innozenz Achleitner, once a Director of Music in Salzburg, a few hours would have seen the score distributed over a large part of the city it had been written to honour in the form of wrapping-paper.)

Later in England, Handel was responsible for another mammoth musical gathering when he wrote his *Musick for the Royal Fireworks* in 1749. The original idea was for the work to be played in the open air, and for this a massive assembly of woodwind, brass, and percussion was required: nine trumpets, three timpanists, nine horns, 24 oboes (ie three parts of respectively twelve, eight, and four per part), and twelve bassoons, a **total of 57.** For later performances indoors the wind/brass complement was reduced and a string band added.

Early in the 19th century the Czech composer Antonín Reicha conducted experiments with unusual positioning of orchestral forces, and with non-musical adjuncts (see Section IV); he also proposed an 'ideal' orchestra of twelve flutes, twelve oboes, twelve clarinets, twelve bassoons, twelve horns, six trumpets, six trombones, six pairs of timpani (tuned to accommodate all possible key combinations–an early move towards twelve-tone thinking), 60 violins, 18 violas, 18 cellos, and 18 double basses: **Total: 192.**

With the revival in popularity of Bach's oratorios under the guiding hand of Mendelssohn, and the increase in choral societies in England and on the Continent, concerts involving **300 performers** became commonplace. In 1833, for instance, a performance of *St Matthew Passion* was given in Leipzig by **230 singers** and an orchestra enlarged to over **100 players,** including eight each of oboes and clarinets, 46 violins, and ten double basses. Considerations of authenticity were put last (viz the clarinets).

Performances of Handel's *Messiah* at the Crystal Palace Handel Festivals (1857, then every year from 1859 to 1926 with the exceptions of war years) regularly attracted choirs of **between 3000 and 4000** but here again the degree of fidelity to Handel's intentions was in inverse proportion to the size of the forces.

The largest amateur orchestra numbered a total of 13 500 instrumentalists at the University of Michigan Band Day celebrations, an annual event between 1958 and 1965.

The largest amateur choir numbered 40 000 in the Vasco da Gama Stadium in Rio de Janeiro in 1940. Leading the singers was the Brazilian composer Heitor Villa-Lobos who for many years had been interested in mammoth-sized groups. In 1931 he had amassed a **choir of 12000 voices** in São Paulo, four years later he led a **choir of 30000, plus 1000 instrumentalists** and thereafter increased the numbers for each successive annual patriotic display until the 1940 record.

In this connection should be mentioned also the experiments of Patrick Sarsfield Gilmore, a bandmaster of Irish origin, who assembled an orchestra of **2000 instrumentalists and a choir of 20000** for the World Peace Jubilee at Boston, Massachusetts, on 17 June 1872, the conductor being Johann Strauss II. The violinists numbered more than 350 on this occasion. This assembly followed a previous gathering in 1869 when the forces were merely 1000 instrumentalists and 10000 voices.

The most massive musical gathering of all time occurred in 1971 in Bethlehem, Pennsylvania. Both amateur and professional performers took part in a performance of *Alleluja* by the American composer Robert Moran. It involved rock groups, marching bands, gospel singing groups, church bells, firework displays, light shows, and the entire population of the town of Bethlehem which, in 1960, numbered 75408. With an assumed population increase during the intervening eleven years, plus the numerous artists imported for the occasion, a conservative estimate would put the number of 'performers' involved in the performance in excess of **76000.**

The first concert to attempt to popularise the Negro spiritual among white people took place in June 1872 at the Coliseum, Boston, Massachusetts. The concert was given by the Fisk Jubilee Singers conducted by Johann Strauss II.

Section VII

MUSIC LITERATURE

Without the facility of rendering on to the written or printed page a precise indication of what music sounds like, the entire art would rely for its continuity on improvisation and memory. Performances of large-scale works would be impossible, and instrumental groups would have to invent anew each time they performed. There would be no such thing as a 'standard classic' because nothing would be standard for more than a few performances, and no single piece of music would be given the opportunity to become a classic; its spread would be restricted to a local audience, temporally and geographically.

This is one aspect of 'written music'. The literature of music goes much wider than this, however, into the realms of musical dictionaries, encylopaedias, biographies, periodicals, criticism, and musicology–all, be it noted, impossible if precise indications of the sound of music were not able to be transferred to paper.

The oldest surviving musical notation. In Section V we discussed the oldest song in the world, dating from 1400 BC. Some 400 years earlier there existed a heptatonic scale which was deciphered from a clay tablet by Dr Duchesne Guillemin in 1966–67. The tablet was discovered at Nippur Sumer, now Iraq.

The beginnings of the present notation system were created about the year 1020 by the Italian monk Guido d'Arezzo (*c* 990–1050). He saw the need for a method by which to teach his singing pupils to sing unfamiliar songs at sight, and the system he invented has the genius of simplicity. He realised that his singers knew many hymns extremely well from memory (indeed, there was no other way of performing the tunes at that time) and, by taking various prominent syllables from a well-known hymn, the relative pitches of which were well implanted in the minds of his pupils, he devised a scale based on the vocal sounds 'ut–re–mi–fa–sol–la(te–ut)', those notes in parenthesis being added later to complete the scale. This method is still used to indicate the octave C–C, sometimes the syllable 'doh' replacing 'ut'.

The text of the hymn which d'Arezzo used runs: 'UTqueant laxis REsonare fibris MIra gestorum FAmuli tuorum, SOLve polluti LAbii reatum, Sancte Iohannes'.

His next step was to establish a bass line in red ink to indicate the note 'fa' (F), another above it in yellow for 'ut' (C), and between them a scratched line made with a needle for 'la' (A). Using the lines, and all the spaces below, between, and above them, d'Arezzo was able to indicate positions for all the notes in the range from E to D. Rather later another line was added, clefs were invented to establish registers, and the other conventions were introduced to lead, by the mid 17th century, to the musical notation we know now.

MODERN NOTATION

Explanations of some familiar symbols:

Clef = **key,** ie indication of the register

= **G clef.** A representation of a medieval letter G, the focal point of which indicates the line G.

= **F clef.** A relic of the medieval letter F, centred on the F line.

= **C clef.** Its centre point, which may be fixed on any line, indicates the position of middle C.

♭ = **Flat.** This sign flattens all the notes of the pitch indicated which follows it in the bar.

♯ = **Sharp.** This sign sharpens all the notes of the pitch indicated which follow it in the bar.

♮ = **Natural.** Indicating that a previously flattened or sharpened note is to return to its natural pitch.

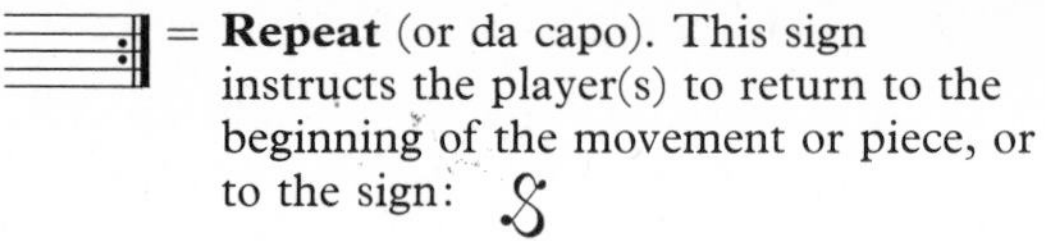

= **Repeat** (or da capo). This sign instructs the player(s) to return to the beginning of the movement or piece, or to the sign: 𝄋

= Repeat the section shown between the signs.

NOTE LENGTHS AND THEIR EQUIVALENT RESTS

In the early days of musical notation there were four note lengths: the double long (a black rectangle with a tail), the long (a black square with a tail), the breve, ie 'short' (a black square without a tail), and the semibreve, ie 'half-short' (a black diamond). A diminution of values has occurred since then so that we have today reached a situation in which the very longest note ever to be encountered is called 'short', and the longest generally used note is called 'half-short'.

Note	*Rest*	*Names*	*Meaning*
		breve; double whole note	short
		semibreve; whole note	half-short
		minim; half-note	shortest (ie minimum)
		crotchet; quarter-note	hook or crook from its old appearance
		quaver; eighth-note	to trill, or quaver (quiver) in very short notes
		semiquaver; sixteenth-note	half-quaver
		demisemiquaver; thirty-second-note	half of half a quaver
		hemidemisemi-quaver; sixty-fourth-note	half of half of half a quaver
		semihemidemi-semiquaver; hundred-and-twenty-eighth-note	half of half of half of half a quaver

TIME SIGNATURES

$\frac{3}{4}$ = three quarter-notes (crotchets) to the bar

$\frac{4}{4}$ or C = four quarter-notes to the bar

$\frac{3}{8}$ = three eighth-notes to the bar.

Other time signature meanings may be inferred from these examples.

During the present century composers have felt the need to extend all the above symbols and meanings in order to bring ever-more strict specifications of their requirements to the notice of their performers. One of the simplest extensions was made by the Romanian composer Xenakis who, in order to reduce the difficulty in reading many leger lines (additional lines above or below the staves to carry higher or lower notes), adopted the practice where necessary of adding a continuous line to represent the note B above the B above the treble clef, and another line to represent the D below the D below the bass clef, thus:

MUSIC IN PRINT

The earliest printed music is a book of plainsong issued in southern Germany in 1473. It is a *Graduale* by an unknown composer, printed by an unknown printer.

The earliest publishing house devoted almost entirely to music-printing was established in Venice in 1501 by Ottaviano dei Petrucci (1466–1539).

The first British song-book contained one of the most famous of English songs. It was published in 1530 by Wynken de Worde (? – *c* 1534) and contained the following songs:

'Pastime with Good Company', by Henry VIII.
'O Death Rocke me on Slepe', by Anne Boleyn.
'Hey Ding-a-Ding'.
'Have With You to Florida'.
'Bonnie Lass upon a Green'.
'By a Bank as I Lay'.
'As I Went to Walsingham'.
'Pepper is Black'.
'Go From My Garden'.
'Greensleeves'.

The oldest American printed music is the Bay Psalm Book of 1698. In its first three-quarters of a century it ran to more than 70 editions.

MUSICAL DICTIONARIES

Activity by publishing houses in the sphere of music has not been restricted to the dissemination of music itself, as the present volume testifies. One of the most useful branches of musical literature is the section which contains works which explain and clarify the terms, often obscure and usually foreign, for the benefit of the non-specialist reader. While usually fulfilling this function admirably, it should not be overlooked that, except for the most basic, these volumes are of prime value to the professional musician as a depository of facts necessary to his work. Such works of reference have a long and noble history.

The first musical dictionary is the *Terminorum Musicae Diffinitorium,* compiled by Johannes Tinctoris and published at Treviso about 1498. It defines 291 terms related to Renaissance musical practice and theory, and has been considered so vital to the correct understanding of this period that it has been translated into German (1863), French (1951), English (1963), and Italian (1965).

The first combined musical dictionary and collection of musical biographies was Johann Gottfried Walther's *Musikalisches Lexicon, oder musikalische Bibliothek,* first published in Berlin in 1732 and reprinted by Bärenreiter in 1953.

The first biographical music dictionary was *Grundlage einer Ehren-Pforte . . . ,* by Johann Mattheson who also published the first music criticism (see below) in 1740. The majority of the biographies were first-hand contributions by the subjects themselves.

MODERN MUSIC ENCYCLOPAEDIAS

The latest, and the largest, in the succession of musical cyclopaedias come from Germany and England.

1. *Die Musik in Geschichte und Gegenwart. Allgemeine Enzyklopädie der Musik,* edited by Friedrich Blume and published by Bärenreiter. Volume I appeared in 1949, and thirteen volumes have appeared since to complete the work, the last in 1968. Written throughout in German but giving a world-wide coverage, it seeks to incorporate the very latest in musical research in its composer biographies and comprehensive lists of works, but since the first volume was issued so many years ago it is clear that musicology has outrun the entries in the early part of the alphabet. Nevertheless, it is an unrivalled source-book of information containing often greatly extended articles of intricate detail.

2. *Grove's Dictionary of Music and Musicians,* founded by Sir George Grove. A multi-volume reference work in English, covering much the same ground as *Die Musik* . . . above, but with less attention paid to lesser composers, particularly in the matter of their composition lists. Five editions have appeared to date, each one greater and more extensive than the last:

I: Edited by Sir George Grove: 4 volumes, 1878-89.
II: Edited by J A Fuller-Maitland: 5 volumes, 1904–10.
III: Edited by H C Colles: 5 volumes, 1927–28.
IV: Edited by H C Colles: 5 volumes, plus supplement to the third edition, 1940.
V: Edited by Eric Blom: 9 volumes, 1954 plus Supplement 1961.

The sixth edition is in preparation and is promised for 'about 1978'. It will probably be in fourteen volumes, and the Editor is Stanley Sadie.

In addition to these long-lasting reference works there is a healthy business in musical magazines in all the musically aware countries of the world. Essentially journalistic, these publications nevertheless carry a vast amount of information which fails to find a place between hard covers: many of the articles, particularly those dealing with musicological subjects by some of the most eminent writers in the field, should achieve a more secure permanency. Fortunately, Detroit Information Service Inc publishes its own periodical which is devoted to indexing the material in others, thereby preventing this valuable material from being buried unknown in library basements.

The first musical journal was *Musica Critica,* edited by Johann Mattheson. The first number was published in Hamburg in 1722; it contained **the first published music criticisms.**

After this date the useful if not always responsible practice of musical criticism was slow to spread.

The first French musical journal: *Journal de Musique Française et Italienne,* appeared in 1764.

The first British musical journal: *The New Musical and Universal Magazine,* appeared in 1774.

The first American musical journal: *American Musical Magazine,* appeared in 1786.

But by the end of the 18th century the art of criticism was well established, particularly in Germany, where the really serious business of discussing the art of music in scientific detail was begun by the *Allgemeine Musikalische Zeitung,* first published in Leipzig in 1798.

The oldest still-existing British musical magazine is *The Musical Times,* which first appeared in 1844. The present editor is Stanley Sadie.

MUSICAL CRITICISM

We have already noted, above, the first printed musical criticisms (in Mattheson's *Musica Critica)* in 1722.

The first English music criticism of any consequence appeared in 1752, when Charles Avison published his *Essay on Musical Expression.*

The first French music criticism appeared in a pamphlet *Letter on French Music,* written by Jean-Jacques Rousseau and published in 1753. It was written specifically to attack the French operatic school and to praise the Italian. A sharp divide had been caused in

The Sydney Opera House (Stan Greenberg)

Sir Charles Groves conducting the BBC Symphony Orchestra at the Promenade Concerts, London (BBC)

Parisian taste by the performance the previous year of an old opera by Destouches, very much in the old-fashioned French style, and the rival appearance of Italian artists in Pergolesi's *La Serva Padrona* (1733). This led to **one of the first musical hoaxes:** the performance of an opera said to be by an Italian composer living in Vienna but actually, as was later revealed, by the Frenchman Dauvergne. After this opera, *Les Trocqueurs* (1753) written in imitation of the Italian style, Dauvergne reverted to the French method, feeling perhaps that he had won the day by having an Italian-style French opera acclaimed and that he could now return to the serious matter of making real French operas.

The first American music criticism did not appear until *Dwight's Journal of Music* in 1852.

MUSICOLOGY

This activity may be described as the study in depth of subjects peripheral to the practice and performance of music; alternatively, the pursuit of information on all aspects of music and musicians except that of actual performance. The value of such study is not always evident at first, but the gradual building up of a large body of facts surrounding music is useful in establishing other facts directly concerning the music, even though the usefulness of this peripheral information might not become apparent for many years after its publication. To take an example, it is well known that Brahms liked to smoke strong cigars. The actual make of these cigars can be of little interest to future generations since the cigars themselves no longer exist and Brahms was foremost a composer, not a cigar-smoker. However, if it can be proved that, in order to obtain his favourite make of cigar, Brahms travelled to another town on a given date, that much more is known about his life, and his appearance in that town on a certain date may assist in establishing the date of a piece of music. This imaginary example can be paralleled by real ones. For instance, the records of doctors who attended Schumann prove that his hand injury was not caused by his invention and use of a mechanical device to strengthen the third finger: there was already a deterioration in his hand action brought about by mercury poisoning (due to the then accepted treatment for syphilis) which led him to try to strengthen the hand mechanically (see Eric Sams's closely reasoned article in *The Musical Times*, December 1971).

The most obviously useful musicological study is into the background of the actual music of a composer, and one of the most obvious benefits to come from this kind of study is the thematic catalogue (see below).

The first stirrings of musicology were published in 1798 in the Leipzig magazine *Allgemeine Musikalische Zeitung*. The magazine *Cäcilia,* printed in Mainz by Schott from 1824 to 1850 went into musicological subjects even more deeply, and the contemporary *Neue Zeitschrift für Musik,* edited by Schumann, appeared in Leipzig from 1835. It dealt almost exclusively with the then modern movements in music.

The first use of the term 'musicology', or the German equivalent *Musikwissenschaft,* was in 1863, when Friedrich Chrysander published his periodical *Jahrbuch fur musikalische Wissenschaft*.

The ultimate in musicology may be said to have been reached with the private publication of volume I of the *Life of Wagner* in 1898. It was assembled from a huge collection of manuscripts, letters, and other paraphernalia, by Mary Burrell, a life-long admirer of the composer's music, and was engraved in script, with countless reproductions and photographs included. This first volume was 7·5 cm (3 in) thick, 76 cm (30 in) tall, and 53 cm (21 in) wide, and covered merely the first 21 years of Wagner's life. The planned succeeding volumes did not appear, due no doubt to the removal of the driving force with the death of Miss Burrell in 1898, but much of the material she so assiduously collected was made available to the public in *Letters of Richard Wagner,* published in America in 1950.

ITALIAN MUSICAL INDICATIONS

A few words might be said in explanation of those Italian musical terms which, because of their frequent appearance on concert programmes and record sleeves, have become part of the English language.

That Italian is by tradition the language of music is understandable since virtually all the important forms of music (the only notable exceptions being the symphonic, or tone, poem, and serial music) had their origins in that country. The convention is so well established world-wide that even Russian programme notes printed in Cyrillic, revert to the Roman type when words such as 'andante' appear in the text. During concert intervals in England it is not uncommon for these directions to merge into the conversation, to the complete understanding of all parties no doubt, in criticisms such as 'I don't think his finale was as cantabile as it might have been.'

It is entertaining to compare the musical meanings, as accepted for centuries, with the common Italian usage. Where there is no significant difference between the two, the latter has been omitted, and only the most common terms are included. The less common directions will be found in reference books of a more specialist nature than the present volume. Abbreviations, where commonly recognised, are given in brackets.

Direction	*Musical use*	*Common Italian use*
A Capella	in the style of Church music (ie voices without instruments)	at chapel
Accelerando	increasing the tempo gradually	making haste
Acciaccatura	a short grace-note	something crushed
Adagietto	a short (small) adagio	–
Adagio (Ad^{o})	slow; faster than largo and grave	slowly; at leisure
Affettuoso	tender, affectionate, pathetic	–
Allegretto (All^{tto})	light, cheerful; in tempo between allegro and andante	diminutive of allegro
Allegro (All^{o})	lively, briskly	gay, cheerful, merry
Amoroso	tenderly, gently, affectionately	lover; loving
Andante (And^{te})	moving easily; flowing; at a walking pace	going, current, flowing; (a) fair (price)
Andantino (And^{tno})	slightly slower than andante	diminutive of andante
Appassionato	passionate, intense	eager, enthusiastic
Appoggiatura	long grace-note	something which leans
Aria	tune, song, usually for a single voice	air, wind, song
Assai	very, more, extremely	much, copiously
Attacca	commence the next movement immediately	attack
Brillante	bright, sparkling, brilliant	–
Brio	fire, vigour	fire, vivacity
Cadenza	a solo showpiece usually near the end of a piece	–
Cantabile	in the singing style	–
Canzona	a graceful and elaborate song	ballad, song
Capriccio(so)	a capricious or fanciful composition	caprice, whim
Coda	an ending piece	end, queue, tail
Col	with	–
Comodo	with ease, comfortably	convenience, ease, leisure
Con	with	by, with
Crescendo	with a gradually increasing tone	growing
Decrescendo	opposite of crescendo	–
Diminuendo	decrease of power	abatement
Dolce	sweetly, softly, gently	dessert, sweet, soft
Dolente	sorrowful, pathetic	–
Energ(et)ico	energetic, emphatic	energetic, powerful
Espressivo	expressively	–
Fantasia	fancy, caprice	–
Finale	final section or movement	–

Direction	*Musical use*	*Common Italian use*
Forte (*f*)	loud	forcible, heavy, high, loud, strong
Fortissimo (*ff*)	very loud	augmentative of forte
Fuga	a strict contrapuntal work	escape, flight
Fugato	in fugal style	–
Fuoco	fire, energy, passion	fire
Garbo	simplicity, grace, elegance	courtesy grace, politeness
Gentile	noble, pleasing, graceful	courteous, kind, polite
Giocoso	humorous, merry	facetious, jocose
Grave	majestical, serious, slow	heavy, serious
Grazia	grace, elegance	favour, grace, mercy
Grazioso	graceful, smooth, elegant	dainty, gracious, pretty
Intermezzo	an interlude	–
Lamentoso	lamenting, mournful	–
Larghetto	slow, but not as slow as largo	–
Largo	slow, broad, solemn	breadth, width, room
Legato	smooth, slurred	tied, connected
Lento	slow	loose, slow, sluggish
Maestoso	majestically, dignified	–
Marcato	strongly marked emphasised	–
Mesto	melancholy	–
Mezzo	middle (mezzo *f*=half loud)	–
Moderato (Mod^{to})	moderately quick	–
Molto	much	–
Moto	movement	agitation, exercise, impulse, motion
Obbligato	necessary, obligatory	–
Pesante	weighty, heavy, ponderous	–
Pianissimo (*pp*)	very quiet	augmentative of piano

Direction	*Musical use*	*Common Italian use*
Piano (*p*)	quiet	–
Più	more (più forte=louder)	–
Pizzicato (pizz)	the strings are to be plucked instead of bowed	pinched
Poco	little	–
Pomposo	stately, grand	pompous
Prestissimo	very quickly	augmentative of presto
Presto (P^{o})	quickly, rapidly	soon, quick
Quasi	like, as it were	–
Ralentando (ral)	a gradual slowing of the tempo	–
Ricercare	any musical work employing novelty in design	to enquire into; seek, research into
Risoluto	resolutely, boldly	–
Ritardando (rit; ritard)	a gradual slowing of the tempo	–
Ritenuto (rit)	a sudden slowing of the tempo	–

(Because of the common abbreviation of 'rit' for both 'ritardando' and 'ritenuto' it is better to use 'ralentando' instead of the former to avoid error)

Direction	*Musical use*	*Common Italian use*
Scherzo	jest, a lively piece	freak, jest, trick
Sempre	always	–
Senza	without	–
Sforzando	forced, greatly stressed	–
Sordino	a mute, muted	–
Sostenuto	sustained, sonorous	–
Sotto voce	with half the voice	in an undertone
Spiccato	very detached, bouncing the bow	to stand out, be prominent
Spirito	energy, spirit	courage, ghost, spirit, wit
Spiritoso	energy, spirit	alchoholic, witty
Staccato	pointed, distinctly separated	–
Tanto	so much, as much	
Tosto	quick, swift	hard
Tranquillo	tranquilly, quiet	–
Tutti	all, the entire group	–
Vivace	lively, briskly	bright, sprightly

Some extremes

The slowest tempo indication is 'Adagio molto assai'. This is rarely used, 'Adagio assai' usually sufficing.

The fastest would be some such combination as 'Prestissimo assai possibile' (literally, 'as extremely very fast as possible').

The quietest indication was *pppp* (literally (più più più piano', or 'more more more quiet') at the end of Tchaikovsky's Symphony No 6, but it is assumed that this direction has been surpassed in more recent music, in which no extreme seems too extraordinary.

The ultimate in quiet music must be silence itself. Silence has been used as an integral part of music from the earliest days: one thinks of the effective use of pauses towards the ends of certain Bach fugues, and the dramatic silences in many of Haydn's works (the first movements of Symphonies 39 in G minor (*c* 1768), and 80 in D minor (*c* 1783/84), are particularly effective examples).

The present century has seen many extensions of this use of silence. Gyorgy Ligeti's Chamber Concerto (1969) ends with two whole bars of silence, carefully conducted, presumably to avoid the destruction of the effect of the close by the sudden, and aurally shattering, intrusion of applause. It is when silence is used, not as an adjunct to music, but instead of it, that one must question the validity of certain pieces of so-called 'music'. John Cage, in 1952, 'wrote' a work entitled *4′ 33″*, this being the length of, to quote the composer, 'a piece in three movements during which no sounds are intentionally produced'. Any group of instruments, and presumably singers, may join in provided only that they make no musical sound for the duration of the three 'movements'. Cage's contention is that there is always something to hear so long as one is alive and has ears to hear it. He has a valid point there, but as far as the writer is aware he has not explained why, in order to hear this silence, one has to pay to sit watching motionless artists; nor does it explain the presence of those artists. It would be an interesting exercise, perhaps, to arrange for an encore of the piece–surely the Musicians' Union could not object.

The loudest indication will coincide with the occasion on which a composer tires of writing the letter *f*. Indications such as *ffff* are quite common in modern music, sometimes with the addition of *fz* to add force to the power: *fffffz*. The addition or subtraction of one *f* in such indications makes no difference in actual performance because, by the time the players reach *fff* they are playing as loud as they know how anyway. It becomes a matter of degree, and of judgement by the conductor: if he sees a piece of music with *fff*, building up to a final *fffz*, it is up to him to ensure that the players are not stretched to the utmost for the *fff*, and that something is in reserve for the additional *z*.

The first accelerando in music occurs in Haydn's Symphony No 60 in C, *Il Distratto* (1774). At the end of the fifth movement (Adagio) a repeated phrase occurs four times, over the third of which Haydn writes 'Allegro'. It is evident from the nature of the music and the character of the symphony as a whole that Haydn intended some bizarre effect here, and although he did not specify 'accelerando' it is safe to assume that that is what he meant.

The first crescendo. As with accelerando, we may conjecture that the first crescendo in music was not marked as such but its existence is indicated unmistakably in the music.

Rossini earned the nickname 'Signor Crescendo' because of his striking use of the effect (known irreverently as 'the Rossini steamroller'), not least in his popular overtures. However, the invention of the device is credited to Johann Simon Mayer (1763–1845), who constructed greatly extended crescendi lasting over a number of bars and built up by successive entries of instruments. The true origin of the crescendo dates back much further than this in fact. The Mannheim orchestra under Jan Vačlav Stamič (1717–57) employed the effect frequently as part of its internationally famous virtuosity while the operas of Nicolo Jommelli (1714–74) also incorporated it as a structural entity. Many passages of repeated figuration in the earlier Italians such as Vivaldi (1675–1741) and Albinoni (1671–1745) invite this swelling treatment without actually calling for it in the music. It may be assumed that performances would include the effect as a matter of course (it is difficult to imagine a completely deadpan rendering of some of Vivaldi's symphonies, for instance) so the composers saw little point in stating the obvious in the scores. The dynamic succession *f*, *più f*, *ff* (literally 'loud', 'more loud', 'very loud') appears occasionally in Vivaldi's music, but the concept of a gradual tonal increase was doubtless well known before then in choral music, in which graded dynamics were required for expressive purposes.

The first 'hairpins'
indicating minute crescendi and diminuendi are found in the violin sonatas of Giovanni Antonio Piani (*c* 1690–1760+), published in 1712.

THEMATIC CATALOGUES

In appearance there are few less musical of music publications than a thematic catalogue. For the most part it consists of a series of musical staves, each giving the beginning of a piece of music (the *incipit*, or 'beginning') interspersed with virtually unreadable lines of abbreviations indicating sources. Careful reading of the introduction and foreword, and a valiant effort to memorise the list of abbreviations will help to unravel some of the meaning of these supposedly elucidatory lines of letters and numbers, but the production as a whole is likely to remain daunting in the extreme to the ordinary music-lover.

In fact, the thematic catalogue is one of the most vitally useful tools the musicologist has in his perpetual struggle to classify and codify the formidable quantity of music since the first pieces were written down (see the beginning of this Section). It lists, in some kind of logical order, the contents of a group of works by one composer or a group of composers, and it identifies each work in a way as near foolproof as possible: by actually quoting the start of each piece of music. The opening theme or incipit of a piece of music is almost as unique to that work as is a person's fingerprint–it is extremely rare to find two pieces of music in which the opening two or three bars are alike in every particular, and the longer the quoted *incipit* the less likely even that remote circumstance becomes. To illustrate this point, let us take the example of Haydn's Symphony No 70, which was used as a model for a Symphony in D by the Polish composer Karol Pietrowsky. A listener knowing one of these works and then coming afresh to the other would be struck by the extraordinary resemblances between the music of the works' respective first and last movements, but an examination of the incipits of each, although indicating a resemblance, unfailingly identifies the two pieces of music as absolutely distinct. The incipits quoted are of the first violin part only, and the examples are limited to the first three bars of each movement.

Haydn: Symphony 70: first movement:

Pietrowsky: Symphony in D: first movement:

Haydn: Symphony 70: last movement:

Pietrowsky: Symphony in D: last movement:

Once the uniqueness of each piece of music is recognised it will be seen how useful a thematic catalogue can be. As another example, let us take Beethoven's symphonies. In referring to the Symphony in A, we can mean only Symphony No 7 since that is the only symphony he wrote in that key; similarly, all the other symphonies may be identified explicitly by key only, except Nos 6 and 8, which are both in F major. In this case, however, No 6 is known as the 'Pastoral' Symphony whereas No 8 has no sub-title, therefore confusion is again avoided. When we turn to Vivaldi's concertos we are faced with a completely different and inherently defeating situation in which there are more than twenty Violin Concertos in C, only two of them with sub-titles. Of the remainder, sixteen are in the standard three-movement form of fast–slow–fast, and eight of these have the identical movement markings of Allegro; Largo; Allegro. Of these, several are without even the notoriously misleading opus numbers. Clearly, some method of visual identification is required to distinguish between these works, and between the similar potential confusions among Vivaldi's concertos in G, D, A. etc. The thematic catalogue rescues us from this confusion, and by referring to the numerical position of the work in the standard thematic catalogue of Vivaldi's concertos it is possible to pinpoint which work is meant with unmistakeable accuracy.

It is only during the present century that the value of the thematic catalogue has been widely appreciated, but it is so well established as a research implement today that any deep research into a composer of the past loses much of its usefulness without one. The following examination of the field will illustrate just how widely accepted is the thematic catalogue, not only in the dusty corridors of music research but also in the general identification requirements of concert programmes and the catalogues of music-publishers and record companies.

The first thematic catalogue is a single-page list giving 22 Psalm themes, published as part of *The Book of Psalms in Metre* in London in 1645.

The largest thematic catalogue is that issued in parts and supplements over a quarter of a century from 1762 to 1787 by the Leipzig music-publisher Johann Gottlob Immanuel Breitkopf (1719–94). In total, the catalogue contains some 14 000 incipits of music ranging in form from song to symphony, and its 888 pages include the identification of music by over 1000 composers. Breitkopf's catalogue was intended to advertise the manuscript and printed music for sale at his Leipzig premises; he was not to know that it was to prove an almost priceless source of information for researchers into the musical scene of the 18th century, and that its value is considered to be so great today that the entire catalogue and supplements were republished in fascimile by Dover in New York in 1966, under the guiding influence of Professor Barry S Brook of the City University of New York.

A much larger thematic catalogue is in preparation in New York by Professor Jan la Rue, who has been collecting material for a Union Thematic Catalogue of 18th Century Symphonies and Concertos for more than 20 years. Some 25 000 incipits are listed so far; in order to cross-reference these incipits efficiently, assistance is being sought of electronic data-processing techniques. The future holds promise of a thematic catalogue of potentially infinite proportions: see RISM below.

The best-known thematic catalogue is the *Chronologisch-thematisches Verzeichniss sämmtlicher Tonwerke W A Mozart's* by Ludwig Ritter von Köchel, the first edition of which was published by Breitkopf and Härtel in Leipzig in 1862 (just 100 years after the beginning of Breitkopf's own thematic house catalogue, see above). The latest edition of more than 1000 pages (nearly double the page-count of the original) incorporates the work put in on the catalogue by Alfred Einstein and was published in 1964 under the editorship of Franz Geigling, Alexander Weinmann, and Gerd Sievers, but it is still referred to as 'The Köchel Catalogue', or just 'K'. For years it has been known by the concert-going public that, whereas most composers' music is identified by 'opus', Mozart's are known by the letter 'K' and a number. These numbers have become so identified with the works to which they attach that it is common in musical circles to hear comments such as 'What do you think of Klemperer's K 550?'

The thematic catalogue with the most beautiful title-page is the first of the two catalogues prepared in about 1785 for the music collection of the Comte d'Ogny (1757–90). This first catalogue lists orchestral and instrumental music (the second is devoted to vocal works) and it was written anonymously by someone who had a better eye for calligraphic excellence than for musicological detail. The hand-painted title-page is a production of extreme beauty –see Frontispiece–and is of further interest in that it depicts among the details of its border a triangle equipped with a jingle: see Section II.

A List of Thematic Catalogues

In the following chart are listed the most important published thematic catalogues which give all or a major part of the works of their chosen composers. The works of those composers identified by an asterisk are also often listed with opus numbers but except in the cases marked with a dagger, these opus numbers are misleading, often seriously, and should be disregarded in favour of the specialised thematic catalogue listed. It is relevant to note that the opus numbers originally appended to Mozart's works are nowadays never encountered, and those by which Schubert's music is identified have almost entirely given way to 'D' numbers.

Each entry commences with the composer's name, continues to the accepted or suggested abbreviation for the catalogue covering his work (these abbreviations are used throughout this book where necessary for identification purposes), proceeds to the author and year of publication, and concludes with a brief indication of the catalogue type. There are four basic types of catalogue:

1. Chronological, in which the composer's works are arranged in their proved or surmised order of composition (often by reference only to the opus numbers), regardless of genre.
2. Genre, in which the works are grouped according to type and regardless of chronology.
3. Chronological within genre.
4. Tonality within genre.

Composer	*Symbol*	*Compiler*	*Type*
Abel*	Kn	Walter Knape, 1971	2
Albinoni*†	Gia	Remo Giazotto, 1945	2
Albrechtsberger	Som	László Somfai, 1961–67	3
C P E Bach	Wq	Alfred Wotquenne, 1905 (reprint, 1964)	3
J C Bach*	Terry	Charles Sanford Terry 1929 (reprint, 1967)	3
J S Bach	BWV or S	Wolfgang Schmieder, 1950 (BWV = *Bach-Werke-Verzeichnis*)	2
W F Bach	F	Martin Falck, 1913	4
Beethoven*†	Kinsky	Georg Kinsky and Hans Halm, 1955	1
Boccherini*	Gér	Yves Gérard, 1969	3
Camerloher	Z	Benno Ziegler, 1919	2
Chopin*†	Fr	E W Fritsch, 1870	2
	Brown	Maurice E J Brown, 1960	1
Clementi*	Allorto	Riccardo Allorto, 1959	1
	Tyson	Alan Tyson, 1967	1
F. Couperin	Cauchie	Maurice Cauchie, 1949	1
Dittersdorf	Kr	Carl Krebs, 1900	3
F X Dušek	Şýkora	Václav Jan Sýkora, 1958	2
Dvořák*	Sourek	Otakar Sourek, 1917	1
Field	Hop	Cecil Hopkinson, 1961	1
Franck	Mohr	Wilhelm Mohr, 1969	2
Fux	Köchel	Ludwig Köchel, 1872	2
G Gabrieli	Kenton	Egon Kenton, 1967	1
Gluck	Wq	Alfred Wotquenne, 1904	1
J G Graun	M	Carl H Mennicke, 1906	4
K H Graun	M	Carl H Mennicke, 1906	4

Composer	*Symbol*	*Compiler*	*Type*
Handel	B	Berend Baselt, 1974	3
F J Haydn*	Hob	Anthony van Hoboken, Vol I: Instrumental music, 1957 Vol II: Vocal music, 1971	3
J M Haydn	Perger	Lothar Perger, 1907 (instrumental)	2
	Klafsky	Anton Klafsky, 1925 (vocal)	2
Hasse	M	Carl H Mennicke, 1906	4
Hoffstetter* (J U A and R)	Gottron	Adam Gottron, Alan Tyson, and Hubert Unverricht, 1968	2
L Koželuh	Post	Milan Poštolka, 1964	3
Locatelli*†	Koole	Arend Koole, 1949	1
J-B Loeillet*	Priestman	Brian Priestman, 1952	1
J Loeillet*	Priestman	Brian Priestman, 1952	1
Mahler	Martner	Knud Martner, in preparation	1
Martinů	Saf	Miloš Safranek, 1961	1
Monteverdi	Zimm	Franklin B Zimmermann, in preparation	2
L Mozart	DTB IX/2	Max Seiffert, 1908 (included in a volume of *Denkmäler der Tonkunst in Bayern)*	2
W A Mozart	K, or KV	Ludwig Ritter von Köchel, 1862 (reprinted and revised 1964, see p 217)	1
Offenbach	Al	Antonio de Almeida, 1974	1
Pugnani	Zsch	Elsa M Zschinsky-Troxler, 1939	2
Purcell	Zimm	Franklin B Zimmermann, 1963	2
Roman	Bengtsson	Ingmar Bengtsson, 1955	2
Rosetti	Kaul	Oskar Kaul, 1912	2
D Scarlatti	Longo	Alessandro Longo, 1937	4
	Kk	Ralph Kirkpatrick, 1970	1
Schubert*	D	Otto Erich Deutsch, 1951	1
Sibelius*†	T	Ernst Tanzberger, 1962	2
Soler	M	Frederick Marvin, 1963–?	4
	R	Father Samuel Rubio, 1960–?	2
J Strauss I	S/R	Max Schönherr and Karl Reinöhl, 1954	3
R Strauss	MvA	Erich H Müller von Asow, 1955–68	1
Tartini	Dounias	Minos Dounias, 1935	4
Tchaikovsky*†	J	Boris Jurgenson, 1897	2
Telemann	SS	Käthe Schaefer-Schmuck, 1932 (keyboard works)	2
	Hörner	Hans Hörner, 1933 (Passion music)	2/3
	Hoff	Adolf Hoffmann, 1969 (orchestral suites)	4
	Kross	Siegfried Kross, 1969 (concertos)	2
	(A complete catalogue of Telemann's music, incorporating the above catalogues in revised form and to be known as TWV – *Telemann-Werke-Verzeichnis* – is in preparation by Bärenreiter Verlag of Kassel).		
Torelli*	Gie	Franz Giegling, 1949	2
Viotti*	Pou	Arthur Pougin, 1888	2
	Gia	Remo Giazotto, 1956	1
Vivaldi*[1]	P	Marc Pincherle, 1948	4
	Fanna	Antonio Fanna, 1968	2
Wagenseil	Mich	Helga Michelitsch, 1966 (keyboard works)	2
Wagner	Kast	Emerich Kastner, 1878	1
Weber*	J	Friedrich Wilhelm Jähns, 1871	1+2
Zach	Komma	Karl Michael Komma, 1938	2

[1] A catalogue of type 4, by Peter Ryom and designated RV (*Répertoire des œuvres d'Antonio Vivaldi*) contains the results of much recent research and may well supplant the catalogues of Pincherle and Fanna in time.

The following thematic catalogues each dealing with the works of more than one composer should also be mentioned as being of particular value to the music-researcher. It should be noted, however, that once again it has proved necessary to be arbitrarily selective since there is now such an enormous literature of thematic catalogues available to the specialist that nothing less than a separate book would do justice to the subject. Such a book exists (see the Bibliography under Brook, Barry S); it may come as a surprise to those with an awareness in this field only of Köchel's Mozart catalogue that Professor Brook's bibliography contains no less than 1444 annotated entries.

Basel University Library: list of manuscript music of the 18th century (1957).

Breitkopf: see above.

Brook, Barry S: *Catalogue of French Symphonies* (and associated works; also of some foreign symphonies published in France) *of the second half of the 18th century* (1962).

Duckles and Elmer: *Thematic catalogue of a manuscript collection of 18th-century Italian instrumental music in the University of California, Berkeley Music Library,* (1963). Although mainly of Italian music, other countries' composers are not entirely excluded.

Dunwalt: a manuscript catalogue compiled by, or under the direction of, Gottfried Dunwalt in 1770. It lists over 500 orchestral and instrumental works in Dunwalt's possession at that time. The catalogue is preserved in the British Museum.

Hummel: a publisher's catalogue with six supplements (a seventh was announced but apparently not issued) of music published between 1754 and 1774. The catalogue and the known supplements were published in facsimile with an introduction by Cari Johansson in 1973.

Kade, Otto: a catalogue with supplements of the music libraries of Duke Friedrich Franz III and the Mecklenburg-Schwerin Collections (1893–1908).

Karlsruhe: four manuscript catalogues of the collections of early music in the Badische Landesbibliothek at Karlsruhe.

Mannheim: a list of the symphonies written in the 18th century by composers of the Mannheim School. See p. 65f.

d'Ogny: two manuscript catalogues of instrumental and vocal music in the collection of Comte d'Ogny (1757–90). The catalogues were prepared about 1785 with the utmost attention to beauty of presentation, and the first catalogue (of orchestral and instrumental music) was graced with a finely executed title-page (see above and Frontispiece).

RISM: the initials stand for 'Répertoire International des Sources Musicales'. This organisation's ambition is to gather together for international availability a thematic listing of nothing less than the entire musical printed and manuscript holdings of all the sources (libraries, museums, etc) of the world. An international project of this magnitude, requiring the goodwill and funds of many separate institutions, will require very many years of patience and tenacity before beginning to approach useful completion, and the number of incipits to be included will run into millions. The Czechoslovakian affiliate has reported that cataloguing has been completed for 186000 works, and the holdings of other collections still awaiting thematic cataloguing is formidable: East Germany: 53000; West Germany: 88000; Hungary: 20000, etc.

MUSIC APPRECIATION

The first step towards the establishment of music appreciation as a regular subject in school curriculae could be said to be an article written by Agnes Mary Langdale in 1908, published that year in *The Crucible.*

The most powerful forces in the widening of musical appreciation were the writings of Sir Donald Francis Tovey, whose carefully argued and imaginative writings on music were originally used as programme notes mostly for the Reid Concerts Orchestra in Edinburgh earlier this century.

As *Essays in Musical Analysis,* they were first published in hard-back form by the Oxford University Press in 1935 and have achieved enormous and totally justified popularity, serving as an unattainable standard for later writers.

Section VIII

THE 20TH-CENTURY SCENE

While the main stream of serious music continued into the 20th century from roots established and precepts suggested during the 19th (and even, in some instances, before that, for example, the Neo-classicism of the 1920s and Vaughan Williams's interest in the music of Tudor composers), the field of musical art in this century has been extended and enriched by new and vital forces: popular music and jazz.

NOTABLE FIRSTS IN JAZZ AND POPULAR MUSIC

The first use of the word jazz in print seems to have been in the *San Francisco Bulletin,* 6 March 1913, by Peter Tamony, referring to an enthusiastic baseball-player. **The first use in connection with any kind of dance music** goes back to a song used in the Deep South during the 1880s, part of which ran thus:

Ol' man Johnson's jazzin' around,
Don't stop him, don't stop him or
he'll fall to the ground.

It appears to have had an obscene sexual connotation in Chicago, where anyone causing irritation or annoyance could be told to 'jazz off', but D J 'Nick' LaRocca, leader and cornetist of the Original Dixieland Jazz Band, explained that he never heard the word in his home city of New Orleans, nor anywhere else until he reached Chicago with what was then (1916) called simply the Original Dixieland Band. One night while the band was playing a slow number for dancing, an excited (?inebriated) member of the audience got up from his seat and yelled, 'Jazz it up, boys! Jazz it up!' meaning, presumably, play faster and/or louder. The name was at once adopted to describe the improvised, rhythmically stimulating music the band played, which was quite unlike any other heard up to that time. The music of the New Orleans street parades, as remembered and re-created decades later by survivors of the early years of the century, was much more loosely syncopated in the manner of ragtime, and the improvisation seems to have been limited to the clarinettist, who wove an impromptu obbligato to the melody played by the cornet(s) and on the harmonies supplied by the trombones, horns and, sometimes, saxophones.

The story of the Negro drummer named Charles (abbreviated to 'Chas'–or in a different account, James, abbreviated to 'Jas') who could produce a propulsive rhythm on his assorted kitchenware as well as his regular drums is probably apocryphal; he is further alleged to have been addressed by his Italian (or was he French?) leader when required to perform this diverting act, 'Chas! Chas! I want Chas! Play it, Chas!' and so on. The likelihood of a white European leading a dance band including a member of the Negro race in the Deep South seems remote, to say the least, even in those days.

GREATEST INFLUENCES IN JAZZ

Nick LaRocca (cornet)–leader and manager of the Original Dixieland Jazz Band. By his attack, phrasing, and tone he greatly influenced the

CHRONOLOGICAL CHART ILLUSTRATING THE EFFECTS OF OUTSIDE INFLUENCES ON THE DEVELOPMENT OF 20th-CENTURY POPULAR MUSIC

(One or two representative examples of each trend are given)

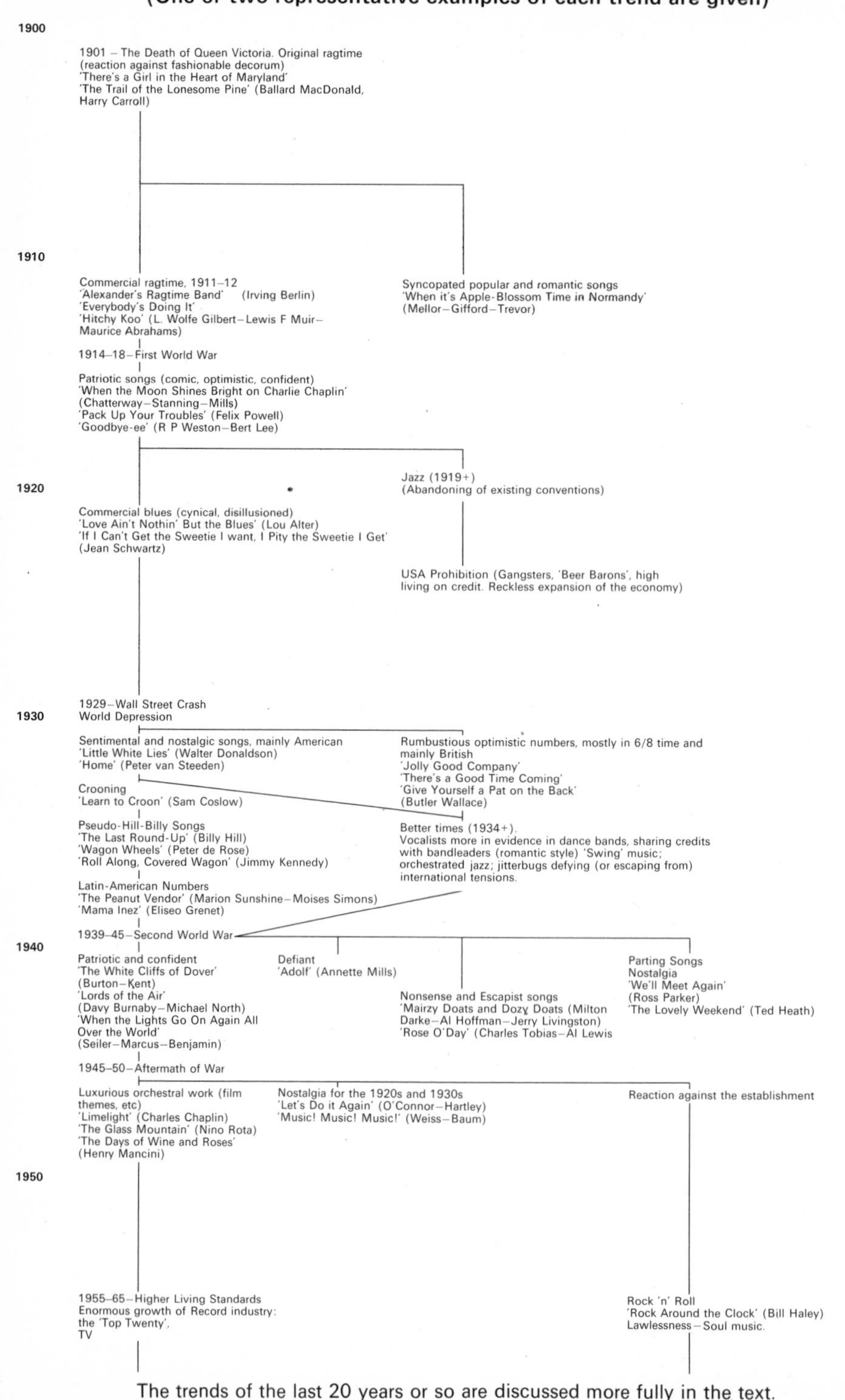

Louis Armstrong (Popperfoto)

teenage Bix Beiderbecke who later influenced many younger musicians, among them Red Nichols from Utah; Andy Secrest from Indiana; and Bobby Hackett from Massachusetts.

Louis Armstrong (cornet and trumpet) – Negro virtuoso, bandleader, and comedian, regarded by most as *the* outstanding influence over all jazzmen, at least subsequent to the mid -1920s, even some who did not play cornet or trumpet.

Miff Mole (trombone)–a superb technician who could make a straight and commonplace arrangement interesting by just a short, brilliantly constructed 'break' or a four-bar solo. He influenced many trombonists such as Tommy Dorsey, Jimmy Harrison, Abe Lincoln, and Don McIlvaine (the last of whom played with Warner's Seven Aces in Atlanta in the mid 1920s).

HARD TIMES EXPERIENCED BY JAZZ MUSICIANS

Most jazz musicians underwent varying degrees of privation during the Depression years as the kind of music that had made them prosperous a decade earlier went out of fashion generally, at least in America. Those who were technically able to adapt to the more orthodox methods of playing dance music from prepared scores did so, and began a new era of prosperity for themselves (notably the bandleaders Benny Goodman, Glenn Miller, Jimmy and Tommy Dorsey, Artie Shaw, Jack Teagarden, etc). Those who were not usually took up other employment or joined the bands of other leaders whose penchant was for the occasional 'hot' solo (eg Ted Lewis used Muggsy Spanier, cornet and Don Murray, clarinets and saxophones; Paul Whiteman employed Bunny Berigan, trumpet and Jack Teagarden, trombone; and Leo Reisman even used the services of Duke Ellington's ex-trumpet soloist, James 'Bubber' Miley). Despite the rather precarious, somewhat hand-to-mouth existence ('scufflin'' as it was known) these musicians led at that time particularly, there are very few cases of anyone straining beyond endurance and committing suicide as a result. It is thought that Jack Purvis, a trumpet-player much influenced by Louis Armstrong, who played with the Hal Kemp Orchestra and the California Ramblers in 1929–31, may have committed suicide in 1962; Sterling Bose did so in 1952 (he was a New Orleans trumpet-player who worked with the Arcadian Serenaders in St Louis in the mid-1920s, and Ray Noble in New York a decade

Benny Goodman (Popperfoto)

Another notable band-leader/pianist, Count Basie (Popperfoto)

later); Ben Pollack hanged himself in 1971 while apparently prosperous as a *restaurateur* and occasional musician, aged 68. The most outlandish example of a suicide among dance musicians was the British clarinettist and saxophonist Arthur Lally, who had worked with Bert Ambrose in the 1920s and 1930s. He was a licensed pilot, and had a bitter hatred of Adolf Hitler and his works. After failing his medical examination for the Royal Air Force in 1940, he volunteered to fly a bomber, solo if need be, over Berchtesgaden, Hitler's 'retreat', and destroy it utterly by aerial bombardment. When this was refused by the War Office, the disconsolate but hate-filled Arthur Lally, convinced he was useless, returned home and gassed himself. Harry Berly, a brilliant violist and tenor saxophonist, who had recorded string quartets for the National Gramophonic Society label in the mid 1920s and hundreds of sides of dance music with Ray Noble, Lew Stone, and others, in the 1930s, became likewise obsessed with the idea that he could do better, and better, but that he was an inferior musician and no one wanted to know about him. He threw himself under an Underground train entering Kennington Station in 1937. Similarly, under the strain of bills he could not meet, Tommy Smith, trumpet-player first with Jack Hylton's Kit-Kat Band (1925 and later) and latterly with Jack Payne and the BBC Dance Orchestra, threw himself under a train entering Victoria Station on 21 June 1931.

INSTRUMENTS USED PREDOMINANTLY OR EXCLUSIVELY IN JAZZ AND DANCE MUSIC

Banjo

The most popular instrument in the 19th-century 'nigger minstrel' troupes became one of the most customary soloists in the very earliest days of sound recording, due to its plangent

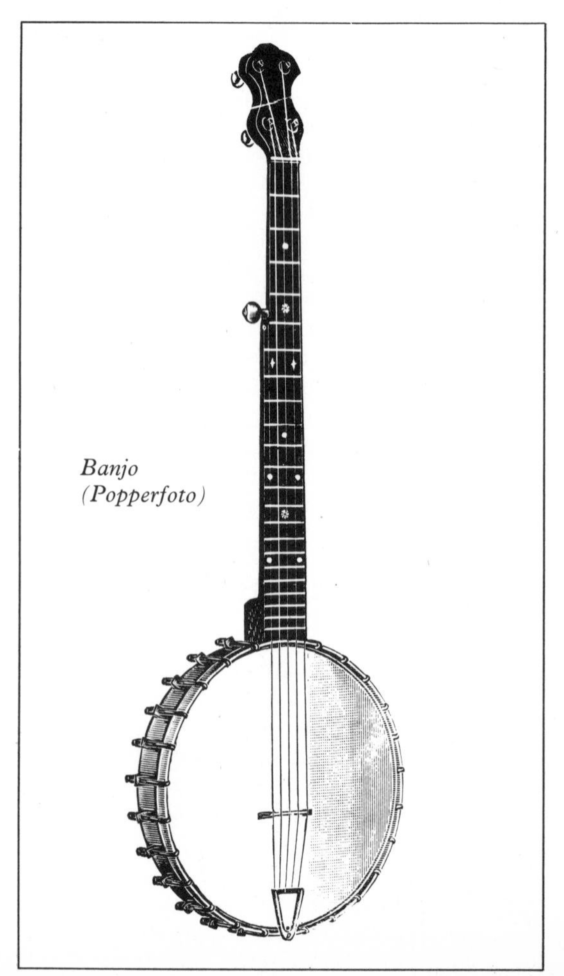

Banjo (Popperfoto)

The original Barnstormers Spasm Band in 1958. l to r : John Wadley, harmonica ; John Gunn, kazoo ; Peter Wadley, bass ; Brian Rust, percussion ; John Denning, banjo ; Jim Robinson, guitar

tone that made a lifelike impression in the crude wax blocks and cylinders then in use. Coincident with the invention of sound recording (see Section IX) came the development of ragtime from Negro dances, revivalist meetings, and white American folk-song, in the accompaniment to which the easily portable, easily learned, widely audible banjo figured very largely. When jazz superseded ragtime as a national dance fashion, the banjo continued to provide the basic rhythm for many years, partly because it could be heard above the 'front line' of brass and saxophones, and partly because of its established superiority as a recording voice under pre-electric conditions. As dance music and, to some extent, jazz became more sophisticated towards the end of the 1920s, and as electric recording became the accepted method, the banjo quite rapidly lost favour to the guitar, until by the mid 1930s, it was practically never used except when a band was playing a 'country-style' number, or deliberately trying to sound old-fashioned. With the revival of interest in original jazz and ragtime that arose after the Second World War and culminated in the 'trad boom' of the late 1950s and early 1960s, the banjo became a *sine qua non* of the 'traditional jazz' bands, the first of which (Lu Watters's Yerba Buena Jazz Band of San Francisco) used two.

Bottle

Ordinary glass bottles have been used in jazz of the more basic kind in two ways: certain cornettists have been known to mute their instruments with 'Coke' bottles in the absence of a more conventional device, and recordings exist of empty bottles being used as percussion instruments. An outstanding example of this is a record made in 1929 in New York for OKeh under the name of 'Blind Willie Dunn's Gin Bottle Four,' on which the bottle is 'played' by no less a celebrity than song-writer Hoagy Carmichael, in company with Joe 'King' Oliver on cornet, Eddie Lang (who was in fact Blind Willie Dunn) and Lonnie Johnson on guitars, and J C Johnson, composer of many popular successes of the time, on piano. Tuned bottles were blown in a performance of the Andante of Haydn's 'Surprise' Symphony (No 94 in G) in the Hoffnung Music Festival Concert on 13 November 1956, perhaps **the only 'serious' use of the instrument.**

Glass

Glass drinking-tumblers have been used in jazz in the following contexts: Herman 'Woodie' Walder, clarinettist of Bennie Moten's Kansas City Orchestra, during the mid 1920s, was often featured as soloist playing–if that is the word–his mouthpiece into a glass, with rather bizarre effect, and on at least one recording session (for Victor in 1929) the great trombonist Jack Teagarden substituted a glass for the bell of his horn, thereby giving the sound a rather restricted, muted character, but very acceptable within the context of the rest of the band that consisted of paper-and-comb, banjo, string bass (played pizzicato), and drums. Instruments made of glass, other than the bottle referred to above, are not known to have been used in popular music, other than what the recording files describe as 'glass xylophone', recorded experimentally in 1908 by Chris Chapman playing the ragtime classic 'Dill Pickles Rag,' with such astonishing tonal realism that it could pass for electric recording.

Goofus

A strange hybrid instrument, made to resemble a saxophone by sight, but sounding like a harmonica. It was built on similar lines to the former instrument, and the reeds were arranged in such a way that the keys of the 'saxophone' operated them and produced a rather thin, wheezy mouth-organ sound, wind pressure being supplied by either the player's lungs or a pair of bellows. Also known as the 'couesnophone' (after the French musical instrument-makers Couesnod) or 'queenophone', it became fashionable in some dance bands from 1924 to the end of the decade; the principal exponents were Don Redman, one of the saxophonists in Fletcher Henderson's Negro orchestra, and the white bass saxophonist Adrian Rollini, who used it on many of the casual recording sessions in which he took part, and in Fred Elizalde's Orchestra in the Savoy Hotel, London, where he played during 1928 (see also Section II).

Harmonica

The humble 'mouth-organ', although comparatively recently elevated to concert-platform status by Larry Adler, has always featured prominently in small country-style dance and jazz bands, but rarely in urban groups. One of the few city-based harmonica-players to achieve any sort of recognition through recordings is Robert Cooksey, who made a remarkable series of delightful records for Victor in 1926 and 1927 accompanied by guitarist Bobby Leecan, or by the latter's Need-More Band. Cooksey (from Philadelphia) also recorded in 1927 for Pathé as a member of the Dixie Jazzers Washboard Band, and in 1926 for Victor as one of the South Street Trio (one of these was also Bobby Leecan). 'Field recordings' made on location by the major American companies during the later 1920s often used harmonica-players, mostly Negroes such as the leader of the Memphis Jug Band, Will Shade, and the soloist of Cannon's Jug Stompers, Noah Lewis, but also the white New Orleansian Alvin Gautreaux, who took part in one Victor recording in that city in 1927 under the leadership of John Hyman, cornetist of an otherwise conventional Dixieland unit. Among the country blues artists who made many records as harmonica-players, the best known is 'Sonny' Terry, who has made frequent visits to Great Britain in the company of his guitar-playing partner Brownie McGhee; Terry's Surrealistic, almost nightmarish

'Hootin' Blues' became a best-seller in England during the mid-1950s. The white harmonica virtuoso Borrah Minevitch, American based but formerly a frequent visitor to Britain also, began his recording career as the soloist of a group called the 'Dizzy Trio', on Victor in 1924, playing a number called 'Hayseed Rag'. The country-style singer Carson Robison, also known as a guitarist and whistler, was also often used as a harmonica-player on dance records during the 1920s, but the instrument's voice lacks the carrying power to enable it to match successfully the combined efforts of a brass team or saxophone section so that, in former times, it was used only sparingly in such small groups as mentioned above; but modern amplification has enabled harmonica-players to compete with more conventional wind instruments on equal terms.

Hot Fountain Pen

A miniature clarinet, with a range of one octave, devised by Adrian Rollini as a 'stunt' for use in small jazz bands; it was not a generally accepted instrument, hardly surprisingly, as like the harmonica, its tone was soft and its carrying power very limited. Rollini is the only well-known exponent of it, usually on records by Joe Venuti's Blue Four and sometimes with Fred Elizalde's Orchestra.

Jew's Harp

Most often found in country-style dance bands or in conventional urban orchestras when playing commercial numbers with a rural flavour; very rarely used at all in jazz. Records by city-based professional recording artists such as Carson Robison, Vernon Dalhart, and Frank Luther sometimes use a jew's harp, as its curiously nasal, restricted tonal range and limited carrying power make it acceptable when the only other instruments present are two or three strings, but there is obviously no point in attempting its use in even a small jazz or dance band using several brass and woodwind instruments.

Jug

The widely used substitute for expensive conventional brass or string bass instruments among the less affluent members of Negro dance bands throughout the Southern States during the first half of the century was a stone or metal jug, with narrow neck and wide capacity. By blowing across the opening with varying degrees of wind-pressure, it was found possible to reproduce accurately and effectively the sound of both the more conventional types of bass. Some jug-blowers blew or hummed into beer- or even oil-cans, and could thus assume the role of trombonist in addition, and records by the Dixeland Jug Blowers, made in Chicago for Victor in 1926, have two jug-players, Earl MacDonald and Henry Clifford, who produce the trombone and tuba parts with remarkable fidelity. Victor and OKeh records between 1927 and 1934 often featured an outstanding unit known as the Memphis Jug Band, which varied instrumentally from session to session and often from one title to the next, and which included, besides the one jug and the usual banjo and/or guitar, other unusual instruments such as harmonica and kazoo. Clarence Williams, the pianist from Louisiana who directed hundreds of recordings in New York between 1921 and 1941, was also something of a jug-blower, though he confined his activities in this direction principally to marking the off-beat on a limited number of notes. One of the best of the Memphis jug men was Gus Cannon, whose Jug Stompers (a trio of jug, harmonica, and guitar) made many Victor recordings between 1928 and 1930. The leader also played banjo simultaneously with the jug, having the latter attached by a metal rod to the neck of the banjo. It may be a point of sociological significance that there are virtually no white jug-blowers in the history of American popular music.

Kazoo

A 'toy' instrument well known to most children, consisting basically of a metal lozenge-shaped device, with an orifice covered by a membrane, into which the performer hums or imitates the approximate sound of a muted trumpet or cornet, the body of the instrument acting as an acoustic amplifier. Although principally (and more effectively) used by Negro country-based bands, and by some units recording in New York under the direction of such as Clarence Williams, some white musicians have developed the art of kazoo-playing to a degree of accuracy enabling the instrument to participate in full-sized jazz bands. Among these is the clarinet- and saxophone-player Larry Abbott, who made hundreds of records with Harry Reser, the banjoist, and his various bands (such as the Clicquot Club Eskimos, the Jazz Pilots, the Six Jumping Jacks, and others); his playing is not at all strident, but it fits the context of the band perfectly. The drummer of the California Ramblers in the 1920s was usually Stan King, who was also an occasional kazoo-player, but the most outstanding performer was also a drummer–Tony Sbarbaro, latterly known as 'Tony Spargo', formerly of the Original Dixieland Jazz Band, and, until not long before his death in 1969 at the age of 72, drummer with Phil Napoleon's Original Memphis Five. He had constructed a kazoo shaped like a small bugle, from which he could produce the most amazing impressions of a first-class Negro cornetist, and on records by the Napoleon Band on Victor and Columbia in 1956 and thereafter, as well as on records made under the name of the Original Dixieland Jazz Band for Vocalion in 1935, and for Commodore in 1946, and others, he does so without losing the rhythm he maintains as drummer in the normal way. The pioneer kazoo man was Dick Slevin, of the Mound City Blue Blowers, consisting of paper-and-comb, banjo, and guitar besides kazoo, which played in London at the Piccadilly Grill in the spring of 1925; he too was more of the muted variety. Mention should be made of an Englishman named John Gunn, whose kazoo-playing with the Original Barnstormers Spasm Band between 1957 and 1960 rivalled Tony Sbarbaro's for its realistic impressionism. He too constructed a sophisticated piece of equipment from a large biscuit-tin, from which a substitute trombone effect could be produced, acoustically amplified, but his usual method was to use a kazoo with a small horn attached for amplification of the 'trumpet' sound (see also Section II).

Mellophone

A member of the French horn family occasionally used in jazz and dance music and usually played by Dudley Fosdick. He was a member of Ted Weems's Orchestra during the late 1920s and early 1930s, and afterwards played with Guy Lombardo's Royal Canadians, as well as recording groups under such names as the All Star Orchestra (Victor, 1927–28), Miff Mole's Molers and Red Nichols's Five Pennies (1928); his broad, rich tone and wide range added an interesting sound to the ensemble passages, and he was a capable soloist. Bill Trone, trombonist with Don Voorhees and his Orchestra in 1927, also sometimes used a mellophone, and a decade later, Eddie Sauter doubled on this and trumpet with various bands before joining Benny Goodman as arranger. One other performer on the mellophone who can be judged from his records was the bandleader and trombonist Blue Steele (whose band played in Memphis) on Victor records in the late 1920s.

Ocarina

The 'sweet potato' is rarely used in conventional jazz or dance music, though, perhaps rather oddly, one of the foremost exponents was the late Harry Berly, violist with Roy Fox's Band at the Monseigneur Restaurant, Piccadilly, London, late of a chamber music group and tenor saxophonist with Roy Fox and Lew Stone, also at the Monseigneur. The ocarina is more often found in country-and-western groups, although dance bands wishing to produce a rural effect have sometimes employed it, and the famous quartet of ocarinas used on stage in 'Bidin' My Time' (from the show *Girl Crazy*, New York, 1930) was reproduced on various dance-band recordings of the number.

Paper-and-Comb

The most primitive of all 'melody' instruments has one outstanding performer in jazz: the late William 'Red' McKenzie, leader of the Mound City Blue Blowers, who recorded with his comb on many sessions, producing a pleasantly cloudy effect, suggesting a distant muted cornet.

Suitcase

The substitute for a bass drum used by Josh Billings on some of the later records of the Mound City Blue Blowers.

Swanee (or Slide) Whistle

Another instrument whose normally dulcet tones are incompatible with a brass or saxophone section in a jazz or dance band, but which has been used to good effect as a solo voice to give an extra and distinctive sound to a performance. The first recording session undertaken by Paul Whiteman and his orchestra (Camden, New Jersey, 9 August 1920) featured a swanee-whistle on the best-seller *Whispering*, and the player (Warren Luce) was used by Whiteman on several subsequent recordings. Other performers, but much better known for their work on conventional instruments, are Louis Armstrong, cornet and trumpet master, who appeared as swanee-whistle soloist on a record made in 1926 of his Hot Five *(Woosit)*, and his colleague in Joe 'King' Oliver's Jazz Band three years before, Warren 'Baby' Dodds, the drummer, who plays swanee-whistle on Oliver's records of *Sobbin' Blues* and *Buddy's Habit*.

Washboard

The old-fashioned metal or wooden board with ridges used by humbler members of society for removing dirt from clothes in the washtub became a useful substitute for a drum when it was discovered that a sound similar to a drum-roll could be produced by running the fingers, each wearing a thimble, up and down the ridges. It was not long before 'refinements' such as small cymbals and tap-boxes were screwed or clamped to the board which turned it into a miniature drum kit for those not in a financial position to buy a real full-sized one. Such Negro artists as Floyd Casey (with Clarence Williams), Eddie Edinborough (with Bobby Leecan), Bruce Johnson (with the Washboard Serenaders), Jimmy Bertrand and Jasper Taylor (with many bands in Chicago) could give as good a rhythmic backing to a full-scale band as many of their more conventionally equipped colleagues. The British comedian-actor Deryck Guyler, a life-long connoisseur of jazz, is Britain's most proficient washboard performer.

PARTNERSHIPS

In the popular music world of the 20th century, the composition of words and music has been generally rather a matter of *ad hoc* arrangement between lyric-writer and composer rather than of teams of writers working almost indissolubly. The following exceptions, however, produced some remarkable results over the years.

De Sylva–Brown–Henderson

'Bud' de Sylva, Lew Brown, and Ray Henderson composed a large number of extremely popular songs in the years of their partnership from 1926 to 1931. All had written successful numbers individually prior to this period (de Sylva wrote ''N' Everything' in 1918 with Al Jolson and Gus Kahn; Lew Brown produced 'Chili Bean' in 1919 with Albert von Tilzer, and 'Why Did I Kiss That Girl?' in 1923 with Ray Henderson, who in turn had written 'Humming' in 1920 with Louis Breau and 'Georgette' in 1922 also with Lew Brown). Their best-known numbers, many of them composed for Broadway shows and the early talking pictures, are as follows:

1926 'Black Bottom' *(George White's Scandals)*
'Lucky Day' *(George White's Scandals)*
'The Birth of the Blues' *(George White's Scandals)*
'It All Depends on You'

1927 'So Blue'
'Just a Memory'
'Broken Hearted'
('Here Am I, Broken Hearted')
'Magnolia' ('Mix the Lot – What Have You Got?')
'The Best Things in Life are Free' *(Good News)*
'The 'Varsity Drag' *(Good News)*
'Good News' *(Good News)*
'Lucky in Love' *(Good News)*

1928 'Together'
'I'm on the Crest of a Wave'
'That's Just My Way of Forgetting You'
'The Song I Love'
'Sonny Boy' (Film *The Singing Fool)*
'You're the Cream in my Coffee' *(Hold Everything)*
'For Old Times' Sake'

1929 'Turn On the Heat (Film *Sunny Side Up)*
'If I Had a Talking Picture of You' (Film *Sunny Side Up)*

'I'm a Dreamer–Aren't We All?' (Film *Sunny Side Up*)
'You've Got Me Pickin' Petals Off o' Daisies' (Film *Sunny Side Up*)
'I'm in Seventh Heaven' (Film *Song of Songs*)
'Little Pal' (Film *Song of Songs*)
'Why Can't You?' (Film *Song of Songs*)
'Used to You' (Film *Song of Songs*)
1930 'Thank Your Father'
1931 'Come to Me' (Film *Indiscreet*)
'One More Time'
'You Try Somebody Else'

Dubin–Warren

Al Dubin and Harry Warren worked as a team for many years during the 1930s; Harry Warren had already written big successes such as 'Pasadena' (1924), and during the late 1930s he composed a wordless number for the trumpeter-bandleader 'Red' Nichols to use as a signature tune (*Wail of the Winds*). Dubin–Warren successes include:

1932 'Shuffle Off to Buffalo' (Film *42nd Street*)
'42nd Street' (Film *42nd Street*)
'Young and Healthy' (Film *42nd Street*)
'You're Getting to be a Habit with Me' (Film *42nd Street*)
1933 'The Boulevard of Broken Dreams' (Film *Moulin Rouge*)
'Shadow Waltz' (Film *Gold Diggers of 1933*)
'We're in the Money' (Film *Gold Diggers of 1933*)
'Keep Young and Beautiful' (Film *Roman Scandals*)
'Build a Little Home' (Film *Roman Scandals*)
'Shanghai Lil' (Film *Footlight Parade*)
'By a Waterfall' (Film *Footlight Parade*)
1934 'I'll String Along With You' (Film *Twenty Million Sweethearts*)
'Wonder Bar' (Film *Wonder Bar*)
1935 'She's a Latin From Manhattan' (Film *Go Into Your Dance*)
'About a Quarter to Nine' (Film *Go Into Your Dance*)
'Lulu's Back In Town' (Film *Broadway Gondolier*)
'The Rose In Her Hair' (Film *Broadway Gondolier*)
'The Words Are in My Heart' (Film *Gold Diggers of 1935*)
'Lullaby of Broadway' (Film *Gold Diggers of 1935*)
1936 'I'll Sing You a Thousand Love Songs' (Film *Cain and Mabel*)
'With Plenty of Money and You' (Film *Gold Diggers of 1937*)
1937 'September in the Rain' (Film *Melody for Two*)

George and Ira Gershwin

Although George Gershwin composed the music for many songs *without* lyrics by his brother Ira, and though Ira survived him to supply words to the music of other composers, as a team they provided the words and music to the following well-remembered and often-revived musical productions and films:

1924 *Lady, Be Good* (including 'Fascinating Rhythm'; 'I'd Rather Charleston'; 'The Half of it Dearie Blues'; and the title-song; also originally 'The Man I Love').

George Gershwin (Popperfoto)

1925 *Tell Me More* (including 'Why Do I Love You?' and the title-song); *Tip-Toes* (including 'Looking For a Boy'; 'When Do We Dance?'; 'That Certain Feeling'; 'Sweet and Low Down').
1926 Oh, Kay! (including 'Someone to Watch Over Me'; 'Maybe'; 'Clap Yo' Hands'; 'Do Do Do')
1927 *Funny Face* (including ''S Wonderful'; 'My One and Only'; 'He Loves and She Loves'; 'High Hat')
1930 *Strike Up The Band* (including 'The Man I Love'; and the title-song); *Girl Crazy* (including 'I Got Rhythm' and 'Embraceable You')
1931 *Delicious* (film including the title-song).
1936 *Shall We Dance?* (film including 'They Can't Take that Away from Me'; 'I've Got Beginner's Luck'; Let's Call the Whole Thing Off'; 'Slap that Bass'; 'They All Laughed').
1937 *The Goldwyn Follies* (film including 'Love Walked In'; 'Our Love is Here to Stay').

Richard Rodgers–Lorenz Hart

American team who contributed words and music to the following musical productions between 1925 and 1942, when the partnership split up (Hart died the following year):

1925 Garrick Gaieties (first edition – 'Manhattan'; 'Sentimental Me').
1926 *The Girl Friend* (including 'The Blue Room' and the title-number); *Garrick Gaieties* (second edition–'Mountain Greenery'); *Peggy Ann* (including 'A Tree in the Park').
1927 *A Connecticut Yankee* (produced in London as *A Yankee at the Court of King Arthur)* (including 'Thou Swell'; 'My Heart Stood Still', the latter not in the London production, but used instead in *One Dam Thing after Another)*.
1928 *Present Arms* (including 'You Took Advantage of Me'; 'Do I Hear You Saying "I Love You"?').
1929 *Spring is Here* (including 'With a Song in My Heart'; 'Yours Sincerely'); *Heads Up!* (including 'A Ship Without a Sail').
1930 *Simple Simon* (including 'Ten Cents a Dance'; 'Dancing on the Ceiling').
1931 *America's Sweetheart* (including 'I've Got Five Dollars').
1932 *Love Me Tonight* (film, including 'Mimi').
1933 'Lover' (independent waltz song).
1934 'Blue Moon' (independent slow fox-trot ballad).
1935 *Jumbo* (including 'My Romance').
1936 *On Your Toes* (including 'There's a Small Hotel'; 'Slaughter on Tenth Avenue'; and the title-song).
1937 *Babes in Arms* (including 'Where or When'; 'Johnny One Note'; 'The Lady is a Tramp'; *I'd Rather be Right* (including 'Have You Met Miss Jones?').
1938 *I Married an Angel* (including title-song); *The Boys from Syracuse* (including 'This Can't Be Love'; 'Sing for Your Supper').
1940 *Pal Joey* (including 'I Could Write a Book'; 'Bewitched (Bothered and Bewildered)').
1942 *By Jupiter* (including 'Wait Till You See Her'; 'Nobody's Heart').

Richard Rodgers – Oscar Hammerstein II

Upon the death of Lorenz Hart, Richard Rodgers teamed up for another successful partnership with Oscar Hammerstein II.

1943 *Oklahoma* (including 'Oh! What a Beautiful Morning'; 'People will say We're in Love'; 'The Surrey With the Fringe on Top').
1945 *Carousel* (including 'June is Bustin' Out all Over'; 'If I Loved You'; 'You'll Never Walk Alone').
1945 *State Fair* (20th Century Fox film; including 'It Might as Well be Spring'; 'It's a Grand Night for Singing').
1947 *Allegro* (including 'Money Isn't Everything'; 'The Gentleman is a Dope').
1949 *South Pacific* (including 'Some Enchanted Evening'; 'Younger than Springtime'; 'This Nearly Was Mine').
1951 *The King and I* (including 'Hello Young Lovers'; 'Getting to Know You'; 'Shall We Dance?'').
1953 *Me and Juliet* (including 'No Other Love'; 'I'm Your Girl').
1955 *Pipe Dream* (including 'All Kinds of People'; 'All at Once You Have Her').

SONGS THAT WERE SUCCESSFUL AFTER A TITLE CHANGE OR THE ADDITION OF LYRICS

Original title and date	*Successful title and date*	*Composer(s)*
'Lookin' for Another Sweetie' (1929)	'Confessin' (That I Love You)' (1930)	Marty Symes; Al J Neiburg; Jerry Levison
'Deep Purple' (1934)	'Deep Purple' (1938) (Lyrics: Mitchell Parrish)	Peter de Rose
'Chansonette' (1923)	'The Donkey Serenade' (1937)	Rudolf Friml
'Concerto For Cootie' (1936)	'Do Nothin' Till You Hear From Me' (1944)	Duke Ellington (Lyrics: Bob Russell)
'Never No Lament' (former title 'Foxy') (1940)	'Don't Get Around Much Any More' (1943)	Duke Ellington (Lyrics: Bob Russell)
'Smile And Show Your Dimple' (1917)	'Easter Parade' (1933)	Irving Berlin
'A Jazz Nocturne' (1931)	'My Silent Love' (1932)	Dana Suesse
'Star Dust' (1927)	'Star Dust' (1931) (Lyrics: Mitchell Parrish)	Hoagy Carmichael
'Panama' (1924)	'When Day Is Done' (1926)	Robert Katscher (Lyrics: Bud de Sylva)
'El Abanico' (pre-1914)	'You'll Be Far Better Off In A Home' (1941)	Javaloyes (Lyrics: Box; Cox; Osborne)
'Quiereme mucho' (1922)	'Yours' (1939)	Gonzalo Roig (Lyrics: Shirr)

1957 *Cinderella* (CBS Television show, including 'Ten Minuets Ago'; 'Do I Love You Because You're Beautiful?'). This show was watched in all by between 75 000 000 and 100 000 000 people.
1958 *Flower Drum Song* (including 'I Enjoy Being a Girl'; 'Don't Marry Me').
1959 *The Sound of Music* (including 'My Favourite Things'; 'Climb Ev'ry Mountain'; 'Edelweiss').

JAZZ AND DANCE MUSICIANS WHO DIED IN UNUSUAL CIRCUMSTANCES

Barnes, Walter. Burned to death with eight members of his band when the club where they were playing in Natchez, Mississippi, caught fire on 23 April 1940; aged 33.

Bowlly, Al. Popular British vocalist who was killed by a land-mine during an air raid on London in the early hours of 17 April 1941, aged (probably) 43.

Green, Charlie. Negro trombonist who found himself locked out of his house in New York on 29 February 1936, and froze to death while sleeping on the doorstep, aged about 36.

Johnson, Ken. Trinidadian bandleader who was killed with several members of his band, as well as many patrons, when the Café de Paris, London, was hit during an air raid on 8 March 1941.

Martin, Carroll. Trombonist with Isham Jones's Orchestra in Chicago for many years, killed when the car in which he was being driven with his instrument, probably to play at an engagement, pulled up suddenly throwing him forward on to his trombone (which he was apparently examining) with such force that it buckled under the impact, penetrating his chest and lungs. Date unknown, but about 1940.

McMurray, Loring. Prominent New York alto saxophonist with Sam Lanin's Orchestra during the early 1920s who made his nose bleed by blowing it, contracted septicaemia and died, while still around 30 years old, date unknown but believed to be about 1925.

Melrose, Frank. Chicago pianist of great ability whose mutilated body was found by a roadside out of Hammond, Indiana, 1 September 1941; aged 33. Cause of death still uncertain (murder or road accident?).

Glenn Miller (Popperfoto)

Miller, Glenn. Trombonist and bandleader who, as Major Glenn Miller, left an English airfield to fly to newly liberated Paris on the morning of 15 December 1944, to direct the American Expeditionary Force Band which had preceded him there. Neither he nor his plane was ever seen again.

Moten, Bennie. Ragtime pianist and bandleader from Kansas City (Negro) who died there aged 40 on 3 April 1935, following complications and loss of blood as a result of a tonsillectomy.

Smith, Bessie. 'The Empress of the Blues', who died from loss of blood and severe arm, head, and chest injuries after a road accident, 26 September 1937. She was found in the road by a local surgeon who took her to hospital, where she died the next morning, aged 42.

Smith, Clarence. 'Pine Top' the Negro pianist who pioneered the boogie-woogie style of playing, was killed by a gunman's bullet not intended for him as he played in a Chicago night-club on 14 March 1929, aged 24.

Thomas, Hersal. Teenage Negro pianist whose death on 3 July 1926 at the age of 17 may have been due to food poisoning, but whether this was because of the unfit condition of the food, or to poison having been introduced into it by a jealous girl-friend has never been finally settled.

Vincent, Eddie. Negro trombonist pioneer who was working in Chicago in 1927; going down a rickety wooden staircase one night after playing, his trombone fell from his grasp. He tried to save it, the balustrade collapsed and he was killed in the fall.

Waller, Thomas 'Fats'. World-famous Negro pianist who contracted pneumonia while returning home after a tiring tour, and died aboard the *Santa Fé Chief,* aged 39, on 15 December 1943. Twelve years earlier, he had recorded 'Dallas Blues' and sung the lyrics as follows: 'Gonna put myself on the Santa Fé and go, go, go . . . '.

WOMEN COMPOSERS AND MUSICIANS IN JAZZ AND DANCE MUSIC

Benson, Ivy. British bandleader during the Second World War who achieved considerable popularity with her all-girls' band, with which she played alto saxophone.

Dickstein, Barbara. American tuba-player of considerable ability, in her twenties at this writing, frequently plays with Negro veteran jazz musicians, the only white member of the band and the only girl in it.

Donegan, Dorothy. Negro pianist of the boogie-woogie persuasion who worked in Chicago in the late 1930s and early 1940s; an artist of considerable talent, but very little recorded.

Hardin, Lil. Second wife of Louis Armstrong, whom she met when they both played in Joe 'King' Oliver's famous Creole Jazz Band in Chicago in 1922 (married 5 February 1924, divorced 1932). Trained at Fisk University, piano abilities not restricted to the jazz idiom. Died on stage in St Louis while taking part in a memorial concert to her ex-husband, August 1971.

Hutton, Ina Ray. Blonde bandleader of all-girls' band that was very popular in America during the mid 1930s, but which recorded strangely little; she appeared in several films.

Ronell, Ann. American composer of such great successes as 'Willow, Weep for Me'; 'Rain on the Roof' (both 1932); 'Who's Afraid of the Big, Bad Wolf?' (1933).

Snow, Valaida. Negro trumpet-player in the virtuoso style who became very popular in Europe during the five years prior to the

Larry Adler (Popperfoto)

outbreak of the Second World War. She was interned by the Nazis in Denmark in 1940, repatriated in 1943, and resumed her musical career in America, where she died in 1956, aged 56.

Stobart, Kathleen. British tenor saxophonist in the modern idiom who achieved great popularity during the 1940s and 1950s.

Suesse, Dana. American composer of many light pieces, not all in the dance idiom, but best known for 'Ho Hum!' and 'Whistling in the Dark' (1931) and 'My Silent Love' (1932) (strangely sub-titled 'A Jazz Nocturne').

Terry, Thelma. Diminutive American string bass player of an outstanding ability that rivalled her male colleagues; led a band known as her 'Play Boys' in Chicago in the late 1920s, all of them being men.

Wayne, Mabel. American composer of many colossal hits, such as 'In a Little Spanish Town' (1926), 'Ramona' (1927), 'Chiquita' (1928), 'It Happened in Monterey' (1929), 'Alone on the Range' (1933), 'Little Man, You've Had a Busy Day' (1934), and 'Home Again' (1935).

Williams, Mary Lou. One of the most versatile of all American jazz pianists, a Negro girl with a gift for playing ragtime, swing, or 'modern' jazz; also composed a piano suite *The Zodiac*, arranged for many outstanding bands, Negro and white, including Andy Kirk's, Benny Goodman's, Earl Hines's, Tommy Dorsey's, Glen Gray's, and Gus Arnheim's; lived in England, 1952–54 and has devoted much of her life to religious study and the Bel Canto Charity Organisation.

EARLY STARTERS AND LONG-LIVED MUSICIANS

Adler, Larry. Born Baltimore, 1914; began playing harmonica while still at school, and made his first record with Bob Haring's Colonial Club Orchestra in July 1930 ('Hittin' the Bottle'); thereafter in much demand, leading to London début in C B Cochran's revue *Streamline* (Palace, 28 September 1934), and subsequent world fame as the premier virtuoso harmonica-player, for whom Ralph Vaughan Williams composed a rhapsody for harmonica, piano, and orchestra (1952).

Blake, Eubie. Born Baltimore, 1883; was playing ragtime during its formative years and composed 'Charleston Rag' (published 1899); subsequently wrote many first-class rags, and the score of the long-running all-Negro revue *Shuffle Along* (opened at 63rd Street Theatre, New York, 23 May 1921, and ran for 504 performances); also composed 'Memories of You' (1930), a permanent best-seller; toured England with (then) partner Noble Sissle, popular singer, 1925–26; during his 80s he made LP albums of his own and other composers' works, and at 92 appeared on BBC Television demonstrating an amazingly flexible piano style and a dance routine he had been using for over 70 years.

Goodman, Benny. Born Chicago 1909; played first professional job (and recorded) with Ben Pollack's Californians there in 1926; left Pollack in 1929 and has since become identified as the most widely and generously gifted clarinettist in jazz, for whom Bela Bartók wrote a trio for clarinet, violin, and piano, who has recorded and frequently broadcast works such as Mozart's Concerto for clarinet and orchestra and works by Weber, J S Bach, and others; may be said to have launched the 'Swing era' in 1935 when his band, after a very shaky start, became a national, then an international favourite; many films, including *Hollywood Hotel* (1938), *Stage Door Canteen* (1943), and *Sweet and Low Down* (1945); provided part of the sound-track of the Walt Disney cartoon *Make Mine Music* (1945).

Hampton, Lionel. Born Louisville, Kentucky, 1909; first records and first work with important band in 1929 as drummer with Paul Howard's Quality Serenaders in Culver City, California; joined Benny Goodman's Trio to make it a Quartet, on vibraphone, 1936, later formed a big band and embraced the 'modern' idiom.

Hanshaw, Annette. Born New York, 1910, self-taught as singer of current popular songs, discovered by recording executive at the age of fifteen and for the next eight years recorded, filmed and was 'The Personality Girl of Radio'. Enormously popular for her musicianly, shy style; played piano and ukulele and composed own extra words for many of her songs.

Johnson, Bill. Born New Orleans, Louisiana, 1872; played bass with the Original Creole Orchestra that toured the country about 1911, and bass and banjo with 'King' Oliver's Jazz Band in Chicago in 1923; still playing occasionally until his 90s; died 1969 aged 97.

Kaufman, Irving. Born New York, 1890; began singing as a boy. His keen sense of pitch, prodigious memory of lyrics, and the ability to sing them with expression made him ideal for dance band and other vocal recording work; perfect diction and mellow tenor can be heard on (he estimates) some 6000 recordings made between 1913 and 1974; at 84 he contributed some contemporary singing to two albums of his earlier work, sounding very little different despite his advanced age.

Osmond, Jimmy. At nine, one of the principal attractions of the Osmond family group that made sensational success with American and British children of about the same age.

Robinson, Sugar Chile. Negro boy pianist who made a great success in 1951 in London at the age of nine, but little has been heard of him since.

Rose Marie. Born 1925; recording and doing radio work at seven, continued this through her teens and still makes occasional night-club, radio, and television appearances.

Selvin, Ben. Born 1900; a bandleader at seventeen, made first records with his Novelty Orchestra at nineteen, and between then and 1934 recorded thousands of sides with many front-rank musicians on all labels, great and small; became an executive for RCA Victor, now retired.

Shapiro, Helen. Born London, 1946, a star at fourteen, with a strangely deep, almost masculine voice. Her popularity began to fade as 'rock' music took over in the mid-1960s.

Tormé, Mel. Born Chicago, 1924; appeared as child prodigy vocalist at three with the Coon-Sanders Orchestra; as teenager sang with Artie Shaw's Orchestra and during the 1950s made many very successful tours on both sides of the Atlantic as soloist (nicknamed 'The Velvet Fog' from the huskiness of his voice).

Van Eps, Fred, Sr. Began recording in 1897 as banjo soloist on Edison wax cylinders, made hundreds of records of all kinds during the next 30 to 40 years, then crowned his career in 1950 by making a long-playing record at 80.

Waller, Thomas, 'Fats'. Born New York, 1904; wrote first song 'Squeeze Me' at fifteen in 1919, began recording career on discs and piano rolls at eighteen in 1922. Made hundreds more during 39 years of life, many as pipe-organ solos of popular songs, blues, and arrangements of Negro spirituals.

Wonder, Stevie. Negro rock singer (blind) who burst into popularity at the age of twelve during the late 1960s, offering the raw material of the idiom with little refinement but with considerable success, especially among connoisseurs of the style.

Stevie Wonder (Popperfoto)

MUSICIANS WHO CHANGED INSTRUMENTS AND/OR CAREERS, OR WHO PLAYED MANY DIFFERENT INSTRUMENTS

Bechet, Sidney. One of the greatest jazz soloists of all, born in New Orleans, 14 May 1897, died in Paris, 14 May 1959, Sidney Bechet played with musicians of all persuasions in the jazz spectrum, white and Negro, pioneer and modern. As one of the principal soloists of the Southern Syncopated Orchestra that played in England between the summer of 1919 and the autumn of 1921, he attracted the attention of Ernest Ansermet, the French conductor, who almost alone among his colleagues recognised the artistic merit of Bechet's music. Sidney Bechet usually played clarinet and soprano saxophone, but recorded using tenor saxophone, piano, string bass, and drums on a multi-recording date for Victor in 1941, and on one session in 1924 with Clarence Williams's Blue Five on OKeh, he played sarrusophone; legend has it he noticed the instrument in a second-hand shop on his way to the studio, impulsively bought it and insisted on trying it out on the record ('Mandy, Make Up Your Mind') much to the amusement of his colleagues.

Beiderbecke, Bix. One of the best-known and most-respected white jazz musicians, Bix Beiderbecke was a cornet-player from Davenport, Iowa, who received his inspiration from records of the Original Dixieland Jazz Band while still a schoolboy. Although only 28 when he died (in New York on 6 August 1931), he had played with two of the finest dance organisations in the USA, those of Jean Goldkette and Paul Whiteman, and had expanded his love of jazz to include the impressionist work of Maurice Ravel, Claude Debussy, Eastwood Lane, Igor Stravinsky, and others. He loved to play piano, and does so on four records–one made with his first professional band, the Wolverine Orchestra (*Big Boy,* 1924), two informal trio records with his friends, saxophonist Frank Trumbauer and guitarist Eddie Lang (*For No Reason At All in C* and *Wringin' and Twistin',* 1927) and one entirely solo (*In a Mist,* or *Bixology,* 1927). In all his other records he played cornet, despite the trend among his colleagues to using trumpet, preferring the broader tone.

Brilhart, Arnold. An outstandingly versatile and talented musician who played all the members of the saxophone family, in addition to flute and oboe; able to sight-read and thus very much in demand for work on all kinds of recording sessions, radio and theatre work. He recorded principally with Yerkes's SS Flotilla Orchestra; the California Ramblers; Ben Selvin's Orchestra; Roger Wolfe Kahn's Orchestra; and the Dorsey Brothers' Orchestra. He has long been a manufacturer of instruments and accessories.

Buckley, Neil. Vocalist with Don Bestor and his Orchestra during the 1930s. Neil Buckley later forsook the music world and became Mayor of a town in New Jersey.

Colonna, Jerry. The hoarse-voiced mustachioed eccentric comedian of American films was once a 'hot jazz' trombonist with Joe Herlihy's Orchestra in New York during the late 1920s; he recorded thus on Edison Diamond Discs.

Dankworth, John. As the leading alto-sax player, Johnny (as he then was) Dankworth for many years held his Band at or near the top of the profession. His interest in serious music has increased over the years: in 1958 he collaborated with Matyás Seiber on the *Improvisations for Jazz Band and Symphony Orchestra.* More recently (1971) a string quartet by John Dankworth was performed in London, and the previous year he composed a *Folk Mass.* He has also written a Jazz opera: *Sweeney Agonistes.*

Day, Doris. Born Doris Cappelhoff in 1924, Doris Day became vocalist with Barney Rapp's Orchestra in 1940, then joined Les Brown's Orchestra for a year. She branched out as a vocal soloist, as many dance-band singers have done, but after making several successful musical films, she discovered her talent as a non-singing light comedienne, and the majority of her subsequent films (made during the late 1950s and after) show her in this capacity.

Dorsey, Jimmy. The elder of the famous Dorsey brothers, born in Shenandoah, Pennsylvania, 29 February 1904. Jimmy Dorsey was regarded during the late 1920s and 1930s as the greatest saxophonist in the world, but he could also give an excellent performance on trumpet, as Joe Venuti's Blue Six playing *Pink Elephants* (Columbia) attests. Jimmy Dorsey also played clarinet and baritone saxophone, and does so on many records, switching from one to the other easily, sometimes via his usual alto saxophone; he died on 12 June 1957.

Downing, Rex. Trombonist with the Coon-Sanders Orchestra during the latter half of the 1920s and until the end of the band's life, Rex Downing subsequently gave up music and became a magistrate.

Durante, Jimmy 'Schnozzle'. A favourite American comedian with a guttural Bronx accent and a large nose, Jimmy Durante was originally a ragtime pianist who quickly absorbed the 'new' jazz idiom (1918), formed the Original New Orleans Jazz Band (afterwards giving his own name to it) and recorded on Gennett and OKeh with this quintet, in the closest approximation to the pioneer Original Dixieland Jazz Band known at that time. He later recorded with Bailey's Lucky Seven on Gennett (1921), under the direction of Sam Lanin.

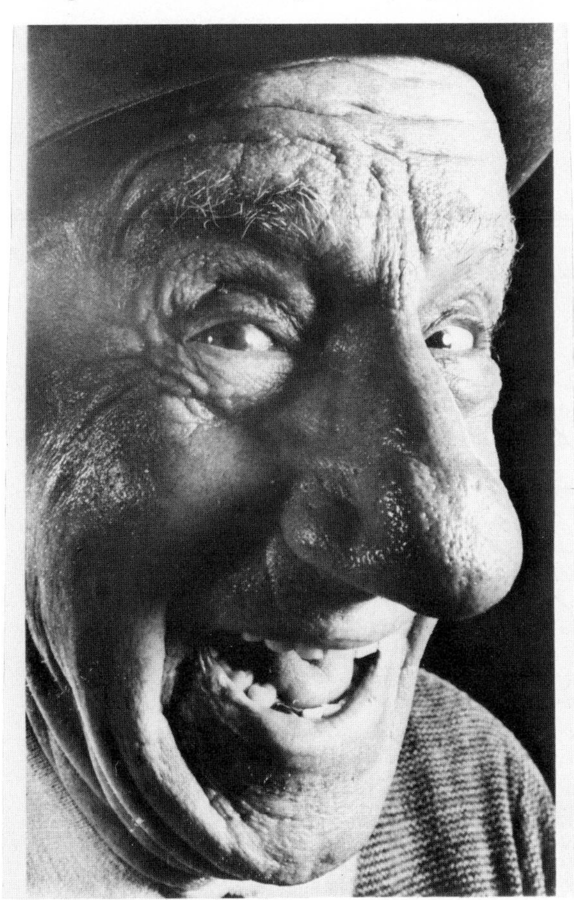

Jimmy 'Schnozzle' Durante (Popperfoto)

Elman, Ziggy. Benny Goodman's high-note trumpet-player of the late 1930s began his career on trombone with Alex Bartha's Hotel Traymore Orchestra in Atlantic City. His style is quite unlike the rather brash trumpet work of the Swing era.

Hughes, David. A successful pop singer in the 1950s, he turned his attention to opera in the mid 1960s. He has sung at Glydebourne and the Welsh National Opera as a tenor, and has made a number of records. He is best remembered perhaps, for his portrayal of Don José in Bizet's *Carmen*.

Johnson, Bob. One of the alto saxophonists in the Harry Yerkes entourage in the early 1920s, later gave up music and became a stockbroker in New York. From the Yerkes records of the time, he appears to have been an excellent musician.

Lindsay, Joe. The trombonist with Armand J Piron's New Orleans Orchestra who in 1925 or 1926 switched to playing string bass, so that the sturdy, melodic trombone of the Piron records for Victor, OKeh, and Columbia in 1923 and 1924 gives way to the athletic, powerful string bass heard on the first three Victor dates in 1926 by Jelly-Roll Morton's Red Hot Peppers.

Nunez, Alcide. New Orleans-born clarinettist with the Original Dixieland Jazz Band (1916), the Louisiana Five (1918–20), and Harry Yerkes's bands (1920) who abandoned the music world in later years and joined the police force.

Ormandy, Dr Eugene. World-famous symphony-orchestra conductor who began his professional career as violinist (Cameo records, 1923–24) and bandleader (OKeh records, 1928–30), also directing accompaniments to OKeh popular vocalists (eg Annette Hanshaw).

Previn, André. German-born conductor of the London Symphony Orchestra, American citizen, recognised as a great authority on all kinds of concert music and a very popular British television personality, albeit sometimes in the role of a comedian, at which he is as expert as he is a conductor. André Previn made many fine records for Victor and other labels in America as a jazz pianist during the late 1940s and early 1950s, and has since embarked on a series of successful classical recordings for RCA, CBS, and EMI.

Rignold, Hugo. For many years conductor of the Liverpool Philharmonic Orchestra, Hugo Rignold was principal violinist and 'hot' jazz soloist on that instrument with Jack Hylton's Orchestra between 1925 and 1930, and was rightly regarded as Britain's foremost exponent of what was then a daringly experimental new style of playing in the jazz idiom. He led his own orchestra during the 1930s, recording dance music for Columbia.

Rollini, Adrian. Born in New York in 1904, Adrian Rollini was the absolute master of the bass saxophone, a seemingly unwieldy instrument for a dance band, but after learning to play piano and xylophone, he added the largest of the saxophone family to his repertoire along with other instruments (goofus, hot fountain pen–see above–drums, and vibraphone). On Joe Venuti's Blue Five record of *Pink Elephants*, made for Columbia in 1933, he plays bass saxophone, vibraphone, piano, and goofus in that order.

UNUSUAL TITLES AND MEANINGS IN JAZZ

Many of the apparently meaningless gibberish titles of jazz numbers are simply an attempt to set down in print the worldless 'scat' (instrumentalised) vocal part, eg Louis Armstrong's 'Skid-dat-de-dat'; Dizzy Gillespie's 'Oo-bop-sh'bam'; Tiny Parham's 'Skag-a-lag' (this has no vocal part, but the phrase occurs in other performances on records as part of the vocal). The following are examples of abstruse titles having an inner meaning, similar to that of Cockney rhyming slang.

Title	*Meaning*
'Dipper Mouth Blues'	'King' Oliver, who composed the number, refused to allow drinking by members of his band while they were on the job, so he provided a bucket of sweetened water with a large dipper. Anyone (eg Louis Armstrong) who could get this in his mouth was known as 'Dipper' or 'Dipper Mouth' (he later became known as 'Satchel Mouth' or more familiarly 'Satchmo'.)
'Feelin' No Pain'	Pleasantly inebriated.
'Flat Foot Floogie with the Floy Floy'	An overworked prostitute.
'Forty and Tight'	The quintessence of sexual prowess or superiority.
'Freakish'	Homosexual.
'Golden Leaf Strut'	'Golden leaf' is marijuana, to which the principal soloist on the record of the number, Leon Roppolo, clarinettist of the Original New Orleans Rhythm Kings, was addicted.
'I'm a Ding-Dong Daddy from Dumas'	I am a man of superior talent and ability in every aspect of human behaviour, principally sexual; Dumas does not exist as far as is known.
'It's Tight Like That'	It is sexually exciting, exceptionally satisfactory.
''Lasses Candy'	New Orleans sweetmeat made of molasses cane sugar.
'Lazy Daddy'	Edwin 'Daddy' Edwards, the only married man in the Original Dixieland Jazz Band who had any offspring at the time (1918), and who could sleep in almost any position at any time.
'Lucky 3–6–9'	The winning combination in illegal dice games.
'Milenberg Joys'	Correct spelling should be 'Milneburg' (slum area of New Orleans near Lake Ponchartrain); original title 'Pee Hole Blues'.

Title	*Meaning*
'Muggin' Lightly'	Playing easily, with a steady beat giving an exciting incentive to dance.
'Pigs' Feet and Slaw'	'Slaw' is cole-slaw, the shredded stems of white cabbage, uncooked, served in white sauce, an inexpensive but popular dish among Southern Negroes.
'Shim-Me-Sha-Wabble'	'Shimmy' (the dance) is derived from 'chemise'; 'Sha-Wabble' is surely self-explanatory; a very seductive dance performed at some speed and involving much body torsion.
'Snake Eyes'	Two dice with a one-spot on each.
'Struggle Buggy'	A small car, commonly used in the 1920s and 1930s, for advanced love-making, despite the restrictions imposed by the confined space.
'Sud Buster's Dream'	A sud buster is a washwomen; also applied to users of various kinds of drugs.
'Sweet Peter'	The male sexual organ. (cf 'Oh Peter, You're So Nice', popular song of 1924 that passed unnoticed).
'Tank Town Bump'	A 'bump' was a dance involving what was then (pre-1930s) regarded as obscene physical contacts and movements; a 'tank town' is one with oil-storage tanks prominent in the topography.
'Top and Bottom'	A nickname given to a ferocious kind of illicit whisky in the Prohibition era.
'To-Wa-Bac-A-Wa'	A chant used in the Mardi Gras celebrations in New Orleans, usually believed to be a simplification of Creole French for 'Go back where you were' ('Tu vais bas que tu vais').
'Viper's Drag, Dream, Moan,' etc	A 'viper' in this sense is a drug addict.
'Warm Valley'	A female sexual organ.
'Yama Yama Blues/Man/Land o' Yamo Yamo'	A bogey man; a never-never land; something imaginary or horrific or delightful, the connotation depending on the context.

THE INFLUENCE OF THE MEDIA

Shortly after the end of the war a new influence emerged which had been hovering in the background for many years. It was in fact the combination of two complementary developments which together reshaped the popular musical scene: radio and records. Hitherto, of course, artists had become popular via these mediums, but the late 1940s saw an unprecedented growth in the popularity of records, spurred on by the proliferation of disc-jockeys serving the post-war Allied Forces abroad (eg the American Forces Network) and the teenage market at home (Radio Luxemburg, etc). Promoters of recordings saw the possibilities which these circumstances opened up and were not slow to exploit them. The age of the 'hit' record had arrived, and at the start of the 1950s popular musical taste was being shaped almost exclusively by record sales and radio plugging, and to a lesser extent by the sales of sheet music. Later came TV appearances to assist in this plugging: personal appearances ('one-night stands') lost their power in the face of this competition, and from then on an artist could be made or broken over the record counter and/or by the attention of the disc-jockeys.

A chronological survey of the last 30 years or

Ella Fitzgerald, one of the greatest women jazz singers of all time (Popperfoto)

Big Bands of the 1930s (dates of first impact)

Louis Armstrong
Count Basie
Jimmy Dorsey
Tommy Dorsey
Duke Ellington
Benny Goodman
Woody Herman
Glenn Miller
Paul Whiteman

Big Bands of the 1940s

Stanley Black
Billy Cotton
Johnny Dankworth
Percy Faith
Geraldo
Ted Heath
Harry James
Stan Kenton
Andre Kostelanetz
Joe Loss
Humphrey Lyttleton
Mantovani
Melachrino
Sid Phillips
Edmundo Ros
Sidney Torch

Instrumental and Novelty Artists of the 1940s and 50s

Instrumental (1940s)
Winifred Atwell
Charlie Kunz

Novelty (1940s)
Mel Blanc
Jimmy Durante
Stan Freberg
Phil Harris
Red Ingle
The Ink Spots
Spike Jones
Danny Kaye
Les Paul and Mary Ford

Instrumental (1950s)
Russ Conway
Liberace

Novelty (1950s)
Victor Borge
The Chipmunks
Jerry Colonna
Flanders and Swann
The Goons
Gerard Hoffnung
Paddy Roberts
Anna Russell

so will illustrate how this influence has developed. Against this chronology its foundations should be recalled: the late 1930s had seen the advent of 'big band' dance and jazz music and alongside had been the popularity of the crooner–male and female. These trends continued through the war and afterwards, giving the listener a much-needed sense of luxury and well-being. By the late 1940s a new social atmosphere had arrived and the way was open to new sounds and their widespread dissemination through records and radio.

The most popular crooner of all time, Bing Crosby (Popperfoto)

Singers of the 1940s

Rosemary Clooney
Nat ('King') Cole
Perry Como
Bing (Harry Lillis) Crosby
Doris Day (Doris Cappelhoff)
Ella Fitzgerald
Peggy Lee (Norma Dolores Egstrom)
Vera Lynn
Dean Martin (Dino Paul Crocetti)
Frank (Albert) Sinatra
Mel(vin Howard) Tormé

Singers of the 1950s

Shirley Bassey
Tony Bennett
Petula Clark
Sacha Distel
Michael Holliday
Teddy Johnson
Eartha Kitt
Frankie Laine
Denis Lotis
Johnny Mathis
Guy Mitchell
Matt Munro
Johnnie Ray
Dickie Valentine
Frankie Vaughan
Andy Williams

Jazz Artists of the 1950s

Modern
Earl Bostic
Dave Brubeck
Steve Lane's Famous Southern Stompers
Modern Jazz Quartet
Thelonious Monk

Traditional
Kenny Ball
Chris Barber
Acker Bilk
Ken Colyer
Dutch Swing College Band

Lonnie Donegan at work in the recording studio in 1957 (Popperfoto)

1949 Skiffle hit England. Skiffle grew out of the so-called 'spasm bands', which were made up of small groups of musicians in deprived areas who were determined to press into service domestic utensils, etc in place of the real musical instruments which they could not afford (see above). Spasm bands can be traced back to New Orleans in 1896 when a zither-playing artist known only as 'Stale Bread' (his main diet?) led such a group. Some of the greatest jazz-players, among them Louis Armstrong, learnt much of their art in spasm bands.

The first spasm band in England was the Original London Blue Blowers headed by Bill Bailey in 1945. It is not known how the word 'spasm' came to be used in this connection; similarly the word 'skiffle', first used in the 1920s, has an equally obscure origin.

The first English skiffle group was founded by Bill Colyer as a part of his Crane River Jazz Band in 1949, but skiffle's great popularity did not arrive until 1952 when his brother Ken formed the Ken Colyer Jazzmen, its skiffle group consisting of Bill (washboard), Chris Barber or sometimes Jim Bray (bass), Lonnie Donegan (guitar), and Ken Colyer himself (guitar). Lonnie Donegan, to become known as 'The King of Skiffle', went on to lead the skiffle group under Chris Barber from 1954, until the formation of his own group in 1956, after the success of their record 'Rock Island Line'.

Kenny Ball and his Jazzmen, one of the most popular English trad jazz groups (Popperfoto)

Bill Haley and his Comets live on stage (London Features International Ltd)

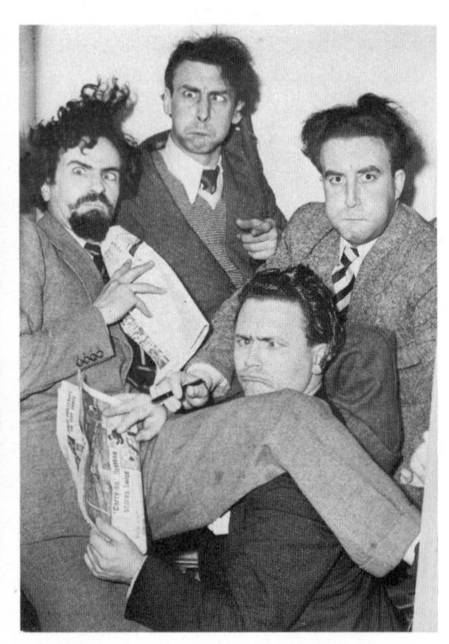

(left) The highest paid musician, Liberace earns more than $2 000 000 each 26-week season with a peak of $138 000 (then £49 285) for a single night's performance at Madison Square Gardens, New York City, USA in 1954.

(centre) Victor Borge, the talented Danish pianist who has shown the funny side of concert life

(right) The original Goons, 1951, l to r: Michael Bentine, Spike Milligan, Harry Secombe and Peter Sellers (Popperfoto)

1954 Rock 'n' Roll. The American disc-jockey Alan Freed is responsible for coining the term 'Rock 'n' Roll' for the new heavy beat pop music which was to dominate the scene for many years, adapting the title of the old blues song 'My Baby Rocks Me With a Steady Roll'.

The first American rock 'n' roll hit was 'Sh-boom', which was originally sung by an unknown Negro group in the spring of 1954, and which soon entered the pop 'charts' in a version by the white group known as 'The Crewcuts'.

The first world-wide rock 'n' roll hit was 'Rock Around the Clock' by Bill Haley and his Comets in July 1955 which was also played behind the credits of the disturbing but successful film *Blackboard Jungle.*

The most successful single rock 'n' roll performer is Elvis (Aaron) Presley who has collected no fewer than 28 individual million-seller awards for his recordings from 1958 to 1975. His first TV appearance was in the autumn of 1955 on the *Tommy Dorsey Show* in America, and his first Golden Disc, 'Heartbreak Hotel', was recorded on 10 February 1956.

Elvis Presley photographed in 1972 (Popperfoto)

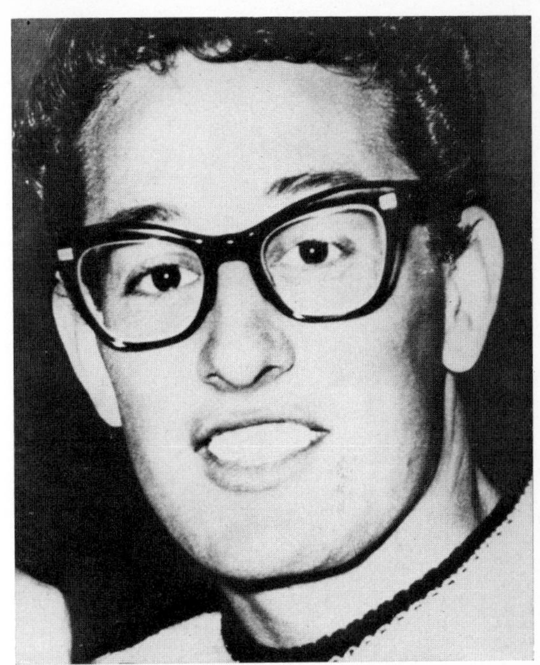

The late Buddy Holly pictured in London in 1957 (Popperfoto)

SOME ROCK 'N' ROLL ARTISTS

1955 Pat Boone, the symbol of pure, youthful, all-American wholesomeness and optimism. His first hit was 'Ain't That a Shame'.

1956 Tommy Steele, the cheeky, Cockney voice of rock 'n' roll. His first recording was 'Rock With the Cavemen'; there followed his first big hit 'Singing the Blues'. He made his TV début on 15 October 1958, and has progressed to become one of the most popular British entertainment personalities.

1957 The Everley Brothers. Two real brothers whose smash hits include 'Bye Bye Love' and 'Wake Up Little Susie'. Their style had a strong influence on that of The Beatles who, at one early stage of their career, called themselves 'The Foreverley Brothers'.

1957 Buddy Holly, the American singer who, with a group called 'The Crickets', made popular recordings of 'That'll Be the Day' and, in 1958, 'Peggy Sue'. He was killed in an air crash in America on 2 February 1959 together with the other rock artists The Big Bopper and Richie Valens.

The late Bobby Darin

1958 Bobby Darin (born Walden Robert Cassotto) recorded 'Splish Splash' and 'Mack the Knife'. Chosen Best New Artist in America (1959) and received the Grammy Award for Best Vocal Performance (Male). He appeared in many films and wrote title-songs and complete scores for *The Lively Set* and *That Funny Feeling*.

1958 Connie Francis, the best-known American female rock 'n' roll artist, from Brooklyn. Her first hit was 'Who's Sorry Now?' followed by 'Stupid Cupid'.

1958 Cliff Richard, a British artist who retains his popularity today, made his first hit with 'Living Doll'. In the early days he was associated with The Shadows, a group of English instrumentalists who changed their name from The Drifters in September 1959 in order to avoid confusion with the American group of that name.

1961 Dusty Springfield, a popular British female artist who was the vocalist in a group called The Springfields. (Her brother Tom Springfield, part of this group, has become a skilful composer of popular music in his own right.) There were several hits as a group, including 'Dear John' and 'Breakaway', before Dusty herself broke away as an independent vocalist in 1963.

Pop and Rock Artists of the 1960s (dates of first impact)

1960	Chubby Checker	1965	Julie Felix
	John Layton		Tom Jones
	The Shadows		Lulu
1961	Ann Margret		The Who
	Anita Harris	1966	Roger Whittaker
	Rolf Harris	1967	The Bee-Gees
1962	Frank Ifield		The Scaffold
	Susan Maughan	1968	Mary Hopkin
1963	The Rolling Stones		Jack Jones
	Kathy Kirby		The Marmalade
	The Searchers	1969	Blue Mink
1964	Cilla Black		
	Val Doonican		
	Herman's Hermits		
	Julie Rogers		

Jazz Artists of the 1960s

John Coltrane
Dudley Moore
The Original Downtown Syncopators
Archie Shepp
The Temperance Seven
Mike Westbrook

1961 Helen Shapiro (see above). Her first record was 'Don't Treat Me Like a Child', but her biggest hit came with 'Walkin' Back To Happiness'.

1961 The Beatles. The rock 'n' roll scene, of which the artists listed above formed only a fraction, if an important one, was transformed and swamped by a group of four youngsters from Liverpool who have been called 'geniuses', 'phenomena', etc (and many less kind things by other artists trying to break into the field), and who have the distinction of being **the most successful group of singers of all time.** They are George Harrison, MBE, John Winston (later John Ono) Lennon, MBE, James Paul McCartney, MBE, and Richard Starkey (Ringo Starr), MBE. They were discovered by Brian Epstein, Manager of the Record Department of Nems Ltd (North Eastern Music Store Ltd), a music shop in Liverpool in 1961 while they were playing in a near-by night-club called 'The Cavern'. After some personnel changes and many attempts to find a group name, John Lennon invented 'The Beatles', a name which took them to the top, where they stayed for a decade.

The history of The Beatles began in 1956 when Paul McCartney, John Lennon, and George Harrison formed a skiffle group known as 'The Quarrymen'. **Their first recording** was made under the name 'The Beat Brothers' in Hamburg for Polydor in 1961 with vocalist Tony Sheridan ('My Bonny' 'When the Saints go Marching In') by which time the original trio had been supplemented by Stuart Sutcliffe and Pete Best. This Polydor disc sold 100000 copies in Germany on its own merits before going on to over a 1000000 in 1964 on the strength of the success of records by the reconstituted group from 1962. After the death of Stuart Sutcliffe and the replacement of drummer Pete Best by Ringo Starr, the Beatles signed a contract with EMI. **The first Beatles disc for EMI** (Parlophone label) was 'Love Me Do'/'PS I Love You', issued late in 1962 which had fair sales; **their first Gold Disc** (1000000 sales) was awarded for 'She Loves You' in April 1963, and orders for **their first LP,** *Please Please Me*

Paul McCartney, once of the Beatles, now of Wings, with a collection of awards bestowed upon them for sales of their chart topping LP 'Band on the Run' (*London Features International Ltd*)

(December 1963), exceeded 250000 in England. The Beatles made **their first TV appearance** on 17 October 1962 on Granada TV England.

Having conquered the UK record market, The Beatles invaded America in February 1964, their disc successes have preceded them: 'I Want To Hold Your Hand' was No 1 in the US hit parade on 24 January of that year. Their personal appearances at Carnegie Hall and on the 'Ed Sullivan Show' (their TV début) confirmed the success of their invasion.

Back home, a new disc, 'Can't Buy Me Love', and 'You Can't Do That', became **the first disc ever to achieve 1000000 sales** (ie firm orders) **before its issue** (20 March 1964).

The Beatles story has been told many times before and there is no room here to deal with more than the salient points among their successes. It should be pointed out, however, that this group has been instrumental in steering the progress of the rock style, influences on The Beatles becoming in turn influences on the main stream of pop music. From the early style based on the Everley Brothers and others, The Beatles later became engaged in the anti-bourgeois sentiments expressed by the American folk-rock singer Bob Dylan in such songs as 'Yellow Submarine' and 'Paperback Writer'. Later still (1964/65), associated with a personal interest in Indian philosophy, The Beatles launched so-called 'Raga-Rock' (more correctly 'Rag-Rock', but thereby running the risk of confusion with 'ragtime', the ragged-rhythmed music of early jazz), in 'Norwegian Wood', etc: a psychedelic music of dream-like imagery. This direction was followed in the first of the super-albums: *Sergeant Pepper's Lonely Hearts Club Band,* four months in the making and issued in June 1967.

Due to their outside interests, among which was the establishment of Apple, their own record company, a gradual dissolution of their style was inevitable; nevertheless they continued to dominate the pop scene until 1970, being unable to do any wrong in the eyes of their fans. John Lennon and Paul McCartney were responsible for writing a number of songs which have entered musical history and are likely to stay there. Among these should be mentioned:

'A Hard Day's Night'
'All My Loving'
'And I Love Her'
'I Want To Hold Your Hand'
'Penny Lane'
'Yesterday'

The Beatles remain **the biggest selling recording artists of all time.** Between February 1963 and June 1972 their sales were estimated at the equivalent of 545000000 'single' discs, including 85000000 LP albums.

1956 Soul grew out of blues via the Gospel-blues singing of Ray Charles (*c* 1954). James Brown, known as 'Soul Brother No 1', was **the first Negro to entertain Negro troops in Vietnam.** Much of the substance of Soul music deals with Civil Rights, the hopeless conditions of the Negro, and other sociological messages. There have been a number of Soul artists since, among them The Righteous Brothers (1963) and Blood, Sweat, and Tears (1968), the latter being the first Soul group to incorporate a horn section–two trumpets, a trombone, and a saxophone.

1961 Folk rock. A white reaction to Soul was inevitable. Bob Dylan's protest rock grew out of rock 'n' roll and the folk revival. Other names to be linked with the folk-rock movement are Peter, Paul, and Mary, Joan Baez, and the Scottish male singer Donovan.

1966 TV pop. The Monkees (deliberately misspelling the root of their group name perhaps in emulation of The Beatles) were an

The Monkees (Popperfoto)

Bob Dylan, probably the greatest influence in 20th-century rock progressive music (London Features International Ltd)

Stephen Stills, David Crosby and Graham Nash. (See p. 250). (London Features International Ltd)

Elton John, who recorded the first album ever to enter the Billboard list at No. 1 with Captain Fantastic and the Brown Dirt Cowboy (Michael Putland, London Features International Ltd)

The Rolling Stones, the most durable Rock 'n Roll group of all time, pictured here on stage in 1976.

American group which established itself at first via the television screen in a series for Screen Gems-Columbia aimed primarily at the younger audience. By introducing pop music in the midst of a story line, the series brought in its wake high sales of Monkees' records, starting with 'Last Train To Clerksville'. The group split up in 1969 amid acrimonious accusations between them and the Columbia company.

1968 Hippie Cult. A new sound emerged in California, springing from the style of Bob Dylan and called 'West Coast Music'. Close-harmony voices and proficient guitar-playing typify this fusing of protest lyrics with country/rock music. The band called 'Crosby, Stills, Nash, and Young' led this movement and performed at the gigantic Woodstock 'love and peace' gathering which attracted nearly 500000 fans. Other important country/rock performers include Buffalo Springfield, The Byrds, Country Gazette, The Flying Buritto Brothers, Joni Mitchell, Jackson Browne, and more recently The Eagles.

1970 Teeny-Boppers. The two elements above, ie television and the younger audience, crystallised into a new craze with an old sound to its title. Bop, as a style of dance music, was a phenomenon of the late 1930s and fits ill with the concept of a crowd of primary school children enjoying themselves to music. The new Teeny-Boppers (also called the 'Bubble-Gum Brigade') stemmed from the followers of David Cassidy (who appeared in the American TV series *The Partridge Family*). The Teeny-Bopper cult spread to England in 1972, in which year Jimmy Osmond made his first hit at the age of eight.

Weeny-Boppers have also hit the headlines with their activities. Ten year old Donna-Marie Newman of England has already achieved success, securing a £100000 recording contract in 1972. One waits expectantly for the next step in juvenile entertainment: Toddle-Boppers and Bottle-Boppers are confidently predicted.

It was in 1970 that **the first pop group ever to appear at the Proms** performed at the Royal Albert Hall in London. The Soft Machine played there on 23 August.

The biggest live audience for a rock concert was in July 1973, when 600000 fans attended a 'Summer Jam' at Watkins Glen, New York, USA, featuring the Allman Brothers Band and the Grateful Dead.

A survey of the post-Beatle years presents a confused picture of the pop scene from which it is too early to pick out salient trends. Cross-fertilisations are common among the styles discussed above, to which should be added Reggae, American Smooth Soul, British Heavy Stomp, Rhythm and Blues, and others. Singers of modern ballads such as Gilbert O'Sullivan and Lynsey de Paul present an honest art in a

A leader in the revival of the Big Band sound in the 1970s, Sid Lawrence (courtesy: Sid Lawrence)

Chris Ellis, vocalist with the New Paul Whiteman Orchestra (Photo: Peter Vernon)

quiet way, but much of the fame, notoriety, and money goes to those artists who exploit the visual possibilities of colour television with exotic clothing, garish make-up, strange equipment, flashing lights, and unconventional camera techniques. They include such entertainers as T Rex (originally called Tyrannosaurus Rex but simplified to enable their fans to overcome pronunciation problems), Gary Glitter, The Slade, David Bowie, Alvin Stardust, Wizard, and Roxy Music. With these and other personalities the way to fame and fortune seems to lie in the ability to scream, shout, stamp, sparkle, shimmer, and sweat, and anything but sing.

The temptation is strong to end on that pessimistic note, but it is encouraging to report a new movement in popular music which looks to the past for its inspiration. The Big Bands of the 1930s and 1940s have enjoyed a revival on records, and this has led to the formation of large bands for the presentation of this music in concert. The Geraldo Orchestra has been re-formed; the Jack Parnell and Woody Herman bands are being listened to with a new interest, together with Stan Kenton's Orchestra. Also appearing are entirely new bands such as the Million-Airs and The New Paul Whiteman Orchestra, with vocalist Chris Ellis, re-creating the sounds of the years between the wars.

David Bowie performing on stage in London in 1976 (Michael Putland, London Features International Ltd)

DANCE TUNES AND POPULAR SONGS BASED PARTIALLY OR WHOLLY ON THEMES FROM 'SERIOUS' MUSIC

Popular song	*Based on*
'Avalon' (Al Jolson–Vincent Rose, 1920)	First eight bars correspond to 'O dolci bacio, languide carezze' in 'E Lucevan Le Stelle' from *Tosca* (Puccini)
'Castle Of Dreams' (Joseph McCarthy – Harry Tierney, 1919)	Waltz No 6 in D flat major, Op 64/1 ('Minute Waltz') (Chopin)
Catherine (Musical comedy by Reginald Arkell and Fred de Crésac, 1923)	Entire score based on melodies by Tchaikovsky
'Concerto For Two' (Bob Haring – Jack Lawrence, 1941)	Piano Concerto No 1 in B flat minor, Op 23, first movement (Tchaikovsky)
'The Echo Told Me a Lie' (Barnes – Fields – John, 1949)	Theme from *Capriccio Italien* (Tchaikovsky) (also known as 'Bella ragazza dalle trecce bionde')
'Full Moon and Empty Arms' (Buddy Kaye – Ted Mossman, 1945)	Piano Concerto No 2 in C minor, Op 18 (Rakhmaninoff)
'Gypsy Moon' (Igor Borganoff, 1932)	'Zigeunerweisen' (Sarasate)
'Horses' (Byron Gay, 1926)	'Troika' (Tchaikovsky)
'I'd Climb the Highest Mountain (If I Knew I'd Find You)' Lew Brown – Sidney Clare, 1926)	*Humoresque* (Dvořák)
'If I Should Lose You' (Earl Burtnett – Robert Stowell, 1927)	Symphony No 5 in E minor, Op 64, second movement (Tchaikovsky)
'If You Are But a Dream' (Jaffe – Fulton – Bonx, 1945)	*Romance* (Rubinstein)
'I'm Always Chasing Rainbows' (Harry Carroll, 1918)	Fantaisie-Impromptu in C sharp minor, Op 66 (posth) (Chopin)
'In an 18th-century Drawing Room' (Raymond Scott, 1939)	Keyboard Sonata in C, K 545, first movement (Mozart)
'Intermezzo' (Bob Haring – Heinz Provost, 1940)	Theme from *Tristan und Isolde* (Wagner)
Kismet (Musical comedy by Robert Wright and George Forrest, 1953)	Entire score based on melodies by Borodin
'The Lamp is Low' (Peter DeRose – Bert Shefter – Mitchell Parrish, 1939)	*Pavane pour une Infante Défunte* (Ravel)
Lilac Time (Musical comedy by Adrian Ross, 1923)	Entire score based on melodies by Schubert
'Mignonette' (Horatio Nicholls, 1926)	Minuet in G (Beethoven)
'Moon Love' (André Kostelanetz, 1939)	Symphony No 5 in E minor, Op 64, second movement (Tchaikovsky)
'My Moonlight Madonna' (William Scotti – Paul Francis Webster, 1933)	*Poème* (Fibich)
'Night' (Seymour Simons, 1922)	'Dance of the Little Swans', from *Swan Lake Ballet* (Tchaikovsky)
'One Night in June' (Ted Snyder – Henry Lange, 1922)	Verse taken from the melody of *Barcarolle* (Tchaikovsky)
'One Summer Night' (Sam Coslow – Larry Spier, 1927)	*Songs My Mother Taught Me* (Dvořák)
'On the Isle of May' (Mack David – André Kostelanetz, 1939)	Quartet No 1 in D major, Op 11, Andante cantabile (Tchaikovsky)
'Our Love' (Larry Clinton – Buddy Bernier – Bob Emmerich, 1939)	*Romeo and Juliet* Fantasy Overture (Tchaikovsky)
'Peter Gink' (George L Cobb)	'Anitra's Dance' from *Peer Gynt* Suite No 1 (Grieg)
'Play That Song of India Again' (Irving Bibo – Leo Wood – Paul Whiteman)	'Chanson Hindoue' from *Sadko* (Rimsky-Korsakov)

Popular song	*Based on*
'Russian Rag' (George L Cobb, 1918)	Prelude in C sharp minor, Op 3/2 (Rakhmaninoff)
Song of Norway (Musical comedy by Robert Wright and George Forrest, 1944)	Entire score based on melodies by Grieg
Summer Song (Musical comedy by Eric Maschwitz, 1956)	Entire score based on melodies by Dvořák
'The Things I Love' (Harold Barlow – Lew Harris, 1941)	Melody in A flat major, Op 42/3 (Tchaikovsky)
'Till the End of Time' (Buddy Kaye – Ted Mossman, 1945)	Polonaise in A flat major, Op 53 (Chopin)
'Tonight We Love' (Bobby Worth – Freddy Martin, 1939)	Piano Concerto No 1 in B flat minor, Op 23, first movement (Tchaikovsky)
'Two Lovely Black Eyes' (Charles Coborn, 1892)	'Vieni sul mar!' (Neapolitan folk-song)
'Wagon Wheels' (Billy Hill – Peter DeRose, 1933)	Symphony No 9 in E minor, Op 95, second movement (Dvořák)
'Wild Horses' (K C Rogan, 1952)	'Die wilde Jagd' (Schumann)

MODERN 'SERIOUS' DEVELOPMENTS

The intention behind jazz and popular music was initially to free the art from the stuffy rules and conventions of the late 19th century, but in so doing it established its own strict formulae. Nevertheless, it led the way to freedom in serious music, a freedom which was seized gratefully by many composers as a licence to compose music which went totally against the conventions of the musical establishment. It is, however, not always evident that audiences seized this new-found freedom with equal gratitude: the 20th century has seen the creation of a wide gulf between the composer and his public, and it is into this gulf that pop, dance, and jazz musicians stepped, bringing music to a public which could not be bothered to follow the intellectual convolutions of 'serious' composers.

The cult of 'anything goes' in modern serious music began early in the century, firstly with a strong move away from the binding restrictions of traditional tonality. This led to the experiments in atonalism of the so-called 'Second Viennese School' (see Section III: Groups of Composers), led by Arnold Schoenberg.

The first composer to write music in the twelve-tone discipline was Josef Matthias Hauer (1882–1959), who postulated the technique in 1912.

Side by side came the predominantly tonality orientated *avant-gardism* of Stravinsky and Bartók, the latter relying greatly upon the untamed musical language of the folk-people of his native Hungary.

The elemental power and the cacophonic effect of some of the music of these and other composers inevitably led to audience reaction. An oft-quoted account of the first performance,

Igor Stravinsky (Popperfoto)

in Paris under Pierre Monteux, of Stravinsky's *Rite of Spring* on 29 May 1913 gives an early example of this reaction, as well as indicating that the 'new' music had its adherents, this in turn indicating that the future for such music, although subject to vicissitudes, was assured. We are told by Carl van Vechen, who attended this first performance of the ballet, that the start of the music was greeted with polite smiles, then a few laughs, but as the music got properly under way the audience divided itself into sharply opposed camps. There were those for whom the noise was intolerable and who left in bewilderment, and others who were angered by the tasteless joke being played on them (the Comtesse de Pourtalès rose to her feet and complained loudly that she had not been so insulted in 60 years). On the other hand there were those for whom the music released feelings of exultant physical emotion, like the man who beat out the rhythm with his fists on the top of van Vechen's head. Afterwards, the composer, the conductor, the impresario (Diaghilev), and the leading dancer (Nijinsky) went to a restaurant to discuss the historic event. They were, in Stravinsky's words, 'excited, angry, disgusted, and . . . happy'.

A large number of excellent recordings of *Rite of Spring* exist, many at a reasonable price: the reader who is unfamiliar with the music and who wishes to understand the reasons behind the furore against, and the wild partisan support for, the music, is invited to obtain one of these recordings. The music's powerful rhythmic impetus, the jagged, mesmeric power of its melodies, and the uncompromising use of severe harmonies will illustrate better than thousands of words the new and disturbing musical influences at work before the First World War, influences which spread dynamically through the music of the next 50 years, affecting branches of the art as diverse as chamber music and big band jazz.

That these influences were indeed disturbing is proved by the events of the early 1920s where concert-halls in Italy and France were transformed into war areas as modernists and traditionalists clashed. Marinetti's concerts, for instance, were frequently accompanied by flying vegetables and crockery, brought in presumably by fanatics expecting trouble. In Germany, modern music also experienced growing pains: Kurt Weill's opera *The Rise and Fall of the City of Mahagony* was met with stink-bombs at first, but as feelings rose the event turned to tragedy. A man was struck with a beer-mug (in an opera-house?) and killed outright.

Of course, in an era of musical anarchy, there are always musicians for whom the established forms of the past provide all the material they need to compose their greatest thoughts. In their way, these 'traditionalist' composers exercise an expanding influence on music. Travelling by a less violent and radical road, taking shorter steps and producing music which is less initially disagreeable, they gradually bring the art of music to a pitch at which the experimentation of the *avant-gardistes*, although obviously retaining their position, are not impossibly separated from the traditional pulse of musical development.

Among the important composers of the 20th century are:

Avant-Gardistes/ Experimenters	*Traditionalists*
Schoenberg (1874–1951)	Elgar (1857–1934)
Ives (1874–1954)	R Strauss (1864–1949)
Bartók (1881–1945)	Nielsen (1865–1931)
Stravinsky (1882–1971)	Sibelius (1865–1957)
Dallapiccola (1904–75)	Vaughan Williams (1872–1958)
Messiaen (b 1908)	Rakhmaninoff (1873–1943)
Cage (b 1912)	Prokofiev (1891–1953)
Xenakis (b 1922)	Shostakovitch (1903–75)
Nono (b 1924)	Barber (b 1910)
Stockhausen (b 1928)	Britten (b 1913)

(Some composers in the above list could be regarded as having a foot in each camp.)

This list purposely has not been brought too close to the present because it is simply not possible to perceive today which of the composers who have come to prominence during the last decade or so will prove to be influential forces tomorrow.

For the sake of interest rather than to infer importance, a selection of extravagances of the so-called 'serious' modern composers are listed here.

Henri Pousseur, the Belgian composer born in 1929 has written a piano work, *Caractères I,* in which a piece of paper with holes cut in it is placed over the music. The pianist plays only the portions of music he can read through the holes.

This idea is symptomatic of the modern attitude whereby the composer puts the responsibility of much of the composing on to the creative artist. Other composers who allow, or insist on, the artists' imagination, co-operation, or luck to create the music they, the composers, have ostensibly composed include John Cage, Morton Feldman, Toshi Ichiyamggi, Terry Riley, Christian Wolff, LaMonte Young, and Cornelius Cardew. An extreme among extremes of non-composition is reached in Wolfgang Fortner's *Marginalien* for orchestra. It consists of a few basic ideas–little more than motific fragments–upon which the performers have to improvise. The score has a great many completely empty staves to allow for this improvisation. A visual equivalent of the work would be a jigsaw puzzle with no ultimate solution in terms of a recognisable picture, in which the puzzler is free to create his own patterns.

A rather more imaginative idea on the part of the composer occurs in Pierre Boulez's *Domaines* of 1968. The leading player is a solo clarinettist; distributed round the stage are small groups of instrumentalists ready to be brought into musical life as the clarinettist, roving freely among them, approaches each in turn at random, playing his instrument and inviting them to join in with impromptu playing of their own based on what the leader is playing.

Of course, many of these works result in music emerging in different keys simultaneously. This effect, bitonality or polytonality, is a regular ingredient of modern music, but it is not generally realised that it is not new. As long ago as the late 17th century H I F Biber included in his Suite in D, *Battalia,* a descriptive movement in which the strings each play a different melody in a different key to imitate a wild gathering in an inn: the soldiers, more than a little merry, sing folk-tunes against each other on the night before the battle. Much later, early in the 19th century, further bitonal experiments were carried out by Antonín Reicha. It was Reicha, too, who explored possibilities of microtones in music, experimenting with intervals of less than a semitone. This idea has been taken up during the 20th century by a number of composers, among them the Russian Vishnegradsky, the Moravian Hába brothers Alois and Karel, and the Englishman John Herbert Foulds.

The first microtonal opera was written in 1910 (but not performed until 1927) by the Italian Vittorio Gnecchi: *La Rosiera.*

John Cage, the American experimental composer, has been responsible for a great many innovations in a century of novelties, some of which approach the magnitude of hoaxes. On 7 February 1943, at the Museum of Modern Art in New York, he mounted a programme of purely percussion music including works by Lou Harrison, Henry Cowell, José Ardevol, Amadeo Roldan, and himself. The instruments included a bewildering mass of objects both expected and unexpected on a concert platform: orchestral bells, temple gongs, cymbals, tam-tams, marimba, thundersheets, oxen bells, cowbells, car brake drums (when suspended and struck, these give off a resounding bell-like note), anvils, dragons' mouths, woodblocks, rice-bowls, claves, buzzer, wind glass, flower-pots, tin cans, Niger drum, button gongs, and an audio-frequency oscillator. A note was inserted at the foot of the programme: 'Sound equipment furnished by the Sound Effects Department of the Columbia Broadcasting System.'

It must seriously be wondered what artistic value might be gained from some of John Cage's extravagancies, as in his *4′ 33″* (see Section VII) and perhaps even more particularly in his Piano Concerto of 1963. During the performance of this work it is directed that turkeys be released from a coffin. Much earlier, in 1942, Cage wrote a piece for voice and piano entitled *The Wonderful Widow of Eighteen Springs.* For the performance, the pianist is instructed to keep the keyboard lid closed and to hit various parts of the outside and inside of the instrument in accordance with directions in the score.

John Cage is a mycologist. If he had been able to exchange certain of his skills with Schobert (see p 62) the musical world might have been the better off.

Other strange occurrences in the age of 'anything goes', chosen at random: In *Terretektorh* by the Romanian composer Xenakis, the 60 instrumentalists are distributed among the audience.

Stockhausen's *Momente* (1962–72) calls for instrumentalists and singers, but the singers are expected to play various percussion instruments, to scrape their feet on the floor, to tongue-click, stamp, shuffle, finger-click, hand-clap, and knee-slap, in addition to making a variety of vocalisations from unvoiced ssssh-ings and prrrr-ings to screaming.

The Canadian composer Udo Kosemets composed in 1966 a piece entitled *Variations (on Variations [on Variations])*. A few words and syllables varied into a poetic text is then varied by Kosemets. Further variation is encouraged when the work is performed, the responsibility for this final variational step once again devolving on to the performers.

Having relied upon the performer to create his work for him, the composer then treats him badly: for a performance of 'Goldstaub', from *Aus dem Sieben Tagen* by Stockhausen, the four performers are required to live in isolation without food for four days before the concert. This calls for a dedication altogether beyond the call of duty.

There are reports of rock groups smashing their instruments after their performances, but **the only work during which an 'instrument' is smashed for a purely musical effect** at the climax is *Home Made,* written in 1967 by the American Alvin Curran, a pupil of Eliot Carter. *Home Made* is full of bizarre effects, among them fragments of texts taken from Shakespeare, Clark Coolidge, Chaucer, and Lewis Carroll: at one point there is a coloratura rendering of the first line only of 'In Your Easter Bonnet'. The instruments are flute, alto flute, piccolo, double bass, and percussion, to which are added whistles, piano and organ played by the soprano, squeaky tubber toys, and a pane of glass. At the height of the piece the pane of glass is smashed.

The use of unconventional materials for musical effects is widely practised by both 'serious' and 'popular' artists and composers. One of the strangest combinations was invented in 1974 by Tristram Cary in his sound-track for Richard Williams's animated feature film *I Vor Pittfalks*. A condom was stretched over a microphone and then scratched with the fingernails. The resulting sound would defy accurate identification by even the most acute listener.

Each one of these odd methods of producing new music breaks some kind of record, which is why this section has departed from the presentation used elsewhere in this book. The reader is invited to decide for himself whether, for instance, Alvin Curran's *Home Made* is the first piece to include a soprano playing keyboard instruments, set Lewis Carroll to music, make use of the timbre of squeaky rubber toys, or incorporate the sound of smashing glass. Perhaps it breaks all these records; or none of them. The modern composer in his quest for new sounds, or notoriety, or money, often takes literally the rule-breaking techniques of Beethoven, Wagner, Stravinsky, and Stockhausen, believing, perhaps rightly, that posterity will acclaim his latest gimmick, and that he will be instrumental, as were those great men before him, in altering the course of musical development. We should hesitate to blame him for trying, reserving our strictures for the works which do not 'come off'. If enough works in a particular style, or employing a particular technique or philosophy, are met with silence or hostility, that track of development will die out no matter how strong the impulse and publicity which set it off. The public is the deciding factor. If the listener wants to hear more of a certain style, that style will flourish. If not, it will join the many thousands of defunct notions with which musical history is littered.

Section IX

MECHANICAL MUSIC-MAKING

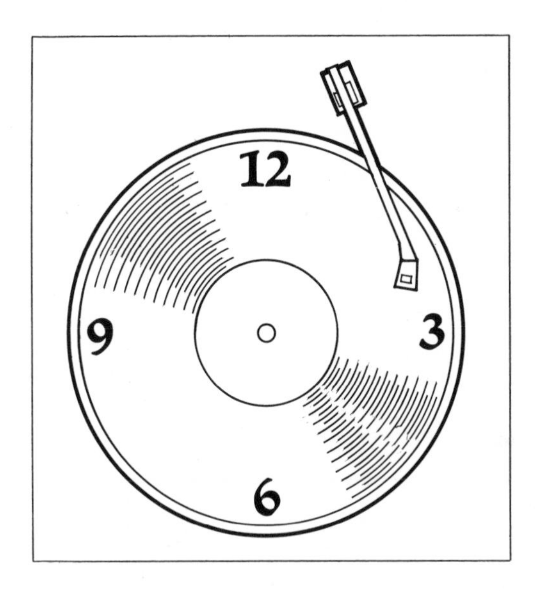

In Section I: Setting the Scene, we discussed the probable way in which the mind of emerging man was fascinated from the start with music-making. There, we assumed without evidence, simply because evidence is not available, that the drive to make music was so strong that it might almost be equated with the urge to communicate verbally; in fact, music is generally regarded as an extension of speech and, therefore, a more sophisticated way of making contact with other humans.

As the gregarious nature of man, and later his artistic nature, drove him to make music, so his ingenious mind impelled him to find ways of making it without direct contact with instruments. In this sphere, however, we do not have to resort to guesswork since mechanical music-making, being more recent than 'natural' music-making, is fairly well documented.

For our purposes we have cast the net wide to include, even if only as a passing mention, all forms of making music mechanically–therefore we have drawn up the following definition: mechanical music-making covers any process in which, or by which, music may be made at will by an individual without his direct contact with a musical instrument.

Within this concept, surprisingly, falls one of the earliest and most primitive of all instruments–although it cannot really be regarded as 'mechanical'–upon which the player did not play, and over which he had little control. **The earliest mechanical musical instrument** within our terms of reference, then, is the æolian harp (see Section II).

The earliest concept of mechanical music, as such, dates from the 3rd century BC.

The great philosopher Plato, in one of his inspired flashes of genius, discovered that, as it was not possible to tell the time at night, sundials being off-duty and sand-clocks difficult to see in the dark, the only means of knowing the time would be by a mechanism which made a noise at each hour. Borrowing his ideas from the Egyptians and the Romans, Plato designed a water-organ which would produce a little tune from its pipes when the flow of water reached a certain weight, this timed to take one hour. It remains a mystery whether this musical clock was ever built since no example has been preserved, but water-organs of about the same period have been discovered, none so far apparently having any connection with time-telling.

The oldest water-powered organ still in playing condition is the so-called 'Salzburg Hornwerk', also called 'Stier' (or 'bull') because of its characteristic loud chord of F–A–C included in each piece of music. Built in 1502, it was owned by Archbishop L von Kreutschach and its 350 pipes were used for only one tune, an old chorale, until the instrument aroused the interest of Leopold Mozart, father of the great Wolfgang Amadeus, in 1759. Leopold wrote a set of variations on the chorale, called the resulting piece *March,* composed further pieces, *February, May, June, July, September,* and *October,* and invited his friend Johann Ernst Eberlin to contribute tunes for the rest of the months. The pieces are still to be heard on the same instrument in Salzburg today.

The first barrel-and-pin mechanism for producing music was invented shortly after, and perhaps concomitant with, the appearance of clockwork in about 1000. This mechanism served as the heart of most types of mechanical instrument for many years, including organs, carillons, snuff-boxes, jewel-cases, sewing-boxes, and the like, until the appearance of the pneumatic drive. It may be taken that the majority of the following inventions use the barrel-and-pin principle or a variation of it.

The oldest musical clock still in working order in which the chimes are struck by an automatic man dates from 1392 and is in Wells Cathedral, Somerset. Automatic men which perform this duty are always called 'Jack'; the one at Wells is known by the name 'Jack Blandifer'.

The water-powered barrel-organ was invented at the latest in 1615 by Solomon de Caus. In 1618, Robert Fludd (known a 'Fluctibus') published designs in *De Naturae Simia* for mechanical music-makers, but no practical models are known to have been built as a result.

The first chiming watch was invented in 1686 by either Daniel Quare or Charles Clay, the court case of 1717 apparently not deciding the issue. These early chiming watches were rather bulky: a much slimmer design was possible with the invention of the helical spring gong by Julien le Roy of Paris in about 1780.

The first mechanical bird-song was invented in 1765 in France. The idea soon became popular and different styles were built into small square boxes which stood beside, or inside, canaries' cages to teach the birds to sing. The name of the device, 'Serinette', comes from the French word for canary: *serin,* but models were designed also for blackbirds, and even curlews. A later development was the imitation singing-bird made by the firm of Jaquet-Droz (father and son) in the late 18th century, in which the little birds had not only a lifelike song but also realistic movements of head and tail.

The first musical box was made by the Swiss watch-maker Antoine Favre, who re-

A sophisticated Victorian music-box (Popperfoto)

A collection of mechanical music-boxes in the Science Museum, South Kensington, London. A group of three working models: the castanet girl on the left moves her head, arms and castanets; the guitarist moves his legs, head, and while playing the guitar, winks his eye and puts his tongue out; the ballerina moves her head, arms and legs (Popperfoto)

gistered his invention on 15 February 1796 in Geneva. The barrel-and-pin arrangement was developed to a high degree of sophistication, but the resulting cylinder-and-tongue principle was the same.

The first manufactory specifically founded for making musical watches, snuff-boxes, etc, was opened in Geneva in about 1810 by Henri Capt, the Longchamps Brothers, Moise Aubert, and Pierre Rochat, following on from a cottage industry started there a few years earlier by Philippe Mayland and Isaac Piquet. It was Philippe Mayland who invented **the radial-tooth disc,** as a variation on the pinned barrel, in about 1810.

The first mechanical orchestra was the Panharmonicon, which Maelzel invented about 1811. It was designed to produce a very wide range of sounds to approach the then modern symphony orchestra of two each of flutes, oboes, clarinets, bassoons, trumpets, horns, trombones, drums, and the usual complement of strings. In 1812 Beethoven wrote for Maelzel's instrument his 'Battle of Vittoria' Symphony, Op 91, later rescoring it for live orchestra.

The 'barrel-organ' which used to be such a familiar sight and sound on the streets of London was invented by Mr Hicks of that city about 1820. It was in fact not a barrel-organ of the accepted type: basically a barrel-and-pin design, no organ pipes are involved. Leather-covered hammers strike the strings much in the manner of a pianoforte but the player has much less control over volume and 'touch' than with a conventional piano. A better name for the instrument which ironically is the best-known barrel-organ of all would be the street-piano. Prints and period films of the 19th-century London scene are rarely complete without the organ-grinder (usually apparently of Italian origin), his monkey and his cup.

The first paper-roll organs were made in 1827. These replaced the usual mechanical tracker actions with pneumatic levers, and it was found that a paper roll of indefinite length could replace the barrel with pins. Although experiments were successful and patents were secured in the 1840s in both England and France, the idea was slow to catch on, and it was

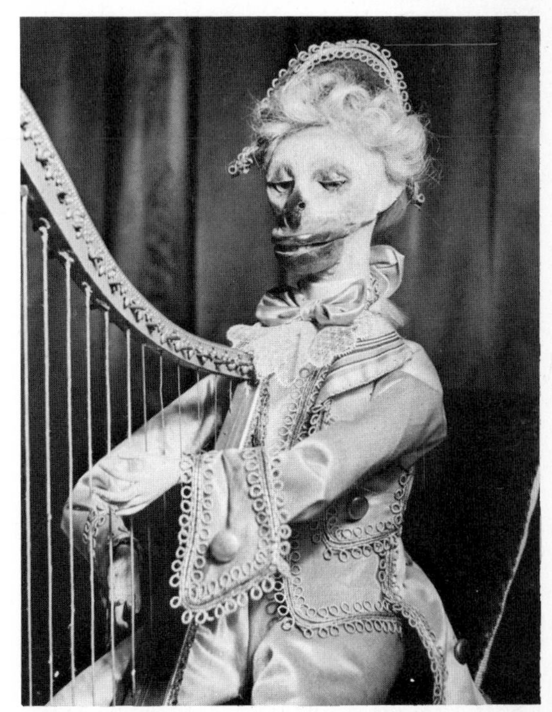

This monkey harpist was made c *1800. When wound up he runs his fingers up and down the harp; his eyes and mouth open and shut in time to the music which comes from the plush seat upon which he is sitting (Popperfoto)*

not until the appearance of the Organette in 1878 that the paper-roll model became commercially viable. The most famous makers were Mignon, Celestina, and Seraphone, all from the late 19th century.

The first musical omnibus followed the invention of that method of transport very quickly, in 1827. The presence of the vehicle was announced by an automatic coach-horn fanfare triggered off by the driver's foot. This mobile musical box was invented by Davrainville in Paris.

Musical clothing, as opposed to artefacts worn on the person such as watches, seems to have been invented in 1875. Queen Victoria was presented with a musical bustle which played the National Anthem when she sat down. Fortunately, the monarch is excused from the convention which dictates that all should rise in the presence of the royal tune; otherwise a certain amount of oscillation might have resulted.

The first pinned disc with pins affixed to one of its flat surfaces (and therefore not to be confused with the radial-tooth disc of about 1810) was invented in 1886. The inventors Ellis Pan and Paul Lochmann, working independently in London and Leipzig respectively, seem to have hit upon the idea virtually simultaneously. The English version was called the 'Symphonion', and the German 'Polyphon'. The inventors decided to pool resources and produce the Symphonion from about 1890.

The first player-pianos and organs, operated by paper rolls and pneumatic action, were invented in Freiburg-am-Breisgau by Emil Welte in 1887. Known at first as the 'Orchestrion', they sometimes were equipped with Turkish military instruments: triangle, cymbals, and bass drum.

The automatic piano-player was invented by the American E S Votey in 1897. It was an eerie machine with felt-covered fingers, and it had to be pushed up to the piano so that these fingers might play upon the keys. A later development was to incorporate the mechanism inside the piano, and this invention was called the 'Pianola'. This in turn led to the reproducing piano on which, instead of the paper roll activating the keys, a live pianist punched holes in a blank roll as he played. Grieg, Paderewski, Busoni, and other famous players of the period made paper rolls in this way which still survive. **The most famous maker of this type of instrument** was Welte-Mignon of Freiburg-am-Breisgau.

The Æolian Orchestrelle was invented about 1900. Basically a paper-roll organ, this had many additional facilities for varying the performance at the will of the operator. It was marketed by the Æolian Company of London.

The Etherophone was invented in 1924 by Leo Theremin. As the player's hand approaches the antenna a pitch sounds and rises as the hand gets nearer. The other hand operates a cut-out device to separate the successive notes if required, and a pedal controls volume. Descendants of this instrument are the Ondes Martinot (see p 42), invented by Maurice Martinot in 1928, and first used in a symphony in Koechlin's No 2; N Langer's and J Halmagyi's Emicon of about 1930, Friedrich Trautwein's Trautonium (1930), and others.

The Superpiano of 1927, invented by E Spielmann. Depression of a key operates a lamp the light of which is turned into electrical vibrations via a photocell.

The Neo-Bechstein, marketed by Bechstein of Berlin from 1931, is an electronic piano which will delay the decay of a note and even increase its intensity in a crescendo by the means of a system of eighteen microphones and an amplifier.

From this stage, and with the rise in popularity of the gramophone, the reign of mechanical musical instruments subsided until the end of the 1950s, when various mechanical organs appeared. They use the more recent invention of tape in their construction and are really sophisticated versions of the electronic organ, requiring a certain amount of skill from the performer. Recent examples are almost unbelievably complicated, with keys offering a variety of dance or march rhythms merely upon their depression, switches modifying the tones to produce imitations of orchestral instruments, further keys to give slow or rapid vibrato, and many other refinements. Such instruments have found their way into 'pop' recording studios on many occasions, and it is nowadays difficult to decide whether, for instance, a bossa nova beat is the work of a sweating rhythm group or a depressed key.

The longest electronic organ marathon was set up in February 1973 by Vincent Bull of Scunthorpe, Lincs, who established a record of 122 hr continuous playing. Some kind of sartorial record may have been set up at the same time since the musical feat was achieved in 'drag', Mr Bull being known locally as 'Vanessa'.

The most elaborate barrel-organ ever to be constructed was called the 'Apollonicon' and it was on exhibition in Regent's Park, London, between 1817 and 1840. It possessed three barrels, but could also be played manually from six consoles.

We have omitted very many inventions of merit (and otherwise) which flooded the music-shops between the wars and since. Many of these instruments have passed into history, but one still has a wide use, particularly in the lighter music fields: the Hammond Organ. Invented during the early 1930s by Laurens Hammond and marketed by his company in Chicago for the first time in 1935, it is cleverly designed so that an extremely wide variety of sounds may be obtained from a relatively small console instrument. Like the Neo-Bechstein, for instance, the Hammond Organ is not a mechanical instrument in the true sense since it requires to be played by a musician before it will make music. It is included here simply because its method of sound production (rotating wheels inducing currents which are amplified and modified electronically) differs from the acoustic mechanics of conventional instruments.

Before concluding this survey of mechanical instruments, it should be mentioned that the mechanical carillon was extremely popular in the 18th century. Handel composed for one belonging to Queen Caroline, but one of the most famous was installed in the Cathedral Tower overlooking the Market Square in Bruges, Belgium, in 1743.

COMPOSERS WHO WROTE FOR MECHANICAL INSTRUMENTS

When considering this, one must remember that many of the actual makers of the instruments concerned produced their own music while others took popular airs of their period. In this way, many operatic transcriptions have issued from piano rolls, musical-boxes, and jewel-cases without the composers being aware that their music was being put to such use.

The earliest composer specifically to write for a mechanical instrument was Peter Philips (*c* 1565–*c* 1630), the English composer who spent much of his working life on the European continent. He wrote and arranged music for the water-powered barrel-organ of Solomon de Caus. Other prominent composers who have turned their attention to mechanical instruments include:

C P E Bach: Pieces for musical clock, Wq 193/5–10.

Beethoven: The 'Battle of Vittoria' Symphony mentioned above; also a scherzo for mechanical organ.

Eberlin: The music for the Salzburg Hornwerk mentioned above; also pieces for a hydraulic organ at Heilbrunn.

Handel: Pieces for Clay's Musical Clock owned by Queen Caroline.

Haydn: His 32 Pieces for *flötenuhr* ('flute-clock') were written for clocks made in 1772, 1792, and 1793 by Father Primitivus Niemecz, Prince Esterházy's Librarian. Haydn called the instrument *laufwerk* ('barrel-work').

Hindemith: His Op 42 is incidental music for mechanical organ for the film *Felix the Cat* (1927). His works also include pieces for gramophone, pianola, and 'electric ether-wave apparatus' (Etherophone?).

L Mozart: The Salzburg Hornwerk pieces mentioned above.

W A Mozart: Including Fantasias in F minor, K 594 and 608 (1790/1) for flötenuhr.

Pieces for mechanical instruments also exist by W F Bach, H L Hassler, J M Haydn, Kirnberger, and Quantz. The modern English composer John White has shown an imaginative interest in mechanical instruments, mounting a Concert of Automata at the New Arts Laboratory, London, on 11 October 1970. The audience was encouraged to wander round the instruments, or exhibits, which included a steam kettle blowing a chord, an electric mandolin, bells being dragged along the floor, and water dripping on to a cymbal. The same composer's *C major Machine* is a work in which a steam-operated machine plays a toy piano (ignoring the black notes) in an endless series of permutations.

Composers who wrote for the player-piano

Eugene Goossens, Hindemith, Howells, Stravinsky.

Composers who imitated mechanical instruments in conventional music

Bartók: in his String Quartet No 3.
Liadov: *The Musical Snuff-box.*
Mahler: street organ imitations often play a dramatic role in his symphonies.

Mechanical imitations of musical instruments

The inventions discussed so far, although sometimes superficially similar to conventional instruments, were all conceived primarily as independent creations. A completely different category takes the real thing as a starting-point and mechanises it:

Mechanical virginals, operated by barrel-and-pin mechanism and owned by King Henry VIII in the 1540s.

Mechanical organ combined with a carillon was sent by Queen Elizabeth I to the Turkish Sultan in 1599.

Mechanical trumpeter invented by Maelzel in about 1810.

Mechanical accordion, called 'Tanzbar' ('dancing bear'), made in Germany about 1892.

Mechanical banjos and mandolins made in America about 1894 by the Wurlitzer Company. They were partly automatic, partly manual.

Mechanical violin produced about 1908 by the American Mills Novelty Company. The strings were vibrated by a circular bow which ran round the body of the instrument. Shortly afterwards the Hupfield Company in Germany constructed an entirely mechanical **string quartet:** two violins, viola, and cello.

In this connection reference must be made to probably one of the most ingenious inventors of all time who happened to turn his brilliant mind to mechanical musical instruments. He was Jacques de Vaucanson who was born in 1709 in southern France and who moved to Paris in 1735. In 1738 he astonished the French capital with a model of a man which actually played a flute by expelling air across the mouthpiece through the lips and playing a tune by stopping the holes with minute fingers. A little later Vaucanson produced an even more complicated model of a fife-drummer which blew on a pipe and beat a drum simultaneously. Later still Vaucanson was involved in the development of weaving machines, but his most famous piece, his greatest work of genius, was the mechanical duck of 1738. Apart from the lifelike cry of the duck, this machine has no connection with the main subject of this book which deals in sounds, but the Vaucanson duck is so famous and so remarkable that a few words about it should be said.

At a demonstration in Paris, the inventor, who had claimed that his toy duck would eat, drink, quack, and paddle in water, proved that it did all these things and more in an extraordinarily lifelike manner, so much so that some of the audience suspected trickery involving the use of a live bird. At a touch from Vaucanson, the duck would raise its head, survey the scene, quack a few times and stretch its wings. The feathers on the wings and tail were attached and hinged separately in such a way that all the movements of the bird were incredibly lifelike. Treating the startled watchers to a few more cries, the bird would then perform what for many was a feat of magic for a machine: it would eat from a pile of grain, drink water from a bowl, and–excrete waste matter from a standing position. The only lifelike function which the model appeared not to be able to perform was that of flight; if Vaucanson had conquered this particular problem, as no doubt he tried, he might well have gone on to secure for himself an honoured place in the sister publication: *The Guinness Book of Air Facts and Feats.*

RECORDED SOUNDS

Today the best-known type of mechanical music-making is the gramophone record, alongside which, and gradually growing in prominence, is the pre-recorded tape. The record began humbly in the late 19th century as an aid to office dictation, but its usefulness as a home-entertainment commodity was quickly realised while its business use faded out, ironically to be brought back in the mid 20th century as an offshoot of the domestic product.

For 120 years the record has undergone an almost continuous process of gradual improvement, the progress of which may best be illustrated by the following chronology, which details other important events surrounding this amazing growth.

1857 Leon Scott built a device which he called 'phonautograph'. It registered movements made by a vibrating body on to a smoked cylinder.

1877 The phonograph invented by Thomas Edison. A foil coating stretched round a cylinder was engraved with a stylus. In June of that year, Lillie Moulton (*née* Greenough and later Hagermann-Lindencrone), the singer born in Cambridge, Mass, wrote: 'There is also another invention called phonograph, where the human voice is reproduced, and can go on forever being reproduced. I sung in one through a horn and they transposed this on a platina roll and wound it off. . . . The intonation–the pronunciation–I could recognise as my own, but the *voice*–dear me!'

Edison's historic 'Mary Had a Little Lamb' was the **first piece of poetry ever to be recorded;** Mrs Moulton's was **the first song.** Edison's invention was patented on 19 February 1878 (patent No 200 521).

Charles Cros working independently in Paris, proposed a very similar invention utilising a disc instead of a cylinder, but Cros's gadget was probably never built.

Thomas Edison in his study (Popperfoto)

1884 Emile Berliner recorded 'The Lord's Prayer' on a cylinder now preserved in the BBC Record Library. This is **the oldest surviving gramophone record.**

1886 Patent (No 341 214) taken out for a cylinder in which a wax coating replaced the foil.

1887 The gramophone invented by Berliner. Patent taken out for **the first disc:** glass, coated with lamp-black.

The first record company founded: North American Phonograph Company, on 14 July.

1890 **First recording studios** set up on Fifth Avenue, New York, by the New York Phonograph Company.

1891 **First record catalogue** produced by Columbia Phonograph Company. It was ten pages in length.

1897 **First operatic arias recorded** in Milan.

1898 **First UK record company,** The Gramophone Company, was established in Maiden Lane in London. Deutsche Grammophon Gesellschaft in Hanover.

The Gramophone Company, Maiden Lane, London, in 1898 (EMI)

Enrico Caruso (Radio Times Hulton Picture Library)

The telegraphone, forerunner of the tape recorder, invented by Valdemar Poulsen of Denmark using steel wire and tape.

1899 **First factory devoted exclusively to the production of gramophone records** was set up in Hanover. It had fourteen presses and produced discs of 12·7 cm (5 in) and 17·8 cm (7 in) diameter.

First French record company established in May: Compagnie Française du Gramophone, in Paris.

Painting by Francis Barraud, **His Master's Voice,** was modified by the artist (replacing its cylinder with a disc) and bought by The Gramophone Company and in time became **the most famous trade-mark in the world.** The painting was taken from life: the dog's name was Nipper, and a memorial plaque was placed over his grave in Eden Street, Kingston-upon-Thames by The Gramophone Company in 1949.

1900 A catalogue of 5000 recordings published by The Gramophone Company. **Paper labels introduced** (hitherto, the record contents were scratched into the centre wax by hand), with black print on a red background.

The first 25·4 cm (10 in) discs made. The Gramophone and Typewriter Company founded.

1901 International Zonophone Company and the Victor Talking Machine Company founded.

1902 **March 18: first Caruso recordings made. First Melba records issued,** with a

One of the most famous trade-marks in the world heading a 'His Master's Voice' advertisement, May 1923

specially designed 'Melba' label **First Gramophone Company Red Label catalogue issued,** consisting entirely of operatic artists with one exception: Jan Kubelik, the violinist. It is worth mentioning at this point a curious development in instrument-building: in order to amplify the tone to assist recording, the Stroh-violin (and other stringed instruments) was developed in London. In this design, the soundbox of the instrument is replaced by a diaphragm and trumpet. Later designs used a microphone and loudspeaker, with a pedal to control the volume.

1903 First complete opera recording: Verdi's *Ernani* by Italian HMV, issued on 40 single-sided discs.

1904 First record company to be devoted entirely to serious music: Societá Italiana di Fonotipia.

1905 First recordings of chamber music (isolated movements by Mendelssohn and Schumann). **First double-sided discs** issued by German Odeon.

1906 First console gramophone, the Victrola, 1·22 m (4 ft) high and with a downward-pointing horn.

1907 Dame Nellie Melba laid the foundation-stone of HMV factory at Hayes, Middlesex.

1909 First recording of a complete symphony: Beethoven's No 5 in C minor, with the Berlin Philharmonic Orchestra conducted by Arthur Nikitsch.

Dame Nellie Melba lays the foundation stone of the HMV factory at Hayes, Middlesex, in 1907 (EMI)

1912 The last cylinder records produced, except for a small output destined for underdeveloped American areas.

1913 The Decca portable gramophone introduced.

1917 First jazz recordings: 'Canary Cottage', by the Frisco Jazz Band, featuring saxophonist Rudy Wiedoeft, recorded 10 May and issued on cylinder: Edison Blue Amberol 3241; 'Darktown Strutters' Ball'/'Indiana', by the Original Dixieland Jazz Band, recorded 30 January, and issued 31 May on Columbia A-2297.

1918 First vocal refrain on a dance record: 'Mary', sung by Harry Macdonough, Charles Hart, and Lewis James, with Joseph C Smith's Orchestra, recorded in New York on 29 July and issued in November on Victor 18500 (USA), and in October 1920 in the UK on HMV B-1100.

1919 The first jazz record to be released in the UK: 'At the Jazz Band Ball'/'Barnyard Blues', by the Original Dixieland Jazz Band, recorded on 16 April and released on Columbia 735.

1920 First experiments with electrical recording.

The first million-seller was Paul Whiteman and his Ambassador Orchestra playing 'The Japanese Sandman' and 'Whispering'. issued in November on Victor 18690 and in UK in January 1921 on HMV B-1160.

First English recording of a dance band with vocal refrain was 'Puck-a-Pu', sung by Eric Courtland (pseudonym of Ernest Pike), with the Mayfair Dance Orchestra conducted by George W Byng, recorded at Hayes, Middlesex on 9 November and issued the following February. (There were various other records made with vocal chorus effects prior to the above, especially in England by the Savoy Quartet on HMV, but these were more in the nature of 'novelty' groups where the star performer was a vocalist who also played one of the two banjos used.)

1923 First magazine devoted to gramophone records: *The Gramophone,* founded by Sir Compton Mackenzie. **First royal**

Two gramophone record advertisements published in the magazine The Gramophone, *May 1923 (General Gramophone Publications)*

recording made by King George V and Queen Mary at Buckingham Palace.

1924 The smallest functional gramophone record, of which 250 copies were pressed, was made by HMV. It was 3·5 cm ($1\frac{3}{8}$ in) diameter and contained a performance of 'God Save the King'.

1925 First electrical recordings issued: 'Adeste Fideles' by a 4850-strong choir at the Metropolitan Opera House, New York; Tchaikovsky: Symphony No 4 in F minor, by the Royal Albert Hall Orchestra conducted by Sir Landon Ronald. *Joan of Arkensaw,* by the Mask and Wig Club Orchestra and Double Male Quartet, recorded in New York on 16 March (issued on Victor 19626); 'Feelin' Kind o' Blue' by Jack Hylton and his Orchestra with vocal refrain by Jack Hylton, recorded in Hayes on 24 June (issued on HMV B-2072). (One title made electrically immediately prior to this, on the same session, was never issued; it was called

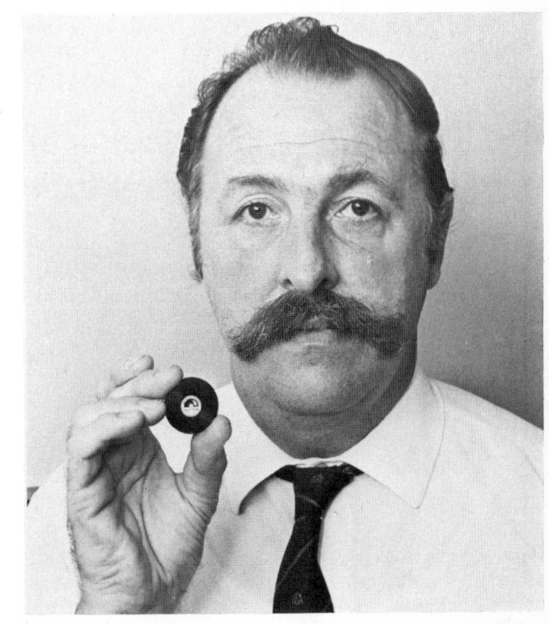

*The smallest functional gramophone record (*Evening Argus, *Brighton)*

'Ah-Ha!'). **First location recording** was made in the Arcadia Ballroom, Detroit, on the night of 29 January, in the presence of some 5000 dancers, by Finzel's Arcadia Orchestra of Detroit, and issued on OKeh 40298. The title was 'Laff it Off', and the vocalist was Charlotte Meyers.

1927 First disc-jockey: Christopher Stone. Ernest Lough recorded 'Oh, For the Wings of a Dove'/'Hear My Prayer', one of the most popular classical discs of all time.

1928 First serious piece of music to be issued on disc before being heard in live performance was Kurt Atterburg's Symphony No 6. It was written to commemorate Schubert's centenary, and with it the composer won a £2000 prize offered for the occasion by the Columbia Gramophone Company.

1929 Decca Gramophone Company launched in February. It grew out of the musical instrument makers Barnett Samuel and Sons Ltd, and took its name from the Decca portable gramophone of 1914.

1931 HMV and Columbia joined forces in March to produce Electrical and Musical Industries (EMI). HMV issued **the first Society issues** (dependent upon prior subscription: the first was the Hugo Wolf Song Society). **First experiments in long-playing records.** The first recording sessions made at 33⅓ rpm specifically for LP were: Classical and semi-classical: Victor L 24000, recorded 21 May and issued later that year, made by the Victor Concert Orchestra. The titles included:
MacDowell: 'To a Wild Rose'
Brahms: 'Lullaby'
Beethoven: Minuet in G
Léhar: 'Vilja', from *The Merry Widow*
Gossec: Gavotte.

Sir Edward Elgar conducting 'The Symphony Orchestra' in the HMV Recording Laboratory at Hayes in the early 1930s (EMI)

1932 LP experiments continued with a jazz record: Victor L 16007, recorded New York 9 February by Duke Ellington and his Orchestra. The titles were: 'East St Louis Toodle-Oo'; 'Lots o' Fingers'; 'Black and Tan Fantasy'. (Other jazz LPs appeared at the same time but were composed of dubbings of existing 78s. The first jazz LPs in UK were entirely of dubbings from 78s of various ages and no jazz made specifically for LP seems to have been issued until some considerable time had elapsed after Decca's launch of LP in the UK in June 1950.) The 1931–32 LPs were close-grooved shellac pressings.

1933 First stereo discs made experimentally by EMI after a process designed by A D Blumlein of that Company. The method used was that finally chosen in refined form for the first commercial release of stereo discs 25 years later.

1938 Cellulose acetate tape developed for recording music.

1939 Decca enters the field of navigational aids.

1940 The first purchase tax levied on gramophone records: 33⅓ per cent. Decca introduced 'ffrr' records made after a new process designed by Arthur Haddy (ffrr = 'full frequency range recording').

1941 First public jam session recording took place in the EMI studios, Abbey Road, St John's Wood, London, on the afternoon of Sunday, 16 November, organised by *The Melody Maker*. Four items from the considerable number played were issued in January 1942 as follows:

25·4 cm (10 in) HMV B-9249 'Tea For Two'.
25·4 cm (10 in) HMV B-9250 'St Louis Blues'.
30·5 cm (12 in) HMV C-3269 'Honeysuckle Rose'/'I've Found a New Baby'.

1942 First golden disc was one sprayed by RCA Victor for presentation to bandleader and trombonist Glenn Miller on 10 February to commemorate the success of his 'Chattanooga Choo-Choo'.

1948 First vinyl records released in America on 21 June. The research which led to their release was headed by Dr Peter Goldmark of the Columbia Broadcasting System Research Laboratories, at which he was in charge of the development of colour television. The gestation of LP took three years (building upon the principles of the early experiments of 1932) and cost $250 000' Disc sizes were 25·4 cm (10 in) and 30·5 cm (12 in); speed 33⅓ rpm.

1949 First 17·8 cm (7 in) 45 rpm discs issued in January by RCA in America.

1950 First LPs issued in the UK in June by Decca.

1951 First public demonstration of 'stereosonic' (later stereophonic) **tapes** by EMI.

1952 First UK release of 45 rpm 17.8 cm (7 in) discs by HMV in October; EMI also announced their first 33⅓ long-playing discs in the same month.

1953 Philips Electrical Industries of Holland entered the record-producing market.

1954 First releases of Deutsche Grammophon records (Archive Series) in UK.

1958 First stereo records introduced in the UK by Pye Group Records in June. Decca and EMI followed later the same year. First LP of any kind to reach 1 000 000 sales was the original cast recording of *My Fair Lady*, issued by Philips in May. First classical record to reach 1 000 000 sales was issued by RCA in America and the UK: Tchaikovsky's Piano Concerto No 1 in B flat minor, played by the winner of the first International Tchaikovsky Competition held in Moscow in April of that year: Van Cliburn, with an orchestra conducted by Kiril Kondrashin.

1959 First magazine tape cassettes issued by the Garrard Engineering and Mechanical Co, Ltd, in September. These magazines, using standard 6·3 mm (¼ in) tape at a playing speed of 3¾ ips were the ancestors of the modern cassette.

1963 First tape cassette with 3.2 mm (⅛ in) recording at 1⅞ ips announced by Philips Electrical at the Berlin Audio Show.

1965 First pre-recorded cassettes announced at Eindhoven, Holland, by Philips in November. Launch of the tape cartridge, primarily for in-car entertainment.

1966 Invention of the Dolby noise-reduction system, developed by Dr R Dolby of Dolby Laboratories Ltd. This 'stretching' process, whereby the background surface 'mush' of the tape is lowered electronically to below audible range, revolutionised the quality available from tape. When applied to the cassette format for the first time in 1970 it brought the quality of the 'compact cassette' up to a level at which it could compete with the stereo disc.

1966/67 American disc sales during this winter season for the first time exceeded $1 000 000 000.

1971 First quadraphonic discs issued in America in October; the first UK issues took place the following April.

Long Playing

In the foregoing chronology it was noted that the first experiments with long-playing discs occurred in 1931 but the first commercially successful vinyl discs appeared in 1948. The average side-length in 1948, and still regarded as standard, is about 25 minutes, but owing to sophisticated cutting techniques this time-limit has been increased on many records.

The longest long-playing record is CBS Classics 61089, containing the complete Slavonic Dances of Dvořák, the total (two sides) playing time of which is 73 min 5 sec. In the late 1950s, the American Vox Company issued some discs to revolve at 16⅔ rpm, theoretically giving double the playing time of the standard 33⅓ rpm disc, but these met with little success due to the reduction of quality brought about by the slow linear speed; spoken-word discs had rather more success. On the Japanese market are to be found 33⅓ rpm discs with up to 45 min *per side*, and coupling works of the length of Beethoven's 7th Symphony and Tchaikovsky's 'Pathètique' Symphony, but they have not so far been made available in the West.

The golden disc awarded to Bing Crosby by the Hollywood Chamber of Commerce for his Decca recording of 'White Christmas'

Other facts of the record industry

The most successful recording artist (solo) is Bing Crosby. On 9 June 1960 the Hollywood Chamber of Commerce presented him with a platinum disc to commemorate a sale of 200000000 records from the 2600 singles and 125 albums he has recorded. On 15 September 1970 he received a second platinum disc for selling 300 650 000 discs with Decca. His global lifetime sales on 88 labels in 28 countries have totalled, according to his royalty reports, 365000000. His first commercial recording was 'I've Got the Girl', recorded on 18 October 1926, issued on Columbia.

The earliest recorded work to sell 1000000 copies was 'Vesti la giubba,' ('On With the Motley') from Leoncavallo's *I Pagliacci,* performed by Enrico Caruso and first recorded by him on 12 November 1902.

The most often recorded songs are 'St Louis Blues' by W C Handy (written in 1914) and 'Stardust' by Hoagy Carmichael (written in 1927). Each has been recorded between 900 and 1000 times.

The busiest recording artist is Miss Lata Mangeshker who, between 1948 and 1974, has recorded at least 25000 solo, duet, and chorus-backed songs in 20 Indian languages. She frequently has five recording sessions per day and has 'backed' 1800 films.

Best-Selling LPs

1958 'Sing We Now of Christmas' (20th Century Fox), renamed 'The Little Drummer Boy' in 1963. Sales to November 1972: 14000000.

Tchaikovsky's Piano Concerto No 1, played by Van Cliburn, is the top-selling classical LP, reaching a total of 2500000 sales by January 1970.

1963 November: *With the Beatles* (Parlophone) sold 1000000 in the USA up to January 1964, and 1000000 in the UK up to September 1965.

John Fitzgerald Kennedy–A Memorial Album (Premium) sold 4000000 copies in its first six days (7–12 December 1963).

Miss Lata Mangeshker

1965 *The Sound of Music* (RCA Victor) is an **all-time best-seller of musical film shows,** with UK and USA sales totalling 19000000 to 1 January 1973.

1970 October: *Jesus Christ Superstar,* **the best-selling UK LP** (four-sided double-album), the sales of which are about 6000000.

Massive Recording Projects

The longest LP set is the Argo recording of the *Complete Works of William Shakespeare* on 137 double-sided discs, made in 1957–64. The next largest recording project was the complete symphonies of Haydn. This task has been carried out twice, by the Musical Heritage Society (USA) and by Decca (UK). The Musical Heritage Society series, made by the Vienna Chamber Orchestra under Ernst Maerzendorfer, was completed on 49 discs early in 1972, and offered on subscription in the USA; the Decca issues with the Philharmonia Hungarica under Antal Dorati on 48 discs were completed in September 1974. The Dorati is the 'bigger' project (despite its two fewer LP sides) because it includes complete recordings of alternative versions of two symphonies, whereas the Musical Heritage series incorporates these alternatives as 'conflations'.

The Quest for High Fidelity

High Fidelity ('Hi-Fi' for short) has been the aim of technicians involved in sound reproduction almost from the start, but the term itself has gained prominence only since the Second World War. Hi-Fi may be defined as an attempt to reproduce from the speaker(s) a sound as near as possible in quality to that reaching the microphone(s) in the recording studio. The fact that it cannot be measured, and cannot, therefore, be defined other than subjectively has meant that unscrupulous manufacturers may emblazon their electronic products with the legend 'High Fidelity' without fear of prosecution under the British Trades Descriptions Act (1968), and other controls elsewhere, no matter how far from the original sound the results from their products may be.

In the following chart the authors' own subjective impressions have been brought to bear on a graph giving the successive steps attained by manufacturers in the ascent to 'the closed approach to the original sound'. The graph should be used in conjunction with the foregoing chronological chart.

It is possible that the gradual rise in software quality will increase during the coming years: there are, furthermore, strong rumours that a 'breakthrough' in Hi-Fi, and in particular in the manufacture and permanence of software, is imminent, and this will be paralleled by a similar revolution in the design and manufacture of playing equipment. At this stage it is possible to hint only at the demise of the record-playing stylus in favour of the laser beam, and the banishment of signal-carrying wires in favour of radio waves; also that the days of the loudspeaker, as we know it, are numbered in hundreds rather than thousands. In short, it is foreseen that audio equipment in the 1980s will be totally different in design and appearance from what we are used to.

THE QUEST FOR HIGH FIDELITY—
A SUBJECTIVE IMPRESSION

degree of fidelity
100%
90%
80%
70%
60%
50%
40%
30%
20%
10%

KEY
Cylinder
78 rpm disc
Long playing disc (33⅓ rpm)
pre-recorded tape
cassette

quad
stereo disc
Dolby
ffrr
electrical recording

1877 1890 1900 1910 1920 1930 1940 1950 1960 1970 1980

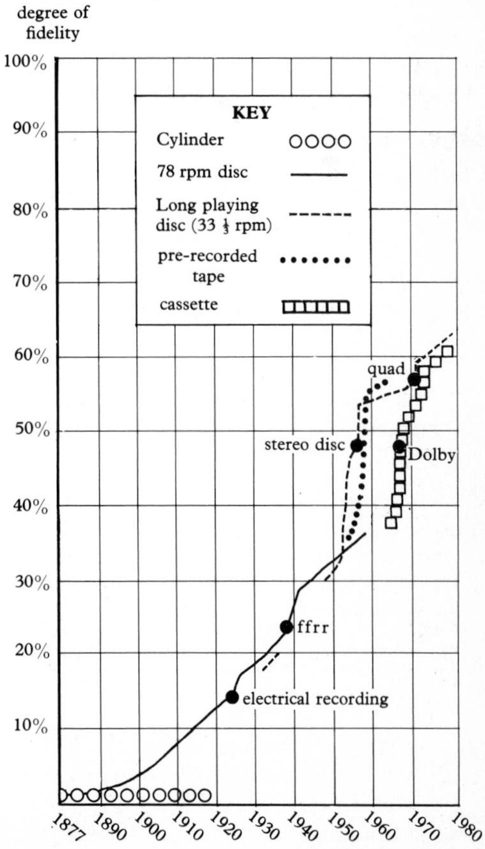

RADIO

In addition to records and tape, direct broadcasting has fulfilled an important role in the broadcasting of music.

The earliest form of mechanical music broadcasting was devised in 1873. In that year a contrivance in the form of a tent with pipes was invented by L J Lefèbre in Holland. Called the 'Kiosk Hollandia', it was designed to convey the sound of the orchestra, via a subterranean pipeline, acoustically 'to great distances'. The music, performed in the tent, was in some manner thrown downwards into the mouth(s) of the pipe(s). Reports at the time promulgated by the manufacturers F J Weygard were in favour of the contraption, some even going so far as to say that the quality of the musical sound issuing from the far end of the tube was an improvement on the original.

The following brief chronological list gives important events in the history of music broadcasting.

1920 February: first public broadcasting station opened by the Marconi Company near Chelmsford, England.

15 June: Dame Nellie Melba became **the first radio artist** when she broadcast from the Marconi Company studios. This was **the first music broadcast in and from England.**

15 September: the first American broadcast by a dance band was given by Paul Spech and his Orchestra.

1922 The British Broadcasting Company formed (British Broadcasting Corporation from 1927).

1923 8 January: the first opera to be broadcast was Mozart's *Die Zauberflöte,* given by the British National Opera Company from Covent Garden.

26 February: the first British broadcast by a dance band was given by Marius B Winter and his Orchestra.

1927 July: the first disc-jockey, Christopher Stone, began a series of programmes of one hour every Friday lunchtime on 2LO from Savoy Hill, London.

1946 November: the BBC opened the Third Programme designed specifically for the performance of serious music, drama, and 'educational' programmes.

A Radio Hoax

The chaotic aspect of much modern music led to an interesting experiment, and the perpetration of a triple musical hoax by Dr Hans Keller of the BBC. On 5 June 1961 a concert was broadcast in which one of the works was *Mobile* for percussion and tape by Pyotr Zak. Later in the same programme the work was given again, as is sometimes done with new works with which it is anticipated that the audience will have difficulties of comprehension. Criticisms of Mr Zak's work were written by the noted critics Donald Mitchell and Jeremy Noble: each found the *Mobile* to be a poor work.

It was later announced that the broadcast had been a hoax. Hans Keller, whose idea it was, explained that the work came about when he and Susan Bradshaw (another member of the BBC Music Department) had wandered round a studio hitting various percussion instruments at random. One microphone was set aside in a corner and attached to an echo chamber for the production of mock electronic sounds. The second performance, later in the same programme, was carried out in the same way, without any reference to the effects produced in the earlier one, and neither was rehearsed in any way. The work was, therefore, a three-way hoax: there was no Pyotr Zak; there were no percussion-players (although perhaps Dr Keller is here underestimating his colleague and himself); and there was no tape. Furthermore, the 'repeat' was merely another impromptu performance.

For a broadcast on Sunday, 13 August 1961, more than two months after the original programme, the critics were invited to discuss this odd hoax with its creator, and it was during this discussion that the reason for the experiment emerged. Apparently, Dr Keller viewed current musical events less than enthusiastically and set out quite deliberately to fool the audience and critics into thinking that they were hearing a new work. The critics were not trapped into believing the work to be good, but they were fooled into taking it seriously. Dr Keller's point was that it was only in the musical climate of that time that such a hoax could be possible, and 'to enquire how far a non-work could be taken for a work'. In the time of Mozart, he explained, any attempt to pass off random noise as music would have been discovered immediately; it could never have been taken seriously, as had the *Mobile*. It might be considered that Dr Keller went to extreme lengths to prove the self-evident fact that music of Mozart's time was organised along stricter lines than music of the mid 20th century.

TELEVISION

Television has proved less successful for serious music broadcasts, but has nevertheless been active in the field.

The first opera ever televised was Act III (only) of Gounod's *Faust* by the BBC in June 1937.

The first TV opera was Menotti's *Amahl and the Night Visitors* (1952); since then there have been several operas designed primarily for the small screen, among them Britten's *Owen Wingrave* (1971) and R Murray-Schafer's *Loving/Toi* (1965) which incorporates advanced production and musical techniques.

The longest-serving TV Musical Director is Bert Hayes of Margate, Kent. He has been in charge of music on TV since the early post-war days of the medium, acting as musical director for series such as 'Crackerjack', 'Lennie the Lion', 'Whistle Stop', and 'Hopscotch', and has been associated with series starring Michael Bentine, Basil Brush, David Nixon, and Shari Wallis.

ELECTRONIC MUSIC AND MUSIQUE CONCRÈTE

It may be necessary for the benefit of some readers to begin by defining these terms, especially now that the origins are obscured by time and the two separate streams have merged.

Musique Concrète: the techniques

Literally, this is music composed of concrete, or natural, as opposed to manufactured, sounds. The real sounds which form its basis are modified electronically, sometimes to the point at which they cease to bear any relation whatever to the original. For instance (see diagram p. 275) a single note played forte on a piano (A) might be recorded and then the tape containing that note manipulated. The initial attack of the note might be removed (B); the reverberation might be extended enormously beyond its natural length, perhaps with alterations to the volume intensity during its length (C); or the natural fall of the volume might be copied and recopied endlessly and segments of the decay placed end to end to form a series of recurring fades, like a shallow saw-tooth edge (D); certain frequencies among the harmonics might be filtered out or exaggerated (E), or the basic sound itself removed to leave only the upper partials (F); pitch might be varied upwards or downwards, or both (G); the initial attack of the note (which we may have removed, remember) might be copied and repeated without its decay (H); any one of these possibilities might be played backwards (J) and/or combined with any others (K), and so on.

These examples by no means exhaust the possibilities of manipulation from just one piano note: imagine the world of sound available to a musique concrète composer with a whole keyboard at his disposal. But these composers need not stop at the piano, or at musical instruments in general. Any natural sound whatsoever, whether man-produced (factory whistle; car engine; spinning top, etc) or natural (animal noises, thunder, sea waves, etc) might be taken and manipulated at the composer's discretion, the only limit being his imagination. The greatest skill seems to be in obtaining the widest spectrum of sounds from the least varied sound sources.

Electronic music: the techniques

This music is likely to appeal more to the purist. No natural sounds are used at all in pure electronic music; every sound is produced electronically from sine waves generated by oscillators. Once recorded on to tape these sine waves may be subjected to manipulation similar to that in musique concrète, but modification of the waves themselves is often inflicted via the controls of the oscillator before recording takes place. Once again extremely wide spectrums of sound are at the disposal of the composer, and as in the case of the composer of musique concrète the results are often of a complexity and dramatic variety not obtainable from conventional instruments.

Shortly after the Second World War, when these two types of music experimentation were still forming into distinct lines of development, the composers collaborated to a certain extent (Stockhausen worked in Paris with Pierre Schaeffer, for instance). By the early 1950s, however, the lines were fully separated, only to come together again later to their mutual advantage. The techniques of electronic composition have progressed so far today that they have outstripped those of the more laborious-to-make musique concrète, and the latter term, apart from certain small cliques which regard the technique as a hobby rather than a viable musical form of expression of future significance, has dropped out of use. Electronic composers may, and do, employ 'concrete' sounds in their quest for sources, but the moulding of these sources is carried out strictly according to electronic music principles. An example is *Relativity,* produced in the BBC Radiophonic Workshop by Lily Greenham (realised by Richard Yeoman-Clark and Peter Howell), and first broadcast on 18 April 1975, in which the basic sound sources are words spoken by actors and then manipulated and juxtaposed electronically.

Musique Concrète: the history

The origins of musique concrète may be said to have begun many years before the introduction of the term itself. The Futurist movement led by Luigi Russolo was working towards the principles of musique concrète and electronic music, ie *away* from the production of music by traditional instruments, but Russolo and his followers still 'played' their instruments according to a score, even though the skills required in playing them seemed to be restricted to those of handle-turning and button-pressing. A few words of explanation are called for.

Balilla Pratella wrote an orchestral work entitled *Musica Futuristica* in 1912. In this piece, Pratella incorporated naïve and banal ideas in an attempt, apparently, to get away from the ever-more complex musical designs of the Late Romantics. This work caught the attention of Russolo, who felt that standard orchestral instruments were unsuitable for the kind of machine-like effects at which Pratella was aiming. Russolo invented an entirely new type of orchestra in 1913, which he called the 'Futurist Orchestra'. Its 'instruments' were machines which generated whistles, hisses, buzzes, and explosions: some were electrically driven, others produced their noise by the turn of a handle. Russolo tried out the first of his noise machines, or 'intonarumori', on 2 June 1913. It was called 'scoppiatore' ('exploder'). In less than a year he had invented and built eighteen more instruments, and in Milan on 21 March 1914 he gave **the first Noise Concert.** The instruments which appeared included *crepitatori* ('cracklers'), *gorgogliatori ('bubblers' or 'gurglers'), rombatori* ('roarers'), *ronzatori* ('buzzers'), *sibilatori* ('hissers'), *stropicciatori* ('rubbers' or 'scrapers'), *ululatori* ('howlers'), and of course the *scoppiatori.* The titles of the works performed, all by Russolo, included *Dawn in the City, Gathering of Aircraft and Automobiles,* and *Battle at the Oasis.* Reports suggest that the weird noises of the machines produced a scene similar to that created at the Paris première of Stravinsky's *Rite of Spring:* the audience made more noise than the performers. Nevertheless, further Noise Concerts were given in many different countries, and the noise-making movement received the attention and a certain amount of verbal support from Stravinsky, Milhaud, Honegger, Varèse, and Ravel, but the only composer outside Russolo's immediate circle to write music to include *intonarumori* was Pratella, whose opera *L'Aviatore Dro* (1915) placed them alongside conventional instruments in the orchestra pit.

Russolo was heartened by the interest, if not by any measure of public acclaim, with which his concerts were received, and he went on to build his most ambitious machine in 1920, a noise-organ called 'Russolofono'.

Unfortunately, the movement passed all too completely into history. Russolo himself seems to have lost interest after a few years, the instruments he took so much trouble to make have disappeared completely, and only one record of *intonarumori* was made: *Chorale* and *Serenata* (HMV R 6919) by Luigi Russolo and

A visual representation of the sound possibilities available from a single pianoforte note using Musique Concrète techniques.

A. A pianoforte note. Vertical measurement approximates to range; thickness of line to sound amplitude.

B. The same note deprived of its initial attack.

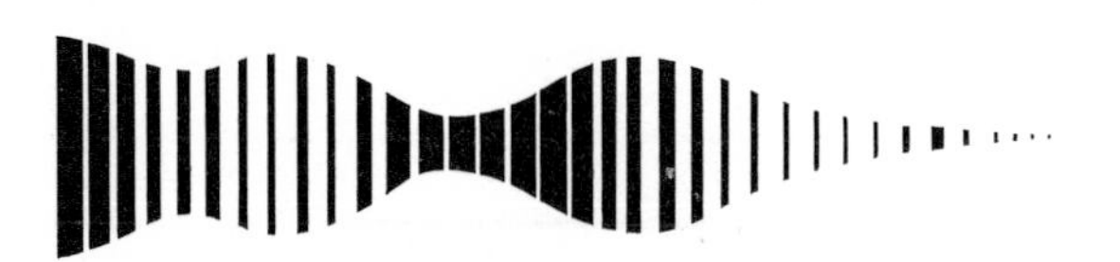

C. The same note, minus attack, but with its decay extended in duration and modified in amplitude and range.

D. The natural fall of the note copied and repeated.

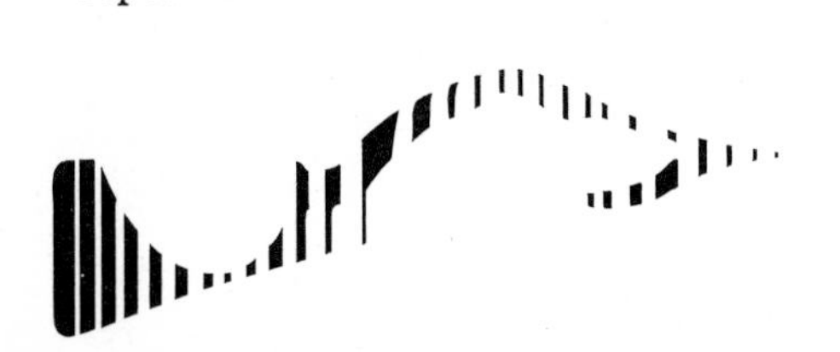

E. The original note with segments of sound filtered out or amplified.

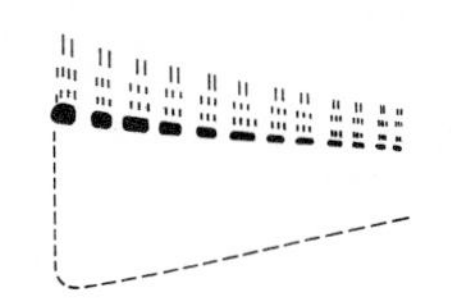

F. The original note filtered out altogether, leaving only the upper partials and harmonics.

G. The original note with pitch variations added to the extended decay.

H. The initial attack of the note repeated in quick succession.

J. A manipulated example (in this case D) played backwards.

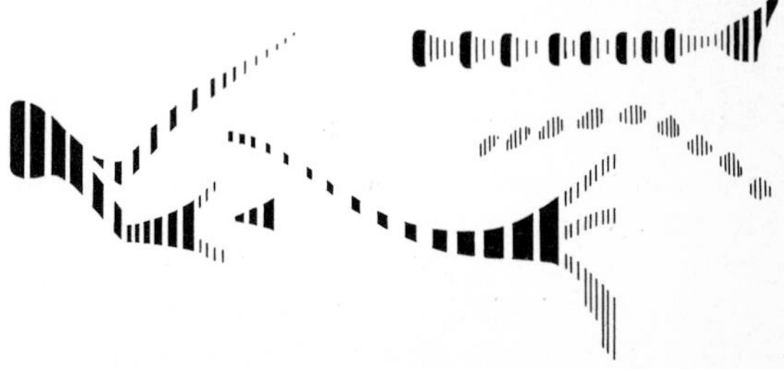

K. An imaginative combination of the above manipulations.

his brother Arturo in 1921. Furthermore, virtually all the music, which was written in an easily understood modification of standard score-writing, has vanished, only seven bars of the opening of *Dawn in the City* surviving.

The next step towards musique concrète was an uncanny mixture of that technique and electronic music: in 1939 John Cage wrote *Imaginary Landscape I* which is a blend of sine waves recorded onto 78 rpm discs.

The first use of the term 'musique concrète' was by Pierre Schaeffer in 1948, when he founded the Groupe de Recherches Musicales at the ORTF studios in Paris. Out of the numerous experiments, **the first work to appear in the new form** was his *Whirligig Study,* made without the aid of a tape recorder and using the sound from a whistling top, recorded on to 78 rpm discs using the 'closed groove', or repeating groove, method. Sound-mixing was carried out with the use of mutliple pick-ups and turntables. Many works were created in this way, but it will be realised that, without the permanence offered by a tape recorder, every performance would be subject to variations and the successful realisation of planned effects would often be a matter of luck.

The Phonogène was invented by Pierre Henry in 1950. This device, based on a complicated principle utilising revolving tape *record* and *playback* heads, enabled composers to alter the speed at which a sound source is recorded.

Pierre Schaeffer's associates who also produced their own works in the early days of musique concrète were Pierre Henry, Philippe Arthuys, and Michel Philippot.

The first recordings of musique concrète were issued by Ducretet Thompson in France in 1955 (DUC 6; DUC 9) and in England the following year (DTL 93090; DTL 93121); they contained pieces by all the composers mentioned above.

Electronic music: the history

It might be claimed that all musique concrète is electronic music since it depends upon electronic apparatus to bring it to performance. As explained above, pure electronic music is that in which the sound sources are made entirely by oscillators, but the earliest steps towards this state were taken in the musique concrète studios of the ORTF in Paris by various assistants and associates of Pierre Schaeffer. Gradually the two movements split apart.

The first studio for the production of electronic music was founded in Cologne by Dr Herbert Eimert in 1951 with the assistance of Cologne Radio. Among those who experimented with the primitive equipment then available were Friedrich Trautwein, Robert Beyer, Meyer-Eppler, Gottfried Michael König, Ernest Křenek, Karlheinz Stockhausen, and Herbert Eimert himself.

The first broadcast of electronic music, in which many of these composers took part, was transmitted on 15 October 1951 by Cologne Radio, but there had been one or two broadcast talks concerning the subject prior to this. **The first record of electronic music** to be issued was a transcript of this broadcast, made available to a limited circle shortly afterwards.

The first commercially issued discs of electronic music were made at the Cologne Studios and issued by Deutsche Grammophon Gesellschaft: they were 25·4 cm (10 in) discs (LP 16132, 16133, and 16134, later to be renumbered as LPE 17242, 17243, and 17244) and appeared in Germany in 1954 and in Britain in 1959. They included music by Křenek, Eimert, König, and Stockhausen. The last-named composer has made the claim that his *Electronic Study I* (on LP 16132) was the first work to make use entirely of sounds generated from sine waves, but its date (1953) seems to put it slightly later than other experiments in the field. That work was, however, undeniably **the earliest electronic work to be issued in a commercial recording.**

Recent developments include the use of electronic music, both taped and live (see below) in conjunction with traditional musicians and instruments.

The longest tape composition is the confusingly titled *Memories of the Future,* Op 79 (1972) by Geoffrey Sentinella, which lasts twelve hours.

Computer Music

The recent history of electronic music has seen a widening of its scope, not only by the admission of 'concrète' sound sources as a

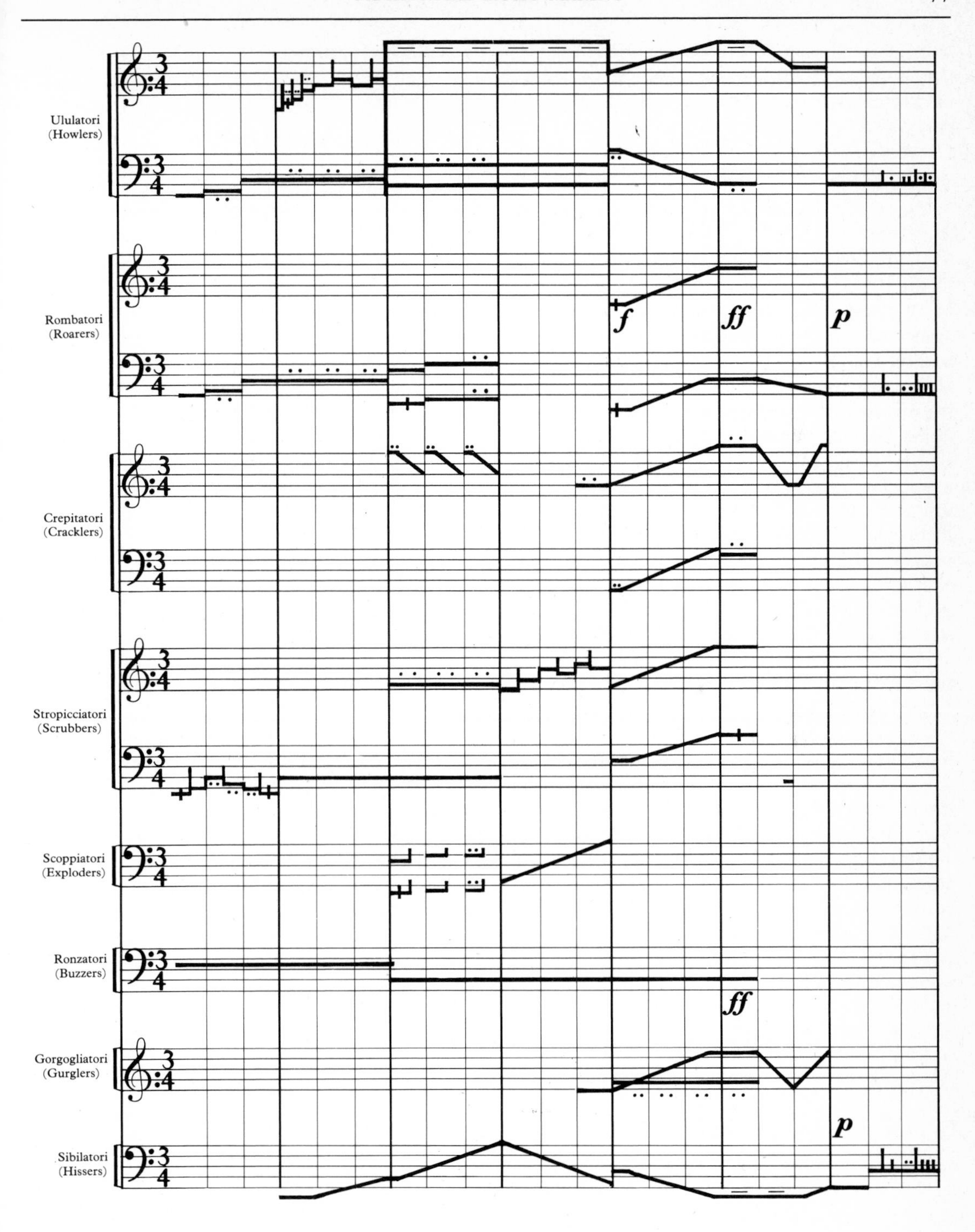

The only surviving music of the Futurist movement: the seven opening bars of Luigi Russolo's 'Down in the City' (1914).

legitimate adjunct to composing, but also into the apparently ubiquitous sphere of EDP: electronic data processing by computer, and even further into a technique known as 'live electronics' (inferring, perhaps, that studio-produced electronic music is moribund).

The first computer music to come before the public was issued by American Decca on a disc (DL 79103; English Brunswick STA 8523) in late 1962. It presented music by Dr J R Pierce of the Bell Telephone Laboratories, and his associates Dr M V Mathews, David Lewin, and others, played by an IBM 7090 computer and converted to music by a digital-to-sound transducer. Possibly the two most remarkable items in this recording are a computerised rendering of a *Fantasia* by Orlando Gibbons in which the sounds of a consort of recorders is imitated so closely as to be almost indistinguishable from the real thing, and 'A Bicycle Built for Two', arranged by Dr Mathews, for which the computer was programmed to sound like a human voice (with a strong American accent) singing one of the verses and accompanying itself on an imitation bar-room piano.

In January 1975 it was announced that a computer had been developed which would, as the operator played upon its keyboard, picture the music on a screen in conventional music type. The machine has been developed by Dr Brian Sykes of the Computer Laboratory of Cambridge University, England. Not only would it project the played notes on its screen; it would also punch holes in a tape so that the instrument could play the music back later–*just* like the reproducing player-piano of the turn of the century.

Live Electronics

Live electronics first appeared about 1966 at the Musica Elettronica Viva studios in Rome, and shortly afterwards in London. In this particular discipline, live performers' voices and the sounds from their instruments are distorted and manipulated electronically in public performance. A good example from 1968 is *Pendulum Music* by Steve Reich. Three pendulum microphones are swung from their leads above loudspeakers which are at the other end of the reproducing chain. The amplifers are then turned up to induce feedback howl which varies and pulses in time to the swings of the microphones. As the movements of the microphones reduce, the variations in feedback are correspondingly lessened until at a stationary position the howl is steady. A fade-out brings the work to an end.

Synthesizers

Mention should be made of the commercial success of the synthesizer pioneered by Dr Robert Moog in America in the 1960s. Both Walter Carlos and Hans Wurman have produced transcriptions of classical and popular music on a Moog (pronounced *Moge*) Synthesizer, starting in 1969, and despite the groans of the critics there can be no denying that some of these arrangements have artistic merit and high entertainment value. The English composer Don Banks has actually written original music for the synthesizer in his *Meeting Place* (1970) for chamber players, jazz group, and live electronics, and synthesisers are part of the standard equipment of 'progressive pop' groups.

BIBLIOGRAPHY

In addition to those books mentioned specifically below, acknowledgement is made to countless indispensable books and scores which have contributed to the collection of facts in this volume, either directly or indirectly, over the years.

Bird, Brian, *Skiffle*, Robert Hale, London, 1958

British Phonographic Committee, The, *The British Record*, London, 1959

Brook, Barry S, *Thematic Catalogues in Music – An Annotated Bibliography*, Pendragon Press, New York, 1972

Charroux, Robert, *The Mysterious Past*, Futura, London, 1974

Clemencic, René, *Old Musical Instruments* (translated by David Hermges), Weidenfeld & Nicolson, London, 1968

Cowell, Henry and Sidney, *Charles Ives and his Music*, Oxford University Press, London, 1955

Murrells, Joseph, *The Daily Mail Book of Golden Discs*, The McWhirter Twins, Ltd, London, 1966

Davidson, Gladys, *Standard Stories from the Operas*, T Werner Laurie, London, 1944

Dent, Edward J, *Alessandro Scarlatti*, Edward Arnold, London, 1905 (second ed 1960)

Dent, Edward J, *Opera*, Penguin, Middlesex, 1940

Ewen, David, *The Complete Book of Classical Music*, Robert Hale, London, 1966

Fétis, F J, *Biographie Universelle des Musiciens*, Didot, Paris, 1862

Foster, Jonathan, 'The Tempora Mutantur Symphony of Joseph Haydn', *The Haydn Yearbook IX*, Universal Edition, Vienna, 1975

Geiringer, Karl, *Musical Instruments, Their History in Western Culture from the Stone Age to the Present Day* (translated by Bernard Miall), George Allen & Unwin, London, 1943

Gérard, Yves, *Thematic, Bibliographical and Critical Catalogue of the Works of Luigi Boccherini* (translated by Andreas Mayor), Oxford University Press, London, 1969

Goodkind, Herbert K, *Violin Iconography of Antonio Stradivari, 1644–1737*, Author, Larchmont, New York, 1972

Green, Stanley, *The Rodgers & Hammerstein Story*, W H Allen, London, 1963

Grove's Dictionary of Music and Musicians, Fifth Edition, Ed Eric Blom, Macmillan, London, 1954

Headington, Christopher, *The Bodley Head History of Western Music*, Bodley Head, London, 1974

Hoboken, Anthony van, *Joseph Haydn: Thematisch-bibliographisches Werkverzeichnis, Band I*, B Schoot's Söhne, Mainz, 1957

Hoffmann, Adolf, *Die Orchestersuiten Georg Philipp Telemann – TWV 55*, Möseler, Wolfenbüttel and Zürich, 1969

Hughes, Gervase, and Thal, Herbert van, *The Music Lover's Companion*, Eyre & Spottiswoode, London, 1971

Jacobs, Arthur, *A New Dictionary of Music*, Penguin, Middlesex, 1967

Jacobs, Arthur, and Sadie, Stanley, *Opera – A Modern Guide*, Pan Books, London, 1964

Jenkins, Jean L, BA, *Musical Instruments (preserved in) The Horniman Museum*, London (second ed), Inner London Education Authority, London, 1970

Internationa Who's Who in Music, Ed Ernest Kay, (seventh ed), International Who's Who in Music, Cambridge, 1975

Qostelanetz, Richard (Ed), *John Cage – Documentary Monographs in Modern Art*, Allen Lane/Penguin, London, 1971

Qühn, Herbert, *On the Track of Prehistoric Man*, (translated by Alan Houghton Broderick), Arrow Books, London, 1958

Loewenberg, Alfred, *Annals of Opera 1597–1940*, Societas Bibliographica, Geneva, 1942; 1955

MacDonald, Malcolm, *The Symphonies of Havergal Brian* (vol 1, Nos 1 to 12), Qahn & Averill, London, 1974

Nettl, Paul, *National Anthems* (translated by Alexander Gode), Ungar, New York, 1952

Ord-Hume, Arthur W J G, *Clockwork Music*, George Allen & Unwin, London, 1972

Palmer, King, *Teach Yourself Orchestration*, English University Press, London, 1964

Pincherle, Marc, *Vivaldi, Genius of the Baroque*, (translated by Christopher Hatch), Gollancz, London, 1958

Robbins L-ndon, Howard Chandler, and Chapman, Roger E, *Studies in Eighteenth Century Music – A Tribute to Karl Geiringer on his 70th Birthday*, George Allen & Unwin, London, 1970

Robbins Landon, Howard Chandler, *The Symphonies of Joseph Haydn*, Universal Edition and Rockliff, London, 1955

Rushmore, Robert, *The Singing Voice*, Hamish Hamilton, London, 1971

Rust, Brian, *American Dance Bands Discography*, Arlington House, New York, 1976

Rust, Brian, and Walker, Edward, *British Dance Bands Discography, 1912–1939*, Storyville Publications, Essex, 1973

Rust, Brian, and Debus, Allen G, PhD, *The Complete Entertainment Discography*, Arlington House, New York, 1973

Rust, Brian, *The Dance Bands*, Ian Allen, London, 1972

Rust, Brian, *Jazz Records, 1897–1942*, Storyville Publications, Essex, 1961; 1962; 1964; 1970

Rust, Brian, and Allen, Walter C, *King Joe Oliver*, Sidgwick & Jackson, London, 1958

Rust, Brian, *London Musical Theatre, 1894–1954*, British Institute of Recorded Sound, London, 1958

Rust, Brian, and Harris, Max, *Recorded Jazz: a Critical Guide*, Pelican, London, 1960

Sachs, Curt, *The History of Musical Instruments*, Dent, London, 1942

Scholes, Percy A, *The Oxford Companion to Music*, (ninth edition), Oxford University Press, London, 1956

Shaw, Arnold, *The Rock Revolution*, Collier-MacMillan, London, 1969

Shaw, Martin, and Coleman, Henry, *National Anthems of the World*, Blandford Press, London, 1963

Spitta, Philipp, *Friedrich des Grossen Musikalische Werke*, Breitkopf und Härtel, Leipzig, 1889

Tallis, David, *Musical Boxes*, Frederick Muller, London, 1971

Vinton, John (Ed), *Dictionary of 20th Century Music*, Thames & Hudson, London, 1974

Warwick, Alan R, *A Noise of Music*, Queen Anne Press, London, 1968

Young, Percy M, *Choral Music of the World*, Abelard-Schuman, London, 1969

Young, Percy M, *The Concert Tradition*, Routledge & Qegan Paul, London, 1965

INDEX